Advances in African American Psychology

Cobb & Henry Titles of Related Interest

African American Identity Development. Reginald L. Jones (Editor)

African American Children, Youth and Parenting. Reginald L. Jones (Editor)

African American Mental Health. Reginald L. Jones (Editor)

Black Adolescents. Reginald L. Jones (Editor)

Black Adult Development and Aging. Reginald L. Jones (Editor)

Black Psychology, 3rd Edition. Reginald L. Jones (Editor)

Handbook of Tests and Measurements for Black Populations. (Volume 1)
    Reginald L. Jones (Editor)

Handbook of Tests and Measurements for Black Populations. (Volume 2)
    Reginald L. Jones (Editor)

Psychoeducational Assessment of Minority Group Children: A Casebook.
    Reginald L. Jones (Editor)

Advances in African American Psychology

Reginald L. Jones, Editor
Hampton University

1999
Cobb & Henry Publishers, Hampton, VA

For information, contact:

Cobb & Henry Publishers
1 Sutton Place
Hampton, VA 23666
Telephone: (757) 827-7213
Fax: (757) 827-1060
E-mail: CobbHenry@aol.com

Manufactured in the United States of America

Advances in African American psychology / Reginald L. Jones, editor.
    p. cm.
  Includes bibliographical references and index.
  ISBN 0-943539-09-9
  1. Afro-Americans--Psychology. I. Jones, Reginald Lanier, 1931-
E185.625.A36 1999
155.8'496073--dc21
                                      97-20669
                                        CIP

*Do not follow
where the path may lead;
go instead
where there is no path and leave a trail.*

This book is dedicated
to the memory of the late
W. Curtis Banks

He left a trail.

Contents

Preface

With the exception of the *Journal of Black Psychology* that focuses upon empirical research, there have been few outlets for advanced theorizing and research on the psychology of African Americans. Early on, I believed it necessary to provide a vehicle for such writing, so I included a number of extensive reviews of research and new paradigms in the Third Edition of *Black Psychology* (1991). In introducing these writings, I wrote the following:

> "because this work (Black Psychology, Third Edition) is expected to be a resource for advanced students and professionals (in addition to those having their first introduction to the subject), I have opted for inclusiveness in subject matter coverage. That is, authors were encouraged to report their ideas, studies and research in detail... so readers can expect solid coverage in any chapter read..."(p. x).

The depth and breadth of advanced research and writing on topics related to the psychology of African Americans has reached a point that justifies publication outlets devoted solely to their explication. To respond to this perceived need, I developed a book series under the generic heading "Advances in African American Psychology." To date two volumes in the series have been published: *African American Mental Health,* and *African American Identity Development*. The present volume, *Advances in African American Psychology*, is the third in the series. A fourth volume, *African American Children, Youth and Parenting*, will follow soon.

In planning the series I sought individuals who had (or were developing) alternative perspectives on the psychology of African Americans, who had interest in substantive psychological topics on issues related to African Americans and were willing to review literature on this topic, and those who were engaged in sustained and programmatic research on topics related to the psychology of African Americans. In seeking authors within these broad parameters, no topics were off limits; I sought individuals who could skillfully present their work and the work of others in a manner that would be informative, enlightening and would point directions for further theorizing and research on the topics.

Overview

The psychological study of African Americans has shown remarkable development. Its growth has been chronicled in the three editions of Black

Psychology (Jones, 1972; Jones, 1980; Jones, 1991), and in a handful of specialized volumes devoted solely to in-depth treatment of one or more areas of psychology related to African Americans. The present volume continues in this vein. Included are 14 chapters in five sections as follows: Part I. Theories and Paradigms; Part II. Methodology; Part III. Research Reviews; Part IV. Health Psychology; and Part V. Mental Health.

Five papers are included in Part I, Theory and Paradigms. These papers advance a number of critiques, perspectives, theories and paradigms that are often alternative to extant theories, research and writings on African Americans. In the first paper, the late W. Curtis Banks (Theory and Method in the Growth of African American Psychology) presents a treatise on theory and method in African American Psychology. He summarizes his arguments as follows: In the growth of the field of African American Psychology, the development of the theory and method has been guided by certain pre-paradigmatic forces rooted in three distinct schools of thought: the Constructionist School, the Reconstructionist School, and the Deconstructionist School. Each School has influenced the development of original theories or innovative methodologies, or both; and each has created certain crises that stem from the areas of development it has ignored. Banks' discussion places these trends in the context of broad philosophy of science frameworks, and addresses the strengths and weaknesses that may be expected to derive from each school. Finally, Banks considers whether these trends suggest progressive or degenerative paradigmatic growth for African American Psychology as a whole.

Myers (Transforming Psychology: An African American Perspective) introduces transpersonal psychology as a platform for presenting her ideas about the need for a paradigm shift in Western Psychology, which she sees as fragmented and not given to global holistic analyses. Arguing that much is to be gained by expanding mainstream psychology to become inclusive of non-dominant and alternate cultural orientations, Myers examines African (and its diaporic) cultural traditions, an underlying worldview that does not fragment spirit. Tracing this [wisdom] tradition to the beginning of human culture and civilization, Myers illustrates ways in which the alternative mindset can "maximize positivity, harmony and balance."

Craig Brookings (Afrikan/Community Psychology: Exploring the Foundation of a Progressive Paradigm) observes that Afrikan psychology and Community psychology are shown to have a common heritage, a parallel developmental history, and similar conceptual and philosophical orientations. Both areas, he notes, emphasize humanitarian values, cultural relativity, and an ecological perspective on social and psychological problems and solutions. Unfortunately, Brookings finds very little theoretical or empirical literature that outlines the basic tenets of this relationship. Brookings suggests that both areas and the African American community can benefit from a conscious understanding of their respective principles, particularly as they relate to what community psychologist refer to as social change and to what is understood as the need for "liberation" by Afrikan psychologists.

Next, Taylor and his colleagues introduce valucation (Valucation: Definition, Theory, and Method) a term they use to reference methods that deepen commitment to values that enhance personal excellence and strength in environments of a wide range: hospitable to hostile, democratic to oppressive, cooperative to competitive, malleable to intractable, ingenious to disingenuous. In the first part of the paper, Taylor, et. al identify seven target values—Love and Respect, Interpersonal Skills, Learning orientation, Self-confidence, Self-persistence, Self-esteem, and Self-reliance—which they contend are survival relevant and imminently implementable. Experiental, historical, political, scriptural, and empirical arguments are used to justify the survival relevance of target values, and prior studies are used to justify the survival relevance of target values and their programmatic implementability. In the second part of this paper, the authors introduce their theory of mediated action—which combines elements of the theory of reasoned action with key constructs from information processing theory—to generate eight basic and four applied propositions which provide the basis for four valucation methods which are then introduced and illustrated. In the final section, research, development, and policy, implications of valucation theory and methods are summarized.

Drawing upon organizational culture, developmental theory, and organizational climate, as well as African philosophy and cultures and African-centered personality theory, Coppock (Afrocentric Organizational Development) presents an African-centered perspective on organizations. Coppock's vision is to use this information to be better able to "create, improve, and intervene with [African Americans] businesses and organizations—making them better suited and harmonious to the root and spirit of African people."

Two papers on Methodology are included in Part II. In the first paper, Caldwell, Jackson, Tucker, and Bowman (Culturally Competent Research Methods) present general conceptual and methodological issues that must be addressed when conducting research on African Americans. Organizing the chapter around several methodological approaches (regional sample surveys, multigeneration family studies, qualitative studies, and studies of clinical diagnosis), Caldwell et al. summarize major conceptual and methodological issues and challenges associated with the approaches, while also calling attention to lifestyle and cultural factors that may affect the quality and meaningfulness of the data collected.

In the second paper, Tucker and Mitchell-Kernan (Mate Availability Among African Americans: Conceptual and Methodological Issues) consider marital trends among African Americans within the framework of a mate availability perspective. They first present an overview of the mate availability perspective and trace its appearance within early paradigms that treated imbalanced sex ratios as a primary force. They then move to more recent formulations which combine the demographic element of sex ratio with socially constructed elements such as eligibility and economic viability or attractiveness. In exploring the utility of the mate availability perspective, the authors reanalyze selected ethnographic case studies of African descended subpopulations in search for evidence of the impact of declining male availability on community and individual adaptation. Finally, Tucker and Mitchell-Kernan offer conceptual and methodological formulations to clarify the relationship between societal processes and individual behavior, as related to changing patterns of family among African Americans.

Reviews of research are the focus of Part III. Papers in this section provide penetrating and comprehensive coverage of their topics and point to directions for further research and investigation. In the first paper, Wyatt (Why We Know So Little About African American Sexuality) provides a historical perspective that describes research on human sexuality in the United States and points to reasons for the dearth of empirically based research with representative samples of African Americans. Wyatt observes that while there has been much interest in, and curiosity about African American sexuality, dating back to the 15th Century, our current knowledge, as we face epidemics such as sexually transmitted diseases, including AIDS, is based more on myth than fact.

In the next paper, Brown, Ward, Lightbourn and Jackson (Skin Tone and Racial Identity Among African Americans: A theoretical and Research Framework) review empirical research on the psychological, social and material importance of skin tone in the life of African Americans. Following their review, the authors explore possible relationships between skin tone and dimensions of racial identity and discuss new directions for research.

In the final paper in Part III, Terrell and Terrell (Cultural Identification and Cultural Mistrust: Some Findings and Implications) examine and critique the literature on Black ideology and suggest additional areas requiring investigation. The authors then propose that a common tendency among African Americans is a mistrust of whites,which they follow with a review of the research exploring the relationship between this trait and the behavior of African Americans in various situations and on different tasks. Finally, the authors present recommendations for further research in this area.

Health Psychology is the focus of Part IV. This is an area to which African American psychologists have paid little attention,so papers in this section provide an introduction to perspectives on health that are African American in origin.

Noting that little attention has been paid by social scientists to the understanding, prevention and treatment of the disorders that African Americans experience, Anderson and Miles (Chronic Pain and Health Psychology: Implications for African Americans) use pain as an exemplar to demonstrate the unique clinical and research contributions social scientists, and in particular health psychologists, can make to health care issues facing African Americans. Their review suggests that an individual's reaction to pain and physical illness is, in part, determined by psychological factors. Anderson and Miles conclude that social scientific knowledge and techniques have tremendous utility for understanding health care behaviors and issues in African American populations.

In the second paper, Martin (Improving the Health of African Americans: Research, Perspectives and Policy) provides a conceptual overview of issues related to the physical and mental health of African Americans,with particular attention given to specific recommendations that respond to the wide array of health challenges African Americans face. In explicating his views, that embrace an Africentric perspective, Martin discusses definitions of health, presents a brief history of African American health and addresses race differences in mortality and morbidity, the role of mental health practitioners in health promotion, health care delivery and approaches to improving the health of African Americans.

Mental Health is the focus of Part V. In the first paper, Edwards (African American Definitions of Self and Psychological Health) addresses the question of how Blacks/African Americans (as an oppressed group) define psychological health for themselves. The methodology is symbolic interaction in that definitions emerged and are shaped by the interaction of the participants, and humanistic in that the introspective perspective of the participants is the focus, from their reference point as actors and self-definers of their reality. Participants also shared information with members of their groups, while self examination and growth were promoted. Participants were taken through a guided fantasy to arrive at the highest ranked characteristics of psychological health. Results were content analyzed. Edwards finally, identifies consistent themes and offers suggestions for further research.

In the final paper, Myers (Therapeutic Processes for Health and Wholeness for the 21st Century: Belief System Analysis and the Paradigm Shift) explicates Belief System Analysis (BSA), a psychotherapeutic approach derived from optimal theory, a theory of human development based on African/American cultural realities and experiences that are designed to meet the mental health needs of oppressed people. Myers observes that mainstream psychology has traditionally ignored the importance of culture and worldview in human functioning. And, as a consequence, a one size fits all orientation in the discipline emphasizes a Western worldview and the experimental frames of reference of the dominant culture. Moreover, Myers observes scholars of African decent have consistently identified needs and concerns vis-à-vis our mental health that traditional models do not and can not address. Myers examines the efficacy of therapeutic practices that are consistent with the needs of oppressed people and are congruent with the strengths of their culture and the realities of their experience. Finally, through case studies, Myers emphasizes the necessity of a multilevel approach to African/African American mental health and the ways in which BSA can be used to enhance individual and collective well-being through spiritual development and "refining the time-tested coping strategies that have sustained our ancestors."

Acknowledgements

An edited work is no stronger than the authors, individually and collectively, who contribute to it. In compiling this volume, I have been extremely fortunate in enlisting the assistance of a group of highly talented, skilled and creative psychologists who are breaking new ground in the theory, research and practice of psychology as related to African Americans. I am indebted, then, first and foremost, to the authors of chapters in this volume. They are: Linda James Myers, Craig C. Brookins, Jerome Taylor, Nsenga Warfield Coppock, Cleopatra H. Caldwell, James S. Jackson, M. Belinda Tucker, Phillip J. Bowman, Claudia Mitchell-Kernan, Gail Elizabeth Wyatt, Kendrick T. Brown, Geoffrey K. Ward, Tiffany Lightbourn, Frances Terrell, Sandra L. Terrell, Louis P. Anderson, Gary T. Miles, Karen Edwards, and the late W. Curtis Banks. These scholars have not only produced groundbreaking work but they have also been most accommodating by revising their manuscripts in response to reviewers, Dr. Aubrey Escoffery, Nancy Boyd-Franklin and Jacquelyne Mattis, who themselves have been generous in sharing their opinions with the authors.

I have also benefited enormously from the assistance of Antoinette Edwards, Katasha Harley and Carmen White for manuscript preparation, Pamela Reilly for proofreading, Wesley Kittling for typesetting and computer work and Michelle Fleitz for the cover design and preparation. This has been a wonderful team that has approached the task of producing the best book possible with skill, professionalism and enthusiasm. I thank one and all for your assistance.

Finally, I acknowledge with love, my wife Michele, who has supported this and all my endeavors in a style that is uniquely her own.

Reginald L. Jones
Hampton, Virginia

Contributors

Louis P. Anderson, Ph.D.
Associate Professor of Psychology, Georgia State University,
Atlanta,Georgia

W. Curtis Banks, Ph.D.
Deceased, was Professor, Department of Psychology, Howard University,
Washington, District of Columbia

Phillip J. Bowman, Ph.D.
Chair, Graduate Program in Counseling Psychology and Associate
Professor, Human Development and Social Policy Program, Northwestern
University, Evanston, Illinois; and Faculty Associate, Program for Research
on Black Americans, University of Michigan, Ann Arbor, Michigan

Craig C. Brookins, Ph.D.
Associate Professor, Department of Psychology, North Carolina State
University, Raleigh, North Carolina

Kendrick T. Brown, Ph.D.
Assistant Professor, Department of Psychology, Macalester College, St.
Paul, Minnesota

Cleopatra Howard Caldwell, Ph.D.
Assistant Professor, Department of Health Behavior and Health Education,
School of Public Health, University of Michigan, Ann Arbor, Michigan

Karen Edwards, Ph.D.
Associate Professor, Department of Psychology, Coordinator, Multi-Ethnic/
Cross-Cultural Psychological Services, Psychological Services Center,
University of Cincinnati, Cincinnati, Ohio

Flavia Eldemire
Univeristy of Massachuetts, Massachuetts

James S. Jackson, Ph.D.
Daniel Katz Distinguished Professor of Psychology and, Director, Program for Research on Black Americans, University of Michigan, Ann Arbor, Michigan

Reginald L. Jones, Ph.D.
Distinguished Professor of Psychology, Hampton University, Hampton, Virginia; and Professor Emeritus, University of California, Berkeley, Berkeley, California

Tiffany Lightbourn
Graduate Student, Department of Psychology, University of Michigan, Ann Arbor, Michigan

William Martin, Psy.D., M.P.H.
Assistant Professor, Tulane School of Public Health, Department of Health Systems Management, New Orleans, Louisiana

Gary T. Miles,
Neuropsychologist, Private Practice, Los Angeles, California

Claudia Mitchell-Kernan, Ph.D.
Vice Chancellor for Academic Affairs; Dean of the Graduate Division; Professor of Anthropology; and Professor of Psychiatry and Biobehavioral Sciences, University of California, Los Angeles, Los Angeles, California

Linda James Myers, Ph.D.
Associate Professor of African American and African Studies and Psychology, The Ohio State University, Columbus, Ohio

Jerome Taylor, Ph.D.
Executive Director, Center for Family Excellence, Pittsburgh, Pennsylvania

Frances Terrell, Ph.D.
Professor, Department of Psychology, University of North Texas, Denton, Texas

Sandra L. Terrell, Ph.D.
Assistant Vice President and Associate Dean, School of Graduate Studies, University of North Texas, Denton, Texas

Contributors

M. Belinda Tucker, Ph.D.
Professor of Psychiatry and Biobehavioral Sciences, University of California Los Angeles, Los Angeles, California

Geoffrey K. Ward
Graduate Student, Department of Sociology, University of Michigan, Ann Arbor, Michigan

Nsenga Warfield-Coppock, Ph.D.
Assistant Visiting Professor, The Catholic University, and President Baobab Associates, Inc., Washington, District of Columbia

Gail Elizabeth Wyatt, Ph.D.
Professor of Psychiatry, Neuropsychiatric Institute, University of California, Los Angeles, Los Angeles, California

Part 1

Theory and Paradigms

Theory and Method in The Growth of African American Psychology

W. Curtis Banks

The most significant aspect of the growth of knowledge in African American Psychology is the historical context in which it is occurring. Two major aspects of that context are the ascendance to an unparalleled status of attention to the political and economic interests of the African diaspora (on one hand), and (on the other) the unprecedented events of what one African American philosopher has described as the "dead, impotent rhetoric of a declining and decaying civilization"—that is, "post modern thought in the West" (West, 1979). The first aspect, in fact, is an explicit feature of the foundation of African American Psychology, as stated in every issue of the *Journal of Black Psychology* through Volume 4. The second has been, at one level, a focus of attention to an array of early and current African American scholars, especially in African American Psychology, though this attention has consisted largely of external commentary and sociological criticism. By that I mean that the major avenue of attack upon Western thought mounted by African American Psychologists has been from outside the system, and from the standpoint of the prerogatives of a particular community to reject as socially, politically, and therefore epistemologically irrelevant a system of ideology, theory and method which fails to advance its interests. These attacks, for the most part, have been eminently valid. In a major way they have been causes as well as effects of the current Western epistemological decline. Where they have fallen short is not in being insufficiently correct, but rather in being insufficiently destructive. And like an animal, only just injured, conventional Western science is dangerously capable of rising up against the tide of refutation, perhaps with new (and more violent) vigor.

One sign of that renewed vigor is the emerging vitality of a "save empiricism" movement. Crosscultural psychology, ethnographic methods, and biculturalism are just some of the dying gasps of a conventionalist scientific community devoted to the preservation of relativistic theory, comparative methodology, and an ideological programme of discriminant self-interest. A central challenge to African American psychologists is precisely that degree of internal penetration into the false structure of conventional thought and an exploitation of the logical invalidities of empirical science that should make such resuscitations untenable. Otherwise, African American science may find itself susceptible to arguments that empiricism, materialism, theoretical formalism, and logical positivism are just good doctrines put to ill-purpose, when they may be no less than ill doctrines put to degenerate purposes.

From a vantage point innocently external to the system and acutely sensitive to the sociological realities, students and practitioners of African American Psychology have advanced two criticisms from the very inception of the field:

1) That science is ideology
2) That empirical research is inherently destined to prove pernicious claims about African American people.

Some empiricists have argued that both these criticisms, while sociologically justified, are not logically valid. And while the "bath water" of poor research, subjectively biased scientists and non-relativized methods should be thrown out, the baby of logical positivist inquiry can be retained. But this attitude of conservation is patently incorrect. Both criticisms cut deeply into the logical foundations of post-modern Western thought, albeit not consciously so. And both criticisms betray the fact that when that core of Western European philosophers of science referred to as the Vienna Circle formulated the canons of modern logical positivism, it was in fact logical negativism that resulted.

That science is indeed ideology is revealed by a close look at the logical structures of inquiring systems and the role of theory and method in them. Logical positivists attempted to save theory from dogma and separate the domains of metaphysics and science. They advanced the verificationist framework as the criterion of meaningfulness for all scientific statements. Within that framework, claims are regarded as scientifically meaningful insofar as their verification is dependent upon the observation of material evidence. What is critical in the end is the extent to which the claims of science must be verified by data which are sought within an empirical methodology. Empirical methods, then, provide the structure within which truth is sought through the confirmation of meaningful theoretical claims. All this sounds highly constructive, positive, and liberal. It was intended to salvage truth from the tyranny of rationalism, which sought communion with God as the ultimate method of verification. At the same time it was intended to preserve the icons of certainty and universality in knowledge which were so acutely threatened by skepticism and relativism.

But this essentially Kantian picture of knowledge has been abandoned by every progressive philosopher of knowledge from Wittgenstein to Kuhn. Popper (1959) has argued that evidence cannot arbitrate theory because it is never independent of theory. Kuhn (1970) has argued that theory is constrained both by certain methodological conventions and by the worldview that governs the monolithic paradigms within which the scientific community operates. Lakatos (1970) has confessed that theories stand on their own quite without consideration to the status of truth accorded them by evidence, that bad theories (or even disproven ones) do not die, and that only methodology defines the doctrines of science and the guidelines of research. And Paul Feyerabend (1978) concludes that in that case "scientific method is (nothing more than) an ornament that makes us forget that a position of anything goes has in fact been adopted."

What each of these points of view expresses implicitly is a recognition of the inherently destructive and negative character of Western thought since Immanuel Kant. It was Kant who first proposed the synthesis of reason and observation that saved Western ideology from Humanean skepticism. But Kant's argument was a diversion. He distinguished claims that have to be true from claims that don't have to be true. But what he advanced was a notion of ideas that separates those that can be false from those that cannot be. Karl Popper (1959) "peeped" this positivist lie when he pointed out that what makes scientific statements scientific is their falsifiability, not their verifiability, so that all scientific knowledge, according to Popper, must logically be uncertain. All inquiry is therefore directed at refutation, not confirmation. And it is the ability of a theory to withstand refutation that determines its integrity. The purpose of theory is, in the strictest and purest sense, to expose ideas maximally to falsification and science is merely religion exposed to criticism.

But this idealistic picture is the opposite of reality. The practice of science in psychology has not been to arbitrate theoretical claims through appeal to evidence, but to protect them from it. The purpose of theory has not been to expose ideas to falsification, it has been to justify the current ideological programme. Like a system of politics, science has sought foremost its own preservation. As we know, legislation does not set forth the ideas which jurisprudence tests and verifies and executive responsibility then carries out in programmes. Rather programmes are adopted which legislation justifies and the judiciary protects from obstruction. Similarly it is not ideological programmes that grow from the theoretical ideas that evidence validates. It is ideological programmes which are set forth and then justified by theory; and the role of methodology is to protect theory from falsification.

Therefore, the most critical considerations for a theory are: 1) What ideological programmes it is capable of justifying; and 2) What methodological framework does its protection and preservation demand. To ignore the current context of epistemological disarray in Western thought is to misunderstand the role of theory in inquiry. Theory does not advance ideas as the positivists (and I might add, misguided optimists) would believe; theory justifies ideas. Empirical methodology is not a tool of revelation and verification as the positivists believed in the early part of this century, but a tool of refutation and a shield of obstruction behind which those ideas which theory justifies are operationalized as programmes.

The result of this framework of conventional empirical science has been the erection of a host of theoretical edifices, which African American Psychology must seek not to improve upon but to thoroughly deconstruct. Negative self-concept, external locus of control, impulsive self-gratification, lack of motivation, low aspirations are the theoretical monsters to which conventional ideological programmes have given birth, and to which conventional empirical methodologies have given protection. The response of African American Psychology has thus far been largely ineffective for this deconstructive task. Two major theoretical schools in our field have pushed for dominance, each without a full enough consideration of the comprehensive responsibilities of theory in knowledge.

The Africanist thrust has been toward a deep appreciation of the role of theory in the justification of ideological programme, with only the barest attention to the protective demands of theory for a methodological framework. The result has been a proliferation of theoretical concepts under virtually constant critical attack. In fact, much of that criticism reflects the real pitfalls into which Africanity's implicit methodological leanings allow it to slip. Growing out of a largely vitalistic ideological programme of African American integrity, that theoretical school has advanced constructs which appeal to the unique characteristics of African peoples. No wonder, then, that conventionalists argue that any such claims are premature in the absence of strictly comparative evidence that whites do not possess the same attributes. Such evidence may indeed be, as I suspect many Africanist theorists would say, programmatically irrelevant (indeed, it would be counterproductive to the ideological programmes on which the theories are based). But such a rebuttal would reveal the adoption by many Africanist theoreticians of the conventional fables about the role of method in advancing theories and verifying ideas. The role of method within the Africanist framework must be to protect theory and programme, not contribute to them. But if the demands of theory are for methodological practices that obstruct rather than defend the ideological programme, the theories (by implication) demand revision.

The Empiricist school has made a similar error in adopting a notion of the preeminence of method. Recognizing the unavoidability of comparative methodology for gaining the esteem of conventional science, Empiricists have attempted to advance an African American Psychology of decidedly humanistic qualities. The role of Empiricist research has been to set forth impeccable methodological credentials for whatever theoretical constructs those methods might defend. The result has been a lack of coherence and unity in the theoretical directions of empiricist research, much less the ideological programmes it seeks to justify and protect. By implication, the only ideological programme associated with the empirical school is that of traditional Western thought, the attainability of certainty, and the viability of ultimately universal psychological constructs—all of which have been abandoned already by Western thinkers themselves. Theoretically, this school seeks the human core which lies beneath the African American veneer and White veneer of African and European peoples, a pursuit which ironically appeals to the most misguided of rationalist endeavors—the search for essences—the antithesis of empiricism and positivism.

Both schools reflect the same basic error, the belief that methodology advances and contributes to theory. Therefore, the Africanists have simply rejected a conventional methodology which would clearly not serve to verify and confirm its claims, but has failed to devise a comprehensive alternative, or come to terms with the essentially negative role it must play in knowledge growth. The Empiricists have made methodological integrity their foremost preoccupation, believing in its ability to lead systematically to a knowledge base from which theory and ideological programmes can spring.

And while we are all trying to be constructive in our push toward the growth of theory, method and knowledge, the traditional edifices continue to stand, to influence the scientific and political communities and to enjoy the protection of a perniciously defensive and destructive framework which too many of us still take to be the salvation of truth and objectivity.

As Friederick Nietzsche (1967) put it when he scared Western Philosophy half to death, "Nihilism stands at the door" and with that foreshadowing of the modern decline of Western thought he advanced an idea that African American scholars have come to regard as unquestionable—that the pursuit of knowledge is the will to power. In this regard I should quote William R. Jones, an African American philosopher, in his defense of African American Philosophy: "Let us be clear in our minds what is at stake here... the authority of blacks to describe reality..." As Nobles has said, power is the ability to define that reality and to have others adopt and act on that definition as if it were their own. But the role of power in knowledge is more negative than Nobles' definition lets on, because the character of knowledge is to advance claims which no person is able to refute. It is ultimately the integrity of the system of justification and defense behind which ideas stand that accords them their power.

There is every reason for us to face the nihilistic task which the Western decline has put before us. The empiricists are right to embrace empirical methodology, but they are wrong to believe in a constructive purpose. Empiricism without an ideological mission is like an army without a position to defend. It exercises its power aggressively against those positions held by others. And empirical methodology has its greatest potential for African American Psychology in the forceful deconstruction of the conventional wisdom, the dominant theories, and the traditional constructs of African American deficiency. Let's not mistake this task for a mere reactionary posture. At the same time, let us not mistake this role as the only one which African American Psychology should adopt.

The Africanist tradition has clearly set out on the right path, if by right we mean a path toward knowledge construction and the justification of ideological programmes. And it should be clear that this activity is ultimately the most important for the growth and health of African American people. But it must be clear in its particularist stance, one that must not be confused with cross-cultural relativism. It must seek to construct its theoretical claims in such a way that the methods required to defend them do not obstruct and divert the ideological programmes which they justify. And it must be vigorous in the establishment of methodologies which insure the proliferation of theory through defense against refutation from outside the system. African American Psychology, therefore, is likely to prosper in direct proportion to its ability to deconstruct conventional falsehood, and its ability to construct particularist theory that stands in contrast to relativism, and a methodology of the absolute rather than the comparative.

References

Feyerabend, P. (1978). *Against method*. London: Verso.

Jones, W. R. (1978). The legitimacy and necessity of Black philosophy. *Philosophical Forum, 9(2-3)*, 149-160.

Kant, I. (1966). *Critique of pure reason*. Garden City, NY: Doubleday.

Kuhn, T. S. (1970). *The structure of scientific revolutions* (2nd ed.). Chicago: University of Chicago Press.

Lakatos, I., & Musgrave, A. (Eds.). (1970). *Criticism and the growth of knowledge*. London: Cambridge University Press.

Nietzsche, F. (1967). *The will to power*. New York: Vintage Books.

Popper, K. R. (1959). *The logic of scientific discovery*. New York: Harper & Row.

West, C. (1978). Introduction. *Union Seminary Quarterly Review, 36(2)*, 67-70.

Wittgenstein, L. (1961). *Tractatus logico philosophicus*. London: Routledge & Kegan Paul Ltd.

Author

W. Curtis Bank, deceased,
was Professor, Department of Psychology
Howard University,
Washington, D.C.

Transforming Psychology: An African American Perspective

Linda James Myers

Brief History of Transpersonal Psychology in the West

Transpersonal psychology seeks to expand the field of psychological inquiry to include the study of optimal psychological health and well-being. The potential for experiencing a broad range of states of consciousness is recognized, allowing identity to extend beyond the usual limits of ego and personality (Walsh & Vaughn, 1980). Within this frame it is understood that the reality one perceives is shaped by an underlying system of beliefs, often implicit, assumed or unquestioned, which serve as self-fulfilling, self-prophetic organizers of experience. From this basis, all psychologies have evolved as implicit or explicit models of human nature. The pervasive dynamic interplay between cultural beliefs and psychological models is now being recognized. The models posed by psychologists are a part of their own beliefs and experience and reflect both the culture and individuals that produce them.

The transpersonal school has not been well accepted by mainstream psychologists in the United States. Taylor (1992) traces the history of its roots as a movement in Western psychology back to its alliance with the origins of humanistic psychology in the 1950's (Vich, 1988). He notes that psychoanalysis came to control almost all clinical teaching in psychology and psychiatry where certification was mandatory from the late 1940's up until the advent of the community psychiatry movement in the early 1960's. At the same time, within academic psychology it became widely recognized that behaviorism and stimulus-response theory was failing as a major organizing paradigm of experimental research. Grand theory construction gave way to tentative model building, yet psychology remained behavioral, not yet having become fully cognitive in its general orientation (Taylor, 1992).

Carl Rogers is cited as positing the first uniquely American challenge to the hegemony of psychoanalytic techniques in clinical practice with his non-directive approach aimed at discovering meaning and value in the normal personality (Rogers, 1942). In the 1950's Abraham Maslow pioneered movement away from pathology and statistical definitions of normality toward a new orientation studying

9

the healthy, fully functioning, self-actualizing human being, which became known as humanistic psychology (Maslow, 1954). By the early 1960's, humanistic psychology became solidified as an academic movement (Taylor, 1992). Taylor describes American folk consciousness as having become indistinguishable from humanistic psychology, as growth centered and alternative psychotherapies proliferated everywhere. Ideas about spirituality and growth-experience were brewing between Maslow and Sutich and in 1969 they founded the *Journal of Transpersonal Psychology* and its own separate supporting association (Sutich,1969).

Early transpersonal psychologists argued that consciousness exists as a phenomenon to be studied by science, claiming that its various levels incorporate the physical, mental, celestial and infinite dimensions of personality (Smith, 1976; Wilber, 1984). A younger generation of leaders in the field of transpersonal psychology emerged after the deaths of Maslow and Sutich. Several important organizations within the transpersonal movement developed during this period. Among them were the Institute of Noetic Science, The International Transpersonal Psychology Association, Naropa Institute, and the California Institute of Transpersonal Psychology.

While humanistic psychologists were able to gain recognition within the American Psychological Association in the mid-1970's, establishing the Division of Humanistic Psychology, the special interest group which urged the formation of a transpersonal division did not meet with success. The idea of a transpersonal division was rejected by the membership of the American Psychological Association. Taylor points out, however, that transpersonal psychology has managed to circumvent mainstream academic and professional organizations, and transpersonal writers and practitioners are able to maintain direct contact with the American public through older established avenues of public lectures, weekend conferences, a well developed network of alternative health clinics, advertising in alternative life-style publications, and widespread sale of mass market books. Public support within various groups is attributed to its ethic of higher consciousness and differentiation into a variety of fields addressing value-oriented issues such as health, ecology, human rights, business, and religion (Taylor, 1992). A similar pattern has been noted with Black Psychology in terms of reception from mainstream psychology and its ability to reach the public through more direct means (Myers,1983).

In sum, the reception of mainstream psychology and academic programs to transpersonal psychology, has not been good, in part because, as we will explore later, it has not been well understood, due to the intellectual and conceptual incarceration of the fragmented mindset dominant in the society and the institutions that support it. However, the needs of humanity are great and in the information age, institutional structures once hegemonous, may find themselves outmoded, if they continue to be unresponsive and become irrelevant.

Transpersonal Psychology Revisited

Budge (1960) notes that all the major ideas in template form that have exercised a profound influence on the history of spiritual thought can be found in the *Egyptian Book of the Dead,* also known as the Papyrus of Ani or *Book of* the *Coming Forth By Day and The Going Forth By Night* from 4000 B.C. (Bynum, 1992). Yet, a cursory review of the literature in the *Journal of Transpersonal Psychology* in the seventies and beyond reveals that for the most part, search for a paradigm has been focused toward Oriental philosophy and modern physics (Myers, 1983, 1988). Conspicuously absent in the literature of transpersonal psychology in its search for a paradigm is an exploration of traditional African culture, much less African American culture (Bynum, in press). While such a legacy of omission from philosophical and psychological endeavors is common, the unity and integration of knowledge sought in a transpersonal paradigm can be identified in the African and African American cultural experience and reality. Despite the continued presence of a void in the science of consciousness and transpersonal literature, little movement has been made toward the inclusion of Afrocentric knowledge in the discussion of psychological theory. Upon exploring this phenomenon in the transpersonal literature, we see it is simply reflecting the mindset dominant in the society-at-large, although it seeks to function at the height of human understanding. The limitation can be understood as a function of the conceptual system of the actors (Myers, 1988).

The worldview implied by modern physics is inconsistent with the dominant view of our present society. The prevailing Western worldview does not reflect the harmonious interrelatedness we observe in nature (Capra, 1975). The worldview is fragmented, not given to global, holistic analyses. Taylor (1992) asserts that the history of the transpersonal movement in psychology is quite new and closely allied with the origins of humanistic psychology in the 1950's (Vich, 1988). Although he mentions the classical traditions of Asia and the mystical traditions of Judeo Christianity, he makes no mention of the African connection and contribution to these traditions.

Transpersonal psychology represents a paradigm shift in Western psychology and the potential to benefit from exposure to cross cultural beliefs about the nature of consciousness and reality is tremendous. Expanding the prevailing monocultural beliefs about our basic nature and our relationship to the world may be one of the most important tasks confronting psychology today. While recognition of the upper reaches of psychological development supports the investigation of maximal positive well-being and higher states of consciousness, this awareness has not been characteristic of Western psychologies. The failure of materialistic, external striving to provide satisfaction, peace, and well-being has led some people to look for a more adequate source. One of the principal aims of transpersonal psychology must be to help us overcome the perceptual distortions identified by the many consciousness disciplines, yielding a view of reality more consistent with that modern physics has shown to be the true nature of the material universe. Rooted in the African/African American cultural reality is the insight necessary to provide that link.

A legacy of omission of Africa from philosophical and psychological endeavors is common (Myers, 1985). Until recently, African culture has been badly misunderstood because of the imposition of an alien worldview in its analysis. The unity and integration of knowledge sought in a transpersonal paradigm has its framework already extant in the African cultural reality. I will discuss this in greater detail, as it relates to optimal psychology, theory rooted in the wisdom tradition of African deep thought.

Bynum (1992; in press) foresees a future in which the field will transcend its almost exclusive preoccupation with "Eastern and Western" methods and will open to dimensions inherent in many forms of ancient African mysticism and the African unconscious (Bynum, in press; King, 1990). He believes the field will turn its attention to a primal root phenomenon of transpersonal experience as old as Kemetic seers and Vodic Rishis of India, and yet as modern as next year's headlines (Bynum, 1992, p.305).

In order to achieve such a state of dynamic balance, a radically different philosophical, social, and economic structure will be needed: a cultural revolution in the true sense of the word. The survival of our whole civilization may depend on whether or not we can bring about such a change. Let us discuss the ways in which African psychology through optimal theory can contribute to our improved understanding and appreciation of the transpersonal dimensions of human experience and can help ameliorate many of the problems so pervasive in our society and the world today.

African Psychology Transforms

Within the past two decades, a number of psychologists have independently converged on an approach to the science of mind and behavior that is rooted in the traditional African worldview (Akbar, 1976, 1981; Baldwin, 1981; Frye, 1980; Khatib & Nobles, 1978; Myers, 1980, 1981; Nobles, 1972, 1974; X Clark, McGee, Nobles & X Weems, 1975). One of the Afrocentric models of psychological functioning grounded in the wisdom tradition of African deep thought,which has been developed, a theory of optimization, is consistent with and reinforces the paradigmatic shift currently taking place in the sciences in Western culture (Bateson, 1979; Capra, 1975, 1982; Gelwick, 1977; Jantsch, 1980; Polyani, 1967) and the 'new philosophy of science' (Bhaskar, 1975; Harre, 1972; Manicas & Secord, 1983). In addition, as psychological theory, it adds the dimension of practical applicability to everyday life.

According to Glaser and Strauss (1967), in discovering theory one generates conceptual categories or their properties from evidence. The evidence, then, from which the category emerged is used to illustrate the concept. In terms of optimal theory, an entire set of conceptual categories and properties have been generated from the evidence presented by an ancient traditional African worldview and its corresponding African American cultural reality. Many scholars have detailed the existence of a generalized African worldview and certain cultural ethos continually predominate (Asante, 1980; Diop, 1978; Forde, 1954; Frye, 1983; Gerhart, 1978; Levine, 1977; Mbiti, 1970; Nobles, 1972; Sowande, 1973; Thompson, 1974; Williams, 1976; Zahan, 1979). Dixon (1971) and Nichols (1976) have been particularly clear in delineating and articulating the philosophical aspects of the worldview. Myers theory of optimization provides a vehicle for the integration of the conceptual system into meaning schemes and meaning perspectives that maximize the potential to achieve positive experience. Finch (1998) documents additional support for the worldview that integrates science and spirituality in his experiments of African cultural tradition and carry over.

The experience of Africans in America during European American enslavement required that they draw upon their capacity to live above conditions, that is tap into a reality beyond that which appeared. Levine (1977) quotes Aunt Aggy, an enslaved African woman, who speaks of being blessed to see things that the slave captor could not see, and experience a reality unknown to the materially powerful captor. The legacy of that awareness is what underpins optimal theory. Knowledge of a spiritual connection that supercedes all manner of abuse and injustice is believed to be the source of the energy that allowed Africans to emerge from enslavement with their humanity fully in tact, with a desire to secure freedom and justice for all people, not just themselves. While some would argue that such compassion and benevolence was not a good thing, optimal theory posits that they, supported by a reasoned faith, will be our saving grace and means to triumph.

Throughout African/African American tradition from ancient times to modern, certain universal laws or principles have been acknowledged, like the law of opposites, the law of reciprocity, and the role of self knowledge in human experience. Djhuti or Thoth, the Egyptian sage, known by the Greeks as Hermes Trismegistus, spoke directly of Seven Hermetic Principles, the first being that "all is mind" or consciousness (Frye, 1978). Such a system of thinking leaves a legacy of the power we have to define our own experience, which optimal theory has identified and built upon to create a psychology of divine consciousness that identifies the nature and order of human development in terms of knowledge of self as a manifestation of spirit. Awareness of the role and value of oppositions, challenges and struggle in human development has long been recognized in African tradition (Some, 1992). The purpose of so-called negativity in human experience based on optimal theory is to provide the opportunity for growth and the development of greater self-knowledge. Understanding and appreciation of this system of reasoning requires the diunital logic characteristic of African thought (Dixon, 1971; Levine, 1977; Myers, 1988).

In outlining the history of humanistic and transpersonal psychology in terms of the strengths and weaknesses of the discipline, Taylor (1992) delineates what he perceives to be the most substantive limits to the discipline. The first limitation Taylor identifies is obviated as optimal theory is engaged. He states that transpersonal psychology appears philosophically naive. Described as perennial philosophy (Huxley, 1949) in Western thought, it is built upon unquestioned monism and all experiences of higher consciousness are considered "the same" (Taylor, 1992). His description fits the worldview to which he is referring, however other worldviews exist which encourage the questioning which insures a deeper understanding and exploration of the infinite manifestations of the one.

The restrictions which exist within the conceptual system dominant in this culture are overcome as an alternative set of assumptions is adopted utilizing an orientation rooted in an African/African American cultural frame of reference; a totally different outcome and analysis is made possible. This section of the paper will explore these ideas more fully. Our objective will be to illustrate the extent to which it is the hegemony of the mindset dominant in this culture that blocks our potential for growth and health, which affects all in the society who would be inclusive and expansive in their vision. The exclusionary bias characterizing sub-optimal mindset predisposes its adherents to racism (as well as, sexism, classism, and so on), making the situation particularly difficult for African Americans and other people of color.

Let me examine some of the issues that continue to resurface, reflecting the incapacity of the dominant mindset to fully comprehend the transpersonal dimensions of human experience, and explore the insights optimal theory provides. I will use humanistic psychologists in example in order to illustrate the impact on even those more forward thinking among the groups in the dominant culture. One critic of transpersonal psychology has been Rollo May (1986). While May conceded that his reading of William James (1985) reaffirmed his conviction about the importance of spiritual life, he feared transpersonal psychology may be a way of avoiding the real issues of being human and living in the world. According to Doyle in conversation with May:

> That's right. I asked, "are you referring to the old days when psychology was criticized for being used in the service of teaching adaptation of the personality to a status quo which may not have been humane or therapeutic?" And he said, "exactly." That was exactly the kind of thing he's always objected to. So he views teaching conformity to certain social values or adaptation to un-tenable life situations as taking a way out that was not for the good of the human. In the case of transpersonal psychology, he added that he felt sometimes it involved taking too easy a way out for the personality,

to go high on the topic and avoid tangling with their own ego level issues as they might, for instance, include the dark side (May, Krippner, & Doyle, 1992).

Optimal theory posits that there can be no growth or development toward higher consciousness without struggle. The premise underlying this principle is revealed in the common sense reality that in order to know good, one must know bad. It is also illuminated in the African American folk belief that God/dess (the name given the omnipotent, omniscient, omnipresent creative Spirit/Force/ Consciousness and source of all good), in order to know God/dess's self more fully, he/she manifests him/herself in an infinite variety of ways, each aspect having the purpose of increasing God/dess's knowledge of self (Gender balance emphasis is mine. In this African American folk culture the feminine is implicitly subsumed in the articulation of the masculine, the fragmentation of not feeling included by terms such as God, he, and so on, has not set in. This integration of feminine is made possible by the realization that all human life begins as female and life is brought forth through the female). Optimal theory posits that the same pattern of development is reflected in human experience; the purpose of life on this plane of existence is to come to know who we are more and more fully as manifestations of Spirit/Force/ Consciousness. This dialectical process, in the individuation phase or in the state of separation from full identity, will by nature be an experience of alienation at which time the ego level issues of the personality must be dealt with for growth or movement back to one's true identity.

According to ancient African tradition, self knowledge is the basis of all knowledge; movement toward higher consciousness requires tangling with ego level issues. "To go high on a topic and avoid tangling with the ego/personality," would be an impossibility without real value; health and growth require confrontation and mastery of the "dark side." Optimal theory emerging from the cultural reality and traditions of Africans/African Americans with full acknowledgment of the role of consciousness in human experience is grounded in an ontological position that supports the capacity to perceive the interrelatedness and interdependence of all things and reason with the unity that contains and transcends oppositions. From this position, the fears expressed by May are unwarranted. Rollo May goes on to say, "when you achieve peace, you are no longer a psychologist. You have left the reality behind you. The reality is made up of the paradox of being human, which contains within it the struggle with the evil or the darkness within one's soul, with the beauty, the spirituality and the other very positive creative aspects. But once you've achieved peace you're no longer in the struggle, you've risen to a realm which is beyond human in his estimation."

Here again we see the consequences of a fragmented mindset which fails to comprehend the *anyo kwelei enyo*, that is, two truths. In order to be the best psychologist one must be at peace, according to optimal theory. Peace is earned through mastery of the struggles with the "dark side." Peace on the human plane manifests at varying levels depending on one's state of development. The psychologist utilizing optimal theory must strive to achieve a peace that passes the understanding of those fixated on conditions, must work through issues of individual ego and personality (the source of separateness) to move to the realm where healing takes place. A good psychologist is a healer in the African tradition.

According to May, Ken Wilbur (1983) says we are all growing toward Eden. We will be happier and happier. We will be freed from our problems. This is impossible and undesirable. We would cease to be human . This is what I fight against... The idea was that we are growing towards increasing perfection. So all a person had to do was sit tight, and these good things will automatically come about. Well I don't believe it at all... It would happen by virtue of our devotion or hard work. You see what I am against is the belief that this comes automatically. High states are not achieved automatically (May, Krippner, & Doyle, 1992).

May's premise is supported by optimal theory. High states are not achieved automatically, but rather by virtue of devotion and hard work, however, the nature and experience of that work at more advanced levels should not preclude the experience of "growing toward Eden," getting, if not happier, more content and joyful. Moving toward bliss does not mean your work ends, as long as there are issues of personal ego and a fallen humanity to uplift, there will be work, but it does mean your experience of your work changes for the better.

Theory Based on the Wisdom Tradition of African Deep Thought

When the spiritual/material ontology is adhered to with devotion of purpose, one loses the sense of individualistic ego/alienated personality and experiences infinite mind or consciousness manifesting as oneself. The assumptions dominant in this culture fall within the realm of non-reality or illusion to one adopting an optimal conceptual system. A theory of divine consciousness based upon the experience and realities of the African/African American cultural tradition, presents a challenge to the fragmented thinking dominant in this culture. However, the purpose of developing such a theory is to push the cultural legacy of our collective humanity to a higher level of realization as we move into the 21st century. African tradition requires that we build upon the knowledge of our ancestors (the consciousness of those revered ones who have gone before us) upon whose shoulders we stand. If we do not, the ancestors are not pleased.

The theory of optimization issues of personal ego and does not seek to replicate all of the surface structure aspects of African culture, but rather go to the root assumptions and explore how the reformulation manifests in present day, given the extreme trials, tribulations, and struggle we Africans in America have experienced.

The anticipation is of extraordinary growth, pushing the height of knowledge to new peaks as the ancestors work with us and through us. What is being articulated is a way to structure consciousness, which will be reflected in the way one views and experiences the world and can be adopted by anyone across cultures and time.

The theory of optimization congruent with the wisdom tradition of African deep thought, fully incorporates the teachings of Djhuti and other African/African American sages. Optimal theory provides a paradigm which unifies the insights of modern physics and Eastern mysticism under the meaning schemes and meaning perspectives of traditional African/African American cultural reality. Drawing from the best of each cultural tradition which can be traced to the teachings of ancient Africans (i.e., earliest historical records of true beginning of all human culture and civilization, [Beatty, 1998]) a conceptual system is identified which will structure reality such that one can achieve eternal peace and well-being (James, 1954). The same meaning schemes and meaning perspectives are extant in the way of life of many African Americans today, as well as others following the tradition. We can now through quantum evidence begin to account for the processes which would for the extracereloral transmission of information across time and space. Giuffre (1998) speaks of the behavior of entangled particles as a refinement that has been well established scientifically. The idea is that similar particles of commom origin can correspond in their behavior even when separated across time and space. Given the principle of correspondence which optimal theory embraces, we would expect to see that anything manifest in nature physically or materially will be manifest in like pattern on other levels of existence (i.e., psychologically, cognitively, affectively, and spiritually and subsequently behaviorally).

The perfectibility process identified seeks to transform the finite, limited cultural conception of human consciousness into an expanded, cohesive, infinite consciousness which unified, contains and transcends oppositions, moving adherents toward the supremely good or divine. In order to accomplish this task one must begin to perceive and understand that everything, including self, is the manifestation of one permeating essence which is the source of all things good. This ontological position although supported by the height of Western science, Eastern philosophies and African common sense, is untenable to those who would adhere to the outmoded worldview of a fragmented, disintegrative, externalized construction of reality, so clearly associated with modernity.

It is important to note in this regard that what is being advocated is a mechanism and method to identify and utilize that which is universal across human cultures in historical content, starting in the beginning, however a self-selection away from acknowledging our collective and unifying African ancestry will likely occur among those for whom a truly holistic, integrative worldview is not possible at this time. The conceptual system being described as optimal originated in Africa (Diop, 1974; James, 1954; ben-Jochannon, 1970), but its essential principles are extant in the sacred teachings of virtually every cultural group. Optimal theory creates a point of identification outside of the context of religion, placing it in an understanding of human functioning based on the worldview of a people who acknowledge the immanent and transcendent nature the forces of consciousness or spirituality.

Consistent with this holistic, integrate worldview, optimal theory emphasizes the multidimensionality of identity. The significance of how one manifests is to be explored in terms of the varios human diversity markers. Subsequently, race, gender, class, regionality, nationality, size, color, and so on become the substance for increasing self-knowledge. Each aspect of self must be examined, worked through and positively integrated into the state of being a whole person (or personality). The various dimensions of self can be thought of as configurations of energy responding and interacting in predictable ways in social contest given the nature of ones worldview. Spiritual development of the human being is from lower to higher consciousness, or from a sub-optimal to more optimal constructions of reality. Optimal refers to that which can sustain the greatest good (love, peace, joy, harmony, balance, health, etc.) the longest. Intra-individual development is fostered by the desire to seek the good and the critical self-reflection needed to forgo a false superficial sense of self. It is supported by interpersonal interactions, which lend themselves itself to the realization of the interrelatedness interdependence of the collective. The concept of extended self also supports a multi-dimensionality inclusive of parents, grandparents, and others who have come before to contribute to your being (ancestors), your children, their children, and others who will come after you (the yet unborn), all of nature, and the entire community. I am because we are; we are therefore, I am, takes on deeper meaning and significance.

In African tradition, one's being did not automatically make one a part of the community, nor admit one to the position of ancestor. A standard of good behavior and attitude was required (Zahan, 1979). Good in this context becomes commitment to the path of greater self knowledge, beauty being understood as the apprehension of the splendor of truth (Furch, 1998). Actions in one incarnation are "held over," such that whatever your level of consciousness at your passing on (dying), without intervention, that same level would be assumed with reincarnation. This interconnectedness reinforces the concept that the universe is just. African American cultural tradition fully acknowledges the law of reciprocity, as seen in the belief in the folk saying, "what goes around comes around." The reward of the wicked is at best an appearance. Those unifying, containing, and transcending all oppositions, that is, achieving mastery of self, are no longer required to come back, save their choice to help others. In general, connection with those loved ones who have passed on is believed to be of value. Wisdom and morality are outcomes in the natural order of this system of structuring consciousness (Myers, 1988).

The idea that all knowing is a form of in dwelling, overthrows centuries of the Western dichotomy that separates mind and body, reason and experience, theory and practice, subject and object, the knower and the known (Gelwick, 1977;

Manicas & Secord, 1983; Polyani, 1963). Optimal psychology embraces the role of consciousness in human experience and our subjective relationship to itself knowledge as the basis of all knowledge. Self is understood to be multi-dimensional. Psychological theory is shaped by autobiography, and the personal history of the theoretician directly influences his/her articulation of and emphasis on theory (Walsh & Vaughn, 1980). This theory of human functioning has evolved as one African American woman has taken the opportunity to give voice in this fashion to her experience based on knowledge, wisdom, and understanding in the light of her cultural reality. This cultural reality is as ancient as humanity inself, thus it fosters a definition of what it used to be human that is trancultural. Optimal theory creates space for "new science of the word" (Cesaire, 1946), "that can complement and complete the natural sciences with a consistency and congruence typically unavailable, became schemes and perspectives driven by socialization are seldom throughly intergrated. The theory of optimization identifies a method and the process of transformation of consciousness which integrates all aspects of being cohesively; from e.g., issues of race, gender, and class to the environment with a common core, a universal naturalistic worldview and value belief ethic consistent with modern science.

Conclusion

Much is to be gained by the expansion of mainstream psychology to become inclusive of non-dominant and alternate cultural orientations. Roger Sperry (1995), Nobel Prize winner in physiology and medicine in 1981, notes that by the mid-1970's it was apparent that research on brain hemisphere, though richly productive, was far outweighed in importance by the potential impact of the revised concept of consciousness as casual and indispensable in scientific explanation. Although often ignored, we have examined the African (and its diasporic) cultural traditions, an underlying worldview that does not fragment spirit, as in consciousness, and science. Tracing this wisdom tradition to the beginnings of human culture and civilization, this paper has sought to illustrate the ways in which the alternate mindset non-dominant in this culture can serve to liberate and cease to perpetuate the hegemony of a fragmented, monocultural, delimiting perspective. The paradigm of the wisdom tradition of African deep thought that has been proposed offers a theory of cohensive consciousness which delineates a method for the structuring of mind to maximize positivity, harmony and balance (Goleman, 1995; Myers, 1988).

According to Homer and Heroditus, in early times Black people were the inhabitants of what we now refer to as the Sudan, Egypt, Arabia, Palestine, Western Asia, and India (James, 1954). As a consequence the characteristics of the consciousness disciplines characterizing people of color throughout the world can be summarized as follows: 1) Consciousness is primary; the source of all pleasure and suffering is in the mind; 2) A mind untrained is vastly less under our control than we imagine, but when trained, provides optimal means for enhancing well-being, enabling us to contribute to the well-being of others; 3) The trained mind is aware of itself as manifestation of God/dess (its true nature and identity), and as such uses this knowledge to avoid destruction and suffering (Walsh, 1983). Ornstein and Ehrlich (1989) suggest that our reactions to the modern world are often inappropriate because the nature of our minds and the training we give them. Currently a mismatch exists between the demands of planetary culture and our capacity to respond (Kegan, 1994). Drawing from the height of the unifying traditions of human culture, optimal theory presents a model of transformative learning, emerging in contemporary times from the realities and experience of African Americans, to foster holistic health and healing for the entire humanity.

In sum the paradigm shift which is occurring in the natural sciences, has tremendous global human and cultural implications. Psychology must be transformed to be responsive and inclusive of the assumption of the worldviews of the majority of the world's population which when approached scientifically, as in optimal theory can provide much-needed solutions. However, the understanding of the knower must be adequate to the thing to be known, and the same phenomenon may hold entirely different grades of meaning and significance to different observers with different degrees of adequation (Schumacher, 1977). Despite these potential limitations on the parts of some, others seeking and embracing an alternate holistic and integrative understanding realizing the values of developing in the wisdom tradition of African deep thought, individually and collectively. This paper has sought to demonstrate how optimal theory can help us address the historic problem of knowing and understanding (Walsh, Elgin, Vaughn, & Wilber, 1981), particularly as it relates to psychology in this social context.

References

Akbar, N. (1976). *Natural psychology and human transformation*. Chicago: World Community of Islam in the West.

Akbar, N. (1981). Mental disorder among African Americans. *Black Books Bulletin, 7(2)*.

Akishige, Y. (Ed.). (1978). *Psychological studies on Zen (2 vols.)*. Tokyo: Komazawa University

Asante, M. (1980). *Afrocentricity: Theory of social change*. Buffalo, New York: Arnulefi Publishing Company.

Asante, M. K. (1984). The African American mode of transcendence. *Journal of Transpersonal Psychology, 16(2)*, 167-178.

Baldwin, J. (1981). Notes on an Afrocentric theory of Black personality. The *Western Journal of Black Studies., 5(3)*, 172-1979.

Bateson, G. (1979). *Mind and nature: A necessary unity.* New York: E. P. Dutton.

ben-Jochannon, Y. (1970). *African origins of major western religions.* New York: Alkebulan Books.

Bernal, M. (1987). *Black Athena: The Afroasiatic roots of classical civilization.* Vol. 1. The fabrication of ancient Greece 1785-1985. New Brunswick, NJ: Rutgers University Press.

Beatty, M. (1998). Secrets and mysteries in ancient Egyptian texts. Presented at the Annual Conference of the Association for the Study of Classical African Civilization in New York (April).

Bhaskar, R. (1975). *A realist theory of science.* Leeds, England: Leeds Books.

Bynum, E. B. (1993a). *Families and the interpretation of Dreams.* Ithaca, NY: The Haworth Press.

Bynum, E. B. (1993b). *Transcending psychoneurotic disturbances: New approaches in psychospirituality and personality development.* Ithaca, NY: The Haworth Press.

Bynum, E. B. (in press). *Oludawan: The African unconscious.* NY: Columbia University Teachers College Press.

Capra F. (1975) *The Tao of physics.* New York: Bantam Books.

Capra, F. (1982) *The turning point: Science, society and the rising culture.* New York: Simon and Schuster.

Cook, N. & Kono, S. (1977). Black psychology: The third great tradition. *Journal of Black Psychology, 3,* 18-28.

deCarvalho, R. J. (1990). A history of the "Third Force" in psychology. *Journal of Humanistic Psychology, 9,* 135-137.

Diop, C. A. (1974). *The African origin of civilization: Myth or reality.* New York: Lawrence Hill and Company.

Diop, C. A. (1974). *The African origin of civilization.* Westport: Lawrence Hill and Company.

Diop C. A. (1991). *Civilization or barharism.* Brooklyn, NY: Lawrence Hill Books.

Dixon, V. (1971). *Beyond Black or White: An alternative America.* Boston: Little Brown Company.

Eddington, A. (1931). *The nature of the physical world.* New York: Macmillan.

Evans-Wentz, W. Y. (1960). *The Tibetan book of the dead.* London: Oxford University Press.

Fadiman, J. (1969). The Council Grove Conference on altered states of consciousness. *Journal of Transpersonal psychology, 9,* 169-174.

Fadiman, J. & Frager, R. (1976). *Personality and personal growth.* New York: Harper & Row.

Fairservis, W. A. (1962). *The ancient kingdoms of the Nile and the doomed monuments of Nubia.* NY: Crowell.

Fields, R. (1981). *How the swans came to the lake: A narrative history of Buddhism in America.* Boulder, Shambhala.

Finch, E. S. (1990). *The African background of medical science.* London: Karnak House.

Finch, E. S. (1998). *The star of deep thought beginnings: The genesis of African science and technology.* Atlanta: Khenti, Inc.

Forde, D. (1954). *African worlds: Studies in the cosmological ideas and social values of African peoples.* London: Oxford University Press.

Frager, R. (1974). A proposed model for a graduate program in Transpersonal psychology. *Journal of Transspersonal Psychology, 6,* 163-166.

Frye, C. (1980). *Level three: A Black philosophy reader.* Lanham: University Press of America.

Gelwick, R. (1977). *The way of discovers.* New York: Oxford University Press.

Gerhart, G. M. (1977). *Black power in South Africa: The evolution of an ideology.* Berkeley: University of California Press.

Giorgi, A. (1970). *Psychology as a human science: A phenomenologically based approach.* New York: Harper & Row.

Giuffre, k. (1998). Supernatural reality with entangled particles: Quantum evidence for the possibility of extracerebral information. Toward a Consciousness Conference. Tuscon, AZ.

Glaser, B. & Strauss, A. (1967). *The discovery of grounded theory: Strategies of qualitative research.* Chicago: Aldine Publishing Company.

Graves, R. (1875). *The world's sixteen crucified saviors: Christianity before Christ.* New York: Free Thought Books.

Greening, T. (1976). Commentary. *Journal of Humanistic Psychology, 16,* 1-3.

Grof, S. (1985). *Beyond the brain: Birth death and transcendence in psychotherapy.* Albany, NY: SUNY Press.

Harman, W. (Ed.) (In preparation). *The metaphysical foundations of modern science: A reassessment.* Palo Alto, California: Institute of Noetic Sciences.

Harre, R. (1972). *Philosophies of science.* Oxford, England: Oxford University Press.

Hornung, E. (1986). The discovery of the unconscious in ancient Egypt. *Annual of Archetypal Psychology and Jungian Thought,* 16-28.

Institute of Noetic Sciences (1990). *Annual Report of the Institute of Noetic Sciences.* Sausalito, California.

Jackson, J. G. (1970). *Introduction to African civilizations.* Secaucas, NJ: Citadel Press.

James, G. (1954). Stolen Legacy. New York: Philosophical Library.

James, W. (1902/1985) *The varieties of religious experience.* Cambridge, MA: Harvard Press.

Jantsch, E. (1980). *The self-organizing universe: Scientific and human implication of the merging emerging paradigm of evolution.* New York: Pergamon Press.

Journal of Transpersonal Psychology. (1988). Cumulative Index, 1969-1988. *Journal of Transpersonal Psychology* , 20, 185-208.

Kegan, R. (1994). *In over our heads: The mental demands of modern life.* Cambridge: Harvard.

Khatib, W. M. & Nobles, W. (1978). Historical foundations of African psychology and their philosophical consequences. *Journal of Black Psychology, 4 (1-2),* 91-102.

King, R. D. (1990). *African origin of biological psychiatry.* Germantown, TN: Seymour Smith.

Kripperm S. (Ed.). (1990). *Dreamtime and dreamwork: Decoding the language of the night.* Los Angeles: Tarcher.

LaBerge, S. (1985). Lucid dreaming: *The power of being awake and aware in your dreams.* Los Angeles: Tarcher.

Levi (1972) . *The aquarian gospel of Jesus Christ.* Marina Del Ray: DeVoris & Company.

Levin, L. W. (1977). *Black culture and Black consciousness.* New York: Oxford University Press.

Manicas, P. & Secord, P. (1983). Implications for psychology of the new philosophy of science. *American Psychologist, 38(4),* 399-413.

Maslow, A. H. (1966). *The psychology of science*: A *reconnaissance* Chicago: Regnary.

Maslow, A. H. (1958). *Motivation and personality* . New York: Harper & Row

May, R. (1972). *Power and Innocence New York*: Dell.

May, R. (1950/1970). *The meaning of anxiety.* New York: Norton.

May, R., (Ed.). (1964). *Existential psychology.* New York: Random House.

May, R., (1958). The origins and significance of the existential movement in psychology. In R. May, E. Angel, & H. F. Ellenberger (Eds.), *Existence: A new dimension in psychiatry and psychology.* New York: Basic Books.

Mbiti, J. (1970). *African religions and philosophy.* New York: Doubleday.

Metzinger, T. (1997). The self model theory subjectively. Conceptually dissolving the first-person perspective under the information processing approach. Toward A Science Consciousness International Conference. Elisnore, Denmark.

Myers, L. (1981). African-American psychology: Another way. Fourteenth Annual National Convention of Black Psychologists, Denver, Colorado.

Myers, L. (1981). The nature of pluralism in the African-American case. *Theory into practice, 20(1),* 3-6.

Myers, L. J. (1985) Transpersonal psychology: The role of the Afrocentric paradigm. *Journal of Black Psychology, 12(1),* 31-42.

Myers, L. J. (1988). *An Afrocentric worldview: Introduction to an optimal psychology.* Dubuque, Iowa: Kendall/Hunt Publishers.

Nichols, E. (1976). The philosophical aspects of cultural differences. World Psychiatric Association, Ibadan, Nigeria.

Nobles, W. (1980). African philosophy: Foundation for Black psychology. In R. L. Jones (Ed.), *Black Psychology,* (2nd ed.). New York: Harper and Row.

Ornstein, R. & Ehrlich, P. (1989). *New world new mind: Moving toward conscious evolution.* New York: Doubleday.

Plyani, M. (1966).*The tactic dimension.* Garden City: Doubleday.

Rogers, C. R. (1942). *Counseling and psychotherapy: Newer concepts in practice.* Boston: Houghton: Mifflin.

Saraswati S. S. (1984). Yoga nidre. Munger India: Bihar School of Yoga.

Schumacher, E. (1968). *A guide for the perlexed.* New York: Harper and Row.

Schwaller de Lubicz, R. A. (1982). Sacred science: *The king of pharaonic theocracy.* Rochester, VT: Inner Traditions

Selye, H. (1974). *Stress without distress.* Philadelphia: Lippincott.

Smith, H. (1976). *Forgotten truth.* New York: Harper & Row.

Sowande, R. (1972). The quest of an African worldview: The utilization of African discourse. In Daniel, J. (Ed.), *Black communication dimensions of research and instruction.* Washington, D.C.: National Endowment for the Humanities.

Sperry, R. (1995). Science for values and solutions. *APA Monitor, 7,* 6.

Sutich, A. J. (1967). The growth-experience and the growth-centered attitude. *Journal of Humanistic Psychology, 7,* 155-162.

Sutich, A. J. (1969). Some considerations regarding transpersonal psychology. *Journal of Transpersonal Psychology, 1,* 11-20.

Sutich, A. J. (1975). Process character of definitions in transpersonal psychology, *Journal of Humanistic Psychology, 15,* 39-40.

Sutich, A. J. (1976). *The founding of humanistic and transpersonal psychology:* A personal account. Unpublished doctoral dissertation, Humanistic Psychology Institute, San Francisco.

Tart, C. (1980). States of consciousness and state specific science. In R. Walsh and F. Vaughn (Eds.), *Beyond ego: Transpersonal dimensions in psychology.* Los Angeles: J. P. Tarcher.

Tart, C. (Ed.). (1969). *Altered states of consciousness.* New York, John Wiley & Sons.

Taylor, E. I. (1978). Psychology of religion and Asian studies: The William James legacy. *Journal of Transpersonal Psychology, 10,* 1.

Taylor, E. I. (1991). William James and the humanistic tradition. *Journal of Transpersonal Psychology 20,* 107-110.

Thompson, R. (1974). *African art in motion.* Los Angeles: University of California.

Vaughn, F. E. (1982). The transpersonal perspective: A personal view. Journal of *Transpersonal Psychology, 14*, 37-45.

Vich, M. A. (1988). Anthony J. Sutich, 1907-1976. *Journal of Humanistic Psychology, 16*, 3.

Walsh, R. (1983). The consciousness disciplines. *Journal of Humanistic psychology, 23(2)*, 28-30.

Walsh, R. N. & Vaughn, F. (1980). *Beyond ego: Transpersonal dimensions in psychology.* Los Angeles: J. P. Tarcher, Inc.

Watts, A. (1961). *Psychotherapy East and West.* New York: Pantheon.

Wilber, K. (1980). *The atman project.* Wheaton, IL: Quest Books.

Wilber, K. (1981). *Up from Eden.* Garden City, NY: Anchor Press/Doubleday

Wilber, K. (1984). The developmental spectrum and psychopathology: Part I, stages and types of pathology, *Journal of Transpersonal Psychology, 16*, 75-118.

William, C. (1976). *The destruction of Black civilization.* Chicago: Third World Press.

X (Clark), C., McGee, P., Nobles, W. & X (Weems) L. (1975). Voodoo or I.Q.: An introduction to African psychology. *Journal of Black Psychology, 1(2)*, 9-30.

Zahan, D. (1979). *The religion, spirituality. and thought of traditional Africa.* Chicago University Press.

Author

Linda James Myers, Ph.D
Department of Black Studies
386 University Hall
The Ohio State University
Columbus, OH 43210
Telephone: (614) 292-3447
Fax: (614) 292-2293

Afrikan/Community Psychology: Exploring the Foundations of a Progressive Paradigm

Craig C. Brookins

Introduction

Social change appears to be at the core of one's being as a contemporary African. This is particularly true for African communities throughout the Diaspora that are too often forced to define a major part of themselves based on their struggles with oppressive circumstances extending from their relationships with non-African peoples. While this has certainly not always been the case, it can be said with some certainty that contemporary issues faced by African communities are greatly linked to the challenges of self-definition based on an African-centered worldview. This attempt to reassert a more humanistic worldview for the betterment of communities is at the core of both African and Community psychology paradigms.

Concern with the capacity of traditional Euro-American psychology to adequately address social and Community problems prompted psychologists and other social scientists from diverse backgrounds to examine and develop alternative psychological paradigms. The catalyst for much of this activity as it related to the African American Community were the socio-political events of the 1960s and early 1970's (Rappaport, 1977; Williams, 1974). For instance, the urban uprisings of the 1960's witnessed a flood of research studies reexamining the sociological and psychological profiles and subsequent political dimensions of the "Negro" and the African American Community (Nobles, 1973; Sikes, 1972; Smith, 1972). Concurrently, another major line of social science research was taking place in the arena of social change and resulted in Community-based intervention work, university-Community involvement, and at least partially, the War on Poverty initiated by the Federal government in 1964 (Clark, 1965; Clark & Hopkins, 1968; Shellow, 1970).

Afrikan psychology and Community psychology originated within this socio-scientific climate with the development of alternative psychological paradigms and the formation of their respective organizations: The Association of Black Psychologists in 1968 (Williams, 1974) and the Division of Community Psychology within the American Psychological Association during the mid to late 60s (Rappaport, 1977). Despite these common origins, the subsequent development of these professional organizations and the perspectives they represent have taken relatively separate, yet parallel paths. Moreover, not until recently has any literature been published in the two main Community psychology journals that reflected an Afrocentric orientation or attempted to contrast that perspective with Community psychology (Watts, 1993).

With the above as a foundation, the purpose of this chapter is to: (a) provide a comparison of the basic principles of each field with particular attention given to the degree to which the core conceptual paradigms are congruent with the needs of the African American Community; (b) examine the relationship between Community psychology and the African American Community, particularly with regard to Community intervention research; (c) identify previous efforts that illustrate the role Community psychology can play in the African American Community; and (d) discuss the opportunities and limitations of both approaches from an Afrocentric perspective. It is not within the scope of this chapter to provide a broad overview of either Community or Afrikan psychology but rather to present a brief survey of each and how they have heretofore addressed issues within the African American Community. I believe an adequate merging of the two fields will lead to a greater understanding of the role psychology can play in the creation of a psychologically healthy African American Community, yet transcend these more circumscribed concerns to create a more optimal social scientific approach benefiting the broader society. To this end the chapter begins with a discussion of the conceptual foundations underlying both areas including the role of spiritualism, axiological considerations, the ecological paradigm and adequate definitions of "Community," promotion of a "sense of Community," diversity, and social change ideology. Strategies for achieving social change objectives are then discussed with particular reference to prevention, empowerment (including liberation ideology), and the role of research methodologies and their uses. Finally, a discussion is presented of how the intersection of these two areas provide a foundation for intervention and research with African communities.

Conceptual Foundations

Community psychology has been defined as a paradigm (Rappaport, 1977) or a "way of thinking" (Levine & Perkins, 1987) that can be used to address the myriad of social problems that exist in contemporary societies. The defining characteristics of Community psychology represent a paradigm shift and is encompassed in a worldview that has as its primary concern the health and well-being of all members within the Community. These characteristics include the necessity for adhering to humanitarian values (Fairweather, 1972), an ecological paradigm (Barker, 1963; Bronfenbrenner, 1979; Rappaport, 1977) and strategies that are consistent with these two perspectives and emphasize individual and group competencies such as Community activism, prevention, and empowerment (Berkowitz, 1992; Kelly, 1978; Rappaport, 1981). From this perspective, planned social change within scientific, political, and social arenas is seen as necessary to accomplish the goals of the Community psychologist.

Although disagreement exists on whether Afrikan psychology should be considered an "emerging perspective" (Jackson, 1982), an "optimal psychology (Myers, 1988), or an emerging discipline (Nobles, 1986), the core characteristics are not in dispute and also represent what can be considered a paradigmatic shift in the psychological arena. Afrikan psychology is also based on an ecological paradigm that recognizes the holistic experiences of human being, and emphasizes the relationships among people and their environments, and the responsibility human beings have for optimizing these relationships. For African Americans, this optimization process occurs in a context of racial and cultural oppression. Afrikan Psychology, therefore, views social change through the lens of a "liberation struggle" that promotes African cultural paradigms and individual and Community transformation.

Spiritual Conceptualizations

Afrikan psychology, more so than Community psychology, emphasizes the spiritual dimension of human beings' existence, as opposed to human/environment relationships, as the defining characteristic of the paradigm (Nobles, 1986). This appears to differ somewhat from the rare discussions of spirituality found in the Community psychology literature on religiosity (Neff & Hoppe, 1993) and what Sarason (1993) has referred to as a "need for transcendence." The former refers to a commitment to religion or religious practices that serves as a social support resource. The latter reflects a belief in the afterlife that also serves a social support function by providing the individual with a "psychological sense of Community" (Sarason, 1993).

According to Myers (1988), the Afrocentric spiritual reality asserts that "there is an all pervasive 'energy' which is the source, the sustainer, and the essence of all phenomena. In this regard everything becomes one thing, spirit manifesting." (p. 34) From this perspective, positive interpersonal relationships are part of one's ontological reality as opposed to solely being a behavioral disposition or social resource. Moreover, the "sense of Community" function of religion that Sarason refers to appears to be limited to the religious group or religion that one practices, whereas, Afrocentric spirituality seeks to connect one with all humanity and every other aspect of the physical world. While some religious beliefs may be viewed in this manner, Sarason is correct in pointing out that discussion of religion or spirituality in the psychological arena, Community psychology included, is relatively non-existent.

Taking into account the fact that many of the social change efforts occurring over the years in the African American Community were initiated by religious groups such as the Southern Christian Leadership Conference and the Nation of Islam (Sawyer, 1988; Wilmore, 1983), the question thus becomes how can the spiritual dimension of the African worldview manifest itself in psychological research and action? Watts (1993) and Lomotey and Brookins (1988) have demonstrated the reported importance of spirituality to many youth-based interventions in the African American Community, and others have pointed out the involvement of religious institutions in the implementation of support programs and empowerment efforts (Billingsley & Caldwell, 1991; McAdoo & Crawford, 1990; Moore, 1991). Yet, few studies have been done to either operationalize the construct nor to clearly describe how spirituality can be integrated into intervention models.

An examination of belief systems and worldviews appears to be one promising way of understanding how spirituality manifests itself within individuals and groups (Myers, 1988). Montgomery, Fine, and Myers (1990) and Brookins (1994) have demonstrated the efficacy as well as the problems with paper and pencil measures in this area. The Belief Systems Analysis Scale (Montgomery, Fine, & Myers, 1990) measures what the authors term an "optimal Afrocentric Worldview that views spirituality as a belief in a non-material reality that underlies all observed material phenomena and that there is a unity of spirit (thoughts/feelings) and matter (five sense perception). The essence of this unity is by nature positive, common to all persons, and unites individuals with one another and with everything else in the universe. Empirical assessments of the optimal Afrocentric worldview has shown it to be negatively related to perceived psychological distress in college students (Montgomery, Fine & Myers, 1990) and higher levels of self-esteem, lower levels of anxiety and depression, and greater satisfaction in being a mother in a sample of single and two parent household mothers (Fine, Schwebel & Myers, 1985).

The limitations of paper and pencil measures in assessing psychological, not to mention behavioral, characteristics are well known. It can probably be assumed that these problems would be magnified on a somewhat more abstract construct such as spirituality. Perhaps multiple method strategies (i.e., interviews, paper and pencil questionnaires, behavioral indicators, etc.) should be employed to most completely measure the construct. Regardless, it is clear that the centrality of spirituality to the worldviews and the liberation activities of most people of color (Watts, 1993) and those living in oppressed circumstances (Evans, 1992; Young, 1986) necessitates a greater focus for both research and action for Community and Afrikan psychologists.

Values Orientation

Both Community and Afrikan psychology operate from value orientations extending from both ecological and humanitarian paradigms. According to

Fairweather (1972), humanitarian values and social action must be the defining force beneath all social change efforts in the social sciences. Humanitarian values emphasize human beings' basic biological (e.g., food, shelter, security) and social (e.g., interpersonal relationships, human dignity, justice) needs. Social action is necessary to insure that these needs are met and maintained despite what Fairweather (1972) points out as the frequent inconsistency between humanitarian rhetoric and objective reality. From this value orientation, Community psychologists recognize the inherent conflicts and needs of a diverse society and attempt to approach social issues from an "emic" perspective that emphasizes cultural relativity and subjective validity (Zane & Sue, 1986). Individuals and groups are acknowledged for the unique perspectives they may bring in their own efforts at creating and maintaining human life. Human experiences are culturally driven and determine the ways in which problems are perceived, analyzed, and acted upon. Consequently, social analysis and action must arise from the group for which the issue is of most direct concern.

These viewpoints most directly parallel the African philosophy of life on which an Afrocentric psychology is based. The African philosophy of life places interpersonal human relationships at the center of a value system that emphasizes humanism, communalism, and the validity of "lived experience" (Mbiti, 1989; Myers, 1988; Nobles, 1986). From this perspective, the efforts of social scientists should be toward optimizing human relationships through the recognition of the historical, political, and broad social experiences of individuals and groups (Butler, et al., 1979) and how that experience interacts with contemporary realities.

Despite the fact that the actual approach to psychology as it relates to African American people has been shown to take on different schools of thought (Karenga, 1982), most of the work by African American psychologists since the turn-of-the-century (Guthrie, 1976) has certainly attempted to redefine psychological paradigms to be more consistent with the "lived experience" of peoples of African descent. In fact, perhaps the most prolific work within Afrikan psychology has been the efforts to examine the influence of historical and cultural experiences on the racial identity development of African Americans (Cross, 1991).

While the use of a socio-historical approach has been used to further understand and analyze the current status of African American communities in psychology and other social science disciplines (Gregory, 1992; Wilson, 1987, 1989), scant literature exists that examines the histories of various socio-psychological efforts to institute change within these communities. For example, little has been done to extract lessons from Kenneth Clark's work on Community action programs (Clark, 1968, 1988) to enhance contemporary Community intervention efforts. In fact, a cursory review of studies published in the *Journal of Black Psychology* since it's inception as well as the representative texts on Black Psychology (Burlew, Banks, McAdoo, & Azibo, 1992; Jenkins, 1982, 1995; Jones, 1972, 1980, 1991; Nobles, 1986; White, 1984; White & Parham, 1990) reveals little attention being given to the many social program efforts that have taken place since the mid-1960's directed at improving the conditions of African American communities. It appears the same can also be said of the Community psychology literature (Loo, Fong, & Iwamasa, 1988).

Fortunately (although primarily non-empirical), valuable information can be obtained from an examination of work in other social science and public policy areas. For instance, Fattah (1987) describes the experiences of a violence prevention intervention begun in the 1960s that is certainly relevant given the current proliferation of such programs. Heath and McLaughlin (1993) studied organizations providing services to inner-city youth (not solely African American) and provide a comprehensive examination of public policy, organizational development, and Community collaboration in addition to increasing understanding of effective intervention models. Butler (1991) provides an excellent sociological overview of the lessons learned through the many entrepreneurial and self-help enterprises within the African American Community since just prior to the 1900s that should prove valuable for those calling for similar efforts directed toward Community development. Finally, a variety of philanthropic foundations, Community agencies, and national organizations have sponsored reports identifying or describing intervention efforts in the areas of Community development (Annie E. Casey, 1992; North Carolina Poverty Project, 1989), environmental racism (Bullard, 1992), and family and child well-being (Kyle, 1987). Again however, since few of these efforts have been implemented along the lines of an action research approach, the valuable lessons they teach us must be supplemented by more systematic empirical studies.

Ecological Paradigm

Community psychology is perhaps best defined by an approach that places the person in the context of his/her environment in an attempt to understand social problems and develop ways to address them. According to Rappaport (1977), the ecological paradigm offers a conceptual alternative to traditional psychological research and practice by emphasizing the strengths of the individual and the belief that most social problems would be more appropriately addressed by individuals who have access to the appropriate resources. Along with the obvious influence of the individual, the structure and status of the Community is seen as both a causal factor in social problems and the necessary venue for interventions to address such problems. Community psychologists attempt to take the work of environmental and ecological psychology (Barker, 1963), organizational climate theory (Moos, 1974), social ecology (Kelly, 1968) general systems theory (Bertanlanffy, 1968), and developmental psychology (Bronfenbrenner, 1979) to develop a coherent approach to understanding the etiology of individual and social problems and define ways in which social problems can be addressed through interventions that recognize the dynamics of social systems. Unfortunately, the Community psychology literature has not quite lived up to these ecological expectations (Speer, et al., 1992; Wolff, 1993) although frameworks for conducting Community-based intervention and research are available (Geller, 1986; Kelly, 1988).

Akbar, Saafir and Granberry-Stewart (1980) applied one of the first ecologically oriented Afrocentric analyses of the study and practice of psychology within the African American Community. Using a systems perspective, Akbar et al. defined three distinct yet overlapping communities: physical, mental, and spiritual.

The physical Community defines relationships among people based on geographic boundaries, affective ties, shared self-definitions, and the distribution of resources. Although many physical communities in the United States continue to be segregated along racial lines, this is becoming less commonplace. Many predominantly African American communities can be defined as much by their lower socio-economic status as by any natural or enforced racial divisions. Nevertheless, defining communities according to the physical proximity of the individuals within them is certainly less than adequate, as it was in the past, and has complicated the question of adequately defining the African American Community.

The mental Community is defined by a system of shared ideas and concepts, ideologies, organizing knowledge, and problem solving. For example, Community psychologists and Afrikan psychologists would represent two distinct mental communities given the worldviews that define their areas of study. Also indicative of a mental Community would be the reactionary and proactive liberatory responses that arise from histories of oppression that have been shown to connect people of color throughout the world both historically and in contemporary times (Bulhan, 1985). Nevertheless, solely defining the African American Community as a mental Community also appears to be inadequate given the various conflicting ideologies that are evidenced throughout the social scientific literature (i.e., "old style" civil rights, neo-conservatism, nationalism, Afrocentrism, etc.)

The spiritual Community, defined by the values and ideals related to human aspirations, and that provide meaning to life, perhaps most completely brings people of African descent together according to a communal framework. The cultural commonalities indicated by Mbiti (1989), Gay and Baber (1987) and others (e.g., poetic and prosaic vernacular, funeral practices, musical styles, etc.) are said to be reflective of the African philosophy of life and essentially suggests a spiritual Community. Although spirituality is often manifested in ones religious or spiritual practices, even seemingly diverse religious affiliations (e.g., Christian, Jewish, Muslim) have been shown to share many commonalities (ben-Jochannon, 1972) at least in doctrine if not in practice.

It appears that neither of these "Community" perspectives alone adequately defines the contemporary African American Community. In fact, Akbar, Saafir and Granberry-Stewart (1980) suggests that for any individual the challenge is to obtain a relative degree of overlap among each of the communities in which one lives while moving toward their ideal integration and consistency (see Figure 1). On a

Figure 1
Illustration of movement from extant to ideal Community relationship as conceptualized by Akbar, et al., (1980)

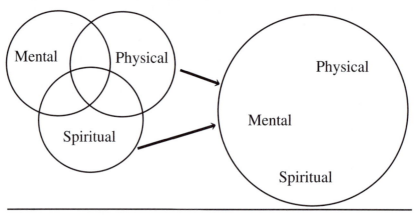

Community level, maximization of these relationships would be incorporated into the institutional structures of society (e.g., family, school, work, government policy, etc.) and provide for the optimal development of each individual.

Contributing to these Community conceptualizations for African Americans is the "Triple Quandary" socialization process as described by Boykin (1986). According to this model, developmental outcomes are influenced by three competing socialization messages, (1) the mainstream society that emphasizes Eurocentric values associated with succeeding within the American system (i.e., competitiveness, individualism, materialism, etc.); (2) the ethnic cultural societal experiences that emphasize values based on ones particular ethnic group. For African Americans, this includes an emphasis on communalism, particular styles of affective expressiveness, adherence to a social time perspective; and (3) minority experiences that are reflective of the values and behaviors often adopted as a result of living in an environment characterized by social, economic, and political oppression. Boykin points to the hegemonic influences of mainstream Euro-American values that deligitimize all other values and create a triple quandary through which affected individuals and groups must struggle to effectively negotiate.

To most fully make use of these ecological paradigms, liberation work on the part of social scientists within the African American Community must recognize and effectively negotiate the dialectics of these competing influences on individual and Community development. Strategies promoted within the Community psychology literature and elsewhere have provided useful frameworks for action research (Geller, 1986; Kelly, 1988), organizing communities (Bogan, Omar, Knobloch, Liburd, & O'Rourke, 1992; Chavis, Florin, & Felix, 1992), and supporting citizen's participation in neighborhoods (Florin, Jones, & Wandersman, 1986;

Unger & Wandersman, 1985). Unfortunately, despite the "liberation" goals advocated in much of the Afrikan psychology literature (Akbar, 1984; Baldwin, 1992; Coppock, 1975), there are few comparable frameworks that provide practical strategies for implementing change other than at the individual level.

Defining Communities

According to Rappaport (1977), Community is defined as "a subgroup within society, which is perceived or perceives itself as distinct in some respects from the larger society." (p. 3). Blackwell (1991) has provided perhaps the most comprehensive analysis of the Black Community and states:

> The Black Community is "a social system engaged in a number of interrelated activities, organized around social institutions, that function to meet specific needs and which parallel those institutions existing in the larger society. It exists in a colonized state. It is unidimensional in both sociopsychological and ecological terms. People are brought together because they share common values and interests." (p. 14)

In addition, Blackwell suggests the Black Community serves five primary functions: (1) production-distribution-consumption, (2) socialization, (3) social control, (4) social participation, and (5) mutual support. These definitions set the parameters around which psychological research and action can be developed and implemented.

Traditionally, however, psychologists within the African American Community have not given adequate attention to the interrelationships of these systemic functions as they impact individuals. For instance, understanding "production-distribution-consumption" to be a major function of the Community that promotes social and psychological health should prompt psychologists to become increasingly involved with interventions that promote economic empowerment and Community development. In an analysis of the role of Black families and Community development, Johnson (1981) makes a case for widespread institution building that will consequently facilitate strong families. While these types of efforts have long term historical precedence in the African American Community, the social technology linking Community development with psychological health remains vague. Moreover, contemporary African American communities have become increasingly diverse and thereby require strategies that may vary considerably from the past. For instance, many social scientists have pointed to the apparent class schism within the African American Community that have resulted from socioeconomic divisions (Lawson, 1992; Wilson, 1987) The differing values and interests brought about by socioeconomic divisions confounds Community development efforts solely along ethnic or racial lines. Considering the trifold conceptualization of Community that Akbar, Saafir & Granberry-Stewart (1980) propose, future Community development intervention will need to be multidimensional in it's focus and goals and attend to issues that African Americans share with other groups within their physical, mental, and spiritual communities.

Sense of Community

Along with the prevailing definitions of what can be considered a Community is the notion conceptualized by Sarason (1974) regarding a psychological sense of Community. This sense of Community is the belief the individual has regarding their belongingness to a collective of others. More specifically, Sarason (1974) has defined it as "the perception of similarity to others, and acknowledged interdependence with others, a willingness to maintain this interdependence by giving to or doing for others what one expects from them, the feeling that one is part of a larger dependable and stable structure" (p. 157). Research has shown sense of Community to be related to psychological well-being and Community activism (Davidson & Cotter, 1989). According to McMillan and Chavis (1986), a sense of Community is thought to be comprised of people's feelings of membership or belonging in their Community; a belief that they can have an influence on what takes place in their Community; a belief that they are integrated into their Community to the extent that their developmental needs will be met by resources available in the Community; and that their historical, temporal, and spatial experiences provides them with an emotional connection to the Community.

Over the years, African Americans have maintained strong and vibrant communities despite being subjected to a myriad of oppressive forces. Given the multi-level challenges that oppression imposes on individuals and communities, however, the degree to which a sense of Community has been maintained is unclear. While it is not difficult to see the sense of membership and emotional connection African Americans have to themselves and their culture, a sense of influence and integration is more elusive given it's greater dependence on forces external to the Community.

Nevertheless, a sense of Community is a concept that lends itself well to operationalizing successful intervention efforts challenging oppressive circumstances. Interventions promoting a sense of Community can incorporate preventive strategies that build individual resistance to oppression as well as empowerment strategies designed to integrate people into the "life" of the Community and maximize their strengths and influence.

Respect for Diversity

The liberation struggle that Africans in America have been engaged in can be seen as one of demanding the opportunity for culturally grounded self-actualization.

To this end, Afrikan psychology has tended to primarily focus on promoting the Afrocentric cultural paradigm while Community psychology has had a somewhat broader focus in it's advocacy for celebrating diversity in all it's manifestations (i.e., sexual orientation, mental illness, physical disabilities, etc.). These approaches are certainly compatible since by definition diversity recognizes that the strength of the overall society is built upon the strength of each of it's components.

Watts (1992) has outlined four principles that must be present if a "Psychology of Human Diversity" is to be achieved. These are human relativism, a sociopolitical orientation, an ecological and social systems approach, and participant methodologies. This chapter attempts to demonstrate how both Afrikan and Community psychology are consistent with these principles and their relative success in achieving social change goals within African American communities. It is clear that each can continue to find mutual benefit as they pursue their respective development. And, as Watts (1992) has pointed out, diversity is not exclusive of a unified frame-of-reference. Consequently, while Afrikan psychology will continue to concentrate on issues most salient to people of African descent, such an approach is necessary to place the African perspective in an empowered position so that mutual understanding and sharing can eventually take place.

Social Change Ideology

Social change can be seen as the process (as opposed to a goal) for actualizing the ideals of Community psychology. Realizing social change, or more correctly, defining social change parameters, is an illusive process that social scientists have struggled with for quite some time. Seidman (1986) has outlined two types of change that generally result from deliberate social change efforts: first order and second order social change. First order social change activities attempt to address social problems (i.e., racism, crime, low educational attainment, etc.) by coming to better understand the system and how individuals and groups can function more effectively within that system. For example, the underachieving child needs to develop attention and study skills to improve performance in the classroom. Or, the profit-oriented organization that has a history of racist treatment of African Americans needs to implement diversity training for it's employees. The results of such interventions, while certainly appropriate and necessary to improve individual functioning, do not fundamentally change the system itself. In short, it helps people to adapt to the system and perpetuates the status quo.

On the other hand, second order change effects the fundamental assumptions and operational order on which social systems are based. Accordingly, the definition of the problem is changed if it is assumed for, instance, the underachieving child has unrecognized strengths that can be used to improve academic performance and supplement other aspects of her development. Instead of low educational attainment, which would objectively remain the case, the more salient question becomes how can the system be changed to accommodate the child's diverse nature? In the case of the racist organization, assuming that racism is a fundamentally different issue than economic exploitation ignores the need to put relationships among human beings at the center of human activity. While diversity training may certainly address this broader issue, it puts the solution primarily in the framework of helping the organization achieve it's profit-making goals.

Myer's (1988) "optimal psychology" represents a shift in paradigms that advocates the need for second order change with regards to relationships among human groups and within social systems. Within the African American Community, first order change is generally conceptualized within the framework of the Black liberation struggle for racial and Community empowerment. Many social change activities are designed to bring African Americans into the mainstream of economic and social activity. Unfortunately, achieving this goal may do little to change a system that has shifted from exploitation of one group to exploitation of others both within and outside the system (e.g., other nations, cultures, and developing countries).

These perhaps extreme examples are used to illustrate the fundamental problems with social change. It requires an honest assessment of the basic premises on which we operate and the goals we seek to achieve. It runs the risk of accepting a "not-in-my-neighborhood" attitude. In other words, as long as our needs appear to be met and we can effectively function within the prevailing culture, then the problem is essentially considered solved. Alternatively, if we maintain focus on second order change, then the questions we ask as social scientists concerning liberation will likely lead us to more appropriate social change strategies.

Social Change Strategies

Community psychologists have adopted several strategies that generally include some combination of advocacy, prevention, and empowerment. Within the Afrikan psychology literature, however, there is very little reference to social change methodologies that translate liberation ideology to practical applications and strategies. A review of these concepts and the approaches taken towards their effective implementation moves us closer to conceptual and practical integration.

Prevention

Prevention is perhaps one of the more popular mental health promotion strategies advocated by Community psychologists to address the myriad problems individuals and groups face in contemporary societies. At it's most basic level, prevention refers to activities directed at the reduction of the incidence of disease or dysfunction in a population. There are three categories of prevention including primary prevention efforts directed toward entire populations, secondary prevention efforts targeting sub-groups thought to be "at-risk" for exposure to the particular disease or dysfunction, and tertiary prevention that refers to treatment of dysfunction in an effort to prevent it's reoccurrence. Successful primary and secondary prevention efforts are believed to decrease the exorbitant costs of tertiary or after-the-fact interventions. For instance, training youth in conflict resolution and violence prevention skills is expected to decrease the numbers of those youth involved in the criminal justice system and the consequent expenditures on prisons and other rehabilitative efforts.

Despite it's seeming usefulness as a concept for policymakers, prevention remains a misunderstood and infrequently used strategy on the part of these groups as well as the general populace (Mann, 1986). Nevertheless, prevention has been a stalwart of the Community psychology arena since it's inception and, although little can be found within the literature, prevention can be seen as a strategy to counter the political and social oppression that African American people encounter (Hilliard, 1988). Unfortunately, prevention is limited in it's ability to effectively address issues of oppression by what Swift and Levin (1987) have described as an interactional philosophical perspective. This perspective, among other things, tends not to view the individual within the context of the environment and values maintenance of the status quo over the need for social change. Most prevention efforts seek to equip the individual for coping with or adapting to their circumstances (Price, Cowen, Lorion, & Ramos-McKay, 1988) as opposed to changing those circumstances. As in the example indicated above, youth trained to better cope with an oppressive environment are typically not trained to change that environment. That is, the causes of the oppression are left in tact and each succeeding generation of youth must learn the same coping skills. While in it's pure form, prevention is certainly a valuable tool for assisting individuals and groups in effectively addressing their circumstances, it's greatest effectiveness can be found in combination with an empowerment ideology.

Empowerment

Unfortunately, empowerment is also an illusive concept that has taken on many manifestations both within and outside the African American Community. Empowerment is grounded in a philosophical perspective that is transactional in nature and sees changing the relationship of people to their social and physical environment as an intrinsic goal (Swift & Levin, 1987). For Community psychology, empowerment is a natural extension of prevention work and can be summarily defined as the process of allowing people to take control of their own lives in an effort to realize justice, integrity, and psychological health (Rappaport, 1981; Swift, 1992).

The Afrikan psychology literature has generally defined empowerment in terms of race consciousness and self-actualization. From this perspective the individual develops the psychosocial competence to become a proactive agent for their own liberation (Akbar, 1994; Jenkins, 1995; Kambon, 1992; Myers, 1988). Accordingly, the role of psychology is to become engaged in the process of mental liberation from the oppressive circumstances African people must contend with due to their racial status. It should be no surprise then that one of the more prolific areas of study for Afrikan psychologists, as stated earlier, is in racial and ethnic identity development and transformation. While this work has managed to provide a fairly rich understanding of the components of a healthy racial identity, developing theoretical and programmatic models for promoting and nurturing those identities among children, youth, and adults is much less forthcoming.

The promotion of race consciousness and self-actualization is a form of sociopolitical education seen as necessary to liberating individuals and groups from their oppressive circumstances. In fact, Watts (1992) has challenged Community psychologists to give much more attention to the conscientization process articulated by Friere (1975). By focusing on an in-depth understanding of oppression, conscientization seeks to transform individuals into proactive social change agents. Further research and understanding of the psychological dynamics of this sociopolitical education process is necessary to effectively translate it into practical social technologies. Brookins (1996) has taken a step in this direction in his delineation of the Adolescent Developmental Pathways Paradigm (ADPP). The ADPP is a culturally-based, developmental and ecological model for promoting identity and self-actualization in African American youth making their transition to adulthood.

Outside of psychology, empowerment for African Americans has a rich history in political science (Bobo & Gilliam, 1990; Hayes, 1992; Jennings, 1992), sociology (LaVeist, 1992; Perry, 1980), theology (Cone, 1970; Sawyer, 1988; West, 1982), and social work (Pinderhughes, 1983). These areas have generally not been given the consideration they deserve within the psychological arena despite the many lessons they can offer. Perhaps one reason for this is that writings in these areas tend to focus on analyses of the political and economic participation and influence of the African American Community and, while offering general guidelines for policy makers, social scientists, and other public servants, they provide little by way of practical interventions that have demonstrated progressive social change.

Another set of writings, however, provides rich narratives of the experiences of grassroots Community development organizations (Annie E. Casey Foundation, 1992; Center for Community Change, 1992; Woodson, 1989). Many Community development efforts extend from economic and political empowerment goals and seek to help Community members to understand their capacity to develop themselves through the process of developing their communities. These include involving people in neighborhood and other volunteer organizations (Florin, Jones &

Wandersman, 1986), Community cooperatives (Levi & Litwin, 1986), educational change strategies (Lomotey & Brookins, 1988), economic development initiatives (Swack & Mason, 1987) environmental issues (Bullard, 1992), political participation (Bobo & Gilliam, 1990; Jennings, 1992), and the elimination of poverty (North Carolina Poverty Project, 1989). Community psychologists have been much more in touch with this literature as seen in their work on citizen participation (Levi & Litwin, 1986; Zimmerman & Rappaport, 1988) and Community development (Chavis, Florin & Felix, 1992).

Research Orientation

Research methodology in Community and African psychology are essentially no different from other areas of study in the social sciences. What does differ is the emphasis placed on cultural relativity with regards to the research process. Adherence to cultural relativity requires that participants in research efforts within the African American Community be involved at every stage of the process, from defining the issues of concern, through the empirical and non-empirical methodologies used, to interpretation of the results. Accordingly, methodology is inclusive of the research design, statistical techniques, and social intervention strategies used to promote social change.

Action research methods that assist the social change process are also emphasized over more basic strategies that simply seek to understand phenomena. Action research strategies include both traditional quantitative methods (i.e., correlational, quasi-experimental, and experimental) as well as an increasing use of qualitative methods (i.e., ethnographic, epidemiological, etc.).

Fairweather and Davidson (1986) describe a comprehensive action research model based on Experimental Social Innovation and Dissemination (ESID) that in practice uses all of the above methodologies to identify the causes of social problems, formulate and evaluate interventions that address the problem, and disseminate effective intervention models to other communities and groups. ESID views the social change process as ongoing and in need of continuous scientific validation. While recognizing diversity within and between communities and cultures, the dissemination stage of ESID seeks to broadly distribute social change technology. Given the urgency of social problems within African American communities, this is a step that researchers too often neglect.

Unfortunately, as is the case with other areas mentioned in this chapter, very little action research within African American communities has been reported in either the Community or Afrikan psychology literature. While some of this may be due to the difficulties in conducting such research (Dolch & Handy, 1985; Vega, 1992) and the limited number of African American and other researchers with these interests, nevertheless, several promising ways in which research can be conducted and social intervention promoted has certainly been demonstrated. For instance,

Watts (1993) has identified the importance of and benefits to be derived from "resident research" that intimately links the researcher, the research process, and the communities of interest. Fawcett, Seekins, Whang, Muiu, & Suarez de Balcazar (1984) describe seven case studies that illustrate the role or researchers in facilitating empowerment strategies in communities; and Curtis (1989) examined the role of ethnography in assisting neighborhood leaders in developing an action plan to address issues in a multi-ethnic, low-income inner-city Community.

With regard to social intervention, even more innovative change strategies should be explored that utilize relatively unconventional but culturally powerful Community-based resources such as theater (Dorsey, 1983) and urban radio (Johnson, 1992).

Summary: Foundations of a Progressive Paradigm

The development and evolution of all social science disciplines is largely dictated by the sociopolitical context in which they exist. It is therefore not surprising that Afrikan and Community psychology share similar conceptual frameworks, value orientations, and scholarly approaches. The parallel development in these two areas has brought many, although at times isolated contributions to our understanding of social and Community change. This chapter has highlighted the similarities and differences between Afrikan and Community psychology primarily in an attempt to further understand social change technology as it relates to the African American Community (see Table 1). In our efforts to understand these relationships and move toward a more progressive paradigm several issues become more apparent.

First, the contrast between "social change" and "liberation" ideology perhaps best demonstrates the departure Afrikan psychology has taken from traditional social scientific paradigms as well as their more progressive offspring such as Community psychology. Moreover, recognizing the spiritual dimension of human communities, moves Afrikan psychology into a realm of inquiry where, as yet, few other disciplines dare to tread. It also appears, however, that the merging of Afrikan psychology principles with those of Community psychology and other areas of study can contribute to the "operationalization" of spirituality (if such a thing is possible).

Secondly, while African American communities cannot be totally defined to the exclusion of other ethnic, social, economic, or political groups, African people share a common spiritual ethos that defines their psychological frame-of-reference and in many ways dictates their similar responses to the widespread oppressive forces that challenge them on a daily basis. This dimension of thought and behavior must be recognized as central to an understanding of communities if any change efforts are to be successful. However, working in communities quickly brings the realization that liberation ideology cannot become too far removed from the tasks

Table 1
Selected Characteristics Derived from Community Psychology and Afrikan Psychology Perspectives[1]

Principles	Community Psychology	Afrikan Psychology
Conceptual Foundations	•Emic vs. Etic Perspective •Social Change •Sense of Community	•African Philosophy of Life •Spirituality •Liberation Ideology
Values Orientation	•Humanitarianism •Respect for Diversity •Cultural Relativity and Subjective Validity	•Humanism("person to person relations") •Lived Experience •Communalism"survial of the tribe
Ecological Paradigm	•Person-Environment Fit •Multiple Ecological Levels •System Orientation •1st and 2nd Order Change	•Akbar's Three Community Perspectives •Cultural Orientation •Boykins Triple Quandary Model
Social Change Strategies	•Prevention •Empowerment •Advocacy •Community Organizing/Citizen Participation •Self-help	•Sociopolitical Education ("Conscientization") •Institution Building •Personal, Social & Political Empowerment •Self-help
Research	•Experimentation and Dissemination •Ethnography	•Conceptual and Theoretical Redefinitions •Basic Research Methodologies

[1]These characteristics are those the author has found to predominate in the literature of each area but they are not meant to reflect mutual exclusivity. In fact, many of these characteristics are shared.

of helping people make the world work for them in their daily context. Making liberation a natural part of Community life is key to successful change efforts.

Thirdly, although Afrikan psychologists have historically been involved with the Community it is not clear to what extent we have been effective in altering the basic nature of communities and individuals' relationships to communities as well as the larger society. Liberation goals seek to change the basic power relationships among people within a society. This is certainly not a simple task and one that goes beyond the individually oriented approaches characteristic of most psychological areas of study, Afrikan psychology included. While the individual is certainly the core change agent, understanding better how to translate individual liberation to liberated communities are tasks yet to be realized.

Finally, the primary struggle for African communities in all their many configurations is toward a liberatory stance that reflects dignity and control of human, economic, social, and political resources. Psychology, as a discipline, has and can continue to play an important role in this process if the approach taken emphasizes the tenets of both Afrikan and Community psychology as discussed here. Change agents must understand that a systematic and scientific liberation and social change model is something that takes place over generations. Psychology and communities tend not to operate according to a long term understanding of change and the change process. As we work with people and communities, it is necessary to articulate long term visions of what our communities should look like and be as specific as possible in outlining the short and long term objectives towards realizing those visions.

References

Akbar, N. (1984). Africentric social sciences for human liberation. *Journal of Black Studies, 14*, 395-414.

Akbar, N. (1994). *Light from ancient Africa*. Tallahassee, FL: Mind Productions.

Akbar, N., Saafir, R. K., & Granberry-Stewart, D. (1980). Community psychology and systems interventions. In The Community Clinical Psychology Project of the Southern Regional Educational Board (Ed.), *Readings for mental health and human service workers in the Black community* (pp. 97-147). Atlanta, GA: Southern Regional Education Board.

Annie E. Casey Foundation. (1992). *Building strong communities: Strategies for change*. New York: Annie E. Casey Foundation.

Baldwin, J. A. (1992). The role of black psychologists in black liberation. In A. K. Burlew, W. C. Banks, H. P. McAdoo, & D. A. Azibo (Eds.), *African American psychology: Theory, research, and practice* (pp. 48-57). Newbury Park, CA: Sage Publications.

Barker, R. G. (1963). On the nature of the environment. *Journal of Social Issues, 19*, 17-38.

ben-Jochanan, Y. (1972). *Black man of the Nile*. NY: Alkebu-Lan Books.

Berkowitz, B. (1992). Revitalizing Community action. *The Community Psychologist, 25(2)*, 5-6.

Billingsley, A., & Caldwell, C. H. (1991). The church, the family, and the school in the African American Community. *Journal of Negro Education, 60*, 427-440. (N)

Blackwell, J. E. (1991). *The Black Community: Diversity and unity* (Third ed.). New York: Harper Collins.

Bobo, L., & Gilliam, F. D. (1990). Race, sociopolitical participation and black empowerment. *American Political Science Review, 84*, 377-393.

Bogan, G., Omar, A., Knobloch, R. S., Liburd, L. C., & O'Rourke, T. W. (1992). Organizing an urban African-American community for health promotion: Lessons from Chicago. *Journal of Health Education, 23*, 157-159.

Boykin, A. W. (1986). The triple quandary and the schooling of Afro-American children. In U. Neisser (Ed.), *The school achievement of minorities: New perspectives* (pp. 57-92). Hillsdale, NJ: Erlbaum.

Bronfenbrenner, U. (1979). *The ecology of human development: Experiments by nature and design*. Cambridge, MA: Harvard University Press.

Brookins, C. C. (1994). The relationship between afrocentric values and racial identity attitudes: Validation of the Belief Systems Analysis Scale on African American College Students. *Journal of Black Psychology, 20*, 128-142.

Brookins, C.C. (1996). Promoting ethnic identity delevopment in African American youth: The role rites of passage. *Journal of Black Psychology, 22*, 388-417.

Bulhan, H. A. (1985). *Frantz Fanon and the psychology of oppression*. New York: Plenum.

Bullard, R. D. (1992). *People of color environmental groups: Directory*. Flint, MI: Charles Stewart Mott Foundation.

Burlew, A. K. H., Banks, W. C., McAdoo, H. P., & Azibo, D. A. ya (Eds.). (1992). *African American Psychology: Theory, research, and practice*. Newbury Park, CA: Sage.

Butler, J. S. (1991). *Entrepreneurship and self-help among Black Americans: A reconsideration of race and economics*. Albany, NY: State University of New York.

Butler, P. A., Khatib, S. M., Hilliard, T. O., Howard, J., Reid, J., Wesson, K., Wade, G., & Williams, O. (1973). *Education in Black psychology: A position paper*. Washington, DC: Association of Black Psychologists.

Center for Community Change. (1992). *Twenty-five years of Community change*. Washington, DC: Center for Community Change.

Chavis, D. M., Florin, P., & Felix, M. R. J. (1992). Nurturing grassroots initiatives for Community development: The role of enabling systems. In T. Mizrahi & J. Morrison (Eds.), *Community organization and social administration: Advances, trends, and emerging principles*. Binghamton, NY: Haworth Press.

Clark, K. B. (1965). *Dark Ghetto: Dilemmas of social power*. New York: Harper & Row.

Clark, K. B. (1988). A Community action program. In G. W. Albee, J. M. Joffe, & L. A. Dusenbury (Eds.), *Prevention, powerlessness, and politics: Readings on social change* (pp. 461-470). Newbury Park, CA: Sage Publications.

Clark, K. B., & Hopkins, J. (1968). *A relevant war against poverty: A study of Community action programs and observable social change.* New York: Harper & Row.

Cone, J. H. (1970). *A Black theology of liberation.* New York: Schocken.

Coppock, N. (1975). Liberation and struggle: Concepts for the Afrikan family. *Journal of Black Psychology, 2,* 44-52.

Cross, W. E. (1991). *Shades of black: Diversity in African-American identity.* Philadelphia: Temple University Press.

Curtis, K. A. (1989). Help from within: Participatory research in a low-income neighborhood. *Urban Anthropology, 18,* 203-217.

Davidson, W. B., & Cotter, P. R. (1989). Sense of Community and political participation. *Journal of Community Psychology, 17,* 119-125.

Dolch, N. A., & Handy, K. M. (1985). Community groups, needs assessments and amiss methods: Reflections on Collaborative research. *Sociological Practice, 5,* 177-192.

Dorsey, F. E. (1983). African Community Theater development: Consciousness, communication, and culture. *The Western Journal of Black Studies, 7,* 78-82.

Evans, E. N. (1992). Liberation theology, empowerment theory and social work practice with the oppressed. *International Social Work, 35,* 135-148.

Fairweather, G. W. (1972). *Social Change: The challenge to survival.* Morristown, NJ: General Learning Press.

Fairweather, G. W., & Davidson, W. S. (1986). *An introduction to community experimentation: Theory, methods, and practice.* New York: McGraw-Hill.

Fawcett, S., Seekins, T., Whang, P. L., Muiu, C., & Suarez de Balcazar, Y. (1984). Creating and using social technologies for Community empowerment. In J. Rappaport, C. Swift, & K. Hess (Eds.), *Studies in empowerment: Steps toward understanding action* (pp. 145-171). New York: Haworth Press.

Fine, M. A., Schwebel, A. I., & Myers, L. J. (1985). The effects of worldview adaptation to single parenthood among middle-class adult women. *Journal of Family Issues, 6,* 107-127.

Florin, P., Jones, E., & Wandersman, A. (1986). Black participation in voluntary organizations. *Journal of Voluntary Action Research, 15,* 65-86.

Gay, G., & Baber, W. L. (Eds.). (1987). *Expressively Black: The cultural basis of ethnic identity.* New York: Praeger.

Gregory, S. (1992). The changing significance of race and class in an African-American Community. *American Ethnologist, 19,* 255-274.

Guthrie, R. V. (1976). *Even the rat was white: A historical view of psychology.* New York: Harper & Row.

Hayes, F. W. (1992). Governmental retreat and the politics of African-American self-reliant development: Public discourse and social policy. *Journal of Black Studies, 22,* 331-348.

Heath, S. B., & McLaughlin, M. W. (Eds.). (1993). *Identity and inner-city youth: Beyond ethnicity and gender*. New York: Teachers College Press.

Hilliard, T. O. (1988). Prevention of psychopathology in Blacks. In G. W. Albee, J. M. Joffe, & L. A. Dusenbury (Eds.), *Prevention, powerlessness, and politics: Readings on social change* (pp. 342-358). Newbury Park, CA: Sage Publications.

Jackson, G. G. (1982). Black psychology: An avenue to the study of Afro-Americans. *Journal of Black Studies, 12*, 241-260.

Jenkins, A. H. (1982). *The psychology of the Afro-American: A humanistic approach*. New York: Pergamon Press.

Jenkins, A. H. (1995). *Psychology and African Americans: A humanistic approach* (2nd ed.). Boston: Allyn and Bacon.

Jennings, J. (1992). *The politics of Black empowerment: The transformation of Black activism in urban America*. Detroit, MI: Wayne State University Press.

Johnson, P. (1992). Black/urban radio is in touch with the inner city: What can educators learn from this popular medium? *Education and Urban Society, 24*, 508-518.

Johnson, R. C. (1981). The Black family and Black community development. *Journal of Black Psychology, 8*, 35-52.

Jones, R. L. (Ed.). (1972). *Black psychology* (1st ed.). New York: Harper & Row.

Jones, R. L. (Ed.). (1980). *Black psychology* (2nd. ed.). New York: Harper & Row.

Jones, R. L. (Ed.). (1991). *Black psychology* (3rd. ed.). Berkeley, CA: Cobb & Henry Publishers.

Kambon, K. K. K. (1992). *The African personality in America: An African-centered framework*. Tallahassee, FL: Nubian Nation Publications.

Karenga, M. (1982). *Introduction to Black studies*. Inglewood, CA: Kawaida Publications.

Kelly, J. G. (1968). Toward and ecological conception of preventative interventions. In J. W. Carter (Ed.), *Research contributions from psychology to Community mental health* (pp. 75-99). New York: Plenum Press.

Kelly, J. G. (1988). *A guide to conducting prevention research in the community: First steps*. New York: Haworth Press.

Kyle, J. E. (1987). Strategic planning and program coordination. In J. E. Kyle (Ed.), *Children, families and cities: Programs that work at the local level* (pp. 7-34). Washington, DC: National League of Cities.

LaVeist, T. A. (1992). The political empowerment and health status of African-Americans: Mapping a new territory. *American Journal of Sociology, 97*, 1080-1095.

Lawson, B. E. (Ed.). (1992). *The underclass question*. Philadelphia: Temple University Press.

Levi, Y., & Litwin, H. (Eds.). (1986). *Communities and cooperatives in participatory development*. Brookfield, VT: Gower Press.

Levine, M., & Perkins, D. V. (1987). *Principles of community psychology: Perspectives and applications*. New York: Oxford University Press.

Lomotey, K., & Brookins, C. C. (1988). Independent Black institutions: A cultural perspective. In D. T. Slaughter & D. J. Johnson (Eds.), *Visible now: Blacks in private schools*. New York: Greenwood Press.

Loo, C., Fong, K. T., & Iwamasa, G. (1988). Ethnicity and cultural diversity: An analysis of work published in community psychology journals, 1965-1985. *Journal of Community Psychology, 16*, 332-349.

Mann, P. A. (1986). Prevention of child abuse: Two contrasting social support services. *Prevention in Human Services, 4*, 73-111.

Mbiti, J. S. (1989). African religions and philosophy (2nd. ed.). Oxford: Heinemann.

McAdoo, H., & Crawford, V. (1990). The Black church and family support programs. *Prevention in Human Services, 9*, 193-203.

McMillan, D. W., & Chavis, D. M. (1986). Sense of community: A definition and theory. *Journal of Community Psychology, 14*, 6-23.

Montgomery, D. E., Fine, M. A., & Myers, L.J. (1990). The development and validation of an instrument to assess an optimal afrocentric worldview. *Journal of Black Psychology, 17*, 37-54.

Moore, T. (1991). The African American church: A source of empowerment, mutual help, and social change. *Prevention in Human Services, 10*, 147-167.

Myers, L. J. (1988). *Understanding an afrocentric worldview: Introduction to an optimal psychology*. Dubuque, IA: Kendall/Hunt.

Neff, J. A., & Hoppe, S. K. (1993). Race/ethnicity, acculturation, and psychological distress: Fatalism and religiosity as cultural resources. *Journal of Community Psychology, 21*, 3.

Nobles, W. W. (1973). Psychological research and the Black self-concept: A critical review. *Journal of Social Issues, 29*, 11-31.

Nobles, W. W. (1986). *African psychology: Towards its reclamation, reascension and revitalization*. Oakland, CA: The Institute for the Advanced Study of Black Family Life and Culture.

North Carolina Poverty Project. (1989). *Twenty-five years of community action in North Carolina 1964-1989*. Greensboro, NC: North Carolina Poverty Project.

Perry, H. L. (1980). The socioeconomic impact of Black political empowerment in a rural southern locality. *Rural Sociology, 45*, 207-222.

Pinderhughes, E. B. (1983). Empowerment for our clients and for ourselves. *Social Casework, 64*, 331-338.

Price, R. H., Cowen, E. L., Lorion, R. P., & Ramos-McKay, J. (Eds.). (1988). *Fourteen ounces of prevention: A casebook for practitioners.* Washington, DC: American Psychological Association.

Rappaport, J. (1977). *Community psychology: Values, research, and action.* New York: Holt, Rinehart and Winston.

Rappaport, J. (1981). In praise of paradox: A social policy of empowerment over prevention. *American Journal of Community Psychology, 9,* 1-25.

Sarason, S. B. (1974). *The psychological sense of community: Prospects for Community psychology.* San Francisco: Jossey-Bass.

Sarason, S. B. (1993). American psychology, and the needs for transcendence and community. *American Journal of Community Psychology, 21,* 185-202.

Sawyer, M. R. (1988). Black ecumenical movements: Proponents of social change. *Review of Religious Research, 30,* 151-161.

Shellow, R. (1970). Social scientists and social action from within the establishment. *Journal of Social Issues, 26,* 207-220.

Sikes, M. P. (1972). Community mental health and community psychology: A Black's perspective. *Interamerican Journal of Psychology, 6,* 131-136.

Smith, W. (1972). Youth-A view from Berkeley: Black youth. In D. Adelson (Ed.), *The community psychology series: Volume 1. Man as the measure: The crossroads* (pp. 78-88). New York: Behavioral Publications.

Speer, P., Dey, A., Griggs, P., Gibson, C., Lubin, B., & Hughey, J. (1992). In search of community: An analysis of community psychology research from 1984 -1988. *American Journal of Community Psychology, 20,* 195-210.

Swack, M., & Mason, D. (1987). Community economic development as a strategy for social intervention. In E. M. Bennett (Ed.), *Social intervention: Theory and practice* (pp. 93-124). Lewiston, NY: Edwin Mellen Press.

Swift, C. F. (1992). Empowerment: The greening of prevention. In M. Kessler, S. E. Goldston, & J. M. Joffe (Eds.), *The present and future of prevention* (pp. 99-114). Newbury Park, CA: Sage Publications.

Swift, C., & Levin, G. (1987). Empowerment: An emerging mental health technology. *Journal of Primary Prevention, 8,* 71-94.

Unger, D., & Wandersman, A. (1985). The importance of neighbors: The social, cognitive, and affective components of neighboring. *American Journal of Community Psychology, 13,* 139-169.

Vega, W. A. (1992). Theoretical and pragmatic implications of cultural diversity for community research. *American Journal of Community Psychology, 20,* 375-392.

Watts, R. J. (1992). Elements of a psychology of human diversity. *Journal of Community Psychology, 20,* 116-131.

Watts, R. J. (1993). Community action through manhood development: A look at concepts and concerns from the front-line. *American Journal of Community Psychology, 21,* 333-360.

West, C. (1982). *Prophesy deliverance!: An Afro-American revolutionary christianity* (1st ed.). Philadelphia: Westminster Press.

White, J. L. (1984). *The psychology of Blacks: An Afro-American perspective.* Englewood Cliffs, NJ: Prentice-Hall.

White, J. L., & Parham, T. A. (1990). *The psychology of Blacks: An African-American perspective (Second ed.).* Englewood Cliffs, NJ: Prentice Hall.

Williams, R. (1974). A history of the Association of Black Psychologists: Early formation and development. *Journal of Black Psychology, 1,* 9-24.

Wilson, J. (1987). *The truly disadvantaged: The inner city, the underclass, and public policy.* Chicago: University of Chicago Press.

Wilson, W. J. (1989, January). The underclass: Issues, perspectives, and public policy. *Annals of The American Academy of Political and Social Science, 501,* 182-192.

Woodson, R. L. (1989). NPI Policy Review Series. Race and economic opportunity. Washington, D.C.: The National Center for Neighborhood Enterprise.

Young, J. U. (1986). *Black and African theologies: Siblings or distant cousins?* Maryknoll, NY: Orbis Books.

Zane, N., & Sue, S. (1986). Reappraisal of ethnic minority issues: Research alternatives. In E. Seidman & J. Rappaport (Eds.), *Redefining social problems* (pp. 289-304). New York: Plenum.

Zimmerman, M. A., & Rappaport, J. (1988). Citizen participation, perceived control, and empowerment. *American Journal of Community Psychology, 16,* 725-750.B

Author

Craig C. Brookins
Department of Psychology
Box 7801
North Carolina State University
Raleigh, NC 27695-7801
Telephone: (919) 515-1725
Fax: (919) 515-1716
E-mail: craig@poe.coe.nscu.edu

Valucation: Definition, Theory, and Methods

Jerome Taylor, Sekai Turner, and Marjorie Lewis

Introduction

The word "value" comes from the Latin verb *valere* which means to be worthy or strong. For us, to be worthy is to be excellent — resourceful and exemplary — and to be strong is to be sturdy — stalwart and tenacious. Here, we are especially interested in excellence and strength which are producible in circumstances of a wide range: Hospitable to hostile, democratic to oppressive, cooperative to competitive, malleable to intractable, ingenuous to disingenuous. We shall use the term *valucation* to identify methods that deepen commitment to values which enhance personal excellence and strength in environments of a wide range.

The importance of valucation is suggested from an examination of two contrasting modes of adaptation. For the snake, body temperature changes as ambient temperature changes (poikilothermic adaptation), and for the hare body temperature remains steady over widely varying ambient temperatures (homeothermic adaptation). Thus the hare's survivability is greater because its body temperature is less environmentally dependent than the snake's. We submit that certain values operate a bit like the adaptive mechanism in homeothermic organisms — their presence enhances survivability in environments of an impressive range.

Which target values are proxies for excellence and strength in diverse environments? How do these values influence cognitive and behavioral processes? And which methods are useful in promoting these values in children and their communities? We attempt to answer the first question under Selection, the second under Theory, and the third under Methods. Future research, development, and policy initiatives are considered under Implications. Although theory and methods introduced here are intended to inculcate values promoting survival across environments of a wide range, we recognize with unabated urgency the need to create more livable and generative environments in the first instance. The latter is the subject of public policy, the former of cultural policy (Jackson-Lowman, 1992; Taylor & Franklin, in press). We believe the coordination of these policy types is in the best interest of African American children and our nation as a whole. We believe neither policy type alone is sufficient.

Selection

When African American and White parents of low to middle income are given opportunity to express how they want their young children to turn out 15 years from now, from 80 to 99 percent of what they say can be compressed into one or more of six categories (Denton, Taylor, Kelly, Ruback, & Feiring, 1977; Taylor, in press; Wilson, 1974):

1a. *Love and Respect* — I want my child to love and be loved, to be obedient to me and cooperative with others having their best interests in mind, to respect my decisions, to be open to constructive advice and assistance during times of trouble.

1b. *Interpersonal Skills* — I want my child to be honest in dealing with her feelings and those of others, to be able to see others as they really are, to be effective in dealing with others, and to be capable of leading others.

2. *Learning Orientation* — I want my child to be savvy, a good thinker and a good learner, to be sharp, smart.

3. *Self-Confidence* — I want my child to be eager to tackle new tasks, explore new places, meet new people, to be daring in constructive ways, to have an excitement about living.

4. *Self-Persistence* — I want my child to be able to stick with a task until it's finished, to be able to stand in a storm, to be able hang in there when the going gets tough and not give up.

5. *Self-Esteem* — I want my child to feel good about herself, to feel beautiful inside, to enjoy who she is, to be proud of her heritage.

6. *Self-Reliance* — I want my child to be able to think and act alone when necessary; when appropriate I want my child to be able to say "no" when everybody else is saying "yes" or to say "yes" when everybody else is saying "no".

In recent papers we have combined 1a and 1b into a magnum category Love and Respect (Taylor, Turner, Franklin, Jackson, & Stagg, 1994) because separating their component scales thus far has proven statistically impossible (Taylor, in press). Because success of valuation efforts is likely to turn on projected outcomes of value to parents, we shall preserve the original intent of parents by referring to seven rather than six categories of valued child outcomes throughout this paper.

Our basic proposition then is this: Love and Respect, Interpersonal Skills, Learning Orientation, Self-Confidence, Self-Persistence, Self-Esteem, and Self-Reliance are target values that promote excellence and strength across diverse environments. We support this proposition on experiential, historical, political, scriptural[1], and empirical grounds.

In projecting their children's future, parents often recalled personal or family experiences in which one or more of the target values played a critical role. As often parents related personal disappointments or failures they felt could have been avoided if only they had more Self-Confidence or Self-Esteem, for example. Experientially, then, target values are survival relevant to parents (Wilson, 1974).

Historically, biographies of male and female African American innovators in political, legal, social, and scientific disciplines provide recurring evidence of exemplary performance on target values. The record indicates that possession and expression of these values were instrumentally related to their success in managing environments of a wide range (Franklin & Meier, 1982; Igus, 1992; Taylor, Denton, Dotson, Mosley, & Smith-Jones, 1985). Politically, the development of local and national organizations to address conditions of adversity was made possible by African American leaders whose vision affirmed target values (Franklin & Meier, 1982; Igus, 1992). Scripturally, we have found that major biblical heroes and heroines exemplified target values which were key to their managing favorable and unfavorable circumstances (Taylor et al., 1985). Finally, two types of evidence are relevant to our empirical claim: (a) results of face-to-face interviews supported the critical importance of target values in the lives of 60 prominent political, educational, and entrepreneurial African American leaders in a large Eastern city and (b) a literature review of empirical studies provided evidence that correlates of identified values were associated with salutary outcomes under environmentally diverse circumstances (Taylor et al., 1985).

For experiential, historical, political, scriptural, and empirical reasons, then, we believe target values Love and Respect, Interpersonal Skills, Learning Orientation, Self-Confidence, Self-Persistence, Self-Esteem, and Self-Reliance promote excellence and strength in diverse environments. Further, we believe that target values are not only survival *relevant* but also immanently *implementable*. We offer three reasons why target values are developmentally and politically implementable.

First, target values are broadly supportable by parents who generated them to begin with. Promotion of narrowly endorsed values would tend to fracture rather than unify a community. Second, target values are transducible, that is, competence on target values is transferable to other areas. Commitment to target values may be associated with better structural outcomes — occupational, educational, and economic. They may be associated with better social outcomes — lower rates of homicide, suicide, teenage pregnancy, chemical dependency, or welfare dependency and higher rates of employment or entrepreneurship. They may be associated with more mature spiritual commitment — with social as well as personal expressions of one's faith. And third, target values are behaviorally achievable. Parents and teachers of young children can be taught how to become more proficient in bringing about behavioral expressions of target values (Taylor, in press; Taylor et al., 1992).

Having examined the case that target values are supportable, transducible, relevant, and achievable, we proceed now to examine how these target values influence cognitive and behavioral processes and outcomes.

Theory

According to Rokeach (1973), values as beliefs reflect preferred means or ends. Love and Respect, Interpersonal Skills, Learning Orientation, Self-Confidence, Self-Persistence, Self-Esteem, and Self-Reliance as target values which affirm parental aspirations are examples of preferred ends which may serve also as means. A closer examination of the literature suggests a more extended meaning: The values construct is used to reference antecedents, consequences, objects, or constructs. Let us take the target value Learning Orientation (commitment to learning) to illustrate these differences: (a) Value as antecedent — "Commitment to learning (X) will lead to a professional occupation (Y)"; (b) Value as consequence — "Weekly visits to the library (X) will enhance commitment to learning (Y)"; (c) Value as object — "Commitment to learning (X) is smart (Y)"; (d) Value as construct — "Commitment to learning (X) is predictive of attitude toward self determination (Y)". That values may serve any to all of these roles at different times perhaps explains why they have such pervasive effects on attitudes and behaviors of an impressive range: Occupational choice (Kempe, 1960), cigarette smoking (Grube, Weir, Getzlaf, & Rokeach, 1984), automobile purchase (Henry, 1976), interracial behavior (Rokeach, 1973), political orientation (Cochrane, Billig, & Hogg, 1979), natural food shopping (Homer & Kahle, 1988), choice of friends (Beech, 1966), and participation in civil rights activities (Rokeach, 1973).

Despite variations in usage, values unexceptionally are expectancies or beliefs which connect identified subjects X to predicate nominatives Y (objects) or to predicate objects Y (antecedents, consequences, or constructs). In the theory of reasoned action (Fishbein & Ajzen, 1975; Ajzen & Fishbein, 1980) expectancies b can be estimated using a unipolar 0 to 1.0 strength-of-belief scale. Let us say, for example, that $b_i = .7$ for the first statement "Commitment to learning will lead to a rewarding occupation." To estimate attitude toward the subject "commitment to learning" requires evaluation of the attribute "professional occupation" inherent in the expectancy b_i. This typically is done using a bipolar -3 (unfavorable) to +3 (favorable) scale. Let us say that evaluation e_i is +2 for the attribute "professional occupation." The attitude toward "commitment to learning" is then estimated from $b_i \times e_i$ or +1.4 in the present instance. Of course in the typical application, multiple rather than single items are used to estimate components b_i and e_i. The advantage of the theory of reasoned action thus far is that it (a) provides a theoretical method for accommodating the several ways in which the value concept is utilized in research and (b) offers a measurement procedure for estimating attitudinal disposition toward the statement in which the value concept occurs.

A further advantage of the theory of reasoned action is that it includes social as well as cognitive and affective factors in the coprediction of behavioral intention. We have just reviewed the cognitive b_i and affective e_i factors of attitude A. To what extent do significant others think I should have a basic commitment to learning (b_i)

and to what extent do I tend to go along with their perception in this regard (m_i)? Answers to these questions go to the issue of subjective norms SN — perceived social pressure to endorse the subject term X — which may be of particular importance to value formation in developmental contexts. The construct b_i of SN can be estimated from the same unipolar 0-to-1.0 scale used to estimate b_i of A (My best friend thinks I should have a basic commitment to learning), and m_i of SN can be estimated using a bipolar scale -3 "strongly disagree" to +3 "strongly agree" (I tend to go along with my best friend's thinking on commitment to learning). Let us say for SN that $b_i = .6$ and that $m_i = +2$. Under the theory of reasoned action, SN = b_i x m_i or +1.2 in the present instance. With an A of +1.4 and SN of +1.2, it would appear that there is moderate cognitive, affective, and normative support for the target value Learning Orientation. As before, however, multiple rather than single items are typically used in estimating components of SN.

Finally, we note that the theory of reasoned action does not include systematic attention to a fundamental construct in cognitive science — information processing. How we decode, encode, retrieve, and judge information may be directly and indirectly influenced by cognitive, affective, and normative factors. A basic commitment to learning (Learning Orientation), for example, may influence what we attend to (decoding), what we remember from what we've attended to (encoding), what we recall from what we've remembered (retrieving), and how we interpret what we've remembered or recalled (judging). Target values, we argue, are critically related to what we think about — information processing — and are vitally important in the coprediction of behavioral intention.

Figure 1 presents our *theory of mediated action* which embeds the theory of reasoned action along with key constructs from information processing theory.

We now proceed to define the ten basic constructs in Figure 1 and to explore their interrelationships through twelve propositions — eight basic, four applied.

Constructs

1. Stimulus Field (SF): The totality of experiences encountered, created, or structured on an ongoing basis. Structured experiences are designed by others, e.g., a parent's dividing a child's evening into scheduled periods of chores, study, and leisure. Created experiences are designed by self, e.g., building model airplanes or playing compact discs, and encountered experiences are not planfully designed by self or other, e.g., an accident on the corner, a murder in the neighborhood, a fight at school, a racist, sexist, classist, or homophobic incident on television.

2. Target Values (TV): Love and Respect, Interpersonal Skills, Learning Orientation, Self-Confidence, Self-Persistence, Self-Esteem, and Self-Reliance which may at a given time occupy the theoretical status of antecedent, consequence, object, or construct.

Figure 1
Toward a Theory of Mediated Action: Implications for Understanding Valucation Processes and Outcomes

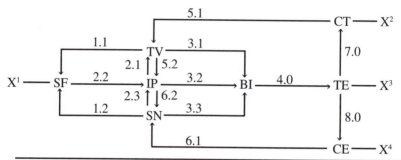

SF=Stimulus Field, TV=Target Values, IP=Information Processing, SN=Subjective Norms, CT=Cumulative Teachings, BI=Behaviorial Intention, TB=Target Behaviors, CE=Current Expectations, X_i=Methods of Valucation directed toward SF (1), CT (2), TB (3), and CE (4).

3. Subjective Norms (SN): Perceived social pressure from significant others —parents, friends, teachers, ministers, youth leaders, media heroes and heroines— to think or behave in certain ways. Of critical interest here is the meta-perception — "I think significant other thinks I should do (or think)..." — and the estimated motivation to comply — "I tend to go along with what significant other thinks I should do (or think)...".

4. Information Processing (IP): What we notice (decoding), what we remember of what we've noticed (encoding), what we recall of what we've remembered (retrieving), and what we make of what we've remembered or recalled (judging). A child notices a particular hero within an otherwise busy Saturday morning cartoon (decoding), and she remembers the hero's cracking his arch enemy over the head (encoding). The following Wednesday she shares her recollection of hero's actions with a friend (retrieving) along with her explanation for hero's actions: "He deserved it for messing with him!" (judging).

5. Behavioral Intention (BI): Basic disposition to perform Target Behaviors reflecting some aspect of Love and Respect, Interpersonal Skills, Learning Orientation, Self-Confidence, Self-Persistence, Self-Esteem, or Self-Reliance.

6. Target Behaviors (TB): Performance which expresses or affirms some aspect of Target Values Love and Respect, Interpersonal Skills, Learning Orientation, Self-Confidence, Self-Persistence, Self-Esteem, or Self-Reliance.

7. Cumulative Teachings (CT): Planned, incidental, or autotelic instruction which affects quality of life. Planned instruction has formal or informal structure — goals with strategies, materials or timeframes. Incidental instruction emerges out of unplanned or uncharted events — a fight, a riot, a gift, a headline, a television program. And autotelic instruction springs from insights gleaned from one's own behavior. These cumulative teachings — planned, incidental, and autotelic — may affect quality of life either positively or negatively.

8. Current Expectations (CE): Designed social pressure from significant others — parents, friends, teachers, ministers, youth leaders, media heroes and heroines — to think or behave in certain ways. The qualifier "designed" for CE complements the qualifier "perceived" for SN, the former referring to intended and the latter to experienced social pressure. The two may not be the same.

9. Valucation Method X_i: X_1 refers to methods designed to regulate the stimulus field, X_2 to methods designed to inform cumulative teachings, X_3 to methods designed to influence target behaviors directly, and X_4 to methods designed to effect current expectations. Together X_1 through X_4 are designed to enhance commitment of children and youth to target values that promote excellence and strength in environments of a wide range.

Propositions

The validity of our model rests on the corroborability of eight propositions which flow directly from our theory of mediated action. These propositions are presented in relationship to their theoretical, empirical, or logical origins. Our basic model is then used as a framework for identifying valucation methods which we anticipate will work as described under four propositions. We first cover our eight basic propositions, then our four applied propositions.

Basic

In relation to constructs introduced in the previous section, the following basic propositions are implied from Figure 1:

1. The stimulus field is influenced by target values (1.1) and subjective norms (1.2).

1.1 A child comfortable with herself and her heritage (Self-Esteem) might be inclined to seek out books, programs, and experiences which deepen her appreciation for her culture of origin (created stimulus field). Noticing these commitments, such a child is likely to be encouraged by parents, relatives, or teachers who themselves identify books, experiences, or programs to deepen the child's cultural appreciation (structured stimulus field). Possibly also the encountered experiences of children high in target values could be different, that is, moment-by-moment decisions they make might well produce a different stimulus field than children low in target values. These expectations are generally consistent with the view that values as cognitions guide the structuring of and response to the stimulus field (Kahle, 1980).

1.2 The structured, created, and encountered stimulus fields of children are influenced by significant others who include their friends and peers. In the process of sharing experiences from their respective stimulus fields, normative expectancies emerge. To varying degrees, children want to try or experience what their friends tried or experienced. These expectations are consistent with developmental theory and clinical observation. To maximize constructive impact on information processing, the best option of course is to deepen the commitment of children to target values and to deepen their appreciation for significant others who are committed to target values.

2. Information processing is influenced by target values (2.1), the stimulus field (2.2), and subjective norms (2.3).

2.1 Target values are cognitive schema which represent an organized collection of beliefs. Self-Reliance as object, for example, may be characterized by such attributes as "courageous," "independent," "inventive," or "strong." We would anticipate, then, that persons highly committed to the value Self-Reliance would tend to notice (decode), remember (encode), and retrieve (recall) information consistent with these attributes which affirm the target value. A particular story of courageous action or a particular movie of inventive genius might be more quickly noticed, remembered, and retrieved by persons committed to the target value Self-Reliance. Moreover, they might tend to interpret behaviors of self or others using dispositional terms such as "courageous" or "strong" (judging). In general effects of schema types on information processing has been well documented for social groups (Hamilton, Sherman, & Ruvolvo, 1990), person types (Amato, 1991), self descriptions (Rholes, Riskind, & Lane, 1987; Dobson & Shaw, 1987), and explanatory constructs (Stewart, 1986).

2.2 What we are exposed to often influences what we think about. Children exposed to experiences that stimulate their "curiosity" (e.g., Children's Museum), spark their "inquisitiveness" (e.g., science project), or encourage their "forwardness" (e.g., tackling a new problem) — all attributes related to Self-Confidence as object — may lead them to notice challenging tasks (decoding), remember their experiences with them (encoding), discuss them with others (retrieval), and assign mastery attributions to them (judging). That sustained exposure can influence information processing is suggested from studies of pornographic violence which demonstrate that repeated exposure can negatively influence how females as well as males think about women (Linz, Donnerstein, & Penrod, 1984; Malamuth, Check, & Briere, 1986; Malamuth & Donnerstein, 1983; Zillman & Bryant, 1984). On the constructive side, we believe sustained exposure to experiences which pique curiosity, inquisitiveness, and forwardness can positively influence how children think about the target value Self-Confidence. An analogous case can be made for each of the remaining target values.

2.3 What we notice and what we remember of what we've noticed is often influenced by significant others who share these moments with us. Through shared exchange and recall these moments are codified in memory. Also, what we make of what we've noticed or remembered may be influenced by significant others. We seek to explain what we've noticed or remembered, and through a process of social comparison we turn to others for self validation (Festinger, 1954). Information processing, then, is influenced by social as well as cognitive factors.

3. Behavioral intention is influenced by target values (3.1), information processing (3.2), and subjective norms (3.3).

3.1 Whether antecedent, consequence, object, or construct we argue that target values as abstract attitudes influence behavioral intention. If Akela is committed to the target value Interpersonal Skills, then when confronting a potential or actual conflict such defining attributes as "honesty," "openness," "accuracy," or "leadership" should be reflected in her behavioral disposition toward working through the conflict. In general the critical role of attitude in copredicting behavioral intention across 87 studies has been affirmed in Sheppard, Hartwick, & Warshaw (1988).

3.2 Continuing the example of 3.1, Akela's behavioral intention is guided not only by the target value Interpersonal Skills but also by active recall and evaluation of similar situations or persons. There is reason to believe that this reflective process which is omitted from the theory of reasoned action affects behavioral intention directly (cf. Sanbonmatsu & Fazio, 1990).

3.3 What we intend to do is partly dependent upon subjectively experienced pressures from significant others. The important role of subjective norms in copredicting behavioral intention has been documented in meta-analyses conducted by Sheppard et al (1988).

4. Target behavior is influenced by behavioral intention (4.0). That what we intend to do is a fair predictor of what we in fact do is suggested by a mean correlation of .53 between behavioral intention and behavioral performance reported for 87 studies involving 11,566 participants (Sheppard et al., 1988). We take, therefore, intention to behave in a value-consistent manner as a fair predictor of behaving in a value-consistent manner. At some subsequent point, it may be necessary to consider additional variables such as perceived control as copredictors of target behaviors (cf. Ajzen, 1985).

5. Target values are influenced by cumulative teachings (5.1) and information processing (5.2).

5.1 Instruction by precept or example provides the structural *anlagen* for whatever values are incorporated by children. Instruction which may be formal or informal can be purveyed by parents, relatives, and peers as well as by educational, religious, and social institutions in addition to the print and electronic media. Instruction can be situational — directed toward specific events — or abstract — directed toward general principles. Whatever the basis (situational or abstract), whoever the purveyor (within or outside the family), and whatever the method (formal or informal), we believe cumulative teachings influence target values one way or another. For example, supporting a child's resolution of conflict through force — one method of teaching — is hardly a way of inspiring others' Love and Respect for the child or the child's Love and Respect for others.

5.2 This subproposition affirms the wisdom of Solomon: "For as a man thinketh in his heart, so is he" (Proverbs 23:7). Recurring preoccupations are likely to influence target values one way or another. Recurring self doubt, for example, will likely diminish one's momentary commitment to the target value Self-Confidence. Here enters of course the importance of personality and nosological variables. We note also that by whatever means the thinking of another is influenced indirectly — through the stimulus field (2.2) or through subjective norms (6.2) as examples — value formation is also influenced indirectly. This structural subproposition is dependent upon the validity of component pathways implied by it, notably but not exclusively 2.2-5.2 and 6.2-5.2.

6. Subjective norms are influenced by current expectations (6.1) and information processing (6.2).

6.1 We anticipate that effects of current expectations on subjective norms will be conditioned by likability and communicability of the source — the person conveying the expectation. The clarity with which the source's beliefs are communicated is likely to affect accuracy of the child's meta-perception: "I think [the source] thinks I should think (or do) ...". A garbled message is likely to produce an inaccurate meta-perception. The attractiveness and acceptability of the meta-perception — the child's perception of the source's beliefs — we expect will increase commensurately with the child's liking of the source. Communicability, then, is relevant to the b_i component and likability to the m_i component of SN. Where both are in place, we anticipate current expectations will affect subjective norms directly.

6.2 We argued previously that cognitive processes are influenced by subjective norms (2.3). Here we argue the converse: subjective norms are influenced by cognitive processes. Mental representation of others — the recall and judgment of positive and negative experiences with them — forms the basis for inferring their beliefs and determining our motivation to comply with them. These intrinsically cognitive processes we believe are foundationally related to subjective norms.

7. Cumulative teachings are influenced by target behaviors (7.0). This proposition suggests we learn from our own behavior as well as from the behavior of others toward us. In general we notice the consequences or implications of our behavior. If Akela's persistence in studying for an exam netted a grade of "A", for example, then instrumental implications of the corresponding target value Self-Persistence are enhanced. Through her own behavior the value of Self-Persistence is affirmed. Positive outcomes associated with this target value then become part of cumulative teachings.

8. Current expectations are influenced by target behaviors (8.0). A student who behaviorally affirms commitment to learning is perceived by others as committed to learning. In turn their value-congruent perception can proactively influence

further commitment to learning through the process of self-fulfilling prophecy (Forsyth, 1987): (a) "the perceiver develops expectations concerning the target; (b) perceiver acts on the basis of this expectation; (c) target person changes his or her behavior in response to perceiver's behavior; and (d) target internalizes the dispositions implied by his or her behavior" (p. 143). Aside from boundary conditions identified by Swann (1984), this four-step process suggests how conceptions of others may constructively reinforce target behaviors in general.

Applied

Under the basic theory, valuation method X_i has multiple mediated effects on target values. In relation to Figure 1 these mediated pathways of influence are now identified for each valuation method:

9. The stimulus field X_1 affects TV over six pathways of influence[2]:

X_1-(SF-IP-TV)
X_1-(SF-IP-SN-IP-TV)
X_1-(SF-IP-TV-SF-IP-TV)
X_1-(SF-IP-BI-TB-CT-TV)
X_1-(SF-IP-BI-TB-CE-SN-IP-TV)
X_1-(SF-IP-BI-TB-CT-TV-BI-TB-CT-TV)

10. Cumulative teachings X_2 affect TV over seven pathways of influence:

X_2-(CT-TV)
X_2-(CT-TV-BI-TB-CT-TV)
X_2-(CT-TV-IP-BI-TB-CT-TV)
X_2-(CT-TV-IP-TV-BI-TB-CT-TV)
X_2-(CT-TV-IP-SN-IP-BI-TB-CT-TV)
X_2-(CT-TV-IP-SN-BI-TB-CE-SN-IP-TV)
X_2-(CT-TV-IP-SN-IP-BI-TB-CE-SN-IP-TV)

11. Target behaviors X_3 affect TV over six pathways of influence:

X_3-(TB-CT-TV)
X_3-(TB-CT-TV-IP-TV)
X_3-(TB-CT-TV-IP-SN-IP-TV)
X_3-(TB-CT-V-IP-BI-TB-CT-TV)
X_3-(TB-CT-TV-IP-TV-BI-TB-CT-TV)
X_3(TB-CT-TV-IP-BI-TB-CE-SN-IP-TV)

12. Current expectations X_4 affect TV over six pathways of influence:

X_4-(CE-SN-IP-TV)
X_4-(CE-SN-IP-BI-TB-CT-TV)
X_4-(CE-SN-IP-SN-BI-TB-CT-TV)
X_4-(CE-SN-IP-TV-BI-TB-CT-TV)

X_4-(CE-SN-IP-SN-BI-TB-CE-SN-IP-TV)

X_4-(CE-SN-IP-TV-BI-TB-CE-SN-IP-TV)

Applied propositions 9 through 12 also offer testable hypotheses about how valuation methods X_1 through X_4 affect target values at different systemic levels.

First, the pattern of relationships have microsystemic implications: to enhance child identification with values that produce excellence and strength in diverse environments, parents must be proficient in influencing the stimulus field X_1, providing cumulative teachings X_2, shaping target behaviors X_3, and optimizing current expectations X_4.

Second, the pattern of relationships have mesosystemic implications: to enhance child identification with values that produce excellence and strength in diverse environments, nurturing environments outside the home — school, church, neighborhood, clubs — must provide complementary proficiencies in influencing the stimulus field X_1, cumulative teachings X_2, target behaviors X_3, and current expectations X_4.

Third, the pattern of relationships have exosystemic implications: to enhance child identification with values that produce excellence and strength in diverse environments, policy initiatives must support microsystemic and mesosystemic proficiencies X_1 through X_4.

And fourth, we note that the lead causal chain is shortest for X_2, longest for X_4, and intermediate for X_1 and X_3. Since the number of causal chains is roughly comparable, 6 to 7 in each instance, this pattern may suggest that X_2 cumulative teachings is the most proficient method for enhancement of valued outcomes and X_4 current expectations the least. Regulating the stimulus field X_1 and influencing target behaviors X_3 fall somewhere in the middle. We bear in mind, however, that these implications are theoretically rather than empirically driven. Indeed on theoretical grounds we justify the inclusion of each identified method of valuation until empirical evidence suggests otherwise.

Methods

In this section we use implications of our basic and applied theory to propose testable interventions that enhance commitment to target values. Implications are drawn at three ecosystemic levels (Bronfrenbrenner, 1979). At the microsystemic level we examine what parents can do to enhance their children's commitment to target values, and at the mesosystemic level we examine what schools, churches, and other community organizations can do. We conclude by examining the role of exosystems — public sector institutions which make or promote social, economic, or educational policies — in affecting valuation processes and outcomes.

Throughout, the attempt is to illustrate the general direction valuation efforts might take. We have not attempted to structure our proposals by developmental age which of course would be required to actually implement them. We have not attempted to direct our proposals toward specific social conditions which also would be required to implement them. Sufficient specificity is provided, however, to guide the structuring of refinements for whatever variations in developmental and social conditions are required.

Microsystemic

Interventions at the microsystemic level are directed toward helping parents influence the stimulus field, cumulative teachings, target behaviors, and current expectations in ways which nurture and reinforce commitment to target values. The importance of interventions at this level have been argued cogently in a series of papers by Spencer (1983, 1987, 1988, 1990).

Stimulus field X_i. Under basic theory, the stimulus field affects target values over six pathways of influence. Here we examine three ways of influencing the stimulus field — the totality of experiences structured, created, or encountered on an ongoing basis.

To enhance structured experiences, *plans* are required. Plans here refer to prearranged experiences which enhance commitment to one or more of the target values, e.g., delivering a favorite drawing to an elderly person to enhance Love and Respect, presenting an interesting book to enhance Learning Orientation, taking dance lessons to enhance Self-Confidence, finding an engaging puzzle to enhance Self-Persistence, displaying the child's drawings to enhance Self-Esteem, or "reading" a story to mother to enhance Self-Reliance. Plans require (a) systematic inventory of available resources that enhance target values and (b) systematic infusion of identified resources into ongoing experiences of children. Requirements (a) and (b) go to the heart of what we have referred to elsewhere as adaptive environments (Jackson & Taylor, 1986; Jackson-Lowman, Franklin, & Underwood, 1992).

To foster created experiences *opportunities* are critical. Here we refer to making available resources within the home to stimulate the child's interest in activities affirming target values. For example, availability of library books would be relevant to Learning Orientation, creative materials to Self-Esteem, or challenging games to Self-Persistence — all chosen at the child's pleasure. Of course these or similar materials could be used to stimulate commitment to more than one target value.

To manage encountered experiences quality *communications* are essential. While largely beyond the control of parent or child, encountered experiences should be processed by parent and child. Three subprocesses are important: (a) parents must understand the event from the child's perspective; (b) parents must help explain the event in a way the child can understand; and (c) parents must help the child understand what to do when again confronted with the event. Under (a) it is important that parents not rush to judgment without fully understanding the child's perception and understanding of the event. Under (b), the many options available to parents depend in part upon their ideological persuasion. One parent, for example, could explain a drive-by shooting in this way: "Young African American males don't have jobs. Drugs are used to make money. If someone messes with their money, they can get killed. But killing someone like that doesn't reflect Love and Respect." Another parent might explain a fight at school in the following way: "Sounds like Robert doesn't have much Self-Confidence." To the degree appropriate, we recommend use of target value labels in conjunction with explanations of encountered experiences. Under (c) the parent in the first example might rehearse with the child what to do upon hearing a gunshot, and the parent in the second example might help her child deal with children having poor Self-Confidence.

Cumulative teachings X_2. Under the basic model there are seven pathways over which cumulative teachings influence target values. Here we identify three strategies for advancing cumulative teachings which are value relevant.

Enrichment entails systematic exposure to and discussion of proverbs, precepts, folk tales, games, and songs of constructive relevance to target values (cf. Daniel, 1979; Jackson & Taylor, 1985; Leslau & Leslau, 1982; Page & Washington, 1987). A Senagalese proverb "it is better to travel alone than with bad company" or the Ashanti proverb "no one tests the depth of a river with both feet" are related to the target value Interpersonal Skills. The familiar saying "sticks and stones can break my bones but words can never hurt me" and the Senagalese proverb "a healthy ear can stand hearing sick words" are relevant to the target value Self-Esteem. Gina Calleja's (1983) *Tobo Hates Purple* wherein a little boy resolves his unhappiness over his skin color also addresses the target value Self-Esteem. "Knowledge is like a garden; if it is not cultivated, it cannot be harvested," a Guinean proverb, and "knowledge is better than riches," a Cameroonian proverb, are both related to the target value Learning Orientation. The civil rights song of inspiration "We Shall Overcome" is akin to the Congolese proverb "No matter how long the night the day is sure to come," both related to the target value Self-Persistence. The African American saying "Right is right if nobody's doing it and wrong is wrong if everybody's doing it" is related to the Ethiopian proverb "one who runs alone can't be outrun by another," both addressing the target value Self-Reliance. While in this analysis we have focused primarily on proverbs and precepts and somewhat less on songs and books, we note that many games for African American children now entering the marketplace are relevant to target values. Whatever the medium selected, enrichment strategies require forethought. First, the parent must planfully select the medium. Second, the parent introduces the selection in ways the child can understand. Third, the parent tests the child's understanding of the selection, making modifications or adjustments to ensure understanding. And fourth, the parent links the selection to the appropriate target value, tests the child's understanding of this linkage, and where necessary makes modifications or adjustments to ensure understanding.

Explanation refers to proactive identification and discussion of contemporary and historical events and movements of relevance to target values. Unlike enrichment strategies, events and movements to be explained are typically provocative and often painful. During the 1940s "life is brighter when skin is lighter" or "do this to get Whiter skin" were advertising motifs for Nadinola, the bleaching cream promising to turn dark skin light. Promising to make African American women more charming and alluring, these advertisements were expressive of negative views of darker skin — a reflection of negative Self-Esteem. Likewise expressive of negative Self-Esteem is a 15 year old African American male's killing an off-duty firefighter in an unprovoked attack because the youth "wanted to get a reputation" (Duggan, 1992). In Johnny Gruelle's (1929) classic *Golden Book*, brown Cocoa-boy is the only character without clothes and a real name — issues which express the negative polarity of Love and Respect. W.F. Bell's "Blackbirds" (1909) depicting naked African American babies contentedly perched in a barren tree likewise is a negative expression of the target value Love and Respect. During the civil rights movement Blacks confronting Bull Connor's fire hoses and vicious dogs were exemplars of Self-Confidence and Self-Persistence. In all instances where provocative or painful events or movements are explained, the basic aim is identical: to assist developing children acquire cognitive frameworks for interpreting and deflecting the ubiquitous claims of racism or sexism or classism on their lives. Whichever the field of application, five steps are entailed. First, the parent must identify the material to present. Second, the parent must prepare the child to receive the material. Here parents must acknowledge the pain and anguish involved before introducing the material. Third, the child must be guided in understanding the material. Parents help the child describe the material and then test the child's understanding of it. Fourth, the parent helps the child express her feelings about the material which must be done patiently and sympathetically. And fifth, the parent links the material to appropriate target values, tests the child's understanding of this linkage, and modifies her input until the child understands it.

Exemplification invites parent modeling of target values. The challenge here is for parents to be what they want their children to become — high in Love and Respect, Interpersonal Skills, Learning Orientation, Self-Confidence, Self-Persistence, Self-Esteem, and Self-Reliance. A parent's taking her child with her to a march against apartheid could be taken as an expression of Love and Respect. A parent's habit of reading in the presence of the child expresses the target value Learning Orientation. Asking for each child's view of a dispute demonstrates the target value Interpersonal Skills. Parents must remain alert to opportunities to provide leadership on target values they prize for their children. This requirement affirms a basic principle of social learning theory.

Target Behaviors X$_3$. Two strategies are examined for changing child performance in the direction of target behaviors. We expect under the basic theory that these strategies will affect target values over six pathways of influence. The first strategy features a values-based approach to instruction and the second a values-based approach to discipline.

Instruction refers to caregiving strategies that bring about developmentally competent performance on each target value — Love and Respect,...,Self-Reliance. Since previous research has identified key parenting and teacher behaviors that enhance performance on target values, we refer the interested reader to these reports (Taylor, in press; Taylor et al., 1992).

Discipline is here defined as strategic efforts to bring child performance in line with target values. We recommend two approaches, the first suggesting what to do when child behaviors are consistent with target values and the second suggesting what to do when they are not. We recognize the deterrence implication typically associated with the term "discipline," but this use alone would seem especially limiting in relation to African American and other children at risk.

Ten year old Akela comes home from school and shares with her mother how her friends Cheryl, Cathy, and Linda tried to get her to join them in unfairly criticizing Wendy who is a classmate of all four girls. Mother listens carefully and then says, "I'm glad you were able to stand up to your friends, although I know it wasn't easy. What you did was show real Self-Reliance, and I'm proud of you for that. As I've said before, 'wrong is wrong if everybody's doing it and right is right if nobody's doing it.' You remember our discussion last week about Frederick Douglass. He was a brave man. He had to stand alone like you many times." This vignette illustrates five principles of values-based discipline applied to instances where child behaviors conform to target values (Taylor, 1981): (a) listen to what the child has to say; (b) summarize the value-consistent behavior — "I'm glad you were able to stand up ...;" (c) reinforce the value-consistent behavior — "What you did was show real Self-Reliance and I'm proud of you for that;" (d) link the value-consistent behavior to a cultural principle — "Wrong is wrong if everybody's doing it and right is right if nobody's doing it;" and (e) link value-consistent behavior to a cultural or religious hero or heroine — "You remember our discussion about Frederick Douglass ... "

Just as value-congruent behavior is rewarded within the cultural idiom, so should value-incongruent behavior be sanctioned within this idiom. There are five parallel principles of values-based discipline applied to instances where child behaviors are inconsistent with target values: (a) listen to what the child has to say; (b) summarize the value-inconsistent behavior — "You found your math problems hard so you gave up trying"; (c) sanction value-inconsistent behavior — "That doesn't show very good Self-Persistence and I'm not very pleased"; (d) relate the value-inconsistent behavior to a cultural principle — "As I've said before, 'A winner never quits and a quitter never wins'"; (e) relate value-inconsistent behavior to a cultural or religious hero or heroine — "I know that math is not your best subject, but do you remember Wilma Rudolph who was born with a crooked leg and a deformed foot. Who would ever think she would make a runner, but she trained hard, mastered her handicap, and went on to win one bronze and three gold metals in the World Olympics." Following this fifth step the parent provides whatever patient and loving support or help is needed to bring the child's behavior into conformity with the target value. As this happens appropriate reinforcement is given.

Current Expectations X_4. By changing objective expectations in the direction of target values we hope to change subjective expectations in the direction of target values over the six pathways of influence identified under basic theory. To this end four strategies are recommended.

Displaying refers to posting pictures, news clippings, or articles of persons exemplifying each value on the refrigerator door, in the child's room, or on the "community bulletin board," or in other conspicuous places within the home. Displayed exemplars provide structured opportunities for recurring discussion between parent and child in relation to target values. The importance of these values and their exemplification in the lives of exemplars should be lifted in ongoing discussion.

Engaging refers to having children talk with local persons who exemplify target values. Through the parents' intimate network of kith and kin and perhaps teachers, ministers, or youth workers, persons exemplifying target values are identified. An aunt, for example, may have a story to tell about how she worked and sacrificed to finish school. Her story may reflect aspects of Self-Persistence and Learning Orientation. However, to pin down this value lesson, five preparatory steps are required. First, the parent must contact friends, relatives, or acquaintances to identify why she wants her child to talk with them. In this regard she gives a spiel about target values and together they decide which target value(s) to feature. Also they agree that a self photograph will be shared with the child to help connect the exemplar to the value(s). Second, they agree on life stories to use in exemplifying the target value(s). Parent participation is vital at this stage because the parent more than anyone knows what types of stories are most likely to capture the child's interest and curiosity. Third, the meeting between and child and friend, relative, or acquaintance takes place and life stories are shared in relation to target values. It is critically important that target values are identified explicitly in relation to life stories shared. At the end of the engagement, the friend, relative, or acquaintance shares a picture of himself or herself with the child. Fourth, the parent asks her child to share collected life stories and corresponding target values. And fifth, the name and picture of persons engaged are displayed along with value labels they exemplify. Displaying routines already described then follow.

Networking involves planfully bringing together for sharing and playing the children of parents who explicitly subscribe to target values. The network could include another child or a party of children who are occasionally invited into the home typically for brief periods of time — no more than 90 minutes. By way of preparation, the children should be primed to have lots of fun. Also they should know that (a) the parents of the children share the same target values, (b) they will learn about some other people who share these same values, and (c) they are expected to be good examples of target values. At the point of actual coming together, it is critically important that activities selected are genuinely fun for participating children. At some point during play, the host child introduces one or two picture displays and corresponding value stories which are discussed with her friends. The play then continues. Through contiguous association — the pleasure of fun and exposure to exemplars — we anticipate that these planned network events can strengthen normative support for target values.

Preceptoring refers to sustained engagement with mature persons who (a) are exemplary models of target values for developing persons and (b) provide ongoing instruction in the importance of target values for developing persons. By "sustained engagement" we mean ongoing association between mature and developing persons and by "mature persons" we mean individuals who exemplify target values and basic commitment to teaching them. A possible list of candidates can be drawn from friends, relatives, teachers, ministers, acquaintances, or youth workers identified for the strategy of engagement. Arrangements for ongoing contact and tutelage are worked out on an individual basis. It's conceivable, for example, that a child could have one preceptor for three of the target values and a second for the remaining three.

Mesosystemic

Interventions at the mesosystemic level are directed toward establishing organizational climates which nurture and reinforce commitment to target values. The challenge here is to help schools, churches, and social, recreational, or health organizations serving the community promote target values. The intent of course is to forge partnerships between home and community around target values having survival implications for children who participate in both systems — micro and meso. The importance of these partnerships for socially marginalized children has been highlighted in a series of papers by Ogbu (1990a, 1990b, 1991; Ogbu & Fordham, 1986). In relation to this documented need we offer two basic strategies.

A *support base* should be created to recognize and nurture those formal and informal organizations of the mesosystem which are committed to target values. Churches subscribing would know other churches subscribing. Recreational organizations subscribing would know other recreational organizations subscribing. And all churches subscribing would know all recreational organizations subscribing, and likewise for schools or other elements of the mesosystem committing to target values. To expedite informed participation of parents in informal and informal organizations of the community, they also would be informed of this network of community support for target values. The overall intent is to create a web of community support for target values which can be accessed by parents as well as children.

The support base should assist participating members establish an *organizational culture* promotive of target values (Deal & Kennedy, 1982; Sackmann, 1991; Taylor, Prettyman, Cunningham, Mewbourne, & Dixon, 1992). Adapting the perspective of organizational culture to the challenge at hand, the leadership of participating organizations would be encouraged to: (a) promote target *V*alues systemwide, (b) recognize *E*xemplars who personify target values, (c) establish *R*outines to deepen commitment to target values, and (d) develop communication *N*etworks to share working strategies, review results stemming from implementation of these strategies, and utilize results to improve strategies for enhancing the commitment of children and youth to target values. We now examine each of these components which together form the acronym VERN.

Values. Currently we have used the term "Values for Life" to promote target values we've argued are relevant to personal survival across diverse environments. To promote this view the leadership and staff of participating organizations must be similarly convinced. The three strategies we recommend are directed toward enhancing Current Expectations (X_4) that support identified values.

First, we recommend using with leadership and staff an adaptation of interview procedures used with parents to identify the seven target values (Taylor, in press-a). Based upon experience in administering adaptations of this interview, administrators and staff affirm the same values for children that parents do. To promote target values they must first be claimed. Adaptation of interview procedures are relevant to this requirement.

Second, positive and negative correlates of each target value are generated by leadership and staff. Positive behavioral correlates of Love and Respect, for example, might include "helpfulness," "cooperativeness," or "affection" and negative behavioral correlates "harmful," "combative," or "rejection." Positive correlates of Self-Confidence might be "curious" or "inquisitive" and negative correlates "inattentive" or "withdrawn." A composite chart of positive and negative attributes is developed and made available to persons at all levels of the organization. Leadership and staff are then invited to develop a list of crises and stressors that confront children within the organization. This list also is made available to persons at all levels of the organization. Finally, leadership and staff are invited to examine the extent to which positive vs. negative correlates of target values foster or impair coping and survival of identified stressors and crises. This exercise should be instrumental in convincing leadership and staff that target values are indeed "Values for Life."

Third, a strategy for marketing target values must be developed by leadership and staff. Should banners be created? Posters? Brochures? How should children be involved in the marketing strategy? Should a certain target value be featured for

September and October, another for November and December? These are decisions to be made by organizational leadership in collaboration with staff, students, and support base.

Exemplars. Participating organizations agree to provide social recognition of value exemplars (Current Expectations X_4) and to offer special assistance to children commiting themselves to becoming value exemplars (Target Behavior X_3). Our first and fifth recommendations are directed toward the former, our second through fourth recommendations toward the latter.

First, standards for recognition on each target value should be spelled out and communicated to all children in the organization. For example, children with perfect attendance in school, those whose grades reflect the greatest improvement, those whose deportment reflects impressive improvement, or those who have made the honor roll should be recognized as affirming the target value Learning Orientation by member organizations. Or children who have developed special relationships with elderly persons at the local nursing home or who have volunteered for the neighborhood cleanup should be recognized by participating organizations for affirming the target value Love and Respect. These achievements could be recognized through special certificates, awards, portfolios, photographs, notes home, or board postings. Second, children should be given opportunity to declare which target value they want to work on especially and why they want to work on it. Third, children should be given an opportunity to indicate what they plan to do to distinguish themselves on target values they've chosen. Fourth, a plan should be developed to track children's progress on chosen values. And fifth, children meeting or exceeding their plan should be given social recognition by participating organizations. Particulars for addressing these tasks should be posted by participating organizations with the support base which should be consulted in their development.

Routines. We argue that organizational routines deepen commitment of children to target values should parallel valuation interventions $X_1,...,X_4$ described for microsystemic methods.

In influencing the Stimulus Field X_1, organizations could develop appropriate adaptations of plans, opportunities, and communications to accommodate possibilities and limitations within their particular settings. Likewise enrichment, explanation, and exemplification could be adapted organizationally to enhance Cumulative Teachings X_2 hypothesized to influence children's commitment to target values. Use of values-guided instruction and discipline to influence Target Behaviors X_3 is quite teachable to program or outreach staff working with children of member organizations, and strategies of displaying and networking can be readily adapted by most organizations to influence Current Expectations X_4. For networking, it's particularly important for children of organization "X" let us say to see that children of organization "Y" also are committed to target values. Networking, then, would entail bringing together children having different organizational ties to broaden normative support for target values. Finally, we note that the support base should be consulted in working through these and other organizational adaptations.

Networks. As we have noted, community and neighborhood organizations participating in Values for Life are organizationally integrated with support base. To ensure implementation of interventions corresponding to X_1 to X_4, participating members must install an intelligence system for progressively improving organizational performance in enhancing commitment to target values. Strategies for deepening commitment must be shared throughout the organization. Specific times in the program year must be established to evaluate the impact of implemented strategies, and specific times must be set aside to review the results and to adjust strategies to improve results. These activities must be put on the organizational timeline. Faithful adherence to these timelines will provide the basis for progressive improvement in organizational performance — enhancement of children's commitment to target values.

Exosystemic

Although exosystems are outside the proximal reach of parents, decisions made there can nonetheless affect things that matter to parents. Social and economic policies that increase the rate and magnitude of poverty, for example, can hobble plans and opportunities to regulate the Stimulus Field X_1. Educational policies that covertly or overtly discourage an Africentric view could weaken enrichment and explanation strategies for enhancing Cumulative Teachings X_2 or displaying, engaging, networking, or Preceptoring strategies for enhancing Current Expectations X_4. Antagonism to the Africentric view would be incompatible with values-based discipline to influence Target Behaviors X_3 in the classroom. Finally, we note that valucation methods proposed are rather demanding. Considerable development work needs to be done, and proposed models need to be tested. Extensive training is implied, and positive results need to be promoted. The multidisciplinarity of African American Studies programs might well provide the intellectual context for bringing together developmentalists, historians, literature specialists, and political scientists to carry out this work of central importance to the future of our families.

Implications

In this section we consider research, development, and policy implications of our basic and applied theory of valucation processes and outcomes. Specific recommendations are made in each area.

Research

Our valuation process and outcome model requires empirical evaluation. An issue of first concern is whether values as antecedent, consequence, object, or construct function similarly or differently on information processing and behavioral outcomes. How this issue is settled may have determinative impact on how values should be structured across methods of valuation. Relatedly, empirical indicators of each primary construct need to be developed and evaluated prior to exploring the validity of the eight basic propositions offered by the model. We believe that comprehensive evaluation of our theory of mediated action is likely to require the use of methods which are quantitative — experimental designs and structural modeling — and qualitative — ethnographies and interviews. Our model therefore invites interdisciplinary collaboration.

Strategically the most likely place to evaluate constructs and propositions entailed by the model is within microsystemic settings. Assuming things go well here, the next logical extension is to evaluate the extent to which target behaviors are enhanced and sustained with mesosystemic participation. Of course here we are evaluating the degree of incremental validity of mesosystemic over microsystemic interventions.

Underlying all preceding questions is the most fundamental one: Do valuation methods produce excellence and strength in diverse environments? Do they help protect children from the ubiquitous effect of racism (Taylor & Grundy, 1996)? Do they help protect children from subsequent hazards of cultural malformation: negative self esteem (Denton, 1986; Taylor, 1998), mental health problems (Taylor, Henderson, & Jackson, 1991; Taylor & Jackson, 1991), alcohol abuse (Taylor & Jackson, 1990a, 1990b), marital maladjustment (Taylor, 1990; Taylor & Zhang, 1990), and African American-on-African American crime (Terrell, Taylor, & Taylor, 1980)? Do they help children thrive in face of adverse economic environments? Do they help prevent problems in chemical dependency, teenage pregnancy, school truancy, academic underachievement, or school drop out? While answers to these essential questions are critical in judging the future utility of valuation theory and method, we reemphasize the importance of addressing policy issues which contribute to identified problems in the first instance.

Finally, we need to examine the extent to which valuation theory and methods described and illustrated here for African American children apply equally to other ethnic minority groups. It might well be that at this level of cross-ethnic comparison and collaboration that discoveries are made which extend and enrich valuation theory and method.

Development

The complete development agenda of coordinated interventions to enhance commitment to target values is summarized in Table 1.

A separate curriculum is required for each Table 1 cell entry under Micro and Meso columns. For the microsystemic level, curricula for plans (1-1-1), opportunities (1-1-2), and communications (1-1-3) must be developed that follow guidelines identified under Stimulus Field. Using guidelines identified under Routines, curricula must be developed for the mesosystemic level to infuse plans (1-2-1), opportunities (1-2-2), and communications (1-2-3) into the organizational culture of schools, churches, and other community groups. In general, development tasks implied by Micro and Meso columns are extensive since at the moment structured curriculum exists only for cells 2-1-1 and 2-2-1 (Jackson & Taylor, 1985) and for cells 3-1-1 (Taylor, 1985) and 3-2-1 (Taylor, et al., 1994). The enormity of the challenge for Micro and Meso would suggest the desirability of spreading development tasks among scholars at different centers and institutions. To ensure uniformity of quality and output, we recommend curriculum development outlined in Taylor et al. (1994). To ensure that the resulting curriculum affirms appropriate cultural ground, we recommend close examination of Jackson-Lowman's (1995) and Daniel's (1979) analyses of African and African American proverbs. And to ensure that the resulting curriculum affirms appropriate spiritual ground, we recommend close examination of the spirituality framework developed by Rogers (1994; 1998). Burgess' (1995) *Values for Life Summer Camp Curriculum* provides an excellent illustration of how curriculum guidelines can be implemented to affirm cultural and spiritual ground.

Policy

Previously we commented on the potential impact of public policies on selective valuation processes. Here we take the larger view— the role of prevailing social paradigms—in affecting these policies to begin with. Conceptually we are concerned, then, with the impact of macrosystemic values on exosystemic processes and outcomes.

Staube (1992) reviewed three paradigms of cultural adaptation. In the first, effort is made to exclude or isolate certain ethnic groups, nationalities, or races from participation in the mainstream. We shall refer to this pattern as *adaptation by exclusion*. In the second, effort is made to homogenize differences across ethnic groups, nationalities, or races through common identification with mainstream ideology. We shall refer to this pattern as *adaptation by absorption* — the familiar melting pot concept. And in the third differences across ethnic groups, nationalities, and races have an emergent quality much like the rich tonality of an orchestra which cannot be predicted from the mere sum of its parts. We shall refer to this pattern as *adaptation by synergy*.

Table 1
Summary of Development Agenda to Enhance Commitment to Target Values

Type of Intervention	Systemic Level		
	Micro	Meso	Exo
Stimulus Field X_1			
Plans	1-1-1	1-2-1	1-3-1
Opportunities	1-1-2	1-2-2	1-3-2
Communications	1-1-3	1-2-3	1-3-3
Cumulative Teachings X_2			
Enrichment	2-1-1	2-2-1	2-3-1
Explanation	2-1-2	2-2-2	2-3-2
Exemplification	2-1-3	3-2-2	2-3-3
Target Behavior X_3			
Instruction	3-1-1	3-2-1	3-3-1
Discipline	3-1-2	3-2-2	3-3-1
Current Expectations X_4			
Displaying	4-1-1	4-2-1	4-3-1
Engaging	4-1-2	4-2-2	4-3-2
Networking	4-1-3	4-2-3	4-3-3
Preceptoring	4-1-4	4-2-4	4-3-4

For each cell i-j-k, i refers to type of valuation method (1=stimluls field, 2=cummulative teachings, 3=target behaviors, 4=currnet expectations), j to systemic level (1=microsystemic, 2=mesosystemic, 3=exosystemic), and k to the particular strategy for implementing valuation method i

We believe that adaptation by synergy may represent the maturest form of cultural adaptation. It requires in the first instance that cultural groups rediscover and transmit values that made their survival possible across environments of a wide range. This effort to valuate is complemented to the degree macrosystemic values (a) provide a supportive context for the rediscovery and celebration of each cultural group, (b) create equitable opportunity structures that allow full expression of cultural uniqueness and commonalties, and (c) establish a climate in which cultural groups can encourage and celebrate communality as well as diversity. The most adaptive policies, then, would simultaneously encourage discovery and celebration of diversity and communality. Within this context of diunital accommodation — public and cultural policies are coordinated *and* complementary — adaptation by synergy should flourish. And to this degree American society should also.

Reference Notes

1. We acknowledge the controversy of explicitly including a scriptural standard in the confirmation of target values. We nonetheless decided to include it because of the central role religion has played in the survival and enhancement of African American and other communities at risk.

2. The first entry X1-(SF-IP-TV) means that valuation method X_1 affects target values over a three-step mediated process: by influencing SF which in turn influences TV through IP. Other mediated pathways here and for other valuation methods are given analogous interpretation.

3. We gratefully acknowledge the creativity of our former Director of Administration Gwendolyn Harris who proposed the phrase "Values for Life".

References

Ajzen, I. (1985). From intentions to actions: a theory of planned action. In J. Kuhland & J. Beckman (Eds.), *Action-control from cognitions to behavior.* Heidelberg: Springer.

Ajzen, I., & Fishbein, M. (1980). *Understanding attitudes and predicting social behavior.* Englewood Cliffs, NJ: Prentice-Hall.

Amato, P.R. (1991). The "child of divorce" as a person prototype: Bias in the recall of information about children in divorced families. *Journal of Marriage and the Family, 53,* 59-69.

Beech, R.P. (1966). *Value systems, attitudes, and interpersonal attraction.* Unpublished doctoral dissertation, Michigan State University.

Bell, W.F. (1909). *Blackbirds.* Memphis, Tenn.

Bronfrenbrenner, U. (1979). *Ecology of human development: experiments by nature and design.* Cambridge: Harvard University Press.

Burgess, B.N. (1995). *Values for Life Summer Camp Curriculum*. Institute for the Black Family, University of Pittsburgh, Pittsburgh, PA.

Calleja, G. (1983). *Tobo hates purple*. Toronto: Annick Press LTD.

Cochrane, R., Billig, M., & Hogg, M. (1979). British politics and the two-value model. In M. Rokeach (Ed.), *Understanding human values: individual and societal*. New York: Free Press.

Daniel, J.L. (1979). *The wisdom of Sixth Mount Zion from the members of Sixth Mount Zion and those who begot them*. University of Pittsburgh.

Deal, T.E., & Kennedy, A.A. (1982). *Corporate cultures: the rites and rituals of corporate life*. Reading, Massachusetts: Addison-Wesley Publishing Company, Inc.

Denton, S.E. (1978). *A systems analysis of parenting behaviors related to valued child outcomes*. Unpublished masters thesis, University of Pittsburgh.

Denton, S.E. (1986). *A methodological refinement and validation analysis of the Developmental Inventory of Black Consciousness*. Unpublished doctoral dissertation, University of Pittsburgh.

Denton, S.E., Taylor, J., Ruback, B., Kelly, L, & Feiring, C. (1977). *Parental values in Black and White families*. Presented at the Eastern Psychological Association.

Dobson, K.S., & Shaw, B.F. (1987). Specificity and stability of self-referent encoding in clinical depression. *Journal of Abnormal Psychology, 96*, 36-40.

Duggan, P. (1992). Shooting called bid for status. *The Washington Post*, B1.

Festinger, L. (1954). A theory of social comparison processes. *Human Relations, 7*, 117-140.

Fishbein, M., & Ajzen, I. (1975). *Belief, attitude, intention, and behavior: an introduction to theory and research*. MA: Addison-Wesley.

Forsyth, D.R. (1987). *Social psychology*. Monterey, California: Brooks/Cole Publishing Company.

Grubb, J.W., Weir, I.L., Getzlaf, S., & Rokeach, M. (1984). Own value system, value images, and cigarette smoking. *Personality and Social Psychology Bulletin, 10*, 306-313.

Gruelle, J. (1929). *Golden book*. New York: M.A. Donohue & Company.

Hamilton, D.L., Sherman, S.J., & Ruvolo, C.M. (1990). Stereotyped-based expectancies: Effects on information processing and social behavior. *Journal of Social Issues, 46*, 35-60.

Henry, W.A. (1976). Cultural values do correlate with consumer behavior. *Journal of Marketing Research, 13*, 121-127.

Homer, P. M., & Kahle, L.R. (1988). A structural equation test of the value-attitude- behavior hierarchy. *Journal of Personal and Social Psychology, 54*, 638-646.

Igus, T. (Ed.) (1992). *Book of Black heroes, Vol. 2: Great women in the struggle*. Orange, New Jersey: Just Us Books.

Jackson, E., & Taylor, J. (1985). *Values-based curriculum guide for infant and preschool centers.* Institute for the Black Family, University of Pittsburgh.

Jackson, E., & Taylor, J. (1986). *SAVE our children: curriculum materials for values-based programming.* Institute for the Black Family, University of Pittsburgh.

Jackson-Lowman, H. (1992). *Prevention strategies: creating family-friendly communities.* Presented at the June Conference of the National League of Cities held in Portland, Oregon.

Jackson-Lowman, H. (1997). Using Afrikan proverbs to provide an Afrikan-Centered narrative for contemporary Afrikan American parental values. In J.K. Adjaye & A.R. Andrews (Eds.), *Language, rhythm and sound: Black popular culture in the twenty-first century.* Pittsburg: University of Pittsburgh Press.

Jackson-Lowman, H., Franklin, A., & Underwood, C. (1992). *Adaptive environments.* A paper presented at the Annual Convention of The Association of Black Psychologists held in Denver, Colorado.

Kahle, L.R. (1980). Stimulus condition self-selection by males in the interaction of locus of control and skill-chance situations. *Journal of Personality and Social Psychology, 38,* 50-56.

Kemp, C.G. (1960). Changes in values in relation to open-closed systems. In M. Rokeach (Ed.), *The open and closed mind.* New York: Basic Books.

Leslau, C., & Leslau, W. (1982). *African proverbs.* New York: The Peter Pauper Press.

Linz, D., Donnerstein, E., & Penrod, S. (1984). The effects of multiple exposure to filmed violence against women. *Journal of Communication, 34,* 130-137.

Malamuth, N.M., Check, J., & Briere, J. (1986). Sexual arousal in response to aggression: ideological, aggressive, and sexual correlates. *Journal of Personality and Social Psychology, 50,* 330-350.

Malamuth, N.M., & Donnerstein, E. (Eds.) (1983). *Pornography and sexual aggression.* New York: Academic Press.

Ogbu, J.U., & Fordham, S. (1986). Black students' school success: coping with the burden of "acting White." *The Urban Review, 18,* 176-206.

Ogbu, J.U. (1990a). Minority education in comparative perspective: the case of Black Americans. *Journal of Negro Education, 59,* 45-57.

Ogbu, J.U. (1990b). Minority status and literacy in comparative perspective. *Daedalus, 119,* 141-168.

Ogbu, J.U. (1991). Cultural diversity and school experience. In C.E. Walsch (Ed.), *Literacy as praxis: culture, language, and pedagogy.* Norwood, New Jersey: ABLEX.

Page, M.H., & Washington, N.B. (1987). Family proverbs and value transmission of single Black mothers. *Journal of Social Psychology, 127,* 49-58.

Rokeach, M. (1973). *The nature of human values.* New York: Free Press.

Rholes, W.S., Riskind, J.H., & Lane, J.W. (1987). Emotional states and memory biases: Effects of cognitive priming and mood. *Journal of Personality and Social Psychology, 52,* 91-99.

Rogers, J.A. (1994). *Spirituality and liberation.* Unpublished doctoral dissertation. Duquesne University, Pittsburgh, PA.

Rogers, J.A. (1998). Spirituality: Questing for well-being. In R.L. Jones (Ed.), *African American Mental Health.* Berkeley, California: Cobb & Henry.

Sackmann, S.A. (1991). *Cultural knowledge in organizations: exploring the collective mind.* Newbury Park, California: Sage Publications.

Sanbonmatsu, D.M., & Fazio, R.H. (1990). The role of attitudes in memory-based decision making. *Journal of Personality and Social Psychology, 59,* 614-622.

Sheppard, B.H., Hartwick, J., & Warshaw, P.R. (1988). The theory of reasoned action: a meta-analysis of past research with recommendations for modifications and future research. *Journal of Consumer Research, 15,* 325-343.

Spencer, M.B. (1983). Children's cultural values and parental child rearing strategies. *Developmental Review, 3,* 351-370.

Spencer, M.B. (1987). Black children's ethnic identity formation: risk and resilience of castelike minorities. In K.S. Phinney & M.J. Rotheram (Eds.), *Children's ethnic socialization.* Beverly Hills: Sage.

Spencer, M.B. (1988). Self-concept development. In D.T. Slaughter (Ed.), *Perspectives on Black child development.* San Francisco: Jossey-Bass.

Spencer, M.B. (1990). Parental values transmission: Implications for Black child development. In J.B. Steward & H. Cheatman (Eds.), *Interdisciplinary perspectives on Black families.* New Brunswick, New Jersey: Transactions.

Staube, S. (1992). *Understanding diversity in American society: From the melting pot to multiculturalism and beyond.* Presentation to the Pittsburgh Board of Education and Board of Visitors for the Multicultural Education Forum, May.

Stewart, J.A. (1986). Drifting continents and colliding interests: A quantitative application of the interests perspective. *Social Studies of Science, 16,* 261-279.

Swann, W.B., Jr. (1984). Quest for accuracy in person perception: A matter of pragmatics. *Psychological Review, 91,* 457-477.

Taylor, J. (1981). *Before access: Six basic competencies.* Presented at the Seminar *Beyond Access: Minority Student Success in Higher Education.*

Taylor, J. (1985). *Values-based intervention manual for [parents of] children between 12 and 60 months.* Institute for the Black Family, University of Pittsburgh.

Taylor, J. (1990). Relationship between internalized racism and marital satisfaction. *The Journal of Black Psychology, 16,* 45-53.

Taylor, J. (1999). Toward a purposeful systems approach to parenting. In R.L. Jones (Ed.) *African American children, youth, and parenting.* Hampton, Virginia: Cobb & Henry.

Taylor, J. (1998). Cultural conversion experiences: implications for mental health research and treatment. In R.L. Jones (Ed.), *African American Identity Development*. Hampton, Virginia: Cobb & Henry.

Taylor, J., Denton, S.E., Dotson, I., Mosley, T., & Smith-Jones, J. (1985). *Cultural, scientific, and scriptural materials for enhancing commitment to values-based approach*. Institute for the Black Family, University of Pittsburgh.

Taylor, J., & Franklin, A. (1994). Psychosocial analysis of Black teenage pregnancies: implications for public and cultural policies. *Policy Studies Review, 31(1-2)*, 157-164.

Taylor, J., & Grundy, C. (1996). Measuring Black internalization of White stereotypes about Blacks: The Nadanolitization Scale. In R.L. Jones (Ed.), *Handbook of tests and measurements for Black populations*. Hampton, Virginia: Cobb & Henry.

Taylor, J., Henderson, D., & Jackson, B.B. (1991). A Holistic model for understanding and predicting depression in African American women. *Journal of Community Psychology, 19*, 306-320.

Taylor, J., & Jackson, B.B. (1990a). Factors affecting alcohol consumption in Black women: Part I. *International Journal of the Addictions, 25*, 1279-1292.

Taylor, J., & Jackson, B.B. (1990b). Factors affecting alcohol consumption in Black women: Part II. *International Journal of the Addictions 25*, 1407-1419.

Taylor, & Jackson, B.B. (1991). Evaluation of a holistic model of mental health symptoms in Black Women. *The Journal of Black Psychology, 18*, 19-45.

Taylor, J., Prettyman, M.G., Cunningham, P., Mewbourne, J.A., & Dixon, C.M. (1992).*CLEM: A leadership development plan for African American students in higher education*. An unpublished manuscript, Afro-American Studies Program, University of Maryland, College Park.

Taylor, J., Turner, S., Underwood, C., Franklin, A., Jackson, E., & Stagg, V. (1994). Values for Life: Preliminary evaluation of the educational component. *Journal of Black Psychology, 20*, 210-233.

Taylor, J., & Zhang, X. (1990). Cultural identity in maritally distressed and nondistressed Black couples. *The Western Journal of Black Studies, 14*, 205-213.

Terrell, F., Taylor, J., & Terrell, S. (1980). Self-concept of juveniles who commit Black on Black crimes. *Corrective and Social Psychiatry, 26*, 107-109.

Wilson, M.T. (1974). *Clarifying values caregivers have for their children and the relationship between those values and caregiver behaviors*. Unpublished doctoral dissertation, University of Pittsburgh.

Zillman, D., & Bryant, J. (1984). Effects of massive exposure to pornography. In N.W. Malamuth & E. Donnerstein (Eds.), *Pornography and sexual aggression*. New York: Academic Press.

Author

Jerome Taylor
Center for Family Excellence, Inc., and
Africana Studies and Psychology in Education
University of Pittsburgh
5CO1, Forbes Quadrangle
Pittsburgh, PA 15260
Telephone: (412) 434-0366
Fax: (412) 434-0393

Afrocentric Organizational Development

Nsenga Warfield-Coppock

In each of us, An Afrikan mind, Will be the basis for creating Anything Afrikan, Nothing Afrikan is created, Without an Afrikan mind, That is creative. (Madhubuti, 1974, p. 1)

Introduction

The field of organizational development is young in contrast to the many established fields of inquiry from which it has emerged—business management, sociology, economics, and psychology. The general goal of the field and its application is the enhancement or improvement of efficiency and profits of organizations and business. In general, this field of study is Eurocentrically-based and appears in the literature as the standard. Aside from Ouchi (1981), who has discussed the cultural history and characteristics of the Japanese organization, there is little acknowledgment of the concept of organizations relying on the "cultural" background of the people who create them. The study of Black organizations including voluntary organizations (Babchuck & Thompson, 1962; Drake, 1940; Layng, 1978; Powell, 1979); self-help organizations (Davis, 1977); churches (Drake, 1940; Mays & Nicholson, 1933); freemasonry (Hall, 1973, 1976; Voorhis, 1940); professional organizations (Johnson, 1975, 1980); the Black experience in organizations (Jones & Willingham, 1970; Killan, & Grigg, 1964; King, 1976); political organizations (Levy & Stroudinger, 1978; Morris, 1980; Peterson, 1979; Scott, 1973; Smith, 1981); social and fraternal organizations (Perlman, 1971); comparative analyses of Black organizations (Rudwick & Meier, 1970; Warfield-Coppock, 1985; Yancy, 1970); and a history of Black organizations (Warfield-Coppock, 1982, 1985; Yearwood, 1976, 1980) has provided fertile ground for the development of an African centered perspective of organizations.

The African centered perspective of organizations and their development is a recent phenomenon (Warfield-Coppock, 1985). Toward this end, this chapter will provide a review of related literature and discussion from the fields of organizational psychology, specifically in the areas of organizational culture, developmental

81

theory, and organizational climate. In addition, as we forge new territory for the African American organization, the areas of African philosophy and culture will be reviewed to provide us with a cultural and organizational interface. African centered personality theory will be touched on as it enriches our view of both individual and collective behavior.

With a better understanding of the characteristics of the culturally-based organizations of African American people, we will be better able to create, improve, and intervene with our businesses and organizations—making them better suited and harmonious to the root and spirit of African people.

Personality Characteristics of the Afrocentric Organization (In Contrast to the Eurocentric Organization)

"Because the water is spilled does not mean that the calabash is broken."

This adage from African culture prepares us for understanding the essential differences between the common characteristics of the African centered and European centered organizational type. Americans of African descent have surely been infused and socialized into American culture. However, our history has proven that the essence of the people remains African—the calabash is not broken.

Organizations are the collective behavior of people. Thus, organizations are imbued with the components of personality (Warfield-Coppock, 1985), which have been shown to be culturally based. An African centered definition of personality therefore, would include the African/Black survivals in both roles and characteristics of African Americans. In contrast, a Eurocentric idea of personality, using the Western tradition would include various structures of personality such as the id, ego, superego, preconscious, conscious and unconscious (Warfield-Coppock, 1981).

The characteristics of African personality have been studied by numerous African American psychologists and researchers. These components of personality invariably include "Black consciousness" or "Black identity" (Akbar, 1976: Atwell & Azibo, 1991; Azibo, 1989; Azibo, 1991; Baldwin, 1976; Baldwin, Brown & Rackley, 1990; Burlew & Smith, 1991; Cross, Parham & Helms, 1991; Curry, 1981; Kambon, 1992; Montgomery, Fine & James Myers, 1990; Nobles, 1980; Phillips, 1990; Thompson, 1990; Warfield-Coppock, 1981; Williams, 1981). A summary of the major characteristics of the African personality identified by these researchers include:

> spiritual foundation — in tune or oneness with the Creator and common
> spirit or force in all things, harmony, balance.
> spiritual principles of cooperation, commonality, similarity, synthesis restraint,
> respect, responsibility, and reciprocity
> racial pride, identity and/or awareness

collective self and affective epistemology
group referent behavior—an essential interconnectedness or
    interdependence
multiplicity of form and movement—musical and rhythmic
a high regard for life
interpersonal connectedness by differences, authenticity

These personality characteristics appear, in varying degrees, in organizations (Warfield-Coppock, 1985, 1993). I theorize here that a continuum of attitudes and behaviors may be expected to be present based on the level of consciousness of the members of the organization. People come to organizations or groups with a set of life experiences, attitudes and behaviors that vary along the lines of "Black consciousness." Therefore, the collective behavior and culture of organizations may also follow the stages of awareness similar to those identified for the individual by African American psychologists and scholars (Cross, 1977; Cross, 1991; Cross, Parham & Helms, 1991). These scholars have identified stages which are typical in the "Black awareness" process. While many persons of African descent may never seek to become more conscious of their cultural identity, it is posited that those who do make the transition struggle through the stages identified below:

- Stage 1: Pre-encounter—identifying the old and unproductive patterns and recognizing a need for change. These may include race image anxieties and/or attitudes of race neutrality, race as a social stigma, anti-Black, assimilation-integrationist, etc.

- Stage 2: Encounter—circumstances or events that cause a metamorphosis causing the release of varied emotions, anxiety and the death of the pre-encounter attitudes.

- Stage 3: Immersion-Emersion—conversion by plunging into new African or Black-oriented behavior and practices.

- Stage 4: Internalization—acceptance and quieting of previous anxiety experienced in the transition stages.

- Stage 5: Internalization-Commitment—extending the sustained internalization into a plan of action which will solidify efforts for change and assist others in their transition.

An organization or a group of people within or in the process of forming an organization may choose to bring a "cultural consciousness" into the organizational setting. The persons or the organization may be at any of the stages identified above. With this knowledge, it is important to assist all members to reach more advanced levels. This is usually accomplished through a training series that can offer new information to the group at the same time facilitate a common history/experience for members.

Organizational culture has been defined as, "the way we do things around here" (p. 277, Burke and Litwin, 1989). According to Lineberry and Carleton's

(1992) review of the literature, an organizational culture may include any or all of the following components:

- the dominant espoused values
- the philosophy which guides organizational policy
- norms for the group
- feelings and climate
- the rules for getting along in the organization.

Few organizational theorists consider the race or ethnicity of those establishing the "culture" of any given organization. I suggest here, then that the cultural background of the persons who have founded or manage an organization or business will appear in the day-to-day operations, regardless of the specific rules or guidelines that have been established. Informal rules may be more dominant and widespread than the formal operating rules.

Many of our scholars and theoreticians (Asante, Nobles) have pointed to clear cultural differences in worldviews, value systems, and behaviors. Asante has suggested differences between the Euro-linear view which seeks to control and predict behavior and the Afro-linear view, which on the other hand, strives to understand and interpret behavior.

Dimpka (1992) suggests that cultural values and worldviews lie at the base of how and why whites and blacks find satisfaction in the businesses or organizations in which they work. White values lie in the object or acquisition of the object leading to an assessment of knowledge through counting and measuring. On the other hand a black value system, based on interpersonal "people" relationships, has a knowledge system based on symbolic imagery and rhythm, while not discounting the importance of measuring and counting.

Organizational culture, according to Lineberry & Carleton (1992) "is primarily a set of response tendencies or behavior patterns that characterize people within an organization" (p. 235). It is also the way people conduct themselves as they complete their work. These behaviors are group-wide and value-driven and may contain components such as heroes, myths, legends, rites, and rituals. For example, the myths, legends and heroes of an organization may be the founders or original leaders. Their story may be displayed or discussed with pride by current members or leaders who feel strongly about carrying on the important values and traditions.

The culture process then focuses on how things should be done (based on historical mission and values). It is possible that with an analysis of the way things are done, they may not meet the needs of the group and/or the consumers of the organization's product. This may call for an intervention to change the way things are done.

We shall now review the brief literature comparing of the cultures of Eurocentric and Afrocentric organizations. The Afrocentric organization by values, philosophies, and behaviors place the African world at the center of their focus. This is differentiated from the Eurocentric organization by its values, philosophies, and behaviors which are consistent with placing the European world at the center of their focus.

Eurocentric organizational characteristics cited by Schiele (1990) include: principle of rationality; maximum productivity (how efficiently, how well, how fast, how plentiful something is produced or persons processed); relationship between worker satisfaction and productivity; emphasis on the individual member; distribution of power; availability of resources; performance; service technologies; relationship between goal displacement and unattainment of formal, official goals. Warfield-Coppock (1993) contrasts the Afrocentric and Eurocentric organization using the following model (see Table 1).

The Afrocentric and Eurocentric organizations are compared along cultural lines. The result is a caring, supportive environment which places people above profits in the Afrocentric organization. Policies of this organization are humanistic and seek to assist members to work cooperatively for the betterment of the entire group. The Eurocentric organizations is supportive of individuals who are highly competitive and have high output. Control, power, influence and large profits provide a structure that supports the few over the many. The political goal for the Eurocentric organization is to influence the legislative branch of government in order to support laws, that will support profits (e.g. National Rifle Association, American Tobacco Lobby, etc.)

Many non-African organizations and business have recognized the advantages in the humanistic policies typical of people of color. Changes are being advanced in this area with the final goals remaining profits, control and power. There is at least one characteristic that sets the Afrocentric organization aside from others that may infuse more humanistic policies and practices. The truly African centered organization understands that the mission of the "people" must be reflected in the groups' goals and work. The ultimate goal for the true African centered organization is the liberation of all people of African descent.

Characteristics of the Healthy Afrocentric Organization

"Learning is like sailing the ocean; no one has ever seen it all."

Every organization functions with a culture and climate that is uniquely their own. The shared values, beliefs, and behaviors provides a cultural process. When these components of the organization are delineated they may be found to be functional, or in other words, they further the mission/vision, goals, objectives and tasks of the group.

The healthy Afrocentric organization reflects basic tenets of the African worldview or perspective in both culture and climate. Among these goals are creating harmony, balance, respect, reciprocity and discipline in the working and

Table 1
Afrocentric and Eurocentric Organizations Model

	Afrocentric Organization	Eurocentric Organization
Cosmology (world view)	Oneness with others	Control
Axiology (values)	Humanistic/people orientation	Materialistic orientation
Ontology (nature of man)	Natural goodness	Do before others do
Epistemology (source of knowing)	Spiritual source	Self
Organization Style / Philosophy	Support/care for group	Large profits
Political Goal	Liberation of Africans	Influence in govt.
Management	Communal team oriented	Hierarchy
Leadership	Guidance and building	Authoritarian
Administrative	Humanistic policies	Based on bottom line
Power/Authority	Spread with positions	In the hierarchy
Decision-making (problem-solving)	Collaborative Win-win	Win-lose handed down
Staff Relations	Familial/Interdependent	Person-to-object
Work Orientation	Sense of excellence	Quantitative output
Productivity	Cooperative teams	Competitive

(Adapted form Warfield-Coppock. N. 1995. Toward the Development of an Afrocentric Theory of Organizations)

personal relationships and provide for mutual benefit to all members. Johnson (1975, 1980) studied a Black professional organization and found that the common characteristics of the healthy organization in this research were their shared beliefs, valuing of people and humanistic quality in both structure and function.

We have discussed the indicators of the Afrocentric organization. The closer one is able to replicate these cultural factors in an organizational setting the more healthy the organization and its members will be. It is important to work collectively to provide a sense of mission and goals for an Afrocentric organization. Members need to familiarize themselves with the components of the Afrocentric organization if that is the goal of the group. In most cases seeking a transition to working more collectively and Afrocentrically will require commitment, time, and resources by the organization and its members; the transition to functioning Afrocentrically is not something that can be handed down from the upper echelon of authority in an organization. It must, like the result, be collective. Revolutionary culture change never works. The only way to make viable long lasting changes or improvements

Table 2
Stages of Organizational Development

Developmental	Critical Concern	Key Issue	Consequences if concerns not met
*Birth	1. To Create a new organization	What to risk	Frustration and inaction
	2. To survive as a viable system	What to sacrifice	Death of organization Further subsidy by faith capital
*Youth	3. To gain stability	How to organize	Reactive, crisis-dominated organization; Opportunistic rather than self-directing attitudes and policies
	4. To gain reputation and develop pride	How to review and evaluate	Difficulty in attracting good personnel and clients. Inappropriate overly aggressive, and distorted image building
*Maturity	5. To achieve uniqueness and adaptability	Whether and how to change	Unnecessarily defensive or competitive attitudes; diffusion of energy. Loss of most creative personnel
	6. To contribute to society	Whether and how to share	Possible lack of public respect and appreciation. Bankruptcy or profit loss

in culture or climate is through evolutionary change, over time as a result of shared experience and common history of the group (Lineberry & Carleton, 1992).

It is also important to understand that organizations, have a developmental cycle and that there are critical times and events that must be worked through to maintain a healthy organization. John W. Gardner (1965) stated, "Like people and plants, organizations have a life cycle. They have a green and supple youth, a time of flourishing strength, and a gnarled old age.... An organization may go from youth to old age in two or three decades, or it may last for centuries." (p. 20). Lippitt and Schmidt (p. 103, 1967) have provided a seminal article to assist in the understanding of this important developmental process for all organizations.

Stages of growth and completion of important developmental tasks should be attended to by the members of the organization. Organizations, like people, can expect to face crises. It is how the crises are handled, collectively that shall determine the health, viability, and life expectancy of an organization.

The latest model of the healthy organization is that the leadership should provide opportunities for the organization to learn (Senge, 1990). Generative learning is about creating and one must set up a "creative tension" coming from the organizational vision. Adaptive learning is about coping. The healthy organization has probably received regular preventive maintenance check-ups, and has good coping skills. This means that it annually reviews the congruence between its mission/values and practices, its developmental progress and its leadership and management style and structure. At the very least the healthy organization should reflect attitudes and behaviors of harmony, respect, balance, mutual benefit, and reciprocity.

Barriers and Constraints to the Development of a Healthy Afrocentric Organization

"Where there is sickness there is death."

Individual and collective behaviors, attitudes, and feelings will emerge as people begin to work and live together. Americans of all ethnic background have been exposed, socialized, and trained, to varying degrees, in the ways of the majority's European cultural perspective. Because of the competitive and survival orientation of the culture in which Americans of all colors have been raised, the major barriers to the development of a healthy Afrocentric organization are generally internal. Imbalance in the organization may be attributed to the inability to embrace an Afrocentric or culturally congruent worldview, philosophy, attitudes and/or behaviors. The barriers to forming, developing, implementing or sustaining the Afrocentric orientation may be caused by individuals, subgroups or it may be systemwide. We will review some of the barriers from this holistic perspective.

Azibo (1989) has provided a nosology of disorders among African Americans. Among the psychological and behavioral disorders identified are: Psychological misorientation: Negromachy, alien-self disorders, anti-self disorders; Mentacide: alienating or peripheral mentacide; Personality disorders: materialistic depression, individualism, sexual misorientation, sex obsession, WEUSI anxiety, reactionary disorders; Reactionary disorders: psychological burn-out, psychological brainwashing, oppression violence reactions, self-destructive disorders, organic disorders, theological misorientation; and Disorders: Jonestown syndrome, theological alienation.

Disorders of the individual may be shifted into the working system of an organization causing similar dysfunctional orientations and imbalance. Persons, for example, who display a anti-self disorder and work with the public may carry the sense of dislike even hatred for others who are poor, of color, disadvantaged. These disadvantaged people may received rude, negative or no services as a result of projection of the worker's self-hatred.

Organizational neurosis has been described by Harvey & Albertson,(1971). Characteristics of the neurotic organization are collectively expressed by its members and may include: frustration; worry and anxiety; backbiting; loss of self-esteem; general sense of impotence; blaming others for the problems; subgroup formation with gossiping; members act contrary to data and information they possess; members act differently outside the organization; members have rich fantasies about possible negative consequences; and members engage in behavior which is individually and organizationally destructive.

The results of the illness in an organization affects both individuals and the organization and may be seen as a general lack of motivation, lowered production, efficiency, absenteeism, turnover, loss of self-esteem and confidence. Workers or members may no longer enjoy their work and the quality of their work and output may decrease.

According to some researchers there may be more than one climate within an organization. Multiple climates generally result from differences in perspectives, for example, first and second generation employees/members or different cultural groups where one is dominant and/or hold the major or all management positions.

If an organization has multiple climates that are culturally divergent, the characteristics of the organization may be particularly tumultuous and the members combative. Very serious neuroses may develop which can virtually shut down any progress. The dysfunctional attitudes and behaviors will in some way impede the goals of the individuals and group.

Assessment of the culture and climate can, however, facilitate an understanding of the problems as well as outlining a plan or treatment strategy to bring the organization back to a state of health. Two such assessments are an analysis of the organization structure by using a chart, and/or a climate survey.

Afrocentric Organizational Chart

"Authority has no sweetness."

An organization chart is a visual diagram which plots the arrangement, flow and distribution of responsibilities in a group working toward a common goal. Structure is the term and typically the way Eurocentric thought conceptualizes the format of the organizational chart. Because the Eurocentric system values the competitive and hierarchical management style, a typical organizational chart has one person at the top. Another layer under the top will contain few slots who answer and are directed by the top person. As one moves down the chart there are more and more persons at each level with the largest quantity of workers generally at the lowest rung of the organizational ladder. Persons at the lower levels obtain their direction and answer to those at the level above them (See Figure 1).

Structure dictates the interactions of the members. The attitudinal and behavioral dynamics consistent with this structure will eventually develop regardless of what is verbally communicated to the members of the organization.

Form, as opposed to structure, is a term typically used in a more flexible and dynamic system that allows for multiple authority and collective decision making. An Afrocentric organizational form or chart may in all likelihood appear circular with concentric circle and/or attached circle representing working teams. The chart may include an elders or advisory council which would provide historical and mindful input as well as appropriate rituals to insure continuity, balance and harmonious working groups and relationships in the organization.

An organizational form that is allowed to evolve and expand will allow for change and variable styles and needs of communication and interactions among the organizational members. Afrocentric components are easily interjected in this system (See Figures 2 and 3).

The form established by the collective will define and assist the working patterns of the group. Review the current organizational chart for an analysis of current structure and potential modifications for improvements.

Climate Assessment of the Afrocentric Organization

"The one who sleeps in the hut, knows where it leaks."

Organizational climate refers to the mood or underlying current found in the business or organization's setting. Factors which effect the climate are the way that the organization is perceived by its employees or participants. Standard climate indicators (Chait, 1974) include: relevancy of training; quality of supervision or hierarchy; communications; a person's sense of belonging; sense of competency; job expectation and satisfaction; and compensation, promotions and benefits.

To assess the cultural climate of an organization one would need to address the characteristics of the Eurocentric or Afrocentric organization which we identified earlier (Warfield-Coppock, 1993). Most groups that seek to make improvements in their organizations use a diagnostic and treatment strategy approach. The diagnosis would begin with identifying the cultural and climate characteristics of the organization. This may be accomplished using a survey, such as a climate survey, or interviews with persons to identify areas of concern or problems. The next step would be to analyze the information collected and devise a plan to make improvements in the organization. Implementation of the plan can be completed in many appropriate ways including staff or group training, retreats, strategic planning sessions with appropriate follow up actions, etc.

Warfield-Coppock, (1993) has identified the characteristics for assessing an organization's cultural-congruence-Afrocentric-climate. These indicators include:
   -A worldview that provides for oneness with all things and people
   -A set of values that are humanistic and people oriented
   -A belief in humankind that all people are naturally good
   -A belief that the source of all knowledge is spiritual
   -An organizational style or philosophy that supports and cares for group over the philosophy of large profits

Figure 1
Eurocentric Organizational Charts (Hierarchies)

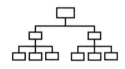

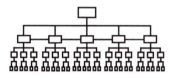

Figures 2-3
Afrocentric Organizational Charts (Working Collectives)

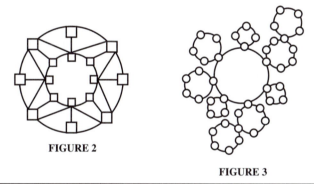

FIGURE 2

FIGURE 3

-A management style that is communal and team oriented
-A leadership style that is guiding, building and supportive
-Administrative policies that are humanistic
-Power and authority is spread among positions rather than located in a few hierarchical jobs (Working Collective Organizational Chart)
-Decision-making is collaborative and problem-solving with a win-win goal
-Staff relations and benefits account for family and interdependence
-Work orientation emphasizes a sense of excellence
-Productivity depends on cooperative teams
-A mission which includes the liberation of people of African descent

In addition to these organizational characteristics, members should be able to identify incidents, events, policies, and practices that have created or increased harmony, balance, respect, reciprocity, and mutual benefit in the organization .

Summary and Conclusion

Organizations are the collective behavior of a people. Organizations carry the personality, cultural consciousness (in levels), philosophy, values, affective orientations, and spirit of a people. An Afrocentric organization would incorporate the best of these components in the collective actions of a group. However, due to barriers of imbalance and lack of understanding, many people and organizations are unaware of the destructive habits they perpetuate. Behavioral disorders and neuroses have been identified as they can exist in the individuals, subgroups or systems of an organization. The structure, identified by an organizational chart, can be used to identify areas of inflexibility and create a working environment more conducive to change and the essence of the people in the organization. Also, the cultural climate of an organization can be diagnosed in order to make needed improvements.

Finally, why study organizations? The best reason to study these institutions of collective action is to understand and make them as useful as they can be to the mission and goals of the people. European descent people and African descent people in America have never had the same missions, goals, or practices. People of African descent have historically used organizations or collective action to fight oppression perpetuated by those of European descent and to advance the goals of the group. It is imperative that our organizations improve, flourish and reflect the essence of our people if we are ever to improve the conditions for all people.

A LUTA CONTINUA

Supplemental Reading

Bowman, P.J. (1991). Organizational psychology: African American perspectives. In R.L. Jones, *Black Psychology,* 3rd Ed. Berkeley, CA.: Cobb & Henry.

Schiele, J.H. (1990). Organizational theory from an Afrocentric perspective. *Journal of Black Studies, 21(2),* 145-161.

References

Akbar, N. (1976). Rhythmic patterns in Afrikan personality. In King, L. et al. (Eds.), *Afrikan philosophy: Assumptions and paradigms for research on Black persons.* Los Angeles: Fanon Center.

Asante, M.K. (1987). *The Afrocentric idea.* Philadelphia, PA.: Temple University Press.

Atwell, I., & Azibo D. A. (1991). Diagnosing personality disorder in Africans (Blacks) using the Azibo nosology: Two case studies. The *Journal of Black Psychology, 17(2),* 1-22;

Azibo, D. A. (1989). African-centered theses on mental health and a nosology of Black/African personality disorder. *The Journal of Black Psychology, 15(1)*, 81-91.

Azibo, D.A. (1991). Commentary: Towards a metatheory of the African personality. *The Journal of Black Psychology, 17(2)*, 37-45.

Babchuck, N., & Thompson, R.V. (1962). The voluntary association of Negroes. *American Sociological Review, 27(5)*, 647-655.

Baldwin, J.A. (1976). Black psychology and Black personality. *Black Books Bulletin, 4(3)*, 6-11.

Baldwin, J.A., Brown, R., & R. Rackley. (1990). Some socio-behavioral correlates of African self-consciousness in African-American college students. *The Journal of Black Psychology, 17(1)*, 1-17.

Bowman, P.J. (1991). Organizational psychology: African American perspectives. In R.L. Jones, *Black Psychology. 3rd Ed.* Hampton, V.A.: Cobb & Henry.

Burlew, A. K., & Smith, L. R. (1991). Measures of racial identity: An overview and a proposed framework. *The Journal of Black Psychology, 17(2)*, 53-71.

Burke, W.W., & Litwin, G. (1989). A causal model of organizational performance. In J.W. Pfieffer (ed.), *The 1989 annual: Developing human resource.* San Diego, CA.: University Associates.

Butt-Thompson, F.W. (1929). *West African secret societies: Their organizations officials and teachings.* London: H.F. & G. Witherby.

Cannon, J.A. (1977). *Re-Africanization: The last alternative for Black America. Phylon, 38(2)*, 203-210.

Carlston, K. (1968). *Social theory and African tribal organization.* Urbana: University of Illinois Press.

Chait, A. (1974). *Manual for organizational climate employee survey instrument.* Washington, D.C. Developmental Publications.

Chinweizu (1975). *The west and the rest of us.* New York: Vintage Books.

Cole, W.S. (1974). The style of John Coltrane, 1955-1967. *Dissertation Abstracts International* 35/04A, 2316. (University Microfilms No. 74-23031)

Counter, S.A., & Evans, D.L. (1981). *I sought my brother: An Afro-American reunion.* Cambridge, Mass.: The MIT Press.

Cox, T.H., Lobel, S.A. & McLeod, P.L. (1991). Effects of ethnic group cultural differences on cooperative and competitive behavior on a group task. *Academy of Management Journal, 34(4)*, 827-847.

Cross, W.E., Jr. (1977). The Thomas and Cross models on psychological nigresence. In Cross, W.E. Jr. (Ed.), Third conference on empirical research in *Black psychology*, 107-121.

Cross, W.E., Jr. (1991). *Shades of Black: Diversity in African-American identity*. Philadelphia: Temple University

Cross, W.E., Jr., Parham, T.A., & J.E. Helms. (I991). The stages of Black identity development: Nigrescence models. In R.L. Jones (ed.), *Black psychology* (3rd Ed.). Berkeley, Ca.: Cobb & Henry.

Curry, A.O. (1981). *An exploratory examination of traditional attitude, values. and personality correlates of Black African people: A study within an Afrikan worldview.* Doctoral dissertation completed for Pennsylvania State University. Ann Arbor, Ml.: University Microfilms Inc.

Danquah, J.B. (1944). Obligation in Akan society. *West African affairs.* A reprint of unknown origin. Other publications include *The Akan doctrine of God.* Oxford: Lutherworth Press.

Davis, L.G. (Ed.). (1977). *A history of Black self-help organizations and institutions in the U.S. 1776-1976: A working bibliography.* Monticello, Illinois: Council of Planning Librarians.

Dimpka, P. (1992). Organizational climate, job expectations and their impact on job satisfaction: Comparing black and white managers. *Journal of Social and Behavioral Sciences, 37(1),* 1-11.

Drake, S. (1940). *Churches and voluntary associations in the Chicago Negro community* (Report of Office Project 465-54-386, Work Project Administration). Chicago: Author.

Fortes, M., & Evans-Pritchard, E.E. (Eds.). (1940). *African political systems.* London: Oxford University Press.

Gardner, J.W. (Oct., 1965). How to prevent organizational dry rot. *Harper's Magazine.*

Gwaltney, J.L.(1993). *Drylongso: A self-portrait of Black America.* New York: Random House.

Hall, M.P. (1973). *Freemasonry of the Ancient Egyptian* (4th ed.). Los Angeles: Philosophical Research Society.

Hall, M.P. (1976). *The lost keys of freemasonry.* Richmond, Virginia: McCoy Publishing and Masonic Supply.

Harvey, J.B., & Albertson, D.R. (1971). *Neurotic organizations: Symptoms, causes, and treatments. Part I & II.* Washington, D.C.: Developmental Publications.

Herskovits, M. (Ed.). (1972). *Cultural relativism.* New York: Random House.

Johnson, A.E. (1975). The National Association of Black Social Workers: Structural and functional assessment by leaders and members. *Dissertation Abstracts International.* 36/04a, 2426. (University Microfilms No. 75-21, 230).

Johnson, A.E. (1980). Black organizations: The extended kinship for survival. In L. Yearwood (Ed.), *Black organizations: Issues on survival techniques* (pp. 103-113) Washington, D.C.: University Press of America.

Johnston, H. R. (1976). A new conceptualization of source of organizational climate. *Administrative Science Quarterly, 21,* 95-103.

Jones, M.E., & Willingham, A. (1970). The white custodians of the black experience: A reply to Rudwick and Meier. *Social Science Quarterly. 51(1),* 31-36.

Kambon, K.K.K. (1992). *The African personality in America: An African-centered framework.* Tallahassee, FL.: Nubian Nation Publication.

Katz, D., & Kahn, R.L. (1978). *The social psychology of organizations* (2nd ed.). New York: John Wiley.

Killan, L.M., & Grigg, C.M. (1964). Negro perceptions of organizational effectiveness. *Social Problems, 11(4),* 380-388.

King, J.R. (1976). African survivals in the Black family: Key factors in stability. *Journal of Afro-American Issues, 4(2),* 153-167.

Layng, A. (1978). Voluntary associations and Black ethnic identity. *Phylon, 39 (2),* 171 -1 79.

Levy, A.B., Stroudinger, S. (1978) The Black caucus in the 92nd Congress: Gauging its success. *Phylon, 39(4),* 322-33.

Lineberry, C. & Carleton, J.R. (1992). Culture change. In H.D. Stolovitch & E.J. Keeps, Eds. *Handbook of human performance technology: A comprehensive guide for analyzing and solving performance problems in organizations.* San Francisco, CA.: Jossey-Bass.

Lippitt, G.L., & Schmidt, W. (1967). Crisis in a developing organization. *Harvard Business Review, 4(6),* 102-112.

Madhubuti, H. R. (1974). *From plan to planet life studies: The need for Afrikan minds and institutions.* Chicago: Broadside Press, Institute for Positive Education.

Mays, B.E., & Nicholson, J.W. (1933). *The Negro's church.* New York: Institute for Social and Religious Research.

Mbiti, J.S. (1970). *African religion and philosophy.* New York: Anchor Books.

Montgomery, D.E., Fine, M.A., & Myers, L.J. (1990). The development and validation of an instrument to assess an optimal Afrocentric worldview. *The Journal of Black Psychology, 17(1),* 37-54.

Morris, A.D. (1980). The rise of the civil rights movement and its movement: Black power structure 1953-1963. *Dissertation Abstracts International, 41/*03A,1241 (University Microfilms No. 80-19971)

Muchinsky, P.M. (1977). Organizational communications: Relationships to organizational climate and job satisfaction. *Academy of Management Journal, 20 (4),* 593-607.

Nobles, W.W. (1980). Extended self: Rethinking the so-called Negro self concept. In R.L. Jones (Ed.), *Black psychology* (2nd. ed.). New York: Harper and Row.

Onwuachi, P.C. (1973). *Black ideology in the African diaspora.* Chicago: Third World Press.

Osei. G.K. (1970). *The African philosophy of life.* London: The African Publication Society.

Ouchi, W.G., & Price, R.L. (1979, Autumn). Hierarchies, clans, and theory : A new perspective on organization development. *Organizational Dynamics,* 24-44.

Ouchi, W.G. (1981). *Theory Z.* Reading, Mass.: Addison-Wesley.

Pasteur, A., & Toldson, I.L. (1982). *Roots of soul: The psychology of Black experiences.* Garden City, New York: Anchor.

Perlman, D. (1971). Organizations of the free Negro in New York City, 1800-1860. *Journal of Negro History, LVI (3),* 181-197.

- Peterson, P.E. (June, 1979). Organizational imperatives and ideological change: The case of Black power. *Urban Affairs Quarterly, 14(4),* 465-484.

Phillips, F. B. (1990). NTU psychotherapy: An Afrocentric approach. *Journal of Black Psychology, 17(1),* 55-74.

Powell, G.B. (I979). Individual traits and Black voluntary associations. *Dissertation Abstracts International.* 40/08B, 4031. (University Microfilms No. 80-021 32)

Rudwick, E., & Meier, A. (1570). Organizational structure and goal succession: A comparative analysis of the NAACP and CORE 1964-1968. *Social Science Quarterly, 51(1),* 9-24.

Schiele, J.H. (1990). Organizational theory from an Afrocentric perspective. *Journal of Black Studies, 21(2),* 145-161.

Schein, E. H. (1985). *Organizational culture and leadership: A dynamic view.* San Francisco, CA.: Jossey-Bass.

Scott, J. (1973). Black science and nation-building. In J. Ladner, (ed.) *The death of white sociology,* 289-309. New York: Random House.

Senge, P.M. (Fall, 1990). The leader's new work: Building learning organizations. *Sloan Management Review,* 7-23.

Sims, H.P., Szilagyi, A.D., & D.R. McKemey. (1976). Antecedents of work related expectancies. *Academy of Management Journal, 19(4),* 547-559.

Smith, R.C. (1981). Black power and the transformation from protest to politics. *Political Science Quarterly, 96,* 431-443.

Sofola, J.A. (1973). *African culture and the African personality.* Ibadan, Nigeria: African Resources Publishers, Co.

Sowande, F. (1973). The quest of an African worldview: Utilization of African discourse. In J. Daniels (Ed.), *Black communications,* (Final report to National Endowment for the Humanities, Project No. EH 6404-72-216). Washington, D.C.: The National Endowment for the Humanities.

Thompson, V.S. (1990). Factors affecting the level of African American identification. *The Journal of Black Psychology, 17(1),* 19-35.

Voorhis, H.V.B. (1940). *Negro Masonry in the United States.* New York: Henry Emerson .

Warfield-Coppock, N. (1981). *Personality and culture.* Unpublished paper for The Fielding Institute.

Warfield-Coppock, N. (1982, August). *Organizational development and the Black organization.* Paper presented at the annual convention of The Association of Black Psychologists, Cincinnati, Ohio.

Warfield-Coppock, N. (1985). *A qualitative study of the African American organization: Investigating Africanisms.* Doctoral dissertation completed at The Fielding Institute, Santa Barbara, CA. Ann Arbor, Ml: University Microfilms, No.88-24, 253.

Warfield-Coppock, N. (1995). Toward an Afrocentric theory of organizations. *Journal of Black Psychology, 21(1),* 30-42.

Warfield-Coppock, N. (1996). Empirical measurements of the Black organization from on Afro-centric prospective. In R.L. Jones (Ed.), *Handbook of tests and measurements for Black populations,* Vol.2 (pp. 519-531). Hampton, VA:Cobb & Henry Publishers.

Williams, R.L. (1981). *The collective Black mind: An Afrocentric theory of Black personality.* St. Louis, MO.: Williams and Associates, Inc.

Wilson, P.G. (1979). Toward a new understanding of the gender of organizations. *Dissertation Abstracts International.* 40/07A, 4273.

Yancy, W.L. (1970). Organization structures and environments: A second look at the NAACP and CORE. *Social Science Quarterly. 51(1),* 25-30.

Yearwood, L. (1976). Black organizations: A study of their community involvement with reference to decision making processes. *Dissertation Abstracts International.* 37/08A, 5375. (University Microfilms No. 77-03601)

Yearwood, L. (1980). *Black organizations: Issues on survival techniques.* Washington, D.C.: University Press.

Zey-Ferrell, M. (1981). Criticisms of the dominant perspective on organizations. *The Sociological Quarterly. 22(2),* 181-205.

Author

Nsenga Warfield-Coppock
Baobab Associates, Inc.
7614 16th Street NW
Washington, D.C. 20012-1406
Telephone: (202) 726-0560
Fax: (202) 829-4784

Part 2

Methodology

Culturally-Competent Research Methods

Cleopatra Howard Caldwell, James S. Jackson, M. Belinda Tucker, and Philip J. Bowman

Introduction

Contrary to the current status of social and behavioral research on most racial-ethnic groups in the United States, there has been a long history of data collection in the African American population (Jackson, 1991; Montero, 1977; Myers, 1977a; 1977b; 1979). A review, however, reveals major conceptual and methodological limitations in these studies. In a previous chapter on survey research methods in African American communities (Jackson, Tucker, & Bowman, 1982), we restricted our comments about these limitations to survey research methodology. In this chapter, we extend our discussion to include additional research approaches for which we have developed procedures to address many of the major deficiencies in previous data collection efforts on African Americans. We also consider the issue of research with multi-cultural samples as a means for understanding African American populations (Freidenberg, Mulvihill & Caraballo, 1993).

Although the research vehicle through which we initially refined our procedures and viewpoints was a cross-sectional, national survey sample, we were concerned with more than the mere technical problems of collecting data from a national probability sample of Blacks.Our main concern was to address the problem of gathering reliable and valid information on a population that had different life experiences than the majority population for whom most theoretical conceptualizations and data collection techniques had been developed (Schwartz, 1970; Sieber, 1973). We found that the utilization of standard concepts, standard instruments and procedures was inappropriate for a population whose cultural perspective and historical experience differ radically from that of the majority (Weiss, 1977; Whiting, 1968). The use of identical procedures, constructs, methods, and approaches from surveys in the majority population yields biased information, masks important relationships, and prevent valid interpretations of findings.

In this chapter we present general conceptual and methodological issues that we feel must be considered when conducting research on African Americans using different approaches. We incorporate many of the issues highlighted in previous research and, where appropriate, use pertinent examples from our current studies for illustrative purposes. The chapter is organized around several methodological approaches: regional sample surveys, multigeneration family studies, qualitative studies, and studies of clinical diagnosis. In the survey research section, we summarize major conceptual and methodological issues. In subsequent sections, we discuss relevant issues based on these concerns and comment on other challenges in conducting research on African American Americans using the specific approach being described. Special consideration is given to life style and cultural factors that may affect the quality and meaningfulness of data collected in African American communities.

Survey Research

We view the survey method as the most efficient way to obtain large, representative samples of the African American population. Other commonly used research methods (e.g., participant observation, field studies, laboratory experiments) are limited to the study of rather small, select groups of people. The amount of information gathered in a well-designed and executed survey permits a level of exploration not possible with other more restricted data gathering procedures (Fowler, 1988).

Although procedures have been proposed to increase the cost-effectiveness of some available survey techniques (e.g., telephone interviews, two-way, mail-in self-reports, etc.), issues involved with face-to-face interviewing are important because face-to-face interviewing has historically yielded proportionately more completed questionnaires than other procedures. On the other hand, telephone interviewing, with its developments over the last twenty years (Connor & Heeringa, 1992; Groves & Kahn, 1979; Inglis, Groves & Heeringa, 1987), provides an efficient alternative that we will discuss later. Additionally, an interviewer can, to some extent, clarify respondent misunderstandings and decrease ambivalent responses and "no" answers. Finally, the interviewer can observe the respondent's behavior throughout the session. Respondent confusion, weariness, enjoyment or hostility is readily seen and can be incorporated into the obtained interview data (See Jackson, Tucker, & Bowman, 1982, for more details).

Even in light of these positive features, a number of methodological problems characterize the use of face-to-face interviewing with African American and other minority populations (Aquilino, 1994). We are concerned with three main categories of problems: 1) the impact of race-related interviewer and respondent characteristics

(Williams, 1964); 2) the influence of language on measurement; and 3) the effects of cultural differences on the meaningfulness of constructs.

Impact of Race-Related Interviewer and Respondent Characteristics on Survey Data

Survey researchers have for some time been aware of the possible contaminating effects of interviewer and respondent characteristics (Rice, 1929; Cannell, 1953; Benney & Hughes, 1956; Kahn & Cannell, 1957; Fowler, 1991). Many of the early findings, however, were related to interviewer expectations conveyed to the respondent in the form of attitudes or beliefs. For example, in a study of the causes of destitution, Rice (1929) discovered that one interviewer tended to elicit responses citing overindulgence of alcohol as the root of their poverty, while another found that social and industrial conditions were at fault. Rice later found that the first interviewer was a prohibitionist, while the other was a socialist.

Interviewers today are thoroughly trained to minimize such sources of bias (Belli & Lepkowski, 1995; Jackson, 1991; Mangione, Fowler & Louis, 1992; National Survey of Black Americans Interviewers' Manual, 1979; Cannell & Kahn, 1968). More visible forms of bias concern us here. The race of the participant in the interview session is an undisguisable fact. The tradition of race relations in this society assures that the race variable will be associated with an assortment of other biasing factors (Anderson, Silver & Abramson, 1988). Informed researchers are now concerned with the effect race of interviewer has on data validity (Anderson & Silver, 1986; 1987). Some researchers have focused on the amount of social distance (i.e., perceived personal or status dissimilarity) between interviewer and respondent as a determinant of response bias (Abramson, 1986; Silver, Abramson &Anderson, 1986). Most agree that a high degree of social distance increases the likelihood of biased responses. Others, however, suggest that very low social distance may well result in as much bias as its alternative (Davis, 1995; Dohrenwend, Colombotos, & Dohrenwend, 1968). That is, when the interviewer and the respondent are too similar, personal involvement may decrease task involvement (Jackson, 1988a, 1988b). A third explanation is simply that on racial matters, people tend to be more frank with members of what they perceive to be their own race (Jackson, 1988b; Schuman & Hatchett, 1974). Some recent research (Davis, 1995), however, suggests that a diametrically opposite effect may be operative in the same-race interview setting.

Clearly, as racial interactions in the society at large change, interviewing situations will reflect the new pattern of behavior (Davis, 1995). This means that research must be a continuous monitoring of societal fluctuations likely to affect the collection of valid data (Jackson, 1991).

The Influence of Language on Measurement

When we consider African American Americans, two issues are relevant: 1) is the language used in the research instrument understood by African Americans; and 2) are words or concepts used on the questionnaire subject to differential interpretation among Blacks, as opposed to the standard research population. For the most part, standardized measures were developed on and for middle-class American White populations (Jackson, 1991). Thus, they contain words, phrases, and concepts used by that population. Some measures have been found to be inappropriate for use with Blacks (e.g. Samuda, 1975; Jackson, 1976). In the National Survey of Black Americans (NSBA), we attempted to develop questionnaire items and measures couched in terms understood by the vast majority of the participants of interest (Jackson, 1991; Sudman & Bradburn, 1974).

The second issue rarely has been addressed empirically. For example, cross-cultural research on the Semantic Differential Scale (Snider & Osgood, 1969) has shown that Blacks and Whites respond very differently to color names and ethnic concepts (Williams, 1966). In our work we asked a sizeable group of African Americans what the words and concepts meant to them; we did not simply assume that all segments of American society interpret or use language identically.

Cultural Influences and Construct Meaningfulness

The behavioral sciences reflect the White, middle-class values that most of the theorists and researchers themselves share. While African Americans certainly have incorporated a good many Western values, clearly a common African heritage and the experiences of slavery and racial oppression have resulted in a shared frame of reference unlike that of any other group. Traditional investigatory procedures in the behavioral sciences, then, might be of questionable legitimacy for Blacks.

A second element of this issue is that of question propriety (Schwarz, 1995a, 1995b). Can all questions ordinarily asked of American Whites be asked of other groups with similar success? Prior national studies which often included Blacks in small numbers, have not typically concerned themselves with these problems. Constructs, instruments and procedures developed primarily for White populations have more often than not been utilized for Blacks in the samples. Differences in response patterns have been attributed to race. While such a conclusion might be valid for some variables, we believe that these differences are often due to erroneous conceptualizations, meaningless constructs, and inappropriate procedures. Historically, even in those studies where Blacks have been of primary focus, little attention has been given to the appropriateness of the methods and the cultural context which we feel is of critical importance (Heiss, 1975; Marx, 1972; Matthews & Prothro, 1966). We have proposed that constructs, instruments, and methods must be considered in light of the experiences and cultural context of Blacks which deviate, often radically for certain subgroups, from that of the White majority. (We address this issue in more detail later in our discussion of qualitative studies).

We have felt it necessary to examine prior assumptions, develop new instruments, and where necessary, develop new approaches. As an illustration we cite the concept of internal-external control which, originally developed by Rotter and his associates in studying the effect of changing reinforcements on learning, became strikingly prominent and popular in research in the 1960's. We have found it necessary to rethink some of the assumptions and implications of internality and externality when used in studies on Blacks (Neighbors, Jackson, Broman & Thompson, 1996). Particularly, we found important two distinctions not typically made in the work in this area. One distinction involves whether the belief in internal or external control reflects an individual's beliefs about the determinants of success and failure generally in our society, and whether it reflects his sense of control over his own life directions. This distinction seemed critical in studying groups whose position in the social structure differentiated their opportunities from those of the majority group.

A second set of distinctions relate to the conceptualization and measurement of externality. It is generally assumed in the internal-external literature that the internal represents the healthier and more effective orientation. This follows partly from the fact that the external orientation has generally been defined as a fatalistic belief in chance. When one applies this concept to Blacks, however, it is clear that there are real external determinants that are not random, that affect successes and failures systematically, and that should be perceived as limiting and constraining. An external orientation that involves a recognition of the constraints imposed by labor market conditions or racial discrimination should promote effectiveness in coping with the reality of being African American in America (Bowman, Jackson, Hatchett & Gurin, 1982).

In studies of Blacks, our colleagues have found that the distinction between personal and general control beliefs leads to differential behavioral predictions, and that externality, defined in terms of a sensitivity to social system determinants, predicts to greater, rather than less, effectiveness (Gurin, Gurin, Lao, & Beattie, 1969; Gurin & Epps, 1975). They were led to these reconceptualizations by analyses of the special meaning of internal and external control in groups deprived of power in our society. This reconceptualization tended to make explicit a set of implicit assumptions in the traditional concept and resulted in the development of a more meaningful construct and method of assessment in studies on Blacks.

As these examples suggest, a concerted and critical examination of the meaning, operationalization, and assessment of substantive constructs could yield more reliable and valid results than in past efforts. We utilized several methods and procedures for increasing our confidence in the quality of the data from the National Survey of Black Americans (Jackson, 1991). Among these were: 1) the random probe (Schuman, 1966); 2) modified back-translation techniques (Anderson, 1967;

Word, 1977); 3) self-defining concepts through open-ended questioning; and, 4) various forms of converging operations (Lehnen, 1971; Andrews & Withey, 1976).

Developing Culturally-Relevant Instruments

In the following paragraphs we examine some of the techniques and approaches that we believe were instrumental in increasing the appropriateness and validity of the survey methods used in the National Survey of Black Americans. Two techniques developed specifically for cross-national studies, the random probe, and back-translation, and their modifications for use in our national survey are described first. We then turn to a presentation of how we proceeded with ascertaining the accuracy of our instruments and methods.

Random Probe. The random probe is a direct technique requiring each interviewer to use predetermined follow-up probes for randomly selected closed ended items in the interview schedule (Schuman, 1966). Following the respondent's choice of the closed-ended alternative, the interviewer asks the respondent to explain what he had in mind when making the particular choice.[1] The respondent's comments are then compared with the intended purpose of the item and the selected closed-ended alternative. Quantitatively, fit can be placed on a five-point scale ranging from the explanation is clear and leads to accurate prediction to unclarity in response. This scoring system and the resulting data can then be used to obtain estimates of items which have little or no meaning to respondents in the interview schedule. The information can also be used in a qualitative manner to assist in understanding the accuracy of the responses.

We found this method particularly helpful during both the pretest phase and the actual survey. Many of the close-ended items were randomly probed across the entire national sample and we have collected a wealth of qualitative and quantitative data.

Back-Translation. Back-translation is a procedure of successive translations to arrive at questions which have the same meaning in two (or more) cultures. This procedure has typically been used in differing language cross-national studies. However, the general logic of the technique seemed appropriate for a study of African Americans, particularly given the recognition of language differences from that of middle-class American culture. In our own application of this procedure, broad areas of concern were generated and open-ended questions were written. Local community members representing varying socioeconomic levels were contacted in the surrounding African American communities and interested groups were formed. All attempts were made to make these groups as heterogeneous as possible (old and young, southern- and northern-born, men and women). Their responses to the open-ended questions were tape recorded and later transcribed. These transcriptions served as the basis of the development of the first pretest instrument for the National Survey of Black Americans. The sessions supplied very rich and detailed information regarding the meaning of many concepts. Questions were written using words whose shared meanings were garnered from the sessions and informal pretests with other indigenous community members were held to ascertain that these questions were working and meaningful to African American community people. Based upon this sort of interchange and input from indigenous community members, preliminary pretest material was developed.

Converging Operations. This procedure involves computing a correlational matrix of responses gathered through different methods and thought to measure the same and different concepts. Campbell and Fiske (1959) proposed that reliability coefficients for concepts could be estimated through the convergence or agreement of items thought to measure the same concept and obtained with highly similar methods. Validity estimates, on the other hand, can be produced through the convergence between items thought to measure the same concept obtained with different methods and the divergence of items thought to measure different concepts obtained with the same methods. Thus, given the various predicted pattern of correlations for conceptually-similar and -dissimilar items measured with different and the same methods, both reliability and validity estimates can be quantitatively obtained.

Given our use of open, closed, and quasi-closed methods as well as interviewer observations for collecting data on a number of convergent and divergent concepts, this multitrait-multimethod matrix approach appears perfectly suited to ascertaining the concept meaningfulness (Lehnen, 1971). We feel that the unique application of these techniques and procedures (Campbell & Fiske, 1959; Schuman, 1966; Warwick & Osherson, 1973), have theoretical and empirical bases that make them viable for determining the meaningfulness and accuracy of substantive concepts and methods for Blacks (Anderson, 1967; Schuman & Hatchett, 1974; Schwarz & Schuman, 1995; Word, 1977). Our results in the National Survey of Black Americans suggest that their application produced a set of questionnaires much more relevant and culturally appropriate than previous efforts.

Field Problems in Survey Research

In addition to developing instruments that are culturally-relevant and appropriate for use in the African American population, we also have to be concerned with the development of data-collection strategies that are sensitive to the peculiar lifestyle situations and conditions of African American people (Jackson, 1988; 1991). We believe that field operations must be structured to minimize the impact of three general problems: low response rates among certain groups of respondents, biasing interviewer-respondent interactions, and response inaccuracy. In this section we discuss pertinent findings relative to each and present our specific techniques to alleviate such difficulties.

Response Rates. One critical determinant of the overall quality of survey data is the obtained response rate (i.e., the actual number of completed interviews gathered over the net sample size) (Babbie, 1973). Low response rates can seriously undermine the representativeness of the data as well as the use of certain more sophisticated analysis techniques. Nonresponse has steadily risen over the years (Cannell, Personal Communication, 1977; Hawkins, 1977; American Statistical Association Conference, 1974) and has only recently been the subject of empirical inquiry (Krysan, Schuman, Scott & Beatty, 1994; Knauper, 1996; Kessler, Mroczek & Belli, 1994). A comprehensive review by Hawkins (1977) indicates that differential responses on the basis of a number of demographic characteristics have been observed. Those of particular relevance are:

1. Blacks tend to exhibit higher response rates than Whites
2. Central city residents tend to exhibit lower response rates than outer city and rural residents.
3. Females tend to exhibit higher response rates than males.

The fact that Blacks as a group are more urbanized than Whites causes overall response rates among Blacks to be lower in some studies than rates among Whites (Bianchi, 1976). This phenomenon in combination with the sex effect, produces dismal expectations for obtaining data on African American males, especially those in the inner city. Traditional practical (as opposed to statistical) efforts to counter nonresponse have consisted primarily of call-back attempts. That is, after the respondent is located, the interviewer will keep trying to schedule or complete the interview until the potential respondent gives an outright refusal or the data collection period ends. In the 1976 Detroit Area Study, for example, the response rate goal of 71% among Blacks was reached by extending the field period by three weeks (Bianchi, 1976). Similar approaches have been used in more recent surveys (Kessler et al, 1994).

Major discussions have centered about the issue of acceptable response rate (Dillman, Singer, Clark & Treat, 1996). Of specific concern is the extent to which the data are biased by non-response. A condition of no bias could exist only in the highly implausible event that nonrespondents form a random subsample of the study population. The question, then, is what response rate represents the thin line between serious and inconsequential error. Certain experts have insisted that even response rates of 80% to 95% seriously bias the results (Deming, 1950; Heneman & Patterson, 1949; Lowe & McCormick, 1955), while others are comfortable with rates of 80% and lower (Sheatsley, 1948; Dinerman, 1948). Unfortunately, there is little empirical evidence to support either position (Hawkins, 1976). In practice, survey scientists have accepted historically far lower rates than these and generally strive to reach 70% (Babbie, 1973) while using statistical correction factors when necessary (Hawkins, 1976). Recent work, however, on the use of incentives has resulted in dramatic increases in response rates (Dillman et al 1996; Kessler et al.,

1995; Krysan, Schuman, Scott, & Beatty, 1994; Willimack, Schuman, Pennell, & Lepkowski, 1995).

Biasing Interviewer-Respondent Interactions. As indicated earlier, our concerns about the possible biasing effect of race-related interviewer-respondent characteristics leads us to believe that African American interviewers should be used to alleviate this difficulty (Schuman & Converse, 1971). We cannot ignore, though, the existence of other potentially biasing factors (e.g., social class, language, age, cognitive ability, and sex differences) which may also inhibit or alter responses (Knauper, 1996; Knauper, Belli, Hill & Herzog, 1995; Markides, Liang, & Jackson, 1990).

Some have found that an observable discrepancy between interviewer and respondent social status may influence respondent behavior (Lenski & Leggett, 1960). This well recognized problem is attended to in the survey methods literature by emphasizing the importance of having interviewers dress in a manner comparable to that of the respondent's while maintaining good grooming.

Some of the same concerns expressed in our decision of language problems inherent in using standard, middle-class-oriented instruments apply here. There are similar status/class distinctions within the national population of Blacks. Furthermore, slang is regional and interviewers unfamiliar with local speech patterns may lose important content in the interview.

Though not well documented, survey methodologists believe that female (and undoubtedly some male) respondents may be less likely to admit a male interviewer into their homes. In addition, certain subjects may be more difficult to discuss openly with persons of the opposite sex (e.g., sex-specific health problems).

Although the potential problem of sex biasing cannot be totally alleviated, we have found in our work that the use of interviewers indigenous to communities tends to alleviate many of the problems of social class distance, language, and similar factors that may influence or inhibit responses. Many of these potential problems can be reduced through careful attention to these matters during interviewer selection (Friedenberg et al., 1993; Jackson, 1991; Mays & Jackson, 1991).

Response Accuracy. In practically all instances, survey researchers are forced to assume that the respondents are being honest, for we rarely have mechanisms of external verification (Schwarz & Hippler, 1995a, 1995b). Medical surveys occasionally have objective evidence derived from physical examinations which can serve as a base for validity checks. When such checks are performed, respondent answers may, at times, evidence surprisingly low validity (Oksenberg & Cannell, 1974; Mangione et al, 1992; Marquis, 1970). Oskenberg and Cannell (1974) conceive of the problem as a consequence of three factors: respondent memory; respondent perception of the importance of the desired information; and the social desirability of certain responses. Of course, depending on the area of investigation, these factors vary in their potential impact on results. For example, memory should have little to do with attitudinal responses (Schwarz & Bless, 1995).

Charles Cannell and his associates at the Institute for Social Research developed very specific procedures that seem to significantly increase the validity of responses (Cannell & Fowler, 1975; Oksenberg & Cannell, 1974; Henson, Cannell, & Lawson, 1976; Marquis, 1970). Their three-pronged strategy consists of: (1) giving the respondents detailed instructions about what they are expected to do in the interview, stressing the importance of accuracy and detail; (2) making the respondents' commitments to give accurate information explicit by having them sign a written form of agreement; and (3) having interviewers acknowledge proper response through the use of positive and negative reinforcement.

Many of these procedures had not been attempted previously with African American respondents in any large numbers. In addressing the problem, however, we felt that many factors needed to be considered and that there were some specific steps that could be taken to address these issues. For example, we believed that payment per interview would serve as an incentive for interview completion and response accuracy by placing value on the respondent's time and information (Dillman, Singer, Clark & Treat, 1996; Warwick & Lininger, 1975). This may also offset possible conflict between the interview and other informal earning activities in lower income groups.

Very often minorities feel that researchers have only personal and political goals and have no intention of returning results to the minority community. Such feelings may inhibit an individual's desire to engage in the study in a meaningful way. We clearly stated at first contact, our intention to share our findings with all respondents as an obligation as well as a desire (Mays & Jackson, 1991).

Our task is made much easier if the goals of the project are endorsed by the respondents. Since we feel that the substantive areas are of significant interest to African Americans generally, respondent participation should be encouraged by a clear statement of our goals, to the extent that findings are not jeopardized, at first contact with the prospective respondent. We also feel that such openness makes the respondent aware of his or her contribution to social science knowledge and, as a consequence, perhaps more willing to take the questions seriously and respond more thoughtfully (Friedenberg et al, 1993). Since response rate and quality are often affected by interviewer motivation, we also acquainted our interviewers with the study's goals (Jackson, 1991). A concerned and supportive field staff can only add to the quality of the data (Belli & Lepkowski, 1995).

A low male response rate may be due in part to their absences during the day hours that many interviewers are likely to prefer. In addition, many Blacks work other than the predominant nine to five shift (often holding night or evening jobs) and may either be asleep or accomplishing other tasks during the regular interviewing hours. We hired field staff who were not reluctant to work during odd hours to accommodate these groups.

Some survey scientists suspect that traditional interviewers, often older White women, have been psychologically, if not physically, reluctant to work in the inner cities (Cannell, Personal Communication, 1977). This, quite naturally, may affect call-back attempts by the interviewer and the interviewer's general commitment to obtain the interview. We believe that African American interviewers familiar with inner city neighborhoods will be less likely to have such qualms and have a better sense of where and when to go.

The use of regionally indigenous field staff also lessened the perceived social distance between interviewers and respondents, particularly in terms of language. Interviewers will be more acquainted with the styles and mannerisms of the area and will be less likely to misconstrue information (Jackson, 1991).

Some respondents have real fears about the admission of total strangers into their homes. Potential respondents who either voice such concerns or appear to have such concerns have the option of being interviewed at a neutral site, possibly a neighborhood church or community center, where she or he will feel less threatened.

While the random household survey technique does not permit predetermined matching by sex, when the refusal is likely to be linked to sex of interviewer (e.g., when a female respondent seems very unwilling to admit a male interviewer), extremely reluctant respondents were given the option of being interviewed by someone of another sex. Generally, we have found that these field procedures have been very productive in eliciting the cooperation of respondents, increasing the motivation of interviewers and contributing overall to the quality of the data. Since all these procedures were used, it is very difficult to accurately pinpoint which was most effective. Our own feeling is that making the goals of the project explicit, using indigenous interviewers, and having instruments with clear face validity to African American Americans contributed importantly to our success.

In addition to the substantive contributions of NSBA, unique survey methods have been developed and implemented. These methods are of general utility and make important contributions to future national and regional surveys, particularly relative to random sampling of racial and ethnic minorities and other high-visibility, geographically-clustered, groups (Gurin, Hatchett, & Jackson, 1989). The development of procedures in the NSBA survey permitted Blacks to be sampled for the first time in a way that insured for individuals in each and every African American household in the continental United States a known probability of selection (Hess, 1985; Jackson, 1991).

Recognizing that other quantitative (e.g., cohort, longitudinal, multigenerational-lineage surveys) and qualitative (e.g., participant observations, systematic observations, focus groups) approaches may be useful to the study of different African American populations, we selected three research methodologies that we have used over the years to complement what we learned while conducting the NSBA. In the remainder of this chapter, we discuss selected conceptual and methodological issues in doing multigeneration family research, focus groups, and studies of clinical diagnosis with African American Americans.

Multigeneration Family Studies

To complement the individual cross-sectional survey-data approach used in NSBA, we launched the National Three-Generation Family Study to gather data from multiple family members (Jackson & Hatchett, 1986). The application of multiplicity sampling procedures produced for the first time in one population group a three-generation-family-lineage, national probability sample. In the three-generation study, national samples of African American elderly, adults, and youth were identified, building on NSBA respondents. In implementing this multigeneration family study, we were faced with an added opportunity for analysis potential provided by a three-generation family lineage sample, as well as new challenges to insure the quality of the data across generations for African American populations. From a methodological perspective (Jackson & Antonucci, 1994), some issues remained the same as with conducting surveys in general (e.g., impact of race-related interviewer and respondent characteristics, influence of language on measurement, cultural influences). Age-related differences in construct meaningfulness, however, was a major concern. The fundamental question was, could we translate social science constructs in a meaningful way across generations of African Americans, while considering the historical context in which different generations had been socalized (Schuman, Belli & Bischoping, 1995)?

In our own work with 510 three-generation African American families (ranging in age from 14-99 years old) we found that the grandparent generation had less formal education and resided in the south more often than persons in the parent and child generations (Jackson, Chatters, & Taylor, 1993). Thus, our concern for question comprehension based on educational attainment and historical experiences with oppression centered on this generation. We modified standard language to frame questions sensitive to the cognitive abilities and cultural context of the oldest generation.

Another example of the need for cultural sensitivity in multigeneration family research may be illustrated by using age as the basis for assessing generational position for African Americans. As Mangen noted in his 1988 publication (Mangen, Bengtson, & Landry, 1988):

> Generational analysis often begins with an age- or cohort-based model assumed to measure generational status accurately and completely. That is, by virtue of membership in some age or cohort group, a respondent individual is assumed to hold a certain generational status (e.g., child, parent, or grandparent) within his or her family. For example, the generational model typically assumes that a 40 year old person has living parents and children, and the questions asked of that individual focus on those two role relationships. It is quite possible that any specific 40 year old might be the oldest generation (G1), the grandchild (G3), or even a great-grandchild (G4). He or she may even be both a grandparent and a grandchild in a five-generation family. (p. 32)

For African American families, the likelihood of experiencing multiple generations within a family is quite high (Burton & Bengtson, 1985; Stack, 1974). Our own analysis of generational position within the three-generation study showed considerable overlap in age across generations, especially among the middle and older lineage positions (Jackson, Jayakody, & Antonucci, 1993). Although the life expectancy of Blacks is significantly less than that of the general population, the potential combination of generational positions within African American families is enormous because of the overall younger age distribution of the African American population (Jackson, et al., 1993) and the 2: 1 early childbearing rates among Blacks teenagers when compared to White teenagers (Allen Guttmacher Institute, 1993).

Like Burton (1995), we found that multigeneration African American families tend to be overwhelmingly female across generations (i.e., G1=72%, G2=69%, G3=54%) (Jackson, Chatters, & Taylor, 1993) which often leads to an underrepresentation of African American males in family studies and inadequate conceptualizations of family roles. Appropriate conceptions of normative roles within families are important considerations in multigeneration family studies. While the socialization of children and adolescents (Burton, 1990; Chase-Lansdale, Brooks-Gunn & Zamsky, 1994; Wilson, 1986) and the father's role as provider (Bowman, 1985; Cazenave, 1984; Christmon, 1990; Marsiglio, 1995; Tucker & Taylor, 1989) have been the focus of some work on African American families, these roles are not well understood. Prior to conducting multigeneration research, attention should be given to defining the nature of normative roles (Burton & Dilworth-Anderson, 1991; Wilson, 1986). Failure to develop theoretical perspectives that include normative features of gender-based family functioning increases the difficulty in assessing the observed structures and functional forms of African American families.

One of the most persistent findings regarding intergenerational relationships within African American families is the pervasiveness of the extended family system. This issue is at the heart of how Blacks define who is part of their family and who is not. The simple nuclear family definition as the most important family form would essentially eliminate any hope of understanding distinctive household living arrangements, patterns of relationships, and provisions of support within African American families (Chatters & Jayakody, 1995). Care must be taken that the inclusion-exclusion criteria in obtaining samples are reflective of the targeted populations to be sampled (Mays & Jackson, 1991). For example, researchers have found that caregiving for grandchildren was a major responsibility of grandmothers within African American multigeneration families (Pearson, Hunter, Ensminger, & Kellman, 1990; Wilson, 1985). This raises the issue of who the focal person should be in studies of childhood socialization and the provision of care within African American families. Although mothers remain the primary socializing agent, consideration also should be given to issues of coparenting (Wilson, 1986) and surrogate parenting (Burton, 1992) within African American families. A misspecification of the target population or inadequate inclusion of caregivers could lead to erroneous interpretation of findings.

Using the three-generation data, we addressed the above concerns by developing the Family Environment Context Model (Jackson, Jayakody, & Antonucci, 1996). This model suggests that the individual family must be considered within an analytic scheme that is responsive to time, process, and context through a multigenerational lineage framework. This is particularly true for African American families that have historically included a broad array of tangible and intangible cross-generational exchanges, horizontally as well as vertically. Cross-sectional or longitudinal research designs alone would not have identified the nature of these exchanges within African American families (Jackson & Antonucci, 1994).

Race-Comparative Research in Family Studies

The appropriate role of race-comparative research is a methodological and substantive issue in studies of Blacks in general, and African American families in particular. Race-comparative studies often result in a lack of attention to possible cultural differences between Blacks and Whites, culminating in inappropriate types of research on African American individuals and families. The importance of within-group differences is frequently overlooked for the sake of racial comparisons. The inappropriate application of this strategy could result in inconsistent findings across studies when careful consideration has not been given to the cultural context of race. For example, identified racial differences may be the result of more subtle socioeconomic or cultural circumstances between Blacks and Whites in America. Chatters and Jayakody (1995) have suggested that a thorough understanding of the interpretation of race differences in financial resources available for support exchanges within families may be best understood with measures of discrepancies in wealth between the races. Given the distribution of wealth within this society, income alone is not sufficient to understand discrepancies in financial exchanges between the races. The search for variations in outcomes cannot be limited to race as the ultimate explanation. Although racial differences in a number of outcomes (e.g., unemployment, health disparities, voting behaviors) may be useful for establishing corrective public policies, it also may be ineffective in race comparison studies in which White family functioning has been accepted as the norm (Billingsley, 1968, 1992). This is not to say that race comparison studies are never appropriate.

Our recently funded (1993-1996) study of teenage mothers and their families is an example of a multigeneration family study that uses race as a context for understanding adaptive responses in African American families experiencing a major family crisis. This study is an initial one-year, two-wave longitudinal investigation of 75 families in which a birth to a mother in her teens has occurred.

Interviews are conducted at two points in time with the teen mother and her mother. As often as is possible, the teen mother's father, grandmother, and her baby's father also are interviewed twice. Three mother/child interactions are video-taped during the one-year period, including an Ainsworth Strange Situation attachment assessment when the infant is 12-months of age. In addition to generational considerations, we are concerned with gender-specific family relationships as they influence mental health outcomes for both African American and White families who have experienced a birth to a teenager.

In conducting this study, we were faced with a number of conceptual and methodological challenges based on racial differences in family life among the included sample. For example, current statistics indicate that African American women are significantly less likely to be married than White women. Thus, the most challenging issue was determining exactly who would be eligible to participate in the study as a father. Although important for determining inclusion criteria for the teenager's mother and grandmother, establishing an operational definition for father of the teen mother was critical. Recent studies have considered the role of different types of fathers in families (Hawkins & Eggebeen, 1990). These studies have been primarily concerned with distinguishing between the influences of biological versus stepfathers. It is rare for these studies to focus on other father figures. However, the fluidity of the lives of African American adolescents, and teen mothers specifically, necessitated a broader definition than biological or stepfathers. Thus, we decided to allow the adolescent mother to nominate the person whom she considered to be her father figure, based in part on who she felt raised her.

We also decided that accepting the adolescent mother's nomination of father would not exclude other prominent adult male figures in her life, such as a stepfather or partner of her mother who lived in the household with the teen mother. Biological fathers who might be available for participation but not nominated by the teen mother were included in the study as well. Thus, this complex definition of father allowed for more than one father figure to participate in the study. The rationale for this complex definition of father is based on the growing body of work which suggests that father figures are important, especially in African American families (Billingsley, 1992), and that the influences of non-residential fathers can affect child outcomes (Marsiglio,1995; Danzinger & Radin, 1990).

In this study, the mother-teen mother dyad represented the biological relationship between mother and daughter in 96% of the cases. The father figures included biological fathers for 64% of the teen mothers. Other family relations such as grandfathers, stepfathers, or uncles represented 36% of these relationships. African American teen mothers were significantly more likely than White teen mothers to nominate a father figure into the study rather than a biological father. Preliminary analyses of these data suggest that relationship status did not affect the nature of associations among variables such as paternal support or conflict and adolescent depressive symptomatology (Caldwell, Antonucci, Jackson, Wolford, & Osofsky,

1997). Future analyses in this area will be necessary to determine the relative influence of father status on racial differences in family adaptational outcomes.

Community Psychiatric Qualitative Studies

Qualitative research can be used to uncover and understand the nature of human experiences (Strauss & Corbin, 1990). From our perspective, qualitative studies offer an opportunity to gather in-depth information on the lives of African Americans. Cultural interpretations of experiences may be placed in the voice of the respondent. It offers several advantages over the survey research approach in that it allows for context to be more fully explored, and meanings to be better understood (Fnedenberg et al, 1993). The primary disadvantage of this approach is that findings may not be generalized due to the use of small, non random samples. Because of our interest in understanding issues from a African American perspective, the use of qualitative data allows us to further explore African American life within a cultural context. It also considers participants as informants rather than objectified subjects (Tripp-Reimer, Sorofman, Peters, & Waterman, 1994). This is especially important when trying to evaluate the appropriateness of measurement tools that have not been validated on African American populations.

According to Berry, Poortinga, Segall, and Dasen (1992), constructs may have both etic and emic meaning. Etic refers to constructs assumed to be universal and equally understood across multiple cultural groups. Emic, on the other hand, refers to constructs having specific culturally-appropriate meaning for use with African Americans. In our view, constructs and measures developed on a predominantly White, middle-class population should not automatically be applied to Blacks because the two groups do not share the same cultural frame of reference (Jackson, Tucker, & Bowman, 1982). In an effort to explore emic constructs related to psychiatric diagnosis, we initiated a series of community psychiatric qualitative studies. Using the focus group strategy, these studies were designed to identify differences in lay explanations of underlying mental health and mental disorder concepts by race, gender, and age. The focus group approach brings together small groups of participants to have in-depth discussions of the phenomenon of interest. Our work with these community psychiatric qualitative studies has resulted in the development of innovative qualitative procedures for examining the conceptual basis and meaning of structured diagnostic material among African American adults, children and adolescents. We are applying quantitative concept-mapping techniques developed in organizational decision-making to the analysis of focus group data in samples of Blacks, Whites, mental health professionals, adults and children and adolescents. We are using standard qualitative analysis techniques on the verbal production from these focus groups as well. Building on this work with focus groups, we are conducting in-depth cognitive interviews with community samples of adults, children, and adolescents. Among adults, we are interested in differences in the meaning of structured diagnostic probes.

In our research on children and adolescents, we are interested in age-related developmental influences on race differences in responses to structured diagnostic material. Like the adult qualitative studies, the purpose of the child qualitative studies is to use a focus group strategy to determine children and adolescents' understanding of terminologies frequently used in standard mental health survey instruments. We are interested in identifying concepts that are understood across multiple cultural groups as well as those that may have a cultural- or gender specific meaning to children and adolescents. Words and questions selected as stimuli come from commonly used measures in child and adolescent mental health research (e.g., the CBCL, DISC, Harter Competency Scale, and the CDI).

Data gathered using these qualitative techniques will be used to develop a set of instruments and procedures for collecting reliable and valid data in the assessment of serious mental disorders among African American adults, children, and adolescents. We believe that this emphasis on empirically verifying the appropriateness and reliability of language used in diagnostic instruments by race, gender, and age is an important undertaking for culturally-sensitive research. To merely utilize existing concepts, measures, and methods would undoubtedly contribute more confusion to an already questionable literature. Obviously, these issues have been raised previously (Drake, 1973; Schuman & Hatchett, 1974; Warwick & Lininger, 1975; Word, 1977). However, studies on African American samples continue to take for granted the need to assess diagnostic instruments validated on White populations before use with African American populations.

Studies of Clinical Diagnosis

In the area of clinical diagnoses, we are engaged in an ongoing clinical study of African American and White inpatients with initial diagnoses of schizophrenia and mood disorder at a local inpatient psychiatric institution. The results of a true experiment on approximately 1,000 patients suggest that race of therapist (and possible cultural differences) may play a major role in the assignment of initial and final diagnoses to African American patients. These findings have important implications for the meaning of diagnostic category assignments across racial and ethnic groups, appropriately prescribed treatment, and follow-up recidivism. Follow-up studies on the qualitative meaning of clinical signs and symptoms, the pathways in and out of treatment, and the nature of patient/therapist interaction, are now underway.

Detroit Psychiatric Institute Diagnostic Study: 1992-1995 (DPIDS used a test/retest format, employing African American and White clinicians and structured and unstructured diagnostic research instruments in an interview sample of over 900 adult inpatients as part of the African American Mental Health Research Center (AAMHRC) study of racial influences on diagnosis. This study is part of the AAMHRC's work on the nature of racial influences on clinical judgement, treatment and treatment follow-up. Inpatient populations in two different clinical sites were interviewed, with a focus on how the color of the therapist affects the stability of diagnoses under both structured and less-structured clinical assessment conditions. Nearly 1,800 inpatients were eligible for this study and approximately 960 participated in the naturalistic experimental study. In addition, a review of patient charts is currently underway, investigating clinical history, influence of related conditions, and other demographic and social factors within the study population. The Chart Review includes coding extensive chart history material on all patients eligible for the Diagnostic Study.

Conclusion

Although no absolute guarantees can be given for the appropriateness of concepts, questions and methods of data collection, we feel confident that our adaptation of (a) cross-cultural approaches; (b) intensive interaction with members of diverse African American communities; and (c) extensive pretesting yield data that are more reliable and valid than that collected in prior surveys. The National Survey of Black Americans was the first study on the African American population that attempted to combine large national probability samples with extensive conceptual and empirical pretesting of instruments and methods of data collection. The results of these efforts are encouraging (Jackson, 1991).

We have learned that the combination of culturally-sensitive questions, indigenous community interviewers and attempts to engage both the interviewer and respondent in the goals of the project are fruitful avenues for data collection. We believe that the meaningfulness of the questions and explicitness of the project goals are the two major factors that contribute to the cooperation of respondents.

Our experiences in doing multigeneration family studies have taught us that in addition to cultural considerations, attention must be paid to construct meaningfulness both within and across generations. Gender-specific issues in family studies may also be brought to the forefront for African American males, if more inclusive procedures are used to broaden traditional definitions of family. Methodologically, the challenge of doing multigeneration studies with African American families must consider the implications of using age as the basis for assessing generational position. The age-condensed family systems that exist for some African American families may allow for overlapping ages across generations. Our Family Environment Context Model considers some of the unique aspects of doing multigeneration research with African American families.

From our qualitative and clinical diagnosis studies, we have learned that understanding differences in the meaning of diagnostic definitions and categorizations may exist based on race, gender, and age. This work has important implications for accurate diagnosis and treatment for African American populations.

Our hope is that greater attention to the issues raised in the present chapter will increase the quality of research and accuracy of data on African Americans. If the concern is with increasing our scientific knowledge and providing relevant social policy data, then social science researchers must be cognizant of and attend to the cultural and life-style factors endemic to the African American community. This sensitivity in theory and research has improved over the past 20 years, based in part on the methods and procedures developed from the National Survey of Black Americans and subsequent Program for Research on Black America (PRBA) studies. We hope that some of our new innovations will influence the nature of future work, not only in the African American population, but in other racial-ethnic groups as well.

Note

1. Schuman indicates that the exact wording is less important than the manner of delivery. He suggests that it is important that the respondent not feel that closed-ended choice is being challenged in any way. Typical probes are: Would you give me an example of what you mean?; I see, why do you say that?; Could you tell me a little more about that?

References

American Statistical Association Conference (1974). Report on the ASA Conference on Surveys of Human Populations. *American Statistician, 23*, 33-34.

Anderson, B. A., & Silver, B. D. (1987j. The vaility of survey responses: Insights from interviews of married couples in a survey of Soviet emigrants. *Social Forces, 66*, 537-554.

Anderson, B. A., & Silver, B. D. (1987). Measurement and mismeasurement of the validity of the self-reported vote. *American Journal of Political Science, 30*, 771-785.

Anderson, B. A., Silver, B.D., & Abramson, P. R. (1988). The effects of race of the interviewer on measures of electoral participation by Blacks in the National Election Studies. *Public Opinion Ouarterly, 52*, 53-83.

Anderson, R. V. W. (1967). On the comparability of meaningful stimuli in cross-cultural research. *Sociometry, 30*, 124-136.

Andrews, F. M., & Withey, S. B. (1976). *Social indicators of well-being: Americans perceptions of life quality.* New York: Plenum Press.

Aquilino, W. S. (1994). Interview mode effects in surveys of drug and alcohol use. *Public Opinion Ouarterly, 58*, 210-240.

Babbie, E. R. (1973). *Survey research methods.* Belmont, CA: Wadsworth Publishing.

Belli, R. F., & Lepkowski, J. M. (1995). *Behavior of survey actors and the accuracy of response.* Survey Methodology Program, Institute for Social Research, University of Michigan: Ann Arbor, MI.

Benney, M., & Hughes, E. C. (1956). Of sociology and the interview: Editorial preface. *American Journal of Sociology, 62*, 137-142.

Berry, J.W., Poortinga, Y.H., Segall, M.H., & Dasen, P.R. (1992). *Cross-cultural psychology: Research and applications.* Cambridge, England: Cambridge University Press.

Bianchi, S. M. (1976). Sampling report for the 1976 Detroit area study. Unpublished manuscript, University of Michigan.

Billingsley, A. (1968). *Black families in White America.* Englewood Cliffs, NJ: Prentice

Billingsley, A. (1992). *Climbing Jacob's ladder: The enduring legacy of African American families.* New York: Simon & Schuster.

Bowman, P.J., & Howard, C.S. (1985). Race-related socialization, motivation, and academic achievement: A study of Black youth in three-generation families. *Journal of the American Academy of Child Psychiatry, 24(2)*, 134-141.

Bowman, P. J., Jackson, J. S., Hatchett, S. J., & Gurin, G. (1982). Joblessness and discouragement among Black Americans. *Economic Outlook USA, 85-88.*

Burton, L.M. (1992). Black grandparents rearing children of drug-addicted parents: Stressors, outcomes, and social service needs. *The Gerontologist, 32*, 744-751.

Burton, L.M. (1990). Teenage childbearing as an alternative life-course strategy in multigeneration Black families. *Human Nature, (1)*, 123-143.

Burton, L. M., & Bengtson, V. L. (1985). Black grandmothers: Issues of timing and continuity of roles. In V.L. Bengtson and J.F. Robertson (Eds.) *Grandparenthood: Research and Policy Perspectives* (pp.61-77). Beverly Hills, CA: Sage.

Burton, L.M., & Dilworth-Anderson, P. (1991). The intergenerational family roles of aged Black Americans. In S.K. Pifer, & M.B. Sussman (Eds.), *Families: Intergenerational and generational connections* (pp. 311-330). New York: Hayworth Press.

Caldwell, C.H., Antonucci, T.C., Jackson, J.S., Wolford, J.L., & Osofsky, J.D. (1997). Perceptions of parental support and depressive symtomatology among African American and White adolescent mothers. *Journal of Emotional and Behavioral Disorders, 5(3)*, 173-183.

Campbell, D. T., & Fiske, D. W. (1959). Convergent and discriminant validation by the multitrait-multimethod matrix. *Psychological Bulletin, 56*, 81-105.

Cannell, C. F. (1953). *A Study of the Effects of Interviewers' Expectations upon Interviewing Results*. Unpublished doctoral dissertation, Ohio State University.

Cannell, C. F., & Fowler, F. J. (1975). Interviewers and interviewing techniques. In *Proceedings of National Invitational Conference on Advances in Health Survey Research Methods* (DHEW Publication No. (HRA) 77-3154). Washington, D.C.: U.S. Department of Health, Education, and Welfare.

Cannell, C. F., & Kahn, R. L. (1968). Interviewing. In G. Lindzey & E. Aronson (Eds.), *The handbook of social psychology: Vol. 2.* Reading, MA: Addison-Wesley.

Chatters, L.M., & Jayakody, R.J. (1995). Concepts and methods in the study of intergenerational support within African American families. In V.L. Bengtson, K.W.Schaie, & L.M. Burton (Eds.), *Intergenerational issues in aging.* New York: Springer.

Chase-Lansdale, P. L., Brooks-Gunn, J., & Zamsky, E. S. (1994). Young African American multigenerational families in poverty: Quality of mothering and grandmothering. *Child Development, 65,* 373-393.

Christmon, K. (1990). Parental responsibility of African American unwed adolescent fathers. *Adolescence, 25,* 645-653.

Connor, J. H., & Heeringa, S. G. (1992). *Evaluation of two cost efficient RDD designs.* Paper presented at the AAPOR 47th Annual Conference. St. Petersburg, FL.

Danziger, S.K., & Radin, N. (1990). Absent does not equal uninvolved: Predictors of fathering in teen mother families. *Jounral of Marriage and the Family, 52,* 636-642.

Davis, D. W. (1995). *The depth and direction of race of interviewer effects: Donning the Black mask.* Unpublished manuscript. Michigan State University, East Lansing, MI.

Deming, W. E. (1950). *Some theory of sampling.* New York: John Wiley & Sons.

Dillman, D. A., Singer, E., Clark, J. R. & Treat, J. B. (1996). Effects of benefits appeals, mandatory appeals, and variations in statements of confidentiality on completion rates for census questionnaires. *Public Opinion Ouarterly, 60,* 376-389.

Dinerman, H. (1948). 1948 Votes in the making. *Public Opinion Ouarterly, 12,* 585-598.

Dohrenwend, B. S., Colombotos, J., & Dohrenwend, B. P. (1968). Social distance and interviewer effects. *Public Opinion Ouarterly, 32,* 410-422.

Drake, H. M. (1973). Survey research in Africa: Its application and limits. In W. M. O'Brien, D. Spain, & M. Tessler (Eds.), *Research methods of culture bound technique.* Evanston, IL.: Northwestern University Press.

Freidenberg, J., Mulvihill, M., & Caraballo, L. R. (1993). From ethnography to survey: Some methodological issues in research on health seeking in East Harlem. *Human Organization, 52,* 151-161.

Groves, R. M., & Kahn, R. (1979). *Surveys by telephone: A national comparison with personal interviews.* New York: Academic Press.

Gurin, P., & Epps. E. G. (1975). *African American consciousness, identity and achievement: A study of students in historically Black colleges.* New York: John Wiley & Sons.

Gurin, P., G. Gurin, R. C. Lao, & Beattie. M. (1969). Internal-external control in the motivational dynamics of Negro youth. *Journal of Social Issues, 25(3)*, 29-53.

Gurin, P., Hatchett, S. J., & Jackson, J. S. (1989). *Hope and independence: Blacks' response to electoral and party politics.* New York: Russell Sage Foundation.

Guttmacher, A. (1993). *Facts in Belief Teenage Sexual and Reproductive Behavior.* New York: Guttmacher Institute.

Hawkins, D. F. (1977). *Nonresponse in Detroit area study surveys: A ten year analysis.* In Working Papers in Methodology, Institute for Research in Social Science. Chapel Hill: University of North Carolina.

Heiss, J. (1975). *The case of the Black family: A sociological inquiry.* New York: Columbia University Press.

Heneman, H. G., & Patterson, D. G. (1949). Refusal rates and interviewer quality. *International Journal of Opinion and Attitudes Research, 3*, 292-298.

Henson, R. M., Cannell, C., & Lawson, S. (1976). Effects of interviewer style on quality of reporting in a survey interview. *The Journal of Psyhology, 93*, 221-227.

Hess, I. (1985). *Sampling for social research surveys*, 1947-1980. Institute for Social Research, University of Michigan: Ann Arbor, MI.

Inglis, K. M., Groves, R.M., & Heeringa, S. G. (1987). Telephone sample designs for the U.S. Black household population. *Survey Methodology, 13*, 1-14.

Jackson, J. S. (1976). *Ethical and psychometric issues in the psychological testing of minorities.* Paper presented at the National Minority Conference on Human Experimentation, Reston, VA, January.

Jackson, J. S. (Ed.) (1991). *Life in Black America.* Newbury Park CA: Sage Publications.

Jackson, J. S. (1988a). Survey research on aging Black populations. In J. S. Jackson (Ed.), *The Black American elderly: Research on physical and psychosocial health* (pp. 327-346). New York: Springer Publishing Co.

Jackson, J. S. (1988b). Methodological issues in survey research on older minority adults. In M. P. Lawton, & A. R. Herzog (Eds.), *Research methods in gerontology* (pp. 137-161). Farmingdale, NY: Baywood Press.

Jackson, J. S., & Antonucci, T. C. (1994). Survey methodology in life-span human development research. In S. H. Cohen & H. W. Reese (Eds.), *Life-span developmental psychology: Methodological interventions* (pp. 65-94). New York: Erlbaum Associates.

Jackson, J.S., & Hatchett, S.J. (1986). Intergenerational research: Methodological considerations. In N. Datan, A.L. Green, & H.W. Reese (Eds.), *Intergenerational relations* (pp. 51-75). Hillsdale, NJ: Erlbaum Associates.

Jackson, J.S., Jayakody, R., & Antonucci, T.C. (1996). Exchanges within Black American three-generation families: The family environment context model. In T.K. Hareven (Ed.), *Aging and generational relations over the life course* (p. 347-377). Berlin: Walter de Gruyter.

Jackson, J.S., Tucker, M.B., & Bowman, P.J. (1982). Conceptual and methodological problems in survey research on black Americans. In W T. Liu (Ed.), Methodological problems in minority research. Chicago: Pacific/Asian American Mental Health Research Center.

Kahn, R. L., & C. F. Cannell (1957). *The dynamics of interviewing.* New York: John Wiley & Sons.

Kessler, R. C., Little, R. J. A., & Groves, R. M. (1995). Advances in strategies for minimizing and adjusting for survey nonresponse. *Epidemiologic Reviews, 17,* 192-204.

Kessler, R. C., Mroczek, D. K., & Belli, R. F. (1994). *Retrospective adult assessment of childhood psychopathology.* Survey Methodology Program, Institute for Social Research, University of Michigan: Ann Arbor, MI.

Knauper, B. (1996). *Age and response effects in attitude measurement.* Survey Methodology Program, Institute for Social Research, University of Michigan: Ann Arbor, MI.

Knauper, B., Belli, R. F., Hill, D. H. & Herzog, A. R. (1995). *Question difficulty and respondents' cognitive ability: The impact on data quality.* Survey Methodology Program, Institute for Social Research, University of Michigan: Ann Arbor, MI.

Krysan, M., Schuman, H., Scott. L. J., & Beatty, P. (1994). Response rates and response content in mail versus face-to-face surveys. *Public Opinion Quarterly, 58,* 381-399.

Lehnen, R. G. (1971) Assessing reliability in sample surveys. *Public Opinion Quarterly, 25,* 578-592.

Lenski, G. E., & Leggett, J. C. (1960). Caste, class and deference in the research interview. *The American Journal of Sociology, 65,* 463-467.

Lowe, F. E., & McCormick, T. C. (1955). Some survey sampling biases. *Public Opinion Ouarterly, 19*: 303-315.

Mangen, D.J., Bengtson, V.L., & Landry, P.H. (1988). *Measurement of intergenerational relations.* Newbury Park, CA: Sage Publications.

Mangione, T.W., Fowler, F. J., & Louis, T.A. (1992). Question characteristics and interviewer effects. *Journal of Official Statistics, 8,* 293-307.

Markides, K. S., Liang, J., & Jackson, J. S. (1990). Race, ethnicity, and aging: Conceptual and methodological issues. In R. H. Binstock, & L. K. George (Eds.),

Handbook of aging and the social sciences. 3rd Edition (pp. 112-129). San Diego, CA: Academic Press.

Marquis, K. H. (1970). Effects of social reinforcement on health reporting in the household interview. *Sociometry, 33,* 203-215.

Marsiglio, W. (1995). Young nonresident biological fathers. *Marriage and Family Review, 20,* 325-348.

Marx, G. T. (1972). *Protest and prejudice.* New York: Harper & Row.

Matthews, D. R., & Protho, J. W., (1966). *Negroes and the new Southern politics.* New York: Harcourt, Brace & World.

Mays, V. M., & Jackson, J. S. (1991). AIDS survey methodology with Black Americans. *Social Science and Medicine, 33,* 47-54.

Montero, D. (1977). Research among racial and cultural minorities: An overview. *Journal of Social Issues, 33,* 1-10.

Myers, V. (1977a). Survey methods for minority communities. *Journal of Social Issues, 33,* 11-19.

Myers, V. (1977b). Toward a synthesis of ethnographic and survey methods. *Human Organization, 36,* 244-251.

Myers, V. (1979). Survey methods and socially distant respondents. *Social Work Research and Abstracts, 15,* 3-9.

National Survey of Black Americans (1977). *Methodological issues: Black identity and mental health.* Research proposal submitted to the National Institute of Mental Health.

National Survey of Black Americans (1979). Interviewers Manual. Ann Arbor, MI, Institute for Social Research.

Neighbors, H., Jackson, J. S., Broman, C., & Thompson, E. (1996). Racism and mental health of African Americans: Self and system blame. *Journal of Ethnicity and Disease, 6(1, 2),* 167-175.

Oksenberg, L., & Cannell, C. F. (1974). *Some factors underlying the validity of response in self-report.* Paper delivered at Conference on Design and Measurement Standards for Research in Political Science, Delevan, Wl.

Pearson, J.L., Hunter, A.G., Ensminger, M.E., & Kellam, S.G. (1990). Black grandmothers in multigenerational households: Diversity in family structure and parenting involvement in the Woodlawn community. *Child Development, 61,* 434-442.

Rice, S. A. (1929). Contagious bias in the interview: A methodological note. *American Journal of Sociology, 35,* 420-423.

Rotter, J. B. (1966). Generalized expectancies for internal versus external control of reinforcement. *Psychological Monographs, 80,* 1-28.

Samuda, R. J. (1975). *Psychological testing of American minorities.* New York: Dodd, Mead & Company.

Schuman, H. (1966). The random probe: A technique for evaluating the validity of closed questions. *American Sociological Review, 31*, 218-222.

Schuman, H., & Converse, J. M. (1971). The effects of Black and White interviewers on Black responses in 1968. *Public Opinion Quarterly, 35*, 44-68.

Schuman, H., & Hatchett, S. J. (1974). *Black racial attitudes: Trends and complexities*. Ann Arbor: Survey Research Center, Institute for Social Research, University of Michigan.

Schuman, H., Belli, R. F. & Bischoping, K. (1995). The generational basis of historical knowledge. In J. W. Pennebaker, D. Paez, & B. Rime (Eds.), *Collective memory of political events: Social Psychological perspectives*. Hillsdale, NJ: Lawrence Erlbaum.

Schwarz, N. (1995a). *Cognition, communication, and survey measurement: Some implications for contingent valuation surveys.* Survey Methodology Program, Institute for Social Research, University of Michigan: Ann Arbor, MI.

Schwarz, N. (1995b). *What respondents learn from questionnaires: The survey interview and the logic of conversation.* Survey Methodology Program Institute for Social Research, University of Michigan: Ann Arbor, MI.

Schwarz, N. & Bless, H. (1995). Mental constructual processes and the emergence of context effects in attitude measurement. *Bulletin de Methodologie Sociologique, 48*, 101 - 119.

Schwarz, N. & Hippler, H. (1995a). Subsequent questions may influence answers to preceding questions in mail surveys. *Public Opinion Ouarterly, 59*, 93-97.

Schwarz, N. & Hippler, H. (1995b). The numeric values of rating scales: A comparison of their impact in mail surveys and telephone interviews. *International Journal of Public Opinion Research, 7*, 72-74.

Schwarz, N. & Schuman, H. (1995). *Political knowledge, attribution, and inferred interest in politics: The operation of buffer items.* Survey Methodology Program Institute for Social Research, University of Michigan: Ann Arbor, MI.

Schwartz, D. A. (1970). Coping with field problems of large surveys among the urban poor. *Public Opinion Ouarterly, 34*, 262-267.

Sheatsley, P. B. (1948). Public relations of the polls. *International Journal of Opinion and Attitude Research, 2*, 453-468.

Sieber, S. D. (1973). The integration of fieldwork and survey methods. *American Journal of Sociology, 78*, 1335-1359.

Silver, B. D., Abramson, P.R. & Anderson, B. A. (1986). The presence of others and overreporting of voting in American National Elections. *Public Opinion Quarterly 50*, 285-239

Snider, J. G., & Osgood, C. E. (Eds.). (1969). Semantic differential technique: A sourcebook. Chicago: Aldine.

Stack, C.B. (1974). *All our kin: Strategies for survival in a Black urban community*. New York: Harper and Row.

Strauss, A., & Schatzman, L. (1955). Cross-class interviewing: An analysis of interaction and communicative styles. *Human Organization, 14*, 28-31.

Sudman, S., & Bradburn, N. M. (1974). *Response effects in surveys*. Chicago: Aldine.

Taylor, R.J., Chatters, L. M., & Jackson, J. S. (1993). A profile of familial relations among three generation black families. *Family Relations, 42*, 332-341.

Tripp-Reimer, T., Sorofman, B., Peters, J., & Waterman, J.E. Research teams: Possibilities and pitfalls in collaborative qualitative research. In J.M. Morse(Ed.), *Critical issues in qualitative research methods (p. 318)*. Thousand Oaks, CA: Sage Publications.

Warwick, D. P., & Lininger, C. A. (1975). *The sample survey: Theory and practice*. New York: McGraw-Hill.

Warwick, D. P., & Osherson, S. (1973). *Comparative research methods*. Englewood Cliffs, NJ: Prentice-Hall.

Weiss, C. (1977). Survey researchers and minority communities. Journal of Social Issues, *33*, 20-35.

Whiting, J. W. M. (1968). Methods and problems in cross-cultural research. In G. Lindzey & E. Aronson (Eds.), *The handbook of social psychology, Vol. 2*. Reading, MA: Addison Wesley.

Williams, J. A. (1964). Interviewer-respondent interaction: A study of bias the information interview. *Sociometry, 27*, 338-352.

Williams, J. E. (1966). Connotations of racial concepts and color names. *Journal of Personality and Social Psychology, 3*, 531-540.

Willimack, D. K., Schuman, H., Pennell, B., & Lepkowski, J. M. (1995). Effects of a prepaid nonmonetary incentive on response rates and response quality in a face-to-face survey. *Public Opinion Ouarterly, 59*, 78-92.

Wilson, M.N. (1986). The black extended family: An analytical consideration. *Developmental Psychology, 22*, 246-256.

Word, C. O. (1977). Cross-cultural methods of survey research in Black urban areas. *The Journal of Black Psychology, 3*, 72-87.

Author

Cleopatra Howard Caldwell
Department of Behavior and Health
Education
School of Public Health
University of Michigan
1420 Washington Heights
Ann Arbor, MI 48109-2029
Telephone: (734) 647-3176
Fax: (734) 763-7379
E-mail: cleoc@umich.educ

MATE AVAILABILITY AMONG AFRICAN AMERICANS: CONCEPTUAL AND METHODOLOGICAL ISSUES

M. Belinda Tucker and Claudia Mitchell-Kernan

The last quarter century has been a period of quite dramatic change in the manner in which African Americans begin families. Compared to earlier periods, African Americans marry later and less and are more likely to separate and divorce. Nonmarital childbearing has also increased. These trends, though more striking in some respects, are consistent with changes in family organization occurring on a global scale in nearly all industrialized as well as developing nations (Brockmann, 1987; Lesthaeghe, 1983; Popenoe, 1988). Indeed, virtually all segments of American society have experienced substantial changes in marital patterns and family organization over the last two decades. Similarity in consequence, however, should not be assumed to reflect commonality in the factors supporting these changes.

In our view, changing patterns of family formation among African Americans can profitably be examined in the context of the decreasing availability of African American males as potential mates for African American females. Our primary objective in this paper is therefore to consider marital trends among African Americans within the framework of a mate availability perspective. We begin by presenting an overview of the mate availability perspective, tracing its appearance within early paradigms that treated imbalanced sex ratios as a primary force to more recent formulations which combine the demographic element of sex ratio with socially constructed elements such as eligibility and economic viability or attractiveness. In exploring the utility of the mate availability perspective, we will reanalyze selected ethnographic case studies of African descended subpopulations in search of evidence of the impact of declining male availability on community and individual adaptation. In the final section of our paper, we will offer some conceptual and methodological formulations intended to clarify the relationship between societal processes and individual behavior, as related to changing patterns of family formation among African Americans. This discussion derives from a program of research underway for mre than decade. Our overall objective in this work is to examine the social context and social and psychological correlates of current family formation behaviors and attitudes.

129

Changing Patterns of Family Formation in the U.S.

Today Americans in general marry later, are less likely to stay married, and are less likely to marry after divorce than in previous times. Between 1970 and 1990, the percent of women married by age 20-24 decreased from 64% to 37%, and the percent of men married by that age declined from 45% to 21%. The divorce rate over the same two decade period nearly tripled—going from 60 to 166 divorces per 1000 married women (U.S. Bureau of the Census, 1991a). The cumulative data suggest that in recent years Americans in general have been as likely to marry eventually as before—but have remained married for significantly shorter periods of time, due to later age of first marriage and a greater likelihood of divorce. Still, some argue that current trends portend substantial decreases in the likelihood of being ever-married for American women (Rodgers & Thornton, 1985; Bloom and Bennett, 1985).

Subpopulation Differences

Although American trends in family formation are pervasive and consistent with worldwide changes, these transitions have not been equally experienced across ethnic groups. In particular, the transformations evident in the family formation patterns and living arrangements of African Americans have been more substantial along certain dimensions. Prior to 1950, African Americans displayed a long established tendency to marry earlier than Whites. That pattern is now reversed (Cherlin, 1981). Between 1970 and 1990, the proportion of women who had ever married declined sharply from nearly 83% to 63% among African Americans; although there was very little change among either Whites (79%) or Latinos (73%) (U.S. Bureau of the Census, 1991b). It has been estimated that only 70% of African American females born in 1954 will ever marry, compared to 86% of African American men and 90% of Whites of both sexes (Rodgers and Thornton, 1985). Of African American women born in the 1930s, 94% eventually married.

Changes of this magnitude raise questions about the structural underpinnings of marriage behavior and marital expectations. What features of social context are related to family formation behaviors, expectations and attitudes?

Conceptual Perspectives

Theoretical discussions of changing family formation patterns have focused primarily on macro-level (as opposed to individual level) processes. A useful conceptual scheme for organizing these formulations is found in the work of Dixon (1971). In attempting to understand cross-cultural differences in marriage behavior, she proposed three mediating factors between social structure and nuptiality: 1) the availability of mates, 2) the feasibility of marriage, and 3) the desirability of marriage.

Mate Availability

Discussions of mate availability have centered on two distinct, but related concepts: marriage squeeze and sex ratio imbalance.

Marriage squeeze. Demographers contend that a "marriage squeeze"—a decrease in the availability of marriage partners—among female members of the "baby boom" has led to delays in marriage and lower marriage rates, particularly for women (Glick, Heer, & Beresford, 1963; Rodgers & Thornton, 1985; Schoen, 1983). This shortage of partners (marriage squeeze) is the result of the ever increasing cohort sizes that characterized the post-World War II "baby boom" years, coupled with the tendency of women to marry men who are two to three years older than themselves. "Baby boom" women were therefore seeking husbands from older but smaller cohorts.

Constrained marital opportunities have been measured several ways as researchers have attempted to approximate the relative sizes of the age cohorts of women most likely to marry particular age cohorts of men (e.g., Akers, 1967; Hirschman & Matras, 1971). More statistically complex formulations of marriage squeeze and related concepts have also been offered (e.g., Schoen, 1983).

Tests of the marriage squeeze hypothesis have been revealing. Using international data on marriage rates and population characteristics, Schoen (1983) demonstrated that marriage squeeze can produce significant changes in the level and distribution of marriage within both developed countries and in the Third World. Glick (1981) found that marriage squeeze contributed to a substantial increase in marital delay among African Americans during the 1970s.

Sex ratio imbalance. Considerably more discussion and research has focused on the much broader concept of sex ratio. Although the marriage squeeze presumably affected all Americans born in the period immediately following World War II, it merely exacerbated the impact of the mortality driven decline in African American sex ratios (i.e., the number of males per 100 females), that had been evident since the 1920s (Cox, 1940; Jackson, 1971; McQueen, 1979; Staples, 1981a,b). Table 1 shows total population sex ratios for Blacks and Whites based on raw Census figures from 1830 through 1990. The figures demonstrate that the overall African American sex ratio has been less than 100 since 1840 (although rising to near 100 in both 1890 and 1920), and declined for the first time to less than 90 in 1980. By 1950 the White sex ratio had also dropped below 100, reaching its lowest level of 94.8 in 1980 (U.S. Bureau of the Census, 1960, 1964, 1973, 1982a, 1983, 1992a).[1]

Sex ratios in the U.S. do vary widely within race, on the basis of geographic region, urbanicity, socioeconomic level and age. This variation is due primarily to differential migration patterns for women and men.[2] State level data indicate that in 1980 African American sex ratios ranged from a statewide low of 82.6 for Alabama (U.S. Bureau of the Census, 1992b) to highs of 154.8 for Hawaii (U.S. Bureau of the Census, 1992c) and 152.9 for South Dakota (U.S. Bureau of the Census, 1992d).

Generally, sex ratios among the younger ages are relatively high, reflecting ratios at birth ranging from 106 among U.S. Whites to 103 among Blacks (National Center for Health Statistics, 1970). [The discrepancy is due primarily to poor prenatal care in low income groups which disproportionately affects male fetuses. (Guttentag & Secord, 1983)] Yet, city level data demonstrate striking variations among young African American adults. According to the 1990 Census, the sex ratio among Blacks aged 20-24 in Denver, Colorado was 100 (i.e., equal numbers of males and females). Yet sex ratios for the same age range in Atlanta, Georgia; Montgomery, Alabama; and Cincinnati, Ohio were 82, 81 and 78, respectively. Stated differently, for every 1,000 African American women aged 20-24 in Cincinnati, there were only 780 males of the same age. Although low sex ratios are to be expected at the upper end of the age scale, such discrepancies among the relatively young are startling.

It appears that the male shortage among Whites of peak marriage age has ended, which suggests that the marriage squeeze was indeed limited to the "baby boom" population. However, analyses of sex ratio trends in the African American population indicate a continuing problem through the end of this century (Guttentag & Secord, 1983). Still, comparisons between 1990 and 1970 population figures show that even among Blacks, sex ratios have increased in many locations. In 1970, "nonWhite" sex ratios for Baltimore and New York residents age 20-24 were in the 70s, while African American sex ratios for both cities in 1990 were close to 90 (Bureau of the Census, 1992e). (Only "nonWhite" figures were available in 1970, but it is unlikely that the small numbers of other races would distort the ratios.)

In fact, the problem of an inadequate supply of males among African Americans has been evident to African American researchers, in particular, for quite some time (Cox, 1940; Cazenave, 1980; Darity & Myers, 1983; Jackson, 1971; McQueen, 1979; Staples, 1981a,b) and has been cited as a factor in an array of social problems (African American researchers may be more attuned to the issue of African American gender imbalance because they experience its effects first hand). In 1908 W. E. B. Du Bois noted that differential economic constraints on the sexes created geographic-specific shortages. He blamed low sex ratios (i.e., more females than males) for "sexual irregularity" among African Americans.

Guttentag and Secord (1983) argued that imbalanced sex ratios throughout time have had major societal consequences, with male shortage leading to higher rates of singlehood, divorce, "out-of-wedlock" births, adultery and transient relationships; less commitment among men to relationships; lower societal value on marriage and the family; and a rise in feminism. They also cite imbalanced sex ratios as a factor in African American marital decline and an increasing out-of-wedlock birth rate. Epenshade (1985) noted, however, that some of the data presented by Guttentag and Secord (1983) appear to challenge their own thesis—e.g., African American sex ratios have declined since 1920, but marital decline has only been evident since the 1960s. Nevertheless, there has been empirical support for some aspects of the Guttentag and Secord speculations from our own research and that of

Table 1
Sex Ratios from Raw Census Data for Blacks and Whites from 1830 through 1990

	Race	
Year	Blacks	Whites
1990	89.6	95.4
1980	89.6	95.3
1970	90.8	95.3
1960	93.4	97.4
1950	94.3	99.1
1940	95.0	101.2
1930	97.0	102.9
1920	99.2	104.4
1910	98.9	106.7
1900	96.8	101.5
1890	99.5	105.4
1880	97.8	104.0
1870	96.2	102.8
1860	99.6	105.3
1850	99.1	105.2
1840	99.5	104.6
1830	100.3	103.7

Sources: U.S. Bureau of the Census (1960, 1964, 1973, 1982b, 1983, 1992).

others (Jemmott, Ashby & Lindenfeld, 1989; Secord & Ghee, 1986; South, 1986; South and Messner, 1988; Tucker, 1987). In our view, the inconsistencies noted by Epenshade stem from the narrow focus on the demographic variable of sex ratio, rather than the range of issues related to mate availability more generally.

Marital Feasibility

There is evidence that constrained economic opportunities in general lead to postponement of marriage and destabilize existing marriages (e.g., Cooney & Hogan, 1991; Liker & Elder, 1983; South, 1985; Wilkie, 1991). Sociologists and economists have been particularly concerned about the relationship between the economic viability of African American males and African American family structure. They have argued that African American marital feasibility has declined because the increasing economic marginality of African American males has made them less attractive as potential husbands, and less interested in becoming husbands, since they are constrained in their ability to perform the provider role in marriage (Darity & Myers, 1986/87; Wilson, 1987). There is empirical support for these arguments (Hatchett, et al., 1989; Testa, et al., 1989; Tucker & Taylor, 1989) although analyses by Mare & Winship (1991) suggest that socioeconomic factors cannot completely explain the drastic marital decline of the last 30 years. Other evidence suggests that the economic fortunes of younger American males of all races have declined (Easterlin, 1980; Lichter, et al., 1991) and that therefore such concerns have affected overall marriage patterns.

Related to these arguments is a theory of marital timing proposed by Oppenheimer (1988) in which late marriage is seen as a function of an elongated search strategy fueled primarily by uncertainty regarding male economic prospects. With the dramatic decrease in young male economic viability generally (i.e., not African Americans only) and the increased training period (e.g., college), there is no incentive to marry before more definitive information is available about the potential economic gains to be had through marriage.

Although the arguments and studies just cited demonstrate the centrality of marital feasibility in marital trends, economic considerations are also a factor in mate availability. That is, to the extent that a given individual is deemed to be less desirable as a mate because of limited economic potential, the pool of eligibles he or she represents is also diminished. If significant numbers of African American males are viewed as incapable of meeting the provider role requirements, they will be not be included in perceptions of availability. William J. Wilson (1987) made this calculation explicit in his Male Marriageability Pool Index (MMPI)—the ratio of employed civilian men to women of the same race and age-group. This formulation therefore combined notions of sex ratio, as well as, economic readiness. Wilson shows that the MMPI for nonWhite men age 16 to 24 declines sharply beginning in the 1960s—about the same time that marital declines began—and continuing through the 1980s.

Desirability of Marriage

Some researchers have questioned the extent which marriage is any longer a valued state in Western society. Studies of Sweden, where marriage declines have been significantly greater than that experienced by any American subpopulation, clearly indicate that a fundamental value shift has occurred (Popenoe, 1988). In contrast, attitudinal studies in the U.S. have not produced evidence that marriage has become significantly devalued. Our own work and that of others indicate that the reported valuation of marriage by Americans in general is quite high (Thornton & Freedman, 1982; Tucker & Mitchell-Kernan, 1995b). Furthermore, African

Americans do not differ from other ethnic groups in the value placed on marriage (Tucker & Mitchell-Kernan, 1995b)

Research on marital desirability has also considered the extent to which cohabitation has become an acceptable substitute for marriage. Such formulations consider increased cohabitation as a cultural change, reflecting greater sexual freedom among adolescents and young adults, the greater availability of relatively effective contraception, increased financial independence of women, and changes in gender roles, among others factors. Studies by Tanfer (1987) and Bumpass, et al. (1991) suggest that while cohabitation may serve as an advanced stage of courtship, or an uncertain stage between dating and marriage, it does not constitute a marital substitute. In fact, Tanfer (1987) reports, on the basis of a national sample of 20-29 year old women, that African American women evidence a *lower* propensity to cohabitate (White women were 1 and 1/2 times more likely to cohabitate), and suggests that this may be due to the relative scarcity of African American men.

Integration and Summary

Several recent studies have attempted to compare the utility of certain of the above perspectives and theories on changing marital behavior–with particular emphasis on diverging African American and White patterns (due to more rapid changes among African Americans). Findings have varied, with support for both availability and feasibility (i.e., economic) arguments (Bennett, Bloom, and Craig,1989; Lichter, McLaughlin, Kephart & Landry, 1992), support for economic theories (Lichter, LeClere, & McLaughlin, 1991), lack of support for feasibility theories (Mare and Winship,1991), and lack of support for availability theories (Schoen and Kluegel,1988). With Current Population Survey (CPS) data, Bennett et al. (1989) found that both demographic and economic factors accounted for the increasing divergence of African American and White marriage patterns. In contrast, however, Mare and Winship's analysis of Census Public Use Sample and CPS data showed little evidence that African American or White marital entry was a function of labor market trends for either men or women, or schooling factors (thought by some to delay marriage). Although, when comparing Census Labor Market Areas, Lichter,et al. (1991) found that spatial variations in marriage rates of both Blacks and Whites could be explained in part by differences in the local supply of economically "attractive" males (though these differences could not completely explain the African American-White marriage differential). Significantly, Lichter et al. (1992) later demonstrated that women's marital timing was directly linked to the availability of men of similar age and race and to male economic circumstances.

There appears to be a considerable degree of inconsistency in the results of these studies. However, several points must be kept in mind. First, none of these studies compared all perspectives. Second, the concept "being explained" is not consistent across these studies. Some studies are focused on explaining the difference between African American and White marriage behavior, while others are concerned with independent prediction of change within each group. Third, there are significant differences in the way that both "economic" (feasibility) forces and "availability" are conceived and measured. Fourth, there is evidence that *perceived* mate availability may be more predictive of attitudes and behaviors than objective (aggregate level) indicators of availability (Jemmott, Ashby, & Lindenfeld, 1989), which indicates a need for more micro-level research in this area. We will elaborate upon this point later in our discussion.

It must be noted that only two studies have found *no* support for either economic (Mare & Winship, 1991) or availability theories (Schoen & Kluegel, 1988), while all of the remaining investigations (including studies that do not explicitly compare perspectives) find some merit in one of these views. In fact, Lichter, et al. (1992) stated that "marriage market factors contribute more in "explaining" the race effect [i.e., differential marriage patterns] than most other factors frequently considered in previous research (p. 27)." We conclude from all of this that there is considerable merit in examining more fully the role of mate availability in family formation.

Clearly, factors other than demographic and economic elements discussed here have played roles in changing patterns of family formation among African Americans. In particular, women's workforce participation, improved contraception, extended period of formal education, the declining gap between African American female and male earnings, and changing conceptions of gender roles, among others have been implicated in the recent transformations (c.f., Cherlin, 1981; Ross & Sawhill, 1975; Blumstein & Schwartz, 1983). As we have argued elsewhere, however, economic decline and high male mortality are targets for social intervention (Tucker & Mitchell-Kernan, 1995a). To understand their precise role in changing family structure could offer significant societal benefits.

Our ultimate goal is to understand the differential involvement of various factors in changing family formation patterns for different groups. That is, similar family formation trends can reflect different historical experiences. For example, we believe that the recent decline in African American marriage can be viewed as a function of a peculiar clustering of factors, including an ever declining sex ratio (that became extremely critical by the 1960s in certain communities), the "baby boom" generated marriage squeeze, the declining economic viability of certain sectors of the African American male population, increasing female employment, and society wide value changes (in regard to gender roles and family formation). Although White American trends are similar, they reflect a different "mix" of influences. Our research program is focused on individual behavior, however, and the extent to which one's behavior and attitudes are associated with one's perception of these societal forces. An impoverished White "baby boom" female may perceive her marital opportunity structure, and the forces that shape it, in a manner remarkably similar to that of a low income African American woman.

Our view, and that explored in this paper, is that availability and economic arguments are interrelated. Economic viability is viewed as one of a number of factors that determine eligibility and therefore availability. Furthermore, differential migration patterns that determine local sex ratios are often in response to economic conditions. For this reason, we focus on a more encompassing notion of mate availability. It should be noted, however, that the presence of "warm bodies" (i.e., sex ratio) and economic viability are but two features of availability. Later in the paper we will present a more fully developed model of availability, as we aim for more precise measurement.

Other Consequences of Constrained Mate Availability

Although seldom empirically based, there have been attempts to link constrained mate availability to other characteristics and features of social organization common to the contemporary African American population. Jackson (1971), Guttentag and Secord (1983), and Staples (1981a) have argued that the increasing numbers of female-headed households, as well as the large numbers of births to unwed mothers in the African American community, are direct consequences of the shortage of male partners. (The Shimkin, Louie, & Frate, 1978, data on rural Southern African Americans [to be discussed in the next section] seem to support this proposition as well.) The situation is compounded by a lower remarriage rate for African American women, relative to White women (Norton & Miller, 1992; Ross & Sawhill, 1975), also most likely due to constrained marital opportunity. That is, White divorcees and widows have a much better chance of exiting the "female-headed household" category than do African American divorcees and widows.

In an analysis of the factors contributing to the existence of African American female single parent households, economists Darity and Myers (1983) demonstrated that the contribution of Aid to Families with Dependent Children (AFDC) to regression models predicting female headship is negligible; rather the most substantial statistical contribution is the African American female to male ratio. They argue that this pattern holds even when the African American undercount (primarily, in the past, of males) is considered. In this perspective, these households may be regarded as adaptive rather than "disorganized" and "pathological" as they are depicted by Frazier (1948) and Moynihan (1967), among others. The Darity and Myers findings also counter theorists who suggest that public welfare policies have driven African American males from their homes and encouraged African American women to have babies and live on their own (e.g., Murray, 1984; Peters & de Ford, 1978).

Some have argued that constrained mate availability has led to a broadening of mate selection standards among African American women. Spanier and Glick

(1980) found that African American women married men who were significantly older, had lower educational attainment, and were more often previously married than their White counterparts. In an interesting parallel development, Guttentag and Secord (1983) have argued that one impact of the marriage squeeze among "baby boom" White women, is their consideration of other pools of eligibles, leading to an increase in interracial marriage. This obviously only serves to worsen the availability problems of African American women, as White women facing constrained availability increasingly consider African American men as potential partners.

Case Studies

Observations of Societies with Gender Imbalance

Ideas about the social structural correlates and consequences of constrained mate availability among African Americans tend to be theoretically derived and lacking in sound empirical support. In particular, *causal* relationships delineated by the conceptual arguments remain to be demonstrated. One problem with the few existing studies on the subject is the global (usually national) perspective employed by most researchers. We favor an approach which centers on the local community level, the context within which people generally meet and marry, to examine the social structural features that seem to accompany the phenomenon. Fortunately, there is a small ethnographic literature that enables us to do just that. Two case studies are described below. Although, neither was presented by its authors as a study of the impact of constrained mate availability, we can examine each to determine whether the hypothesized structural consequences are evident in these localized situations.

Rural Blacks in Holmes County, Mississippi

Shimkin, Louie, and Frate (1978) conducted an ethnographic study of the extended family among rural Blacks in Holmes County, Mississippi and Holmes Countians who resided in Chicago in 1969-1970. Due to severe economic deprivation among Blacks in Holmes County, many residents, particularly men, elected to leave the county in search of employment. This exodus, coupled with a disproportionately high mortality rate for men, left an impoverished community, with few men of working age. Gardening, fishing, and welfare were the basis of subsistence for the women, children, and older men who remained. Interestingly, a number of older men elected to return and retired in Holmes County. All of these factors led to an unusual sex ratio situation. In 1960, the sex ratio for persons aged 30-49 was 72; for the 50-64 age cohort, the sex ratio was 88; and for ages 65 and above it was 94. By 1970, the corresponding sex ratios were 43, 103, and 67! The figures demonstrate two curious trends. In 1960, the sex ratio increased with age (a highly unusual circumstance). By 1970 the 30-49 sex ratio was exceptionally low, while the next older cohort exhibited an exceptionally high ratio, particularly for that age.

It appears that this condition of age differentiated imbalance had a number of consequences: During the 1960-1970 decade, the proportion of husband-wife families (among all families) declined from 75% to 66%. Families with husbands under the age of 45 decreased from 25% of all households to 14%. Among Holmes Countians in Chicago, husbands on average were 4 years older than wives (standard deviation 5.7). In contrast, the Holmes County differential was 7.3 (S.D. 8.3). This configuration also was probably responsible for the fact that 60% of the unmarried 20 to 49 year old African American women in Holmes County were mothers. In addition, male migration began to be accompanied by a later female migration. That is, for most age cohorts, males accounted for over half of the migration total. For ages 30-39 and 50 and over, the migrants were predominantly female.

The Holmes County case appears to isolate several adaptive strategies used by its inhabitants to cope with an abnormal sex and age distribution, including nonmarital births, older husbands, non-marriage, and later female migration. Consistency between the central features of the social profile of Holmes County and the expectations advanced by Guttentag and Secord (1983) lead us to view the sex ratio imbalance, that resulted from constrained economic opportunities, as likely implicated in the observed patterns. Since the focus of the study was not mate availability, information about other behaviors that might also be expected in this kind of situation (e.g., infidelity, man sharing) is not available, nor were the psychological implications of the problem explored.

Garifuna (Black Carib) Communities

The Garifuna (also known as Black Caribs) presently reside in rural settlements and urban centers in Belize, the Honduras and Guatemala. Descended from Africans who had escaped plantation slavery and Carib Indians, Garifuna speak an Arawakan based language and have carried on traditions reflecting both their African and Carib heritages. The Garifuna physically display little of their Indian ancestry and would generally be regarded as a Black population. Fairly large numbers have now settled in Los Angeles and New York.

In 1957-1958 Nancie Solien Gonzalez (1969) conducted a now classic study of Garifuna household structure, focusing primarily on the effects of migration and modernization. She characterized the dominant household structure as consanguineal (i.e., households centered about kin relations, rather than marital ties). In fact, the

Garifuna ideal was the nuclear family household, but the realities of the local economies were such that most found the ideal "difficult to achieve and *maintain*" (Gonzalez, 1969, p. 15). That is, she viewed the lack of economic opportunities as an impediment to the formation and sustained support of nuclear households. While the consanguineal system was considered to be less than ideal, it was preferable to maintaining a household alone because of the difficulties presented by such remote environments for a single woman. Generally, some form of outside assistance was required. In Gonzalez's view, the consanguineal system was in part a response to certain economic and social conditions characteristic of societies undergoing acculturation to Western civilization. She further argues that in the case of the Garifuna, the system was also maintained by the requirements of migrant wage labor and the resultant low sex ratio.

Gonzalez's analysis is based on her observations in Livingston, Guatemala, a predominantly Garifuna settlement. Due to a series of developments (including diseases that ruined the banana industry), little local industry existed. As a result, men were generally required to seek work outside the village. In the past, Garifuna men had become accustomed to working intermittently, as the need arose. Migrant workers could therefore still spend considerable time with their families. After 1930, however, companies began to demand steady employment from their workers. These changes forced many men to take up residence away from their families, resulting in the weakening of many societal ties. In 1956, only the age cohort 2-10 had a sex ratio reaching 100. Due to high infant mortality, the 0-1 ratio was 0.75. Other ratios were: 11-20, 0.67; 21-30, 0.78; 31-40, 0.69; 41-50, 0.69; 51-60, 0.89; 61-70, 0.55; and over 70, 0.54. The sex ratio problem was further compounded by the practice of sending young boys to the city to live with middle or upper class White families (as evidenced by the low 11-20 ratio). These children, who missed their Garifuna socialization, often permanently remained in the larger towns.

Mating systems seemed to be affected by these factors. Marriage could be either the "legal" Western type or of a more informal nature recognized by the Garifuna. The latter was rather easily dissolved when either party grew dissatisfied. Gonzalez enumerated only 65 of the former, usually involving the more well-to-do. While monogamy remained the ideal, most persons had two or more partners over a lifetime. "Extraresidential mating," which entailed the man and woman maintaining independent households, appeared to be the most frequent marital arrangement. A double standard with regard to marriage, divorce, and sex existed, with men being permitted much greater latitude in such areas. A number of men had more than one partner simultaneously. Since most liaisons were recognized in an informal way, there were few "illegitimate" children, as such. Men tended to recognize and provide financial support for their own children. Among the young, marital partners tended to be the same age; among the older, men were often ten or more years older than their wives.

Adaptation to the shortage of men among this particular settlement of Garifuna took some forms now familiar from the sex ratio perspective: flexible male-female relationships, high "divorce" rates, and older husbands for all except the very young. Again, little is known about the psychological reaction of women and men to the situation. The existence of strong cultural traditions and family ties in the Garifuna community seems to have served to blunt the impact of male absence (e.g., no cultural concept of "illegitimacy" with men *expected* to recognize and care for their children). Importantly, many of the absent men were still considered to be residents and spouses who simply were away much of the time. They could still provide financial support and some measure of emotional support in their roles as husband and father. The psychological distinction between permanent and temporary absence is probably highly significant.

Summary

Perhaps the most striking commonality among the communities is the manner in which economic constraints fueled the condition of gender imbalance. In order to enhance their economic viability (which undoubtedly also increased their attractiveness as potential mates), men were forced to leave their homes. Of course, a number of men maintained a position and stake in the community, by becoming partners of women who remained and/or by providing support to family members back home (i.e., partners, children, families of origin). But others became permanently disconnected and could no longer be counted among those available for either relationships or support. These cases are a clear indication of how economic and availability issues are intertwined.

The communities described in these case studies also evidence a number of characteristics hypothesized to be common to societies experiencing a male shortage: 1) Mate selection by the sex in oversupply (females in these cases) was compromised. That is, it appeared that women generally did not have free selection of mates, were at risk of attracting no mate, and may have had to settle for men who were somewhat removed from their ideals; 2) husbands were often considerably older than their wives; 3) high rates of female "singlehood" existed (either through non-marriage or divorce); and 4) children had a high likelihood of not being raised directly by both parents. One imagines that these factors in combination would significantly alter the basic fabric of any society.

It is important to note, however, that these two societies were also quite distinctive in ways which would affect the nature of social and psychological adaptation to the male shortage. They exhibited sociocultural differences (e.g., different marital values, different concepts of "illegitimacy", differences in the nature of male "nonavailability," and differences in the extent to which the male nonavailability was viewed as temporary or permanent). For example, the Garifuna form of marriage permitted the existence of a flexible societally recognized state of union that could absorb the effects of the male shortage more easily than the formal Western manner of union.

Since neither study was designed specifically to examine the phenomenon of mate availability, many unanswered questions remain. For example, what psychological adaptive strategies were developed by both sexes to cope with constrained availability? How do value systems change in response to such a situation? Given that a primary cause of the absence of men in both communities was the nonavailability of local employment, one must consider the characteristics of the men who remained. If they were essentially the infirmed, the aged, and the unmotivated, then how might the societal image of men be affected by the local examples?

In the following section, we will explore the hypothesized connection between mate availability and adaptation and delineate conceptual and methodological issues needed to adequately study the impact of constrained mate availability in African American communities.

Conceptual and Methodological Issues Related to Constrained Mate Availability Among African Americans

As noted earlier, discussions of the consequences of constrained mate availability have been focused almost solely on macro-level processes. Even when relationships between family formation patterns and availability have been empirically documented, the mechanisms by which social structural conditions are translated in individual behavioral decisions have remained unspecified. There have been no attempts to explicate the linkages between macro and micro level processes. One reason for this is the relative absence of individual level theory to address the relationship between mate availability and family formation decisions. However, several social psychological conceptualizations offer promising new directions for future research.

Social exchange theory (Thibaut & Kelley, 1959) has long been used to understand the mate selection process (e.g., Berscheid & Walster, 1969; Murstein, 1973). Sharing similarities with Becker's (1974) utility maximization concept in family economics, the social exchange approach assumes that individuals attempt to maximize rewards and minimize costs when seeking an attractive outcome. Guttentag and Secord (1983) used social exchange theory to explain the role of sex ratio imbalance in romantic involvements. They postulated that gender imbalance combines with the imbalance in the *structural* power held by men versus women (i.e., power associated with the economic, legal, and political structures) "to produce changes in the attitudes and behaviors of men and women in relation to each other, and with sufficient time, to produce changes in the associated sex roles and institutional structures, such as the family" (p. 154). A sex ratio imbalance upsets the balance of social power between the sexes. Using the term *dyadic* power to describe the social power that derives from being the sex in short supply, Guttentag and Secord (1983) argued that when imbalance exists, the sex in greater supply has more difficulty finding a partner and may find relationships less satisfying, since the other partner has more potentially satisfactory alternatives. In their words, conditions of gender imbalance:

> ...generate more dyadic power for the party with more alternatives to the partner, while the partner has fewer. These conditions generate more dyadic power for the party with more alternative sources of satisfaction because of the way they affect the exchange of resources. This party is less dependent on the partner and can turn elsewhere for satisfaction. The partner, on the other hand, has fewer options and thus must provide a level of satisfaction sufficiently above the first party's alternative sources in order to keep the relationship alive. (p. 157)

The partner in greater supply is therefore more dependent and more committed to the relationship than the partner in less supply. Jemmott, et al. (1989) found that college students who perceived a shortage of the opposite sex on their campus were more committed to their romantic relationships, considered their relationships to be more attractive and invested more in their relationships than other students.

Additional clarification of the micro-level aspects of mate availability may be obtained through use of the theory of reasoned action. Our research has shown that although actual marital prevalence varies greatly on the basis of ethnicity, marriage is highly valued by all the ethnic groups studied (Tucker & Mitchell-Kernan, 1995b). The gap between attitudes and actions is addressed by the social psychological theory of reasoned action (Fishbein & Ajzen, 1975; Ajzen & Fishbein, 1980) in which the intention to act is viewed as a function of one's attitude toward the behavior as well as perceived social pressure to perform the behavior. (The complete theory is more complex than this summary formulation, and incorporates other factors including beliefs about the consequences of the behavior, the motivation to conform, and beliefs about the expectations of specific others. A host of studies have sought to further clarify the model.) It could be argued that despite the favorable attitudes of all groups of Americans toward marriage, there has been a decline in the social pressure on people to marry, thus accounting for the decline in marriage. This formulation leaves unexplained why social pressure to marry has lessened. Furthermore, we must also ask why social pressure has decreased even more within certain segments of the African American community.

The concept of causality, in the form of causal attributions, also has potential for improving our understanding of the relationship between mate availability and individual behavior. The notion of internality-externality is a fundamental component of all major theories of attribution (Ross & Fletcher, 1985), and as used here, refers to one's personal sense of control over an event or situation. In a previous study we found that (when controlling for income, education, age and value placed on marriage) single White women with low perceived mate availability were more depressed, anxious, lonely and less satisfied with life; but there were no significant well-being correlates for African American women (Tucker & Mitchell-Kernan, in press). We believe that this is because of the pervasive perception of "male shortage" among African Americans which allows African American women to see the lack of opportunities for dating and the unavailability of men as systemically rooted. White women tended to blame themselves and were therefore psychologically compromised. This may not be the case for White "baby boomers" who have been regaled with media stories detailing their plight, but the sample size in our study was not sufficient to examine such cohort effects.

Micro Theory: Integration

There have been no attempts to either integrate or compare the utility of these theories. However, each has dimensions of relevance to various aspects of our research questions. The addition of notions of causality to social exchange theory seems essential in order to determine consequences of limited mating opportunities for individual social psychological adaptation. Likewise, social exchange theory ignores the processes that define rewards and costs, such as social pressure and expected behavioral consequences. A more complete micro-theory is therefore available by combining aspects of the three formulations.

Conceptual Framework: Linking Macro and Micro Theories

We believe that a more complete understanding of the impact of mate availability on communities and individuals can only be obtained by integrating perspectives on both macro and micro levels. It seems clear that availability concerns of both demographic and economic origin play a role in major shifts in American patterns of family formation generally, and African American patterns specifically. Yet this is only one part of the puzzle.

Linking the macro theories of family formation with the relevant social psychological theories described above depends on specification of a formulation that includes both micro and macro elements. A very promising direction is that outlined by Liska (1984), who critiqued and extended the Fishbein and Ajzen (1975) conceptualization by explicitly incorporating the role of the social structure in a revised model. Liska took issue with the Fishbein and Ajzen theory that most behaviors of interest are under volitional control–which is precisely the point that concerns us with respect to marriage–and argues that most behavior is contingent on the cooperation of others, a number of environmental resources, and one's position in the social structure. The macro theories of availability and feasibility would therefore become linked to notions of behavioral intent. Similarly, the social exchange paradigm depends on both objective and subjective assessments of the mating opportunity structure. In order for social exchange theory to be operative, both potential and current partners are assumed to operate within a defined market context and must be cognizant of their respective marketabilities. These linkages provide the basis for a multi-level analysis.

There are now statistical procedures with which to pursue such a conceptualization. In particular, multi-level analysis (Mason, et al., 1983; Entwistle & Mason 1985) assumes that individuals (the micro level) influence and are influenced by larger units of social organization (the macro level). Although the interdependency between macro and micro levels is implied, the conceptualization also allows for the possibility that micro-level determinants may vary systematically as a result of varying contexts (Mason, Wong & Entwisle, 1983). Technically, this linkage is achieved by treating micro-level regression coefficients as dependent variables in other macro-level regression equations.

The relationship between a societal condition of constrained mate availability and individual attitudes and behavior has never been addressed empirically. Furthermore, interpretation of mate availability in particular societies and situations is still in need of refinement. Several issues concerning the study of the African American male shortage are of particular importance in this regard: 1) measurement of mate availability; 2) objective versus subjective mate availability, and 3) factors influencing mate selection in subpopulations. An elaboration of these issues follows.

Measurement of Mate Availability

How does one adequately operationalize an issue as complex as that of mate availability? Although much discussion has centered on actual numbers of males versus females, regardless of suitability for mating, a number of scholars, including Wilson (1987), have argued that a more realistic conception of mate availability must incorporate the fact that certain categories of men are insufficiently viable, economically, to become husbands or partners of women. We expand this argument, however, and suggest that availability is a function of a number of considerations. In this connection, it is possible to distinguish factors that make potential partners *unavailable*, factors that make potential partners *unattractive*, and factors that make them *ineligible*.

Relative to the first category, Staples (1981a) has noted that the circumstances of incarceration, homosexuality, and interracial marriage have rendered many of the "statistically" eligible African American males unavailable (i.e., these conditions typically involve more African American men than women). Jackson (1971) also cited the greater tendency of African American males (relative to females) to marry members of other races (a situation that is considerably more pronounced today— Tucker and Mitchell-Kernan, 1990).

Even when corrected for "availableness," the absolute number of males relative to females is only one determinant of the complex phenomenon of establishing marriage and family. Mate selection (and family structure as a consequence) is also a function of certain socioculturally defined preferences and proscriptions. For example, social economic status remains an important determinant of marital patterns in the United States. Such sociocultural preferences combine with the deprived economic condition of many African Americans to compromise the attractiveness of a significant portion of the males.

Staples (1981a) suggests that fewer African American men have the superior income, educational, and occupational statuses that are "traditionally" sought by women in American society (although the actual preferences of the various categories of contemporary African American women is a researchable question). A more extreme perspective of attractiveness is presented in Scott's (1980) study of "African American polygamous family formation." Examining wives and "the other women" (not within the same triad, however), he argued that unmarried young low-income women preferred "stable, reliable" married men over the young single unemployed uncommitted males to which they had access. Furthermore, it was noted that such young males, essentially of the "underclass," sought out women who could offer *them* financial security.

Socioculturally defined proscriptions also determine eligibility, or who qualifies as a potential mate. Race or ethnic membership, nationality, and religion are often signal eligibility criteria in this regard. That is, a given individual may be attractive on socioeconomic dimensions and may be a compatible companion on any number of personal attributes, but may be of a race or religion that makes the person essentially "off limits" for marriage.

Needless to say, an accurate assessment of mate availability must incorporate such notions as the above. Neither raw Census based statistics nor "coverage" corrected Census estimates are sufficient indicators of the relative availability or attractiveness of men and women for any population. They account for none of the phenomena mentioned above and the total population figures include the very young and very old who are, for the most part, not involved in mate selection. Age and geographic specific sex ratios are generally more revealing indicators of the situation faced by particular individuals or communities (recall the extremely low African American sex ratios for the 20-24 age group in certain major eastern and midwestern cities.) Although people from different parts of the country (even the world) manage to meet and marry, individuals are ordinarily confined to a specific, limited geographic location for most of their daily interactions. Your pool of eligibles is likely to be limited to persons who dwell within a 50 square mile radius (Catton, 1964).

A number of scholars (notably demographers) have attempted to develop sex ratio based measures that permit determination of the impact of gender imbalance, marriage squeeze, and mate availability more generally. Although most early studies used simple sex ratios (the number of males divided by the number of females times 100), for total populations and for appropriate subsamples (e.g., all adults, selected age ranges), later studies attempted to correct for a number of social and cultural biases. For example, Akers (1967) proposed a marriage squeeze measure based on the ratio of single men to single women at the prime ages of marriage (i.e., males 20-29, females 18-29) weighted by an estimated probability of marriage at each age. Schoen's (1983) measure of marriage squeeze was an attempt to determine the "degree to which the age-sex composition of the given population serves to depress the observed number of marriages below what would have resulted in the absence of an imbalance between the sexes" (p. 65). The formula includes the determination of the "underlying marriage preferences" for the population in question. Although clearly more precise than previous proposals, Schoen's measure is difficult to calculate (e.g., requiring the construction of a two-sex nuptiality life table) and has been criticized for measuring the *consequences* of the sex ratio imbalance rather than the *state* of imbalance separably (D. M. Heer, personal communication, August 21, 1985).

Goldman, Westoff, & Hammerslough (1984) proposed an "availability ratio" (AR) measure that was an attempt to avoid many of the problems associated with the other measures cited above. The ratio, calculated separately for men and women, incorporates into one measure the available pool for mate selection, the *competition* for that pool, and the normative selection patterns involving race, age, and education. (The analytical details are contained in the Goldman et al. [1984] article.) They attempted to "correct" for "ineligibles" and partially account for the level of homosexuality in the population (at least those who never marry) by eliminating persons over 45 who have never been married (under the assumption that such persons never will), and by subtracting the percent of never marrieds over 45 from the younger ages as well. The measure also limits education and age levels of those in the availability pool to realistically expected candidates (e.g., by including all age pairings between men and women which accounted for at least 2% of all marriages of either sex in 1976-78). In addition, only within race estimates were included (using "coverage" corrected figures). The constraints introduced represent useful attempts to account for a number of the major sociocultural preferences and conditions likely to influence mate selection, and ignored in other measures of marital chances.

Goldman, et al. (1984) found a moderate correlation between ARs and more conventionally calculated sex ratios (Goldman, et al., 1984). But the measure presents a view of marital chances that is decidedly more pessimistic for older women. Table 2 shows ARs and two conventional sex ratios for nine cohorts of African American American women in 1980. The AR figures reflect the assumption that older men are free to marry women of all younger ages, therefore increasing the potential competition for such men among older women. When Goldman, et al. compared ARs for women of differing educational levels, in 1980 African American college educated women evidenced the lowest advantage at all ages. ARs for the age 20-24 cohort for African American women with less than high school educations, a high school degree, and at least a college degree were 78, 117, and 71 respectively (p. 18). Female high school graduates among both Whites and Blacks were at the greatest advantage, apparently because they could marry men at all educational levels.

The basic AR assumptions can be questioned. For example, the elimination of all never-marrieds over 45 years of age seems rather drastic. It would seem more appropriate to ascertain the probability of marrying for the first time at that age (which may differ for African Americans). Likewise, permitting all age pairings that account for 2% of all marriages may result in a broader eligibility range than warranted for certain younger age cohorts. Most problematic, marriages between persons who differ greatly in age may be a *consequence* of the phenomenon being measured (thereby biasing the measure). In addition, the assumptions that underly the measure are based on past patterns of behavior and cannot reflect changing societal preferences that may not be adaptations to sex ratio imbalance (e.g., greater acceptance of older female-younger male marriages).

Nevertheless the AR concept appears to provide a basis for the development of a sex ratio index that includes sociocultural realities and preferences specific to the African American population and specific to local communities. For example, although Goldman, et al. dismiss interracial marriage as a major contributor to low sex ratios, as will be demonstrated in the next section, African American male outmarriage is a major factor in certain geographic areas of the United States. There is also reason to believe that African American women may place a greater emphasis on income than education in mate selection. Socioculturally meaningful conceptions of "availability," "attractiveness," and "eligibility" must therefore incorporate these factors.

Our own analysis of 1980 Census data for Los Angeles County shows that African American wives were slightly *more* educated than their husbands, but made substantially less money (see Table 3). Although White wives also displayed much lower incomes than their husbands, they also had less education (and therefore conformed to the societally expected pattern). To the extent that one "traditional" mate selection factor is not fully operative (due to constrained opportunities), another may be substituted. Surely other factors affecting choice of spouse among African Americans vary as well (e.g., value of "legal" marriage versus "common law" arrangements).

Table 2

Availability Ratios (AR) and Conventional Sex Ratios for Black Women by Age

Age	AR	Sex Ratio : Same Age	Sex Ratio : Men 2 Years Older
20 - 24	93	91.3	84.6
25 - 29	60	87.7	81.6
30 - 34	49	85.6	74.3
35 - 39	41	83.3	77.8
40 - 44	38	82.7	78.3
45 - 49	39	82.2	80.8
50 - 54	39	80.7	78.8
55 - 59	39	81.8	77.6
60 - 64	34	79.3	72.9

Sources: Goldman, et al. (1984), U.S. Bureau of the Consus (1983).

This last point raises another issue in the determination of eligibility. That is, since African American males are in shorter supply, both demographically and economically, the focus has been on determinants of male eligibility. However, shifts in male eligibility may also lead to shifts in determinants of female eligibility. Notably, African American female selection criteria are now more likely to include economic viability, as well as an enhanced standard of physical attractiveness.

The Wilson (1987) formulation described earlier—Male Marriageability Pool Index (MMPI), the ratio of employed civilian men to women of the same race and age-group—represents another direction in the assessment of mate availability. Such measures attempt to incorporate economic and demographic constraints.

Through analyses of African American population data from 103 metropolitan areas, Fossett and Kiecolt (1991) examined the efficacy of a range of sex ratio based indicators for use in comparative studies. For all the elegance of the AR, Fossett & Kiecolt (1991) (in contrast to Goldman et al., 1984) observed that it and other such measures were highly correlated with simpler sex ratios. In fact, they found that sex ratios based on broad age ranges (e.g., 15-44) "outperformed" ratios based on very narrow ranges. They also found, however, that measures that incorporated labor force status (e.g., MMPI) produced substantially lower estimates of "male availability." From the analyses of Fossett and Kiecolt, it would appear that comparative research is rarely affected by the differences in the measures, since they are so highly correlated.

It seems that a definitive procedure for measuring "objective" mate availability is yet to be achieved. Indeed, for macro-level comparative research, a particular choice among the available indicators may not significantly affect research outcomes. Nevertheless, techniques for taking into consideration certain socio-culturally based preferences do exist and may be preferable for non-comparative work and for examinations of within-group effects.

Objective vs. Subjective Mate Availability

With few exceptions (Jemmott, et al, 1989; our ongoing research program), the measurement of mate availability has been restricted to macro-level indicators. Yet, the behaviors that tend to be examined as hypothesized consequences are aggregations of individual decisions—i.e., marriage, divorce, childbearing decisions. The question to be considered, then, is whether and how these societal concepts translate into individual perceptions?

These concerns raise the notion of objective vs. subjective mate availability. The measurement procedures described above assume that it is possible to objectively define the pool of eligibles for any given individual. Yet, it is clear that no one can identify potential mates for another without some knowledge of that individual's criteria for mate selection. To be sure, we generally view individual-level mate selection as based on criteria that go beyond socioeconomic factors, including, for example, physical attractiveness, religiosity, personality, even skin color.

In our work, we have developed a concept that we have labeled Subjective Assessment of Mate Availability (SAMA). Although still under development, we have used sets of items that assess an individual's perception of her or his own personal mate opportunity structure—e.g., On a scale of 1 to 10 [difficult to easy], please tell me how easy it is for your to find dates who meet your standards these days?. For women/men like yourself, that is, women/men about your age with a similar education and social background, would you say that there are not enough, enough, or more than enough men/women? This indicator does not tap the factors that contribute to that assessment. We assume, however, that the answers will reflect one's personal calculation (e.g., physical characteristics, economic viability, common interests, personality, etc.). In other questions, we do attempt to ascertain the respondent's weighting of certain specific criteria, such as education, age, income, ethnicity, etc. We have successfully used the SAMA indicator in models of the relationship between perceived mate availability and mental health and in models of the association of perceived mate availability (SAMA) and marital salience with marital attitudes, controlling for background characteristics.

Subjective notions of availability are also often influenced by misinformation and widespread mythology. For example, notions of the severity of the African American gender imbalance in particular geographic locations have been extant in the African American population for some time. African Americans of both sexes, of all socioeconomic classes, and from various regions of the country, have been

Table 3
Mean Years of Schooling and Income for Husbands and Wives in Los Angeles County for Blacks and Whites: 1980 Census

Race	n	Mean	Deviation
Blacks			
Highest Year of School Attended			
Husbands	6,150	14.28	3.25
Wives	5,912	14.50	2.69
Wage/Salary Income in 1979			
Husbands	4,718	15,605.12	9,733.18
Wives	3,651	9,770.58	6,844.84
Whites			
Highest Year of School Attended			
Husbands	52,653	14.92	3.62
Wives	52,604	14.31	3.05
Wage/Salary Income in 1979			
Husbands	40,084	21,551.72	14,673.64
Wives	26,924	9,056.07	7,411.19

Note : Analyses are based on the Five Percent 1980 Census Public Use Sample which contains data on 1% of the population. (The title denotes that the questionnaire was administered to 5% of the population.). Includes only persons with income (i.e. excludes those who reported no wage, salary, or self-employment earnings in 1979.)

heard to comment that African American females outnumber African American males in Washington, D.C. by a ratio of 7:1 (variously reported as 12:1 or 20:1). Obviously, such an imbalance exists for no subgroup of marriage-age African Americans in Washington, D.C. How these quantified notions of imbalance gained such widespread acceptance is a mystery. The problem from the mate availability perspective is that people can only act on the basis of their perceived knowledge of the situation. If African American people in Washington, D.C. believe that women greatly outnumber men, their actions will reflect that belief. We would expect women to behave as if their choices are *extremely* limited (e.g., settling for men with less desirable characteristics, "putting up" with objectionable behavior, feeling undesirable). Alternatively, men would behave as if their options were unlimited (less commitment to relationships, "higher" standards of selection, fewer behavioral controls).

From a methodological perspective, mate availability analyses using demographically based statistics alone provide a rather limited view. That is, we can estimate an individual's actual chances for marriage given certain specific characteristics. But we cannot estimate the impact of a particular individual's beliefs about her or his chances without independent assessment of such attitudes. Furthermore, individual demands in mate selection serve as a self-limiting factor as well. For example, many well-educated, financially secure African American men complain about a paucity of suitable mates, despite the substantial statistical availability of women for such men. Our survey data indicate that African American male assessments of mate availability are much lower than that of White and Latino men in southern California. In accordance with social exchange theory, as the gender in short supply, their selection criteria have become more restrictive. How does such a "raising" of standards affect male-female relationships generally and community well-being? A comprehensive assessment of the underlying individual and community beliefs concerning mate selection and mate availability is a necessary base for understanding this complex and troubling phenomenon.

Factors Influencing Mate Selection in Subpopulations

One distinctive feature of the African American condition in the United States is its subpopulation status. African American social structure is significantly influenced by the behavior and mores of the dominant group. In this basic sense, African Americans are like the other so-called "ethnic minorities" in America. In the area of mate selection, however, that influence has produced some distinctive phenomena. It is widely believed that African Americans have incorporated certain of the mate selection standards endorsed by the dominant population. Many would argue that the use of hair straighteners, curly perms, and skin lighteners reflect an absorption of the dominant population's aesthetic ideals. While we acknowledge that such aesthetic preferences may be implicated in the difficulties faced by some African American women in relationship formation, since there are few data to confirm or deny such contentions, we will focus on the more quantifiable aspects of influence.

Although ethnic groups in the United States are generally endogamous, Blau's (1977) theorem states that minority populations always have higher outmarriage rates than the majority population (i.e., because the same number of marriages in each accounts for a much smaller percentage of the larger group). While this is certainly the case in the United States, all major non-white ethnic groups except Blacks evidence a higher outmarriage rate for women than for men (U.S. Bureau of the Census, 1985). On the basis of internal demographics alone (i.e., the male shortage), one would expect African American women to marry out in greater numbers. However, we suggest that a number of competing factors operate to counter such forces. First, racial attitudes, social stratification, and culturally rooted standards of physical attractiveness affect the degree to which African American women are attracted by and attracted to men of other races. Women are still more likely than men to be chosen on the basis of physical beauty and in America, European standards continue to prevail (the potential impact of African American Miss Americas aside). Perhaps due to historical sexual exploitation, African American women in general do not appear to be especially interested in marriage to men of other races. Another factor possibly affecting the level of African

American outmarriage, however, is the marriage squeeze among "baby boom" Whites. Guttentag and Secord (1983) have suggested that White women from that cohort responded to the shortage of partners by expanding their pools of eligibles and became much more willing to marry non-White men (Guttentag & Secord, 1983). In turn, "baby boom" era White men were not demographically compelled to expand their pools, since they are confronted with an oversupply of White women.

These factors do operate differentially by geographic (and by implication, sociocultural) context, however. As we demonstrated and discussed in a previous publication, African American outmarriage rates vary quite dramatically on the basis of region and gender (Tucker & Mitchell-Kernan, 1990). Among persons who married for the first time between 1970 and 1980, outmarriage was observed among 16.5% of African American men and 4.6% of African American women in the west; among Blacks in the south, only 1.6% of men and .6% of women outmarried.

Racial dynamics in the past have resulted in very different mate selection patterns among Blacks. Allison Davis, Burleigh Gardner, and Mary Gardner (1941) conducted a study of the social system that controlled relations between Blacks and Whites in one southwestern Mississippi community designated as "Old City." It had been observed that the physical characteristics of the African American population in Old City evidenced a greater level of intermixture of the races than was the case elsewhere in the state. It seems that although African American male-White female sexual unions were rare, relatively permanent African American female-White male relationships were an established feature of Old City society. These unions were never legal, but involved a White man's support of his African American mistress and their children. In a number of cases, the White man lived quite openly with his African American family. While White women and African American men in particular expressed outrage at such occurrences, some local Blacks reported that many of the "best" African American women preferred such an arrangement and that many of the "choicest" African American women were therefore unavailable to the African American men (p. 37). The researchers quoted informants who reported that the precarious economic circumstances of African American men diminished their desirability. Furthermore, the nature of the caste system in Old City deemed the offspring of African American-White relationships superior to African American-African American offspring purely on the basis of their physical characteristics. The mistresses also gained from association with a member of the superior caste by having a protector in relations with Whites. Some residents asserted that such a woman had a higher social position in the African American community based on the status of her White associate.

This situation is rather unique among African Americans in several respects: First, a relative shortage of African American females rather than males existed. Second, the shortage was an artifact of racial stratification and sociocultural traditions, rather than a true absence of one sex. Third, the shortage resulted from female rather than male "exogamous" mating. In effect, the perogatives of the superordinate caste extended to sexual rights and "possession" of females, thereby significantly affecting African American familial relations and the basic structure of the community at large. In most circumstances of female shortage, the males of the community would outmarry in response. It is here that the importance of sociohistorical context becomes most apparent. Due to the racial imperatives of the time (as issued by Whites) and the structure of power in that society, one primary adaptive alternative was not available to African American men.

Any meaningful analysis of the impact of constrained mate availability on African American social structure must consider the context in which the phenomenon occurs. The demographic characteristics of the dominant population, as well as its values and interests, may influence the very nature of the phenomenon, as well as the nature of the adaptive responses employed by Blacks.

Discussion

The scholarly literature on African American mate availability suffers from a conceptual and empirical focus that fails to consider the multiple levels of processes involved. Comprehensive, meaningful inquiry is long overdue, given the theorized consequences of imbalance and the likely continuation of demographically based male shortage into the next century and economically compromised communities for who knows how long. The problem seriously affects African American values, family and community structure, and the well-being of individuals and communities.

The mate availability perspective raises a number of questions about social influence on family formation, household structure and family stability. Previous efforts to explain unusual forms of social structure have not been considered here. We have not discussed, for example, efforts to explain African American family forms in terms of African retentions or in terms of socioeconomic adaptation. Some scholars linking African American social forms to African roots have argued that the greater focus among African American women on the maternal rather than the conjugal role (Bell, 1970) is a cultural retention derived from the consanguineal kin preference evident in many African societies (Sudarkasa, 1981) and the centrality of children in African and African American culture (Nobles, 1978). Alternatively, socioeconomic constraints are said to play a role in fostering more instrumental concerns when considering marriage (Ladner, 1971; Stack, 1974). These writings, and others, would suggest that there are some cultural and environmental supports for the unmarried state among African Americans and support for children born out-of-wedlock, at least in some circumstances. Given the findings and theories addressed in this paper, the new perspective derived from mate availability analyses might be incorporated as a significant component in interpreting features of African American family structure and household composition.

One of the factors affecting availability within societies such as our own, where generally endogamous ethnic groups commonly co-exist in close proximity, is the question of how the behavior and practices of other groups affect mate selection within another group, such as Blacks. We have attempted to demonstrate that for African Americans, mate availability over time and in the present has been affected by the attitudes and practices of Whites. In the antebellum period, for example, it is likely that the sex ratio would have favored women in many areas of the plantation south. The need for male labor on the plantation might have resulted in high sex ratios in rural and frontier areas as well. On the other hand, the opposite may have been true in the cities, where female domestic labor may have been more at a premium. This, of course, is speculative. There is evidence, however, that the propensity of southern White males to form liaisons with African American women both during the slavery era and afterward may have been a factor affecting the availability of African American women to marry African American men, at least in certain locations.

More recently, changing racial attitudes and the economic gains experienced by the more highly trained segments of the African American male population have operated to increase the pool of eligible women for African American men. These factors make it possible for White women (as well as non-African American women of other races) to even marry "up" through the selection of African American mates. In turn, the marriage squeeze observed among baby boom White women must be considered a factor in altering White women's attitudes toward the eligibility of African American men as mates and marriage partners. If, in certain areas of the country, as many as one of every six African American men can be expected to outmarry, and so long as the outmarriage rates for African American men and women continue to differ significantly, outmarriage must be considered a factor affecting mate availability. In view of such social realities, we believe that the mate availability perspective offers great promise in achieving a better understanding of the evolution of certain elements of African American social structure and socio-cultural practices.

Conclusion

This discussion has been an attempt to provide a conceptual and methodological context from which to generate additional research questions and models of study. Many major related issues have not been addressed (e.g., adaptation in the form of alternative roles for African American women) in an effort to limit our focus to the issue of model development. Our intent has been to provide a structure that would encourage a major research thrust in this area. A research agenda such as this may help us to understand and begin to address the range of pressing social issues that may be influenced by or rooted in mate availability constraints.

Notes

1. A limitation of raw Census figures is that they are biased by the acknowledged Census undercount of Blacks. The distortion of sex ratios is a consequence of undercount differentials on the basis of gender. A 1985 internal memo from the Census Bureau indicated that African American males age 25 through 54 were particularly likely to be omitted from 1980 Census figures (Passell & Robinson, 1985), although revised population estimates based on the post-enumeration survey following the 1990 Census show that male and female undercounts for Blacks are closer than in previous years, 5.4 for males and 4.3 for females (U.S. Bureau of the Census, 1991c). In order to account for such distortions in 1980, the Census Bureau produced revised population estimates on the basis of independent data sources, including birth and death records and sample surveys. Same age sex ratio charts prepared by the Census Bureau indicate that while actual 1980 Census-based figures show age-specific sex ratios for Blacks ranging from 90 to 80 for ages 25 through 55, sex ratios based on the revised population figures ranged from 97 to 90 for those same ages and years (U.S. Bureau of the Census, 1982a). While these revised figures raise African American sex ratios from seven to ten points, they remain sharply contrasted with those of Whites and all other races, which ranged from 102 to 95 for those same years. That is, even the revised sex ratios reveal that African American sex ratios have been and remain well below that observed for the rest of the American population. Guttentag and Secord (1983) argue that the sex ratio need not fall substantially below 100 in order to have a significant impact. Furthermore, even with undercount adjustments, a male shortage among Blacks is dramatic in certain geographic areas and age groups.

2. Sex ratio imbalance can be the result of a number of factors. In earlier times, the health risks associated with childbirth led to fairly high death rates among women. Mortality associated with childbirth was so high among African American women in the early twentieth century that female death rates exceeded male rates during the childbearing ages (U.S. Bureau of the Census, 1979). Conversely, protracted warfare creates imbalance through differential male mortality and absence while engaged in combat. It has even been noted that specific sexual practices are likely to result in disproportionately high numbers of male births (see Guttentag & Secord's discussion of the sexual behavior of certain communities of Orthodox Jews as related to sex ratios, 1983, pp. 79-111).

Theories about the sources of present day low sex ratios among African Americans vary. Most attribute the problem to a combination of factors. These include inadequate prenatal care (leading to the loss of greater numbers of male fetuses), high infant, childhood, and adolescent male mortality on the one hand, and unequal male and female migration patterns on the other (Guttentag & Secord, 1983; Jackson, 1971).

Throughout history, most cases of sex imbalance have been the result of selective migration (Guttentag & Secord, 1983). This has been a primary influence in African descended populations in the Western hemisphere as well. Blassingame (1972) reports that in the 1830s and 1840s, four out of every five Africans imported into Brazil were male. The 1860 slave sex ratio in Cuba was 156. There is some disagreement about the situation among African American slaves in the U.S. Although Blassingame (1972) believes that the U.S. slave sex ratios were nearly even, Frazier (1948) argues that throughout most of the antebellum period in the U.S. there were many more men than women, a condition which placed tremendous strain on African American family structure. He adds that parity was not reached until 1840. Guttentag and Secord (1983) view the situation as a bit more complex. They argue that in the U.S., African American sex ratios during slavery were to a large degree a function of plantation size and present data to support the view that the slave populations on larger plantations were disproportionately male.

Another source of migratory sex ratio imbalance has been the movement of Blacks in the western hemisphere, most often in search of economic opportunities. During the early twentieth century, West Indian African American migration to the United States and to Great Britain, which initially was substantially male, produced home communities that were disproportionately female, while males in the new country had relatively few female counterparts. The same has been true for many rural African American communities in the United States, as men left for jobs as well as more racially tolerant environments.

3. We acknowledge the fact that throughout our discussion of male shortage, there is the implication that an "ideal" pattern of mating and family formation exists in the African American population. Constrained mate availability is therefore viewed as a contributor to variations from that ideal. Although there is no substantial body of literature in which such ideals are determined for various segments of the African American population, the limited existing research does suggest that Blacks in general—across social classes—share the marriage and family ideals of the larger American culture, desiring nuclear families and children (Hannerz, 1969; Heiss, 1981; Scanzoni, 1971; Scott, 1980).

References

Akers, D. S. (1967). On measuring the marriage squeeze. *Demography, 4(2)*, 907- 924.

Ajzen, I., & Fishbein, M. (1980). *Understanding attitudes and predicting social behavior*. Englewood Cliffs, NJ: Prentice-Hall.

Becker, G. S. (1974). A theory of marriage. In T. W. Schultz (Ed.), *Economics of the family*. Chicago: University of Chicago Press.

Bell, R. (1970). Comparative attitudes about marital sex among Negro women in the United States, Great Britain, and Trinidad. *Journal of Comparative Family Studies, 1,* 71-81.

Bennett, N. G., Bloom, D E., & Craig, P. H. (1989). The divergence of Black and White marriage patterns. *American Journal of Sociology, 95,* 692-722.

Berscheid, E., & Walster, E. (1969). *Interpersonal attraction.* Reading, MA: Addison-Wesley.

Blau, P. M. (1977). *Inequality and heterogeneity: A primitive theory of social structure.* New York: The Free Press.

Blassingame, J. W. (1972). *The slave community: Plantation life in the antebellum south.* New York: Oxford University Press.

Bloom, D. E., & Bennett, N. G. (1985). *Marriage Patterns in the United States. National Bureau of Economic Research Working Paper Series. No. 1701.* Cambridge, MA: National Bureau of Economic Research.

Blumstein, P., & Schwartz, P. (1983). *American couples.* New York: William Morrow & Co., Inc.

Brockmann, C. T. (1987). The Western family and individuation: Convergence with Caribbean patterns. *Journal of Comparative Family Studies, 18(3),* 471-480.

Bumpass, L. L., Sweet, J. A., & Cherlin, A. (1991). The role of cohabitation in declining rates of marriage. *Journal of Marriage and the Family, 53,* 913-927.

Catton, W. R. (1964). A comparison of mathematical models for the effect of residential propinquity on mate selection. *American Sociological Review, 29,* 52-529.

Cazenave, N. (1980). Alternate intimacy, marriage, and family lifestyles among low-income Black Americans. *Alternative Lifestyles, 3(4),* 425-444. Clark (1984).

Cooney, T. M., & Hogan, D. P. (1991). Marriage in an institutionalized life course: First marriage among American men in the twentieth century. *Journal of Marriage and the Family, 53,* 178-190.

Cox, O. C. (1940). Sex ratio and marital status among Negroes. *American Sociological Review, 5,* 937-947.

Darity, W., & Myers, S. L. (1983). Changes in Black family structure: Implications for welfare dependency. *AEA Papers and Proceedings,* May.

Darity, W., & Myers, S. L. (1986/87). Public policy trends and the fate of the Black family. *Humboldt Journal of Social Relations, 14,* 134-164.

Davis, A., Gardner, B. B., & Gardner, M. R. (1941). *Deep south.* Chicago: University of Chicago.

Dixon, R. (1971). Explaining cross-cultural variations in age of marriage and proportion never marrying. *Population Studies, 25,* 215-233.

Du Bois, W. E. B. (1908). *The Negro American family.* Atlanta study No. 13. Atlanta: Atlanta University Publications.

Easterlin, R. A. (1980). *Birth and fortune: The impact of numbers on personal welfare*. New York: Basic Books.

Entwisle, B., & Mason, W. M. (1985). Multilevel effects of socioeconomic development and family planning programs on children ever born. *American Journal of Sociology, 91*, 616-649.

Epenshade, T. J. (1985). Marriage trends in America: Estimates, implications, and underlying causes. *Population and Development Review, 11*, 193-245.

Fishbein, M., & Ajzen, I. (1975). *Belief, attitude, intention and behavior*. Reading, MA: Addison-Wesley.

Frazier, E. F. (1948). *The Negro family in the United States*. (rev. ed.) Chicago: University of Chicago

Glick, P. C. (1981). A demographic picture of Black families. In H. P. MacAdoo (Ed.), *Black families*. Beverly Hills, CA: Sage Publications.

Glick, P. C., Heer, D. M., & Beresford, J. C. (1963). Family formation and family composition: Trends and prospects. In M.B. Sussman (Ed.), *Sourcebook in marriage and the family*. New York: Houghton Mifflin.

Goldman, N., Westoff, C. F., & Hammerslough, C. (1984). Demography of the marriage market in the United States. *Population Index, 50(1)*, 5-25.

Gonzalez, N. O. S. (1969). *Black Carib household structure: A study of migration and modernization*. Monograph 48. The American Ethnological Society. Seattle: University of Washington Press.

Guttentag, M., & Secord, P. F. (1983). *Too many women: The sex ratio question*. Beverly Hills: Sage Publications.

Hannerz, U. (1969). *Soulside: Inquiries into ghetto culture and family*. New York: Columbia University.

Hatchett, S., Veroff, J., & Douvan, E. (1989, June). *Marital Instability among Black and White couples in early marriage*. Paper presented at the conference, "The Decline in Marriage Among African-Americans: Causes, Consequences and Policy Implications," Center for Afro-American Studies, University of California, Los Angeles.

Heiss, J. (1981). Women's values regarding marriage and the family. In H. P. MacAdoo (Ed.), *Black families*. Beverly Hills, CA: Sage Publications.

Hirschman, D., & Matras, J. (1971). A new look at the marriage market and nuptiality rates, 1915-1958. *Demography, 8(4)*, 549-569.

Jackson, J. (1971). But where are all the men? *Black Scholar, 3(4)*, 34-41.

Jemmott, J. B., Ashby, K. L., & Lindenfeld, K. (1989). Romantic commitment and the perceived availability of opposite sex persons: On loving the one you're with. *Journal of Applied Social Psychology, 19*, 1198-1211.

Ladner, J. (1971). *Tomorrow's tomorrow: The Black woman*. Garden City, NY: Doubleday.

Lesthaeghe, R. (1983). A century of demographic and cultural change in Western Europe: An exploration of underlying dimensions. *Population and Development Review, 9,* 411-435.

Lichter, D. T., LeClere, F. B., & McLaughlin, D. K. (1991). Local marriage markets and the marital behavior of Black and White women. *American Journal of Sociology, 96,* 843-867.

Lichter, D. T., McLaughlin, D. K., Kephart, G., & Landry, D. J. (April, 1992). *Race, local mate availability, and transitions to first marriage among young women.* Paper presented at the annual meeting of the Population Association of America, Denver.

Liker, J. K., & Elder, G. H., Jr. (1983). Economic hardship and marital relations in the 1930s. *American Sociological Review, 48,* 343-359.

Liska, A. E. (1984). A critical examination of the causal structure of the Fishbein/Ajzen attitude-behavior model. *Social Psychology Quarterly, 47,* 61-74.

Mare, R. D., & Winship, C. (1991). Socioeconomic change and the decline of marriage for Blacks and Whites. In C. Jencks, & P. Peterson (Eds.), *The urban underclass.* Washington, D.C.: The Brookings Institution.

Mason, W. M., Wong, G., & Entwisle, B. (1983). Contextual analysis through the multilevel linear model. In S. Leinhardt (Ed.), *Sociological methodology. 1983-84.* San Francisco: Jossey-Bass, pp. 71-103.

McAdoo H. P. (Ed.) (1981). *Black families.* Beverly hills: Sage.

McQueen, A. J. (1979). The adaptations of urban Black families: Trends, problems, and issues. In D. Reiss, & H. A. Hoffman (Eds.), *The American family: Dying or developing.* New York: Plenum.

Moynihan, D. P. (1967). The Negro family: The case for national action. In L. Rainwater & W. L. Rainwater (Eds.), *The Moynihan report and the politics of controversy.* Cambridge, MA: MIT Press.

Murray, C. (1984). *Losing ground: American social policy, 1950-1980.* New York: Basic Books.

Murstein, B., (1973). A theory of marital choice applying to interracial marriage. In I. Stuart, & L. Abt (Eds.), *Interracial marriage.* New York: Grossman.

Nobles, W. (1978). Africanity: Its role in Black families. In R. Staples (Ed.), *The Black family: Essays and studies.* Belmont, CA: Wadsworth, 19-15.

Norton, A. J., & Miller, L. F. (1992). *Marriage, divorce, and remarriage in the 1990s.* U.S. Bureau of the Census, Current Population Reports, P23-180, U.S. Washington, D.C.: Government Printing Office.

Oppenheimer, V. K. (1988). A theory of marriage timing. *American Journal of Sociology, 94,* 563-591.

Passell, J. S., & Robinson, J. G. (1985). Internal memorandum for Roger A. Herriot, Chief, Population Division. Subject: *Revised demographic estimates of the coverage of the population by age, sex, and race in the 1980 census.* April 8. Washington: United States Bureau of the Census.

Scott, J. W. (1980). Black polygamous family formation: Case studies of legal wives and consensual "wives." *Alternative Lifestyles, 3*(1), 41-64.

Schoen, R. (1983). Measuring the tightness of the marriage squeeze. *Demography, 20*(1), 61-78.

Schoen, R., & Kluegel, J. R. (1988). The widening gap in Black and White marriage rates: The impact of population composition and differential marriage propensities. *American Sociological Review, 53*, 895-907.

Secord, P., & Ghee, K. (1986). Implications of the Black marriage market for marital conflict. *Journal of Family Issues, 7*, 21-30.

Shimkin, D. B., Louie, G. J., & Frate, D. A. (1978). The Black extended family: A basic rural institution and a mechanism of urban adaptation. In D. B. Shimkin, E. Shimkin, & D. Frate, *The extended family in Black societies*. Chicago: Aldine.

South, S. J. (1985). Economic conditions and the divorce rate: A time-series analysis of the postwar United States. *Journal of Marriage and the Family, 47*, 31-41.

South, S. J. & Messner, S. F. (1988). The sex ratio and women's involvement in crime: A cross-national analysis. *The Sociological Quarterly, 28*, 171-188.

Spanier, G. B., & Glick, P. C. (1980). Mate selection differentials between Whites and Blacks in the United States. *Social Forces, 58*, 707-725.

Stack, C. (1974). *All our kin*. New York: Harper & Row.

Staples, R. (1981a). Race and marital status: An overview. In H. P. MacAdoo (Ed.), *Black families* (pp. 173-175). Beverly Hills, CA: Sage Publications.

Staples, R. (1981b). *The world of Black singles*. Westport, CN: Greenwood Press.

Sudarkasa, N. (1981). Interpreting the African heritage in Afro-American family organization. In H. P. MacAdoo (Ed.), *Black families*. Beverly Hills, CA: Sage Publications.

Tanfer, K. (1987). Patterns of premarital cohabitation among never-married women in the United States. *Journal of Marriage and the Family, 49*, 483-497.

Testa, M. Astone, N. M., Krogh, M., & Neckerman, K. M. (1989). Ethnic variation in employment and marriage among inner-city fathers. *Annals of the American Academy of Political and Social Science, 501*, 79-91.

Thibaut, J. W., & Kelley, H. H. (1959). *The social psychology of groups*. New York: Wiley.

Thorton, A., & Freedman, D. (1982). Changing attitudes toward marriage and single life. *Family Planning Perspectives, 14*, 297-303.

Tucker, M. B. (1987). The Black male shortage in Los Angeles. *Sociology & Social Research, 71*, 221-227.

Tucker, M. B., & Mitchell-Kernan, C. (1990). New trends in Black American interracial marriage: The social structural context. *Journal of Marriage and the Family. 52*, 209-218.

Tucker, M. B. & Mitchell-Kernan, C. (1995a). *The decline in marriage among African American: Causes, consequences, and policy implications.* New York: Russell Sage Foundations.

Tucker, M. B. & Mitchell-Kernan, C. (1995b). Marital behavior and expectations: Ethnic comparisons of attitudinal and structural correlates. In M.B. Tucker & C. Mitchell-Kenan (Eds.), *The Decline in Marriage Among African-Americans: Causes, Consequences & Policy Implications.* New York: Russell Sage Foundations.

Tucker, M. B., & Mitchell-Kernan, C. (in press). Psychological well-being and perceived marital opportunity among single African American, Latina, and White women. *Journal of Comparitive Family Studies.*

Tucker, M. B., & Taylor, R. J. (1989). Demographic correlates of relationship status among Black Americans. *Journal of Marriage and the Family, 51,* 655-665.

U.S. Bureau of the Census. (1960). *Historical statistics of the United States, colonial times to 1957.* Washington, D.C.: U.S. Government Printing Office.

U.S. Bureau of the Census. (1964). *Census of the population: 1960, Vol. 1: Characteristics of the population, Part 1: United States summary.* Washington, D.C.: U.S. Government Printing Office.

U.S. Bureau of the Census. (1973). *Census of the population: 1970, Part 1, United States summary Section 2,* Washington, D.C.: U.S. Government Printing Office.

U.S. Bureau of the Census, (1979). *The social and economic status of the Black population in the United States: An historical view, 1790-1978.* Current population reports (Special studies series P-23, No. 80). Washington, D.C.: U.S. Government Printing Office.

U.S. Bureau of the Census. (1982a). *Coverage of the National Population in the 1980 Census by Age, Sex, and Race.* Current Population Reports, Series P-23, No. 115. Washington, D.C.: U.S. Government Printing Office.

U.S. Bureau of the Census. (1982b). *Statistical abstract of the United States: 1982-83.* (103rd ed.). Washington, D.C.: U.S. Government Printing Office.

U.S. Bureau of the Census. (1983). *Census of the population: 1980, Vol. 1: Characteristics of the population, Chapter B: General population characteristics, Part 1: United States summary.* Washington, D.C.: U.S. Government Printing Office.

U.S. Bureau of the Census. (1984). *Statistical abstract of the United States: 1985.* (105th ed.). Washington, D.C.: U.S. Government Printing Office.

U.S. Bureau of the Census. (1985). *Census of the population: 1980, Vol. 2. Subject reports: Marital characteristics.* Washington, D.C.: U.S. Government Printing Office.

U. S. Bureau of the Census. (1991a). Marital Status and Living Arrangements: March 1990. *Current Population Reports,* (Series P-20, No. 450). Washington, D.C.: U.S. Government Printing Office.

U. S. Bureau of the Census. (1991b). *Stastical Abstract of the United States: 1991*, (111th ed.). Washington, D.C.: U.S. Government Printing Office.

U.S. Bureau of the Census. (1991c). *Census Bureau releases refined estimates from post enumeration survey of 1990 Census coverage.* (Press Release.) United States Department of Commerce News. Washington, D.C., June 13.

U.S. Bureau of the Census. (1992a). *Statistical abstract of the United States: 1992.* (112th ed.). Washington, D.C.: U.S. Government Printing Office.

U.S. Bureau of the Census. (1992b). *Census of the population: 1990, General Population Characteristics: Alabama (CP 1-2).* Washington, D.C.: U.S. Government Printing Office.

U.S. Bureau of the Census. (1992c). *Census of the population: 1990, General Population Characteristics: Hawaii (CP 1-13).* Washington, D.C.: U.S. Department of Commerce, Economics and Statistics Administration.

U.S. Bureau of the Census. (1992d). *Census of the population: 1990, General Population Characteristics: South Dakota (CP 1-43).* Washington, D.C.: U.S. Department of Commerce, Economics and Statistics Administration.

U.S. Bureau of the Census. (1992e). Statistics calculated from data obtained from Bureau of the Census, Van Nuys, California office.

Wilkie, J. R. (1991). The decline in men's labor force participation and income and the changing structure of family economic support. *Journal of Marriage and the Family, 53*, 111-122.

Wilson, W. J. (1987). *The truly disadvantaged.* Chicago: The University of Chicago Press.

Author

M. Belinda Tucker
UCLA Department of Psychiatry and
Behavioral Sciences
SBG Box 62 - NPI
Los Angeles, CA 90024-1579

Part 3

Research Reviews

Why We Know So Little About African American Sexuality

Gail Elizabeth Wyatt

Although the sexuality of African American men and women has always received attention, there is a scarcity of factual information available. In this chapter, I will explore the historical, empirical and political factors that have contributed to why we know so little about African American sexuality. Secondly, a recent study of the sexuality of African American women will serve as a model for the kind of information needed regarding males and females. The importance of this information to understanding health and psychological problems will also be reviewed.

First of all, before I discuss sex research related to African Americans, some history of the field of sex research is necessary to place ethnic-specific research into perspective.

Historical Factors Influencing Sex Research

Several historical factors have affected the scarcity of information regarding American sexual behaviors.

The Judeo-Christian ethic has defined all sexual behavior within the context of the marital relationship (Spilka, Hood and Gorsuch, 1985). Sex was also strongly associated with procreation, so that sex outside of marriage and for the purpose of pleasure were concepts considered by many to be immoral. Sexual behavior which included genital contact to the exclusion of other "auto-erotic" behaviors, was also considered to be the appropriate expression of sexuality in marriage. The body was considered private and discussions of one's sex life, even within marriage, was not condoned. The sexual relationship between a man and his wife was a sacred relationship bound by the sanctity of marriage.

However, Freud's theory of psychosexual development contradicted the Judeo-Christian ethic somewhat, when it described children as interested in and capable of participating in sexual behavior and likely to fantasize about these behaviors with persons known to them, including their parents!

Alfred Kinsey and his colleagues at the Kinsey Institute shocked the American public with the first statistical analysis of American sexual behavior (Kinsey, Pomeroy, Martin & Gebhard, 1953). Their finding that 25% of White women and

50% of African American women engaged in premarital intercourse before age 20 was in direct opposition to the traditional sexual ethics thought to be followed in the 1940's and 50's. They also found that White women as well as men engaged in other "auto-erotic" behaviors such as masturbation, cunnilingus and fellatio more than their African American peers.

However, even though it was obvious that the Judeo-Christian ethic was not operating for everyone, researchers like Kinsey and his associates were not reinforced for their efforts, nor was everyone openly receptive to hearing about them. It was difficult to obtain funds for sex research and much care had to be taken to obtain research participants. Both funding and sampling problems emerged for sex researchers as early as the 1930's; and to some extent, they continue today.

Consequently, although other research has identified sexual patterns in America, there are compromises researchers have had to make. They are listed as follows:

1. Early limitations in funding caused researchers to look for expedient methods of sampling. They have often sacrificed representativeness of the sample for large numbers of subjects (Hunt, 1974; Kinsey, Pomeroy, Martin & Gebhard, 1953). However, in making statements about large populations, their results were often not generalizable to ethnic, age, and religious groups, who were not adequately represented.

2. Efforts to obtain ethnic and non-ethnic group samples often resulted in few similarities between groups. For example, Kinsey obtained a sample of African American women in prison and another sample of rural African American men and women from a farming community in Kansas. Masters and Johnson's sample (1966) of ethnic minority members was too small to identify physiological differences by ethnicity.

3. Members of different ethnic minority groups, albeit small numbers, were often grouped together into one category for some analyses and were labeled as "nonWhite" (see Bell, 1971; Kanther & Zelnik, 1972).

4. Sensitivity to the respondents regarding the discussion of sexual behaviors was often less than desired, particularly years ago when there was little to encourage people to participate in this kind of research. Kinsey used White male interviewers to interview both his African American and White male and female respondents. It is difficult to imagine the level of comfort that could have been established between female respondent and a male interviewer while discussing a sensitive topic, such a methods of masturbation, in the 1940's or 50's.

There is really no wonder that popular magazines meant for the general public, like Playboy, Redbook, Cosmopolitan, Essence and many others, have published their own sex surveys. In light of limited empirical studies, their purpose has been to offer the public information about current sexual practices, as the climate toward sexual behaviors became more acceptable (Grinspoon & Bakalar, 1979; Leary, 1973). However, media sponsored surveys have had their own limitations. Without some control over who actually completed paper pencil mail response questionnaires and some information about the accuracy of the data, it is difficult to make statements about "everyone's sexual behavior," when one could never be sure of who "everyone" was. There are no controls over who returns a magazine survey, nor is there a way to validate the accuracy of the responses given that the respondent is anonymous.

Recently, sex research has utilized non-probability samples to more adequately address issues of generalizability. However, these studies tended to include poor, African American populations who are often clinic or hospital populations (Brunswick, 1971; Castadot, 1975; Ewer & Gibbs, 1975); Graves & Bradshaw, 1975; Teele, Robinson, Schmidth & Rice, 1967); or high school or college students (Reiss, 1964, 1967).

There have also been limitations on the age of individual who have participated in sex research, partly because of difficulties in obtaining samples that were representative across many demographic variables. Most research respondents have ranged in age from adolescence to mid-thirties. There is little, if any, information available about African American children, middle aged males or females, or the elderly. Consequently, what we know often lacks a developmental perspective and the findings of existing research are rarely related to some physical, social, emotional and sexual outcome later in life (Wyatt, 1997).

Thus, although the interest in and permission to discuss sexuality has increased over the years, funding and sampling limitations have severely limited what we know about sex, in general. Now let us examine why we have so little information regarding the sexual behaviors of African Americans.

Historical Factors

At first glance, because so many of the events of slavery have been described in the literature, one might wonder if this author's concern about the scarcity of information about African American sexuality is well founded. There have been descriptions of the sexual behavior and anatomy of African people that date back to the 16th century (Vontress, 1971). Christian missionaries and travelers were shocked to observe practices in Africa that, according to their teachings, would have been engaged in within the marital relationship. Because much of what they labeled those sexual behaviors as immoral and the persons who engaged in them as sexually permissive, as well. However, they failed to understand that sexual behaviors were regulated by tribal customs and traditions in Africa. Although sexual practices vary from African society to society, for the most part, the reproductive aspects of sexual behaviors were controlled by religious values and not sex itself (De Rachewitz, 1964).

Much of what was described about African sexual behavior followed their African American relatives to America. These observations and impressions formed the basis of stereotypes, or preconceived notions regarding various groups or individuals (Baron's & Byrne, 1977). The stereotypes regarding the sexual practices of Africans were reinforced during slavery and were legitimized by literature describing slaves in the new world. For example, African women brought to the new world on slave ships were described as sexually uninhibited (Thomas & Sillen, 1972).

Early social scientists adhered to the biologically determined immorality of the descendents of Africans as a function of their adaptation to the hot climate of Africa (Wyatt, 1982a). The climate was thought to preserve more intense sexual passions and to increase fertility (Dow, 1922). Other descriptions identify the African American culture as one that tolerates promiscuity and readily accepts illegitimacy due to traditions that grew out of slavery (Myrdal, 1944; Liben, 1969).

There are a number of stereotypic descriptions of the treatment of African slaves and their African American descendants by slave masters in the South, beginning in 1690 (Walker, 1976). The breeding of slaves to swell the work force and the subjugation of the female slaves to their slave masters was best described in this passage: "Sexual intercourse between Blacks and Whites seems to have begun a soon as the former were introduced into America. Many White men and women came to think of African American women as basically immoral— loose...easy [and] deliberately indicative of White men. Some Whites still believe this" (Walker, 1976, p. 342).

In general, throughout the following 200 or more years of slavery, African American people were thought to be more primitive, animalistic and sexual than Whites (Davis & Cross, 1979). African American men and women were perceived as having insatiable appetites and in particular, African American men were thought to have oversized genitalia and unusual capacities for endurance during sexual activity.

These stereotypes depicting the impulse-ridden sexual prowess of Blacks may have reinforced some of the practices during the "Jim Crow" era. African American men were often lynched and castrated as a perceived counter assault on their sexual potency and alleged lust for White women (Davis & Cross, 1979).

It seems that the sexuality of American Blacks was perceived as a problem which could be exploited, in the case of African American women, and controlled and punished in African American men. In reality, however, stereotypes of the sexual prowess of African American men created as much interest in them as sexual objects to be taken advantage of, as did stereotypes about African American women (Bell, 1971).

Adherence to stereotypes has been found among the general public and among African American and White mental health professionals, as well. In a study of mental health professional's attitudes towards African American families, African American professionals tended to hold more positive attitudes about family life and sexual behaviors than their European American professional peers. African American professionals however, also tended to believe more stereotypes about their own ethnic group, than their European American cohorts. It is obvious that more educational information is needed regarding the nature of African American sexuality and the differences in sexual practices of various ethnic groups, for the benefit of the general public and the professional community (Powell, Wyatt & Bass, 1983).

Impact of the Media on History of African American Sexuality

The media has seized upon and fostered the endurance of some of the stereotypes of Africans and African Americans. Early roles that African American men and women portrayed in film were often stereotypic of the beastial African native, the asexual, but devoted slave who raised and cared for other people's children and families, or the senseless buffoon whose tastes and lifestyle were basic and uncomplicated. Maykovich, (1971) compared African American stereotypes from the 1930's to the 70's and noted the change of the portrayal of African American people from the negative, passive images of 1932, to the negative, active stereotypes of the 1970's. The following quote captures this new image: "Negative African American stereotypes are more subtle and neatly camouflaged than they were in films of yesterday, but the same insidious message is there: Blacks are violent, criminal, sexy savages who imitate the White man's ways as best they can from their disadvantaged sanctuary in the ghetto" (Poussaint, 1974, p. 26).

Poussaint (1974) expressed concern that African Americans incorporate these negative and destructive images and stereotypes and develop a self-hatred that has made them easy victims for oppression. King (1973) writes that the image of African American women as depreciated sex objects also serves the function of rendering psychological damage upon African American women as unsuitable marital partners of both African American and White men.

In the popular press, there has been a history of mixed messages about African American sexual behavior. For example, one popular magazine exclusively written for African American women described them as more sexually uninhibited and aggressive than White women (Young, 1974). In another publication during that same year, African American women were described as being more sexually restrained and traditional in their sexual expression than White women, particularly in wife swapping and group sex (Staples, 1974).

In the summer of 1978, a top selling album recorded by an English group "The Rolling Stones," included a song regarding the behavior of women of several ethnic group affiliations. In the song "Some Girls," they sang:

White girls are pretty funny,   Sometimes they drive me mad,
African American girls just want to get f——all night
  and don't have that much of a chance.
Chinese girls are so gentle They're really such a tease,
You never know what they're cooking, inside those silky sleeves.
                                        (Rolling Stones Records, 1978)

   This is a dramatic illustration that the stereotype of "sexually uninhibited, but seldom desirable African American women" was being perpetuated even in contemporary music, written and recorded by an English rock group. The song demonstrated how the stereotype has been accepted around the world. Needless to say, a similar stereotype of the African American man would undoubtedly include a mention of his genitalia, sexual capabilities and uninhibited nature (Wyatt, 1982b). Most likely, today, these words would pale compared to some of the rap lyrics regarding African American women. In essence, the stereotypes in contemporary music are as pervasive as ever.

What We Know About Research on African American Sexuality

   The scientific literature has shed little insight on the subject of African American sexuality. Research has often continued to perpetuate stereotypes by identifying differences between African American and White samples and failing to examine the factors contributing to these differences. It is useful to summarize some of the major findings that sex research generated about African American men and women in the areas in which the research has focused prior to the AIDS epidemic.

Sex Education, Birth Control Information, and Use of Contraception

   1. African American adolescents lack knowledge of birth control or contraception (Brunswick,1971; Castadot, 1975; Delcampo, Sporakowski & Delcampo, 1976; Kantner & Zelnik, 1972).
   2. African American adolescents use contraceptives less in the 13 to 19 age group than their White peers (Youth Values Project Report, 1978).
   3. African American men learn about sexual intercourse earlier than White men and when they do, it is through sexual experience (Bell, 1971).

Sexual Attitudes

1. African American men and women attending college have more sexually permissive attitudes than White men, and women with a similar education. (Reiss, 1964, 1967).

2. African American men and women have a single standard of sexual behavior: Sex outside of marriage is equally as acceptable for African American men as it is for African American women (Rainwater, 1966).

3. Sex for African American men has been described as an instrument of power and status (Bernard, 1966).

First Intercourse

1. African American women have higher percentages of premarital coitus and are 3 to 4 times as likely to be exposed to premarital sex as their White female peers (Gebhard, Pomeroy, Martin & Christensen, 1958).

2. African American-American populations have a higher incidence of premarital intercourse (with their finance) than White Americans (Hunt, 1974; Reiss, 1967).

3. By age 16, 29% of African American adolescents have had intercourse (Castadot, 1975).

4. Three-fourths of African American adolescents have intercourse before age 18, as compared to two-thirds of a White sample of 15 to 19 year olds (Kantner & Zelnik, 1972).

5. Fewer than 1% of African American males versus 21% White males were virgins by age 21 (Holman & Schaffner, 1947).

Sexual Behavior

1. African American adolescent females whose parents have college educations have less sexual experience than those of parents with an elementary school education or less (Kantner & Zelnik, 1972).

2. African American adolescent females 15 to 19 years of age, who ascribe to no religion have a higher proportion of coital experience than adolescents with religious affiliations (Kantner & Zelnik, 1972).

3. African American adolescents have sexual intercourse less frequently than White adolescents and with fewer partners (Kantner & Zelnik, 1972; Youth Values Project Report, 1978).

4. African American men and women are less likely to engage in fellatio and cunnilingus than their White peers, regardless of marital status (Bell, 1971; Hunt, 1974).

Sexual Anatomy

1. Three times as many African American males as White males had penises which measured more than seven inches in their erect state, although the difference was not statistically significant (Bell, 1971).

Family Planning, Pregnancy and Abortion

1. African American adolescents desire larger families than White adolescents (Brunswick,1971).

2. African American adolescents who become pregnant tend to keep their children, while four out of five of their White peers tend to give up babies for adoption (Nettleton, 1975).

3. African American women and adolescents tend to have fewer abortions than White women an adolescents (Liben, 1960), particularly among the lesser educated, (Kinsey, et al. 1953). However, Kinsey and his colleagues (1953) also found women of less education to have more spontaneous abortions.

4. Educated African American women are likely to have fewer children than educated White women (Kinsey et al, 1953).

Sexual Abuse

1. African American women are at risk for sexual abuse across all age groups. However, young, unmarried, school-aged African American women of a lower socioeconomic background are at risk for rape (Amir, 1971; Windeland & Davis, 1977; Miller,Moeller, Kaufman, Awasto, Pathak & Christy, 1978; National Crime Panel Survey Report, 1975; Peters, 1976).

Limitations of the Research

These findings are by no means an exhaustive list of all the research that has included African American samples prior to the 1980s. However, it is apparent from these descriptions that differences in sex education information, first coitus, use of contraception, preferences in sexual behaviors, pregnancy and abortion helped to reinforce the notion that African American sexuality was problem oriented.

However, there are other limitations of the above described research, having to do with the definition of ethnic groups included in the research and the manner in which the subjects were designated as "African American."

Ethnicity of Sex Research Samples

One of the major problems found in previous sex research with African American samples is that both racial and ethnic groups have been included together and skin color has been used as a determinant of group identification.

A book by Collins and Ashmore (1970), (pg. 240) provides this definition of the term most frequently confused: "Racial groups are distinguishable solely in terms of genetically determined biological criteria such as skin color and hair texture. Ethnic groups are distinguishable primarily in terms of cultural or learned factors."

Identifying persons of African origin by hair texture and skin color is particularly problematic if the desired sample is to include only people of African origin in the U. S. The history of racial mixing that has occurred between all racial groups over several hundred years in this country makes it virtually impossible to extract a purely Negroid or Caucasoid sample for the purpose of racial comparisons. Furthermore, hair texture or skin color may be misleading features of a group for sex research. The term "ethnic group", used to identify those persons of a racial origin whose socialization and cultural values are similar, appears to be the most useful to designate one group from another, regardless of skin color (Wyatt, 1991).

However, in most research, there is often a conglomeration of groups being included in the research that has described African American sexual practices. While most researchers use the terms "African American" and "White," persons of a variety of other ethnic groups with varying kinds of socialization experiences are often included in these samples. For example, Alan Bell (1971) reported that "orientals" were a part of the sample identified as "African American" in the Kinsey sample. Kantner & Zelnik (1972) also included non-Blacks in their African American sample. Similarly, Jewish Americans are often included in "White" samples without the researcher specifically discussing if any differences have been found between Jewish and other White women's sexual behavior. Additionally, most researchers fail to address how the inclusion of a variety of ethnic groups might influence the results and the empirical documentation regarding how this kind of combination of ethnic groups influences the results. This author, along with Albert Yee, Halford Fairchild and Fred Weizman comprise a task force for the American Psychological Association to study the use of ethnicity rather than race in social science research. Hopefully, guidelines for research will be developed as a beginning attempt to influence the use of these terms for psychologists (Yee, Fairchild, Weizman & Wyatt, 1993).

Thus far, we have discussed some of the reasons why research has contributed to the limited knowledge of *African American* sexuality. However, we know equally as little about *African American* sexuality, because the ethnicity and socialization of samples are seldom described so that the racial origin of the group being studied and the country in which their major socialization experiences took place is clear, in relation to characteristics of the sample and the findings.

For purposes of clarity, let us define the terms "racial" and "ethnic group" that are being used in this chapter. African sexuality includes the variety of sexual practices among the natives of the African continent. African American sexuality includes sexual practices of people of African origin who reside in the West Indies or in other areas where people of African origin may reside. African American sexuality specifically pertains to people of African origin who have been raised in and have spent the majority of their childhoods in the U. S.

This type of ethnic specificity and a discussion of how language, culture, family styles, religion and economics influence behavior, can clarify the relationship of a variety of socio-cultural aspects that are overlooked when ethnic groups are included in research, in general and sex research, in particular.

Political Factors Influencing Sex Research

It is apparent that when the funding problems related to ethnic specific sex research are examined, there are similar problems in the area of sex research, as well.

Many of the problems related to funding have plagued sex researchers over the past 50 years and may have been the reason why Kinsey and his colleagues, Morton Hunt, Masters and Johnson, more recently Michaels, Gagnon, Laumann, and Kolata (1994) and countless others sought private funding for their research. In fact, popular magazines have entered the business of funding sex research because their involvement met a shared need: the publisher was motivated to sell magazines that dealt with a topic of interest and at the same time, coverage of the topic provided funding for sex researchers to collect data on large samples.

Political priorities regarding funding policies have had a powerful impact upon the volume and quality of ethnic specific research. In 1980, the Presidential Administration made a decision to de-emphasize the funding of the social sciences and humanities, in deference to the biological, physical and computer sciences. According to a study of federal research support for African American Studies (Tucker, 1984), much of the research was concentrated in the two areas whose priority was shifted to a lower status. When Tucker (1984) examined lists of federal obligations for research by government agencies, she noted that, over the years 1978 through 1982, and with estimates given for 1983 and 1984, funding for projects involving mathematical and computer sciences increased by 2-1/2 times. However, during the same period, projects related to psychology increased by only 25% and support for the social sciences (i.e., anthropology, sociology, political science, economics and other fields) increased only 10%. Furthermore, the de-emphasis upon social science research focusing upon African American issues came at a time when there was a growing need to conduct research upon other ethnic groups.

Consequently, this effort to balance the attention among a variety of ethnic groups created more competition for the federal dollar.

If we examine the specific agencies where ethnic specific research would be funded, the Department of Health and Human Services (HHS), and the Alcohol, Drug Abuse and Mental Health Administration (ADAMHA) are likely sources of this type of support. While funding for psychology increased through 1982, support for the social sciences declined beginning in 1981, with anticipation that the decline would continue for the next few years. Similarly, support for psychology and the social sciences through HHS declined in 1984, with anticipation for continued decline in the future.

The documentation of changes in support of research related to African American issues is highly dependent upon the data-gathering systems of each agency, making it difficult to assess the status of ethnic specific research for all agencies (Tucker, 1984). However, information from the National Institute of Mental Health (NIMH) can be used as an example of an agency with funds for minority research. The NIMH experiences an increase in funds for support of ethnic research beginning in 1979 (142 projects), but while the number of projects funded increased in 1983 (125 projects), it remained less than the 1979 (142) and 1980 (135) levels. Additionally, when degree of ethnic relevance was considered, by 1983, the number of projects with major relevance to ethnic minorities (a focus on one of five ethnic groups) declined from 54% in 1979 to 33% (Tucker, 1984).

However, unlike other agencies, funding for African American-related NIMH supported research apparently did not decline, as compared to dollars designated for other ethnic groups. For example, in 1978, African American-related research received 44% of funding and 58% of funding in 1983. However, funding for the NIMH Minority Center did reveal a shift between African American and Asian funding, According to Tucker (1984), "African American research dropped from 41% in 1982 to 29% in 1983 while Asian/Pacific funding increased from 7% to 17% during the same period" (p.10). However, most of the research on African Americans today is conducted by European American researchers who are most aware of problems of their samples than their socio-cultural context (Wyatt, 1997).

In summary, the overall shift of focus from the social sciences to the "hard sciences" and the dispersion of funding for ethnic specific research to accommodate the concerns of other ethnic-racial groups places research on African American sexuality in competition with other priorities. It makes the likelihood of funding for this type of research more difficult and places pressure on researchers to return to nonrepresentative samples, experimental designs with methodological limitations, or to research funded by private sources. Unfortunately, private support in the example of funding from popular magazines, often imposes pressure upon the researcher to focus more upon the sensationalism of the findings and less upon other issues such as the representativeness of the sample or the distinctions made between subjects, based upon ethnic group affiliation.

AIDS and Sex Research

A review of the assumptions regarding African American sexuality in the 1970's set the stage for the epidemic of sexually transmitted diseases that proliferated in the 1980's and 90's.

Randy Schilts describes in his book *And the Band Played On* how AIDS spread in the U.S. in the early 1980's. Given that AIDS was primarily identified in gays, IV drug users or unsavory segments of the community (e.g. poor people or prostitutes), political priorities allowed this sexually transmitted disease to spread because of the erroneous assumption that it only affected groups of people who either did not have a critical mass of visable political representation to advocate for them nor the political clout to advocate for themselves (Shilts, 1988). Becoming affected with HIV also had moral overtones and was seen as "God's punishment" for engaging in sinful or socially undesirable sexual practices. Because the capacity to examine the growing epidemic internationally, and to begin behavioral interventions was not fully in place before the mid 1980s, AIDS continued to be perceived as a burden to the U.S. federal budget and to public health officials for far too long.

It is sadly ironic that African American men, women and children are among the groups most likely to be infected with HIV today. We have so little information about sexual practices and the epidemic of STDs is so pervasive that African American sexuality continues to be cast as a "problem oriented" phenomenon. It is of even more concern that the model for sexual behavior intervention has now been altered from a White Christian male model to a White gay male model. The importance of examining African American sexuality within a socio-cultural context still remains as politically charged as it was hundreds of years ago (Wyatt, Myers, Ashing-Guva, & Duwasula, in press).

Obtaining Representativeness in an Ethnic Sample

The historical, research and political factors responsible for our lack of knowledge about African American sexuality and the need for sexual behavior intervention certainly call attention to the need to obtain information regarding the sexual practices of a sample of African Americans, with similar ethnicity and socialization and about whose findings we can generalize to a larger population. While such a sample of African American men in sex research has yet to be collected, a study of the sexual socialization of African American women has recently been collected, which accomplished both sample representativeness and specificity regarding the ethnicity of the subjects (reasonably well). Consider the following description as an example of the effort that needs to be expanded to obtain an adequate sample for ethnic specific sex research.

In order to obtain African American and European American female subjects with comparable demographic characteristics, multi-stage stratified random sampling with quotas was used as the method of selection. Los Angeles County was selected as the site for the research because in it resides a sizable population of African Americans ranging in age, economic and educational levels. The age criteria of 18 to 36 allowed for the examination for the sexual behavior of women born after World War II, before television became a major source of socialization (the 27-36 age group) and women born in the 60's during the Civil Rights Movement, the advent of the sexual revolution and the increased availability of birth control (the 18 to 26 age group). This age criteria also insured that all participants were legal majors and could participate in a sex research project without parental consent.

The sampling procedure was based upon the Los Angeles Metropolitan Area Survey (LAMAS), conducted semi-annually by the UCLA Institute for Social Science Research. It is continually updated to reflect changing residential patterns of Los Angeles County. The actual quotas used for the study were based upon the population of African American women 18 to 36 years of age, ranging in education, marital status and the presence of children. African American women in this study are of African descent, and their parentage also included a variety of other ethnic and racial groups found in America. These women spent at least six of the first 12 years of their childhood in the United States. Women were asked to identify their own ethnic identity.

The respondents were recruited by random-digit dialing of telephone prefixes in Los Angeles County, combined with four randomly generated numbers. The first prefixes were selected to represent specific areas in the County where the various potential subjects might be located. The final set of prefixes represented the remaining areas in the county. While 11,834 telephone numbers were gathered, 6562 were found to be nonresidential or numbers not in service. The remaining 5,272 eventuated to 1,348 households in which a woman was potentially eligible to participate. Of that number, 709 women agreed to participate, 226 refused and 335 women terminated telephone conversations before their eligibility could be determined. There was a 27% refusal rate, based upon women who were eligible to participate. There were 248 women who agreed to be interviewed, 126 of whom were African American. The sample of 122 White women is described elsewhere (Wyatt, 1985).

The number of interviewed women in the quota categories were compared by the same demographic characteristics with 1980 census data for African American women in Los Angeles County (US Bureau of the Census, 1980). The agreement with 1980 census proportions was assessed using a Chi-Square Test as a measure of agreement between the numbers interviewed and the expected count. The results, together with the randomness following from the random-digit dialing method of selection, supported the general representativeness of the sample to African

Table 1

Demographic Characteristics of African-American Women Comparison of Sample and Los Angeles County

Age Range	Sample (126)		LA County (167,880)	
	Number	Percent	Number	Percent
18-26	58	46	90,460	54
27-36	68	54	77,420	46
Education				
llth Grade or less	19	15	29,620	18
High School Graduates	43	34	66,960	40
Partial College	47	37	56,900	34
College Graduate	17	14	14,400	9
Children				
None	38	30	67,220	40
One or more	88	70	l00,660	60
Martial Statisfaction				
Currently Married	35	28	50,900	30
Once Married	38	30	33,140	20
Never Married	53	42	83,840	50

American women ages 18 to 36, with similar demographic characteristics in Los Angeles County as Table 1 illustrates.

Income levels for the sample ranged from below $5,000 to over $40,000 per year. Of those women who were at the poverty level for 1980 (i.e., $9,200 or less for a family of 4), 79% were African American women. This number, however, is proportional to poverty level by ethnicity statistics for L. A. County. Overall, the sample represents a range in income and demographics characteristics of African American women in Los Angeles County.

All researchers cannot afford or do not need to use the kind of sampling procedure described above. However, regardless of the methodology utilized, statements about generalizbility need to be tempered with other limitations of the sample. If the rates of high risk sexual practices for unintended pregnancies and sexually transmitted diseases are being assessed, representative community samples, albeit expensive and time consuming, need some priority, in order to gain information about the population.

Most recently, the Wyatt study has identified non-significant ethnic differences in the age of onset of coitus between African American and European American women (Wyatt, 1987), in the prevalence of child sexual abuse between these groups before age 18 (Wyatt, 1985; Wyatt, Loeb, Vargas-Carmen, Romero, & Solis, 1999) and in adulthood (Wyatt, 1992). These findings are in contrast to previous findings

(Amir, 1971; Castadot, 1975; Hinderlang & Davis, 1977; Hunt, 1974; Kantner & Zelnik. 1972; Kinsey et al., 1953; Miller, Moeller, Kaufman, Awasto, Pathak & Christy, 1978; National Crime Panel Survey Report, 1975; Peters, 1976; Reiss, 1964), and may be due to a variety of reasons: this research includes samples with demographic comparability; specific delineation of the ethnic groups are included; identification and separation of ages of onset of voluntary versus abusive behaviors is made during data collection; or the study identifies more compatible sexual experiences among women who were sexually active from 1960 to the 1990's. More research identifying the factors contributing to these two ethnic groups is needed (Wyatt, 1982a), and is forthcoming (Wyatt, Forge, & Gutherie, 1998).

What We Need to Know About African American Sexuality

Once decisions about sampling and appropriate identification of the ethnic group to be included are resolved, the next task is to obtain data to fill the void of information that examines the nature, circumstances and influential factors relating to sexual behavior ranging in degrees of risks for pregnancy and sexually transmitted diseases (Wyatt, 1997).

The first area that deserves attention is the kind of information that adult males and females recall being taught about their bodies, bow they function and reproduce and appropriate ways to express their sexuality. This information needs to be obtained within three phases: in childhood, from birth to 12 years; adolescence, 13 to 17 years and in adulthood, defined as 18 years and older. Human sexuality information obtained within a developmental perspective allows for changes in educational information to become apparent as the individual grows older, closer to sexual activity and to ages where sex within committed relationships is expected.

Within that context, the source of educational information, parents, peers, formal classes, information learned from religious institutions or elsewhere, needs to be identified, along with the means used to convey information. For example, in the Wyatt study of African American women's sexuality, a few women reported that during adolescence their mothers offered the following, in an effort to convey their disdain for sex outside of marriage or a committed relationship: "Why buy the cow when the milk is free?" Another woman offered this statement as an example of her mother's efforts to stress the physical and psychological ramifications of indiscriminate sex, "When you lay down with dogs, you get fleas." Neither one of: these statements made to women during adolescence was followed by further explanation or discussion. Although the women did not understand the true meaning of the statements at the time they were made, they clearly understood that sex before marriage was not sanctioned by their mothers. It would be interesting to determine what African American males were told about uncommitted sex and multiple partners before and during marriage by parents.

Finally, in addition to information that males and females recall about human sexuality, it is important to know what their current level of knowledge is about the topic. Two studies (Bell, 1971; Kantner & Zelnik, 1972) suggest that African American male and female adolescents appear to have limited information about human sexuality, reproduction and the manner in which disease is spread sexually. The particular areas where factual knowledge is limited need to be identified to help develop human sexuality courses that can be taught where they will reach the maximum number of people: in churches, classes sponsored by youth organizations, those offered to parents and those taught in the public schools on a formal basis, with parental consent (Wyatt, 1997).

The second area that requires more descriptive research data has to do with the sexual practices of African American men and women in childhood, adolescence and adulthood. In addition to behavioral data, including the age at which the behavior was engaged in and the frequency of its occurrence, reasons for engaging or not engaging in certain behaviors can be a valuable contribution towards understanding the decisions that individuals make regarding their sexual practices. Positive and negative feelings about engaging in a sexual behavior can add still another dimension to understanding sexual practices and their effect upon the individual. Sometimes guilt about engaging in a behavior can outweigh the satisfaction derived, but not affect the decision to continue to engage in it. However, feelings of shame and guilt can prevent open discussions of strategies to prevent health related risks.

The circumstances around certain behaviors that are significant to the onset of sexual activity are also useful. What was the situation in which sexual behavior was engaged in? This is particularly important for the experience of first intercourse. For example, when women were asked to describe their first intercourse experience, it became apparent that two-thirds of African Americans reported that it occurred in the home of the subject or the home of the partner. On one hand, while coitus in a familiar environment may be more comfortable, on the other hand, anxiety about being discovered can increase feelings of guilt and even result in sexual problems.

A critical aspect of obtaining information around the circumstances of sexual activity is to inquire as to whether the subject, male or female, engaged in the behavior voluntarily or was coerced into it. Of the 245 African American and European American women interviewed in the recent Wyatt study, 20 women reported that their first experience with intercourse was as a result of sexual abuse, 13 of whom were forcibly raped and 7 of whom had intercourse at age 14 or younger with a much older partner. This serves as an example of the situation wherein, if questions are not asked to identify and separate voluntary from coercive sexual experiences, a subject could be describing a rape encounter in response to a general question about first intercourse (Wyatt, 1987). Optimally, the circumstances around voluntary sexual experiences should be discerned, as well as those that are a result of sexual abuse. Both may have an impact upon the victim's attitudes about sex and the sexual behaviors engaged in after that first experience (Wyatt, 1997).

Included in the set of questions about sexual practices should be questions about behaviors engaged in with someone of the same sex. Far too often it is assumed that because homosexuality tends not to be condoned in the African American community (Wyatt, 1982c), the focus of ethnic specific research includes heterosexual contacts only. The increase in the incidence of AIDS in the African American community strongly suggests that sexual contact is not exclusively heterosexual. However, sexual orientation does not explain sexual practices. It is most critical to assess with whom an individual has sex regardless of gender, as well as the sexual practices engaged in.

The consequences of sexual activity, specifically the use of contraceptives or reasons for their non-use, the responsibility of both partners in dealing with a pregnancy, issues around abortion utilization, the number of abortions and unintended pregnacies, female participants have had and the reasons for them provide additional and much needed information regarding sexual attitudes, behaviors and childbearing patterns of African Americans.

Finally, all of this information should be obtained within an African American cultural context, and the development of the interview or questionnaire utilized should be constructed while taking language (sexual terms used in speaking dialect versus standard English) and literacy into consideration. There is also a need to define body parts as well as sexual behaviors mentioned during the interview process. In the Wyatt study, a variety of terms were used by participants to identify body parts and sexual practices, and the lesser educated African American women were frequently unaware of scientific or anatomical labels.

Under the best of circumstances, face to face interviewing, conducted by an experienced interviewer whose ethnicity and sex are matched with that of the respondent, allows for discussion and clarification about the definition of terms used, feelings of discomfort or embarrassment, and resistance to discuss certain experiences or issues around the confidentiality of material obtained in sex research (Wyatt & Peters, 1986; Wyatt, 1990).

Focus group discussions with participants representing the target group of intent help to identify issues that should be studied and barriers to change. Pilot testing of potential items is also a useful approach to insure clarity of information desired and provides an opportunity to observe how the questioning process in such a sensitive area as sexuality is being perceived by the individual. This is especially vital to research which includes African American males, who are less often respondents of sex research (Wyatt, Myers, Ashing-Guva, & Duwasula, in press). The areas of research that should be included in studies with men will most likely need to be broadened to assess more accurately their sexual socialization experiences, and range of experiences (involving being in prison and on recreational drugs). Focus group discussions and pilot testing can facilitate this process.

Summary and Conclusion

Several factors, including the preponderance of sexual stereotypes regarding the sexual practices of people of African descent, confusion with the terms identifying the ethnicity of the samples, methodological limitations including biased or unrepresentative samples in studies that have included African American populations, and funding limitations that place increasingly less emphasis upon the kind of research which might clarify or improve upon research that has been conducted, have contributed to why we know so little about African American sexuality. And yet, health problems related to early pregnancy and childbearing, psychological problems that African American women encounter, and stressors in male-female relationships that may be related to sexual practices and the consequences of sexual decisions have been identified as areas of concern to researchers and social policymakers (Brunswick 1971; Castadot, 1975; Delcampo, Sporakowski & Delcampo; Dupuy, 1980; Furstenberg, 1979; Johnson, 1974; Kantner & Zelnik, 1972; Liben, 1969; Ralph, 1981; Youth Values Project, 1978). However, the relationship between sexual activity and psychological problems has not been established well enough to call attention to sex research as a national concern and a funding priority. Sexual education, activity and their relationship to the spread of sexually transmitted diseases underlying HIV has brought more attention to this field than it has ever had. Some people, however, equate the volumes of work conducted on persons at risk with AIDS as studies of African American sexuality. This is a problem oriented approach that does not examine a full range of sexual experiences or the context in which they occurred.

If we are to better understand how to prevent psychological and physical health problems, adequate sex research needs to be conducted with African American men and women of all ages and life experiences, beginning with child populations. There are a few researchers who have worked to fill the information gap about African American sexuality including (Butts, 1981; Ladner, 1971; Staples, 1973; Washington, 1981; and Wyatt, 1982a & b, 1985, 1986, 1987, 1990, 1997) among others, but the most damaging factor influencing why we know so little is in the funding of this research, the pathology oriented focus that the research assumes, the samples obtained and the lack of sociocultural focus. As long as research is federally supported, with these problems cited above, limitations in the knowledge base regarding African American sexuality will be apparent until another sexually related health problem emerges. The interest in human sexuality needs to be broadened to substantive levels of information that is specific to health as well as risks for disease.

This chapter is being submitted at a time when increasing numbers of professionals are seeking knowledge and training in the field of human sexuality, pregnancy, STD and HIV prevention. As the review of the literature demonstrates, there is very little accurate information available regarding the sociocultural factors that may differentially affect sexuality and sexual dysfunctions in African American and even European American populations.

Hopefully, the reader of this chapter has become more aware that we do not have adequate information about African American sexuality because of very specific and not coincidental nor mysterious reasons. The reasons for this scarcity of information have to do with a reliance upon stereotypes of sexual behaviors, and not having nearly enough rigorous, empirical documentation of sexual education, attitudes and practices of African American men and women, the factors that contribute to them, and the effects of trauma such as sexual abuse upon sexual behavior, physical and psychological well-being that influence sexual decision making. More research is forthcoming, but the current problem is that research isn't being generated quickly enough to offset the stereotypes, misinformation and ignorance that abounds when the topic of African American sexuality emerges.

References

Amir, M. (1971). *Patterns in forcible rape.* Chicago: University of Chicago: University of Chicago Press.

Baron, D., & Bryne, D. (1977). *Social psychology: Understanding human interaction.* Boston: Allyn & Bacon.

Bell, A. (1971). Black sexuality: Fact and Fancy. In Robert Staples (Ed.), *The Black family.* Blemont: Wadsworth Publishing Co.

Bernard, J. (1966). Marital stability and patterns of status variables. *Journal of Marriage and the Family, 28,* 421-439.

Brunswick, A. (1971). Adolescent health, sex and fertility. *American Journal of Public Health, 61,* 711-729.

Bureau of the Census. (1980). *Statistical abstracts of the United States.* Washington, D.C.: U.S. Department of Commerce.

Butts, J.D. (1981). Adolescent Sexuality and Teenage Pregnancy from a Black Perspective. In T. Ooms (Ed.), *Teenage pregnancy in a family context: Implications for policy.* Philadelphia: Temple University Press.

Castadot, R.G. (1975). Need for, difficulties and experience with sexual behavior questionnaires among teenagers. *Maryland State Medical Journal, 24, (4),* 40-44.

Collins, B.E., & Ashmore, R.D. (1970). *Social psychology, social influences, attitude change, group processes and prejudice.* Reading, MA: Addison-Wesley Publishing Co.

Davis, G.L., & Cross, H.J. (1979). Sexual stereotyping of Black males in interracial sex. *Archives of Sexual Behavior, 8,* 169-279.

Delcampo, R., Sporakowski, M., & Delcampo, D. (1976). Premarital sexual permissiveness and contraceptive knowledge: A racial comparison of college students. *The Journal of Sex Research, 12,* 180-192.

DeRachewitz, B. (1964). *Black eros: Sexual customs of Africa from prehistory to the present day*. New York: Lyle Stuart.

Dow, G.S. ((1922). *Society and its problems*. New York: Crowell.

Dupuy, H.J. (1982). Self-representations of general psychological well-being. American Public Health Association, October 17, 1978, Los Angeles, California.

Ewer, P., & Gibbs, J. (1975). Relationship to punitative father and use of contraception in a population of Black ghetto adolescent mothers. *Public Health Reports, 90*, 417-423.

Furstenberg, F. (1979). *Divorce and separation—context, causes and consequences*. New York: Basic Books Inc.

Gebhard, P. H., Pomeroy, W.B., Martin, G.E., & Christenson, C.V. (1958). *Pregnancy, birth and abortion*. New York: Wiley and Sons.

Graves, W., & Bradshaw, B. (1975). Early reconception and contraception use among Black teenage girls after an illegitimate birth. *American Journal of Public Health, 65*, 738-740.

Grinspoon, L., & Bakalar, J.B. (1979). *Psychedelic drugs reconsidered*. New York: Basic Books.

Hindelang, M.J., & Davis, B.L. (1977). Forcible rape in the United States: A statistical profile. In D. Chappell, R. Geis & G. Geis (Eds.), *Forcible rape: The crime, the victim, and the offender*. New York: Columbia University Press.

Hohman, L.B., & Schaffer, B. (1947). The sex lives of unmarried men. *American Journal of Sociology, 53(6)*, 501-508.

Hunt, M. (1974). *Sexual behavior of the 1970's*. Chicago: Playboy Press.

Johnson, C.L. (1974). Adolescent pregnancy: Intervention into a poverty cycle. *Adolescence, 35*, 391-406.

Kantner, J.F., & Zelnik, M. (1972). Sexual experiences of young unmarried women in the United States. *Family Planning Perspectives, 4*, 9-18.

Kardiner, A., & Ovesey, L. (1951). *The mark of oppression*. Cleveland: World Publishing Co.

King, M. C. (1973). The politics of sexual stereotypes. *The Black Scholar, 4*, 12-23.

Kinsey, A., Pomeroy, W., Martin, C., & Gebhard, P. (1953). *Sexual behavior in the human female*. Philadelphia: W.B. Saunders Co.

Ladner, J. (1972). *Tomorrow's tomorrow*. New York: Doubleday and Co., Inc.

Leary, T. (1973). She comes in colors. In D. Solomon & G. Andrews (Eds.), *Drugs and sexuality*. Frogmore, St. Albans: Panther Books.

Liben, F. (1969). Minority group clinic patients pregnancy out of wedlock. *American Journal of Public Health, 59*, 1968-1981.

Masters, W., & Johnson, V. (1966). *Human sexual response*. Boston: Little, Brown and Co.

Maykovich, M. K. (1971). Changes in racial stereotypes among college students. *Human Relations, 24*, 371-386.

Michael, R.T., Fagnon, J.H., Laumann, E.O., & Kolata, G. (1994). *Sex in America*. New York: Little Brown & Co.

Miller, J., Moller, D., Kaufman, A., Divato, P., Pathak, D., & Christy, J,. (1978). Recidivism among sex assault victims. *American Journal of Psychiatry, 13(9)*, 103-104.

Myrdal, G. (1944). *An American dilemma*. New York: Harper and Row.

National Crime Panel Survey Report. (1975). *Criminal victimization surveys in the nations's five largest cities*. U.S. Department of Justice, Law Enforcement Assistance Administration, National Criminal Justice Information and Statistics Service. Washington, D.C.: U.S. Government Printing Office, April.

Nettleton, C.A. (1975). Dating patterns, sexual relationships and use of contraceptives of 700 unwed mothers during a two- year period following delivery. *Adolescence, 10*, 45-57.

Peters, J. J.(1976). Children who are victims of sexual assault and the psychology of offenders. *American Journal of Psychotherapy, 30*, 395-421.

Poussaint, A.(1974). Cheap thrills that degrade Blacks. *Psychology Today*, 22-33.

Powell, G., Wyatt, G., & Bass, B. (1983). Mental health professionals' views of African American family life and sexuality. *Journal of Sex and Marital Therapy, 9*, 51-66.

Rainwater, L. (1966). Some aspects of lower-class sexual behavior. *Journal of Social Issues, 22*, 96-108.

Ralph, J. (1981). Method issue: Black identity and mental health survey. *Newsletter of the APA/NIMH Fellows, 3(2)*, April-June.

Reiss, I.L. (1964). Premarital sexual permissiveness among Negroes and Whites. *American Sociological Review, 29*, 688-698.

Reiss, I.L. (1967). *The Social Context of Premarital Sexual Permissiveness*. Holt, Rinehardt, and Winston, New York.

Rolling Stones Records. (1978). *Some Girls*. New York: Warner Communications Company.

Shilts, R. (1988). *And the Band Played on*. New York: Penguine Books.

Spilka, B., Hood, R.W., & Gorsuch, R. L. (1985). Religion and morality. In B. Spilka, R. Hood & R. Gorsuch (Eds.), *The psychology of religion* (pp. 257-286). New Jersey: Prentice Hall.

Staples, R. (1973). *The Black woman in America*. Chicago: Nelson-Hall Publishers.

Staples, R. (1974). Is the sexual revolution bypassing Blacks? *Ebony*, 111-114.

Teele, J., Robinson, D., Schmidth, W., & Rice, E. (1967). Factors related to social work services for mothers of babies born out of wedlock. *American Journal of Public Health, 57*, 1300-1307.

Thomas, A., & Sillen, S. (1972). The sexual mystique, In A. Thomas and S. Sillen (Eds.), *Racism and psychiatry*. New York: Bruner-Mazel.

Thomas, W. H. (1910). *The American Negro: What he has, what he is and what he may become*. New York: MacMillan.

Tucker, M.B. (1984). Is African American studies research in jeopardy? A review of recent trends in federal research support. *CAAS Newsletter, 8*(2), 1, 8-12.

U.S. Bureau of the Census (1980). *America's Black population: 1970 to 1982. A Statistical view*. (Special Publication, Series plp/pop. 83). U.S. Government Printing Office, Washington, D.C. 20402.

Vontress, C. (1971). The Black male personality. *Black Scholar, 2*, 10-16.

Walker, E. (1976). The Black woman. In Mabel Smythe (Ed.), *The Black American Reference Book*. Englewood Cliffs: Prentice-Hall.

Washington, A.C. (1981). A cultural and historical perspective on pregnancy-related activity among U.S. teenagers. *The Journal of Black Psychology, 9(1)*, 1-28.

Wyatt, G.E. (1982a). Identifying stereotypes of African American sexuality and their impact upon sexual behavior. In B. Bass, G. Wyatt, & G. Powell. (Eds.), *The African American family: Assessment, treatment and research issues*. New York: Grune & Stratton.

Wyatt, G. E. (1982b). The sexual experience of African American women: A middle income sample. In Martha Kirkpatrick, M.D. (Ed.), *Women's sexual experience: Explorations of the dark continent*. New York: Plenum Press.

Wyatt, G.E. (1982c). Identifying stereotypes of Afro-American sexuality and their impact upon sexual behavior. In B. Bass, G. Wyatt & G. Powell (Eds.), *The Afro-American Family: Assessment, Treatment and Research Issues*. New York: Grune and Stratton.

Wyatt, G.E. (1985). The sexual abuse of Afro-American and White American women in childhood. *Child Abuse & Neglect, 9*, 507-519.

Wyatt, G.E. (1987). Factors affecting adolescent sexuality: Have they changed in 40 years? In J. Bancroft (Ed.), *Adolescence and Puberty*. Cambridge Press.

Wyatt, G.E. (1990). The aftermath of child sexual abuse of African American and White American women: The victim's experience. *Journal of Family Violence, 2*, 403-414.

Wyatt, G.E. (1991). Examining ethnicity versus race in AIDS related research. *Social Science and Medicine, 33(1)*, 37-45.

Wyatt, G.E. (1992). The sociocultural context of African American and White American women's rape. *Journal of Social Issues, 48(1)*, 77-91.

Wyatt, G.E. (1997). *Stolen women: Reclaiming our sexuality, taking back our lives*. New York: John Wiley & Sons Publications.

Wyatt, G.E., & Peters, S. D. (1986). Issues in the definition of child sexual abuse in prevalence research. *Child Abuse and Neglect, 10*, 231-240.

Wyatt, G.E., Lawrence, J., Vodounon, A., & Mickey, M.R. (1992). The Wyatt Sex History Questionnaire: A structured interview for sexual history taking. *Journal of Child Sexual Abuse.*

Wyatt, G.E., Forge, N., & Gutherie, D., (1998). Family constellation and ethnicity: Current and lifetime HIV related risk taking. *Journal of Family Psychology, 12(1),* 93-101.

Wyatt, G.E., Loeb, T.B., Romero, G., Solis, B., & Vargas-Carmona, J. (1999). The prevalence and circumstances of child sexual abuse: Changes across a decade. *Child Abuse and Neglect, 23 (1),* 45-60.

Wyatt, G.E., Myers, H.F., Ashing-Giwa, K., & Durvasula, R. (in press). Socio-cultural factors in sexual risk-taking among black men and women. In R. Staples (Ed.), *The Black family: Essays and studies* (6th ed.).

Yee, A., Fairchild, H., Weizman, F., & Wyatt, G.E. (1993). Addressing psychology's problems with race. *American Psychologist, 48(11),* 1132-1140.

Young, L.C. (1974). Are Black women taking care of business? *Essence,* May.

Youth Values Project. (1978). *The youth values report.* Kelpling Road, Brattlesboro, Vermont: The Experiment.

Author

Gail Elizabeth Wyatt, Ph.D
Neuropsychiatric Instisute, UCLA
760 Westwood Plaza
Los Angeles, CA 90024
Telephone: (310) 825-0193
Fax: (310) 206-9137
E-mail: gwyatt@npih.medsch.ucla.edu

Skin Tone and Racial Identity Among African Americans: A Theoretical and Research Framework

Kendrick T. Brown, Geoffrey K. Ward, Tiffany Lightbourn, and James S. Jackson

Introduction

A wide variety of factors have been shown to influence the quality of life for African Americans. Of these factors, skin tone is one of the most subtle, yet impactful. In the history of African American vernacular, slogans and rhymes have been used to express the linkages among skin tone and Black self- and group images. In the 1960's "Black is Beautiful" replaced the popular turn of the century rhyme, "If you're White you're alright, If you're yellow you're mellow, If you're brown stick around, If you're Black get back." In novels, magazine articles, and personal accounts, individuals of different complexions have expressed the pain, dejection, or guilt associated with unjustified treatment by others because of their skin tone. Despite the popular speculation about the influence which skin tone exerts on the life chances and social outcomes of Black people in the United States, surprisingly little systematic empirical research has been conducted to explore fully the specific mechanisms by which individuals are affected.

This chapter reviews empirical research on the psychological, social, and material importance of skin tone in the lives of African Americans. Following this review, the possible relationships between skin tone and dimensions of racial identity are explored. Finally, critical new directions for research on skin tone and racial identity, as well as other significant psychological aspects of African American life are discussed.

Historically, much of the social and psychological literature on Black Americans directly or indirectly has concerned issues of group identification and consciousness (Jackson, McCullough & Gurin, 1987; Sellers et al., 1998). This interest in group identity derives from the low power minority status of Blacks in this society. In any group experiencing long-term discrimination, a central issue is how individual members relate behaviorally, psychologically, and socially to the group, to its history of discrimination, and, in the case of African Americans, to the active collective struggle to overcome a racist system. Furthermore, how African Americans deal with their low status and relatively low collective power, material, and political circumstances has been viewed as critical determinants of their general social and psychological functioning.

Researchers have focused largely on the pathological consequences of discrimination or the strength of coping in the face of unequal treatment. But all have agreed on the central significance of this psychological relationship to the group — the individual's feelings of attachment, warmth, psychological dependence and behaviors toward cognitive representations of the group. As we discuss in this chapter, we believe that one important historical and contemporary mediating factor in group identity is the physical reality of, as well as individual and in- and out-group reactions to, the varying skin tones of African Americans.

Review of Empirical Studies of Skin Tone

Research on the influence of skin tone can be placed in five major categories: (1) preference for a specific skin tone; (2) stereotyping; (3) social and psychological functioning; (4) mate selection; (5) and resource attainment.

Preferences For Specific Skin Tone

Table 1 presents an overview of empirical studies which have assessed the preferences that African Americans may have for specific skin tones.

Some evidence suggests that an individual's preference for specific skin tone may be related to his or her own skin tone. Hall (1992) showed that light-skinned African American college students value lighter skin tones more so than dark-skinned individuals. Dark-complexioned students value darker skin tones to a greater extent than their lighter-skin counterparts. Similarly, Hamm, Williams and Dalhouse (1973) found subjects to be realistic in their choice of colors that most represented their own skin tones, regardless of the age group to which they belonged. In terms of picking their ideal skin tone, individuals whose skin tone was darker than the median chose darker ideal faces and those whose skin tone was lighter than the median picked lighter ideal faces.

Other studies have found a strong preference for lighter skin tones rather than a preference anchored by one's own skin tone. Bond and Cash (1992) designed a study to examine the relationships between skin color and body image among African American women. They found that when students were asked about their personal ideal skin color, most preferred lighter skin tones, except the dark-skinned women. This bias toward preferring lighter skin tones is also evident in research with children. Children have been shown to exhibit a preference to be lighter-skinned and rate themselves one step lighter on a color scale than interviewers

Table 1
Preference for Specific Skin Color

Study	Sample	Finding(s)
Hall (1992)	83 Black 1st. year college students (33 men and 50 women)	—Self-reported light skinned students valued lighter skin tones more highly, relative to dark-skinned students.
Bond & Cash (1992)	66 Black undergraduate women	—Lighter personal ideals of skin color for sample, except for dark-skinned women.
Seeman (1946)	81 children in 3 all-Black classes (2 - 3rd & 4th grade, 1 - 5th & 6th grade)	—Closer friendship ties (higher acceptability levels) reported by subject for Light Brown and Very Light Brown children in the class.
Porter (1991)	98 self-identified Black American children ages 6-13 years	—Least preferred skin tones were Very Dark Brown and Dark Brown. —Most preferred skin tones were Honey Brown and Very Light Yellow.
Hamm, Williams & Dalhause (1973)	24 Black men age 15-25, 35-45, and 55-65 years	—Those darker than median chose darker real and ideal faces than subjects rated lighter than median.
Goering (1971)	177 Black high school students in 1950; 218 Black high school students in 1970 (same high school)	—From 1950 to 1970, greater acceptance of dark-skinned Blacks as close friends and club members. —Majority of subjects prefer Brown skin color.

(Seeman, 1946), express greater willingness to accept Light Brown and Very Light Brown classmates as close friends (Seeman, 1946), and select Very Dark Brown and Dark Brown as the least preferred and Honey Brown and Light Yellow as the most preferred skin tones in response to a vignette concerning a child unhappy about his or her own skin tone (Porter, 1991). In addition, there has been a long line of research on doll preferences (Clark & Clark, 1946; Cross, 1991 for a review) which suggests that preference exists among young Black children for lighter skin. We will not review that voluminous literature here. The general findings, however, are consistent with other findings (e.g., Porter, 1991).

Finally, one study explored the possible age-related effects associated with skin tone preferences by examining a sample of Black high school students from the 1950's and a second group of students from the 1970's (Goering, 1971). Compared to the 1950 sample, being dark-skinned functioned as less of an impediment in social situations, as evidenced by the increased willingness by the 1970's youth to have dark-skinned close friends, club members, and intimate social relationships.

Also in the 1950 sample, a dark skin tone was least preferred while for the 1970 students being White was least preferred. However in both samples, being a brown tone is almost always preferred to being dark-skinned.

In sum, these studies illustrate interesting twists in the skin tone preference paradigm. While it might be assumed that in general Blacks prefer lighter skin tones, the studies in Table 1 show that these preferences may be mediated by one's own skin tone, the characteristics of the age cohort to which one belongs, and the dominant skin tone ideologies of the period in which an individual lives. Over time the value attached to being light or dark-skinned has changed and it seems that while skin color preferences per se have not diminished, the content of the preferences may vary depending on the historical time period, cohort and skin tone of individuals.

Stereotyping

Referring to the functions of skin color in American society, Russell, Wilson, and Hall (1992) posit that "beneath a surface appearance of Black solidarity lies a matrix of attitudes about skin color and features in which color, not character, establishes friendships; degree of lightness, not expertise, influences hiring; and complexion, not talent, dictates casting for television and film." Skin tone, both immediately obvious and relatively stable as a characteristic, has been used by White and Black Americans alike to stereotype and discriminate against African Americans who fall on different ends of the color spectrum. By stereotyping we are referring to a cognitive representation of a social group (i.e. light or dark-skinned Blacks) by associating particular characteristics, attributes, or emotions with that group. These representations can be overgeneralized, inaccurate, and resistant to new information. Table 2 summarizes the results of studies that have investigated skin tone and stereotyping.

Generally, light-skinned individuals have been associated with positive, favorable characteristics, while darker skin tone is more likely to be linked to derogatory attributes. Marks (1943) found strong correlations between an individual's skin tone rating of a fellow classmate and ratings of the classmate's personal charm and attractiveness. Classmates who were lighter than average, but not at the extreme light end of the color spectrum, were regarded as the most attractive and charming. A similar finding exists for grade-school children as well. Favorable reputational items from the Ohio Recognition Scale are disproportionately directed toward lighter classmates. The unfavorable scale items are more likely to be attributed to darker classmates (Seeman, 1946). Stereotyping based on skin tone may be influenced by the perceiver's gender, especially for traits associated with physical attractiveness (Marks, 1943).

Table 2
Stereotyping

Study	Sample	Finding(s)
Marks (1943)	3 groups of Black college students (2 - undergraduate; 1 - graduate)	—For each group high correlation between light skin tone and personal charm (attractiveness) —For male subjects rating female targets correlation between skin tone and personal charm was twice as strong as female subjects rating male targets.
Seeman (1946)	81 children in 3 all-Black classes (2 - 3rd & 4th grade; 1 - 5th & 6th grade)	—For 2 of 3 classes, significant relationships between interviewer skin color rating and reputational items. Favorable items directed toward lighter classmates; unfavorable items assigned to darker classmates.
Anderson & Cromwell (1977)	350 Black adolescents (7th to senior high school)	—12 positive stereotypical attributes had normal-like distributions with skew toward Light Brown chosen more than Dark Brown. —2 positive stereotypical attributes had normal-like distributions with skew toward Dark Brown. —11 negative stereotypical attributes had bipolar distributions with Black chosen more than Light. —2 negative traits had bipolar distributions with Light chosen more than Black.
Hamm, Williams, & Dalhouse (1973)	24 Black males age 15-25, 35-45, and 55-65 years	—Young (15-25) subjects attributed significantly more positive behavioral attitude to dark skin than subjects in both the intermediate (35-45) and older (55-65) groups.

Work has been done examining the content and valence of stereotypes associated with dark- and light-skinned Blacks. Anderson and Cromwell (1977) focus more specifically on the types of positive and negative stereotypical attributes that are associated with each skin tone group. For items that gauged positive characteristics, overall there was a normal-like distribution favoring the middle skin tone groups with a skew toward Light Brown being chosen more than Dark Brown. Among the positive items that had a skewed distribution, Light Brown skin was chosen more often as being associated with the person in class who was the smartest, the cleanest, the nicest, the one best liked to marry, the one who had the prettiest skin, and the one whose skin color they would prefer to have. Of the items that gauged negative characteristics, having Black skin tone was more often associated with being the dumbest, the dirtiest, the person one would not like to marry, the person with bad hair, and the person with the ugliest skin complexion, than being light-skinned.

Stereotyping of light- and dark-skinned people can vary depending on situational contexts and the age of the individual making the associations. In a convenience sample of Black men aged 15 years to 65 years, Hamm et al. (1973) found that the men did not favor light or dark skin faces as being most beautiful. When asked to chose between a wide spectrum of people in five different situations, however, the respondents were more likely to attribute positive behavioral characteristics to dark-skinned individuals as potential persons to invite to a party, and were least likely to favor dark-skinned individuals as persons who could be successful in business and take care of their property and homes. Also, regardless of the setting, young subjects (15-25 years of age) attributed significantly more positive behavioral attitudes to dark-skinned subjects than older subjects (35 years of age and older).

In sum, what these studies suggest is that when a person has categorized a person as light or dark-skinned these categories develop stereotypical meanings. Light skin tone is generally associated with positive attributes and traits, while dark skin tone is linked to negative characteristics. This general tendency is influenced by the situation in which an individual is being judged and the age-related characteristics of the person making the judgments.

Social and Psychological Functioning

Research addressing the effect of skin tone on African American's social and psychological functioning is scant. Most of the work in this area consists of individual case studies or focus groups (Boyd-Franklin, 1991; Harvey, 1995; Neal & Wilson, 1989; Okazawa-Rey et al., 1987). These studies, combined with the experiments and surveys in Table 3, reveal that a relationship exists between skin tone and factors related to social and psychological functioning.

Three of the studies pertain to social functioning. Dark skin tone has been associated with increased willingness to make sacrifices to get ahead at work for men married less than 6 years (Udry et al., 1969) and weakly linked to feeling powerless to effect change in the political or social environment (Ransford, 1970). Also, individuals rated as Very Dark are least likely to feel that they are competent to affect their college environment or have feelings of mastery over one's self and the environment in general (Holtzman, 1973). These last results, however, are difficult to interpret because only individuals responding favorably to the three highest points of the political efficacy and competence scales were included in the analyses.

Table 3
Social and Psychological Functioning

Study	Sample	Finding(s)
Bond & Cash (1992)	66 Black undergraduate women	—No significant differences by skin color for affective evaluation of overall appearance, facial satisfaction, or skin color satisfaction. —The more discrepancy between self and ideal skin color rating, the less facial satisfaction, but not global appearance evaluation. —Desire to change skin color and dissatisfaction with skin color led to more negative evaluations of overall appearance and lower facial satisfaction.
Udry, Bauman, & Chase (1969)	350 Black married couples	—For married men less than 6 years, dark skin color was associated with increased job mobility orientation.
Ransford (1970)	312 Black male heads of household	—Weak correlation between skin color and powerlessness (having dark skin color contributed to feeling of powerlessness to effect change).
Holtzman (1973)	144 Black students	—Medium-skinned respondents had highest percentage feeling highly competent. Very Dark-skinned people had the lowest percentage, followed closely by Very Light people. —Medium respondents scored highest for High political efficacy. Very light individuals had the lowest percentage, followed by Very Dark people.

Few experiments or surveys have empirically investigated psychological functioning. Bond & Cash (1992) explored how skin tone may affect body image. They did not find differences by skin tone group for evaluations of overall appearance, facial satisfaction, or skin color satisfaction. Discrepancies between how women rate their skin tone and what tone they choose as ideal, however, are associated with less satisfaction with the facial region. Also, if individuals express both a desire to change skin tone and dissatisfaction with their skin tone, they score more negatively for overall appearance and the facial region. Robinson and Ward (1995) investigated the relationship between skin tone satisfaction and self-esteem. Their sample of Black adolescents demonstrated a high correlation between a portion of the Rosenberg Self-Esteem Scale and agreement with the statement "I like my skin color," but no relationships were found between desire to change one's skin tone and self-esteem.

At present the largest body of evidence for the effects of skin tone on African American's psychological functioning comes from personal therapy and focus groups accounts. In such settings, clients speak of the difficulties that they face both outside of, and within, the Black community because of the shades of their skin color. Such difficulties include low self-esteem induced by derogatory comments about physical attractiveness (Neal & Wilson, 1989; Okazawa-Rey et al., 1987; Boyd-Franklin, 1991; Russell et al., 1992), guilt and shame from having to defend one's parentage as being legitimate (Neal & Wilson, 1989; Russell et al., 1992), and reduced personal efficacy due to scapegoating by family members with different skin tones (Russell et al., 1992). Even given these poignant accounts, more research using larger samples of non-therapy populations needs to be completed before definitive statements can be made regarding the effects of skin tone on psychological and social functioning.

Mate Selection

Several studies within the skin tone literature have focused on marriage and, more specifically, mate selection trends, as indicators of skin tone's salience and effects on the lives of African Americans.

In a 1904 newsletter, Nannie H. Burroughs bitterly illuminated a trend that contemporary studies continue to validate, when she wrote, "some Black men would marry the most debased woman, whose only stock in trade is her color, in preference to the most royal queen in ebony" (Gatewood, 1990, p. 154). In *Black Metropolis*, Drake and Cayton (1945) suggested that a darker complexion constituted both a social and economic handicap for women in particular as, "successful Negro men put a premium on marrying a woman who is not Black or very dark-brown" (pp. 498-499). Furthermore, these authors found that some Chicagoland employers maintained policies of "hiring only real light girls with good hair...because they make a good appearance [and] a dark girl has no [customer] drawing power" (Drake & Cayton, 1945, pp. 498-499). As these observations suggest, skin tone's significance among African Americans is not merely its relation to attractiveness ratings and hence, mate selection practices, but indirectly and complexly associated with several resource outcomes vis-à-vis an upwardly mobile spouse, an employment opportunity, or another attainment process. While resource attainment outcomes will be discussed more comprehensively in the next section, it is important to note that research has consistently found mate selection to be a powerful mediating process, in this regard, for African American women and men. Table 4 summarizes the studies that have explored the connection between skin tone and mate selection.

Table 4
Mate Selection

Study	Sample	Finding(s)
Bond & Cash (1992)	66 Black undergraduate women	—Regardless of skin color, most believed that Black men preferred lighter-skinned women. —Lighter the color that subjects assumed men preferred, the lighter they viewed themselves relative to judges' ratings.
Udry, Bauman & Chase (1969)	350 Black married couples	—For men married less than 6 years, significant positive correlation between dark skin color and wife's education. —Dark-skinned women were less likely to have upwardly mobile husbands, regardless of duration of marriage. —For those married 6 or more years, light husbands overselected light wives and underselected medium and dark women.
Freeman, Ross, Armor, & Pettigrew (1966)	250 wives of Black middle-class families	—Husbands in white collar occupations were more likely to marry light-colored wives. —Husbands in blue-collar occupations were more likely to have lighter wife if she was from a blue-collar family. —Husbands in blue-collar occupations had a greater chance of marrying a woman from white collar family if he was lighter.
Porter (1991)	98 self-identified Black children	—Girls chose Honey Brown (44%), Medium Brown (22%), and Very Light Brown (20%) as skin tone that boy in a vignette would want as his own. —Boys chose Very Light Brown (38%), Honey Brown (31%), and Medium Brown (8%) as skin tone that the girl in a vignette would want as her own.
Hughes & Hertel (1990)	1979-80 National Survey of Black Americans (N=2107)	—Controlling for age, gender, education, occupational prestige, and parents' SES, lighter-skinned Blacks had spouses with more education and higher occupational prestige.

Several studies have found relationships between an individual's skin tone and the characteristics and resources possessed by the individual's spouse. Freeman, et al. (1966) found that husbands in blue-collar occupations were more likely to marry a woman from a white-collar family if they were lighter in complexion than the woman. This study also reported an association between light-skinned wives and dark-skinned husbands of higher socio-economic status. Furthermore, they suggested that this relationship between wife's skin tone and husband's socio-economic status did not vary by age of the couple and had not changed significantly over time. In a similar study, Udry et. al.(1969) interviewed 350 married couples in the District of Columbia and controlled for potential period effects by constructing a years-of-marriage cohort variable. As the "Black Power" movement thrived in the late 60's and 70's, social researchers anticipated that dark-skin would cease to be as significant a "handicap" in the lives of Black women. Yet, while educational disadvantage had decreased for darker Black women and their spouses in more recent cohorts, women with dark complexions remained least likely to have upwardly mobile husbands, regardless of when they had married. On the other hand, for those men married less than six years, there was a significant positive correlation between husband's dark skin tone and wife's education. For men married six or more years, significant negative correlations between their darker skin tone, wife's education, and family income were found. While perhaps exaggerating the shift, a Black male respondent in this study anticipated later empirical findings when he offered the observation that, "my Black skin has great value among Negroes today...I remember a time when being as Black as I am did not have much value, but today it is different" (Udry et al., 1971, p. 724). Hughes and Hertel's (1990) study of data from the 1979-80 National Study of Black Americans, one of few national, non-regional skin tone studies, frames this claim of changing skin tone values in its larger context. These authors report that controlling for age, gender, education, occupational prestige, and parental socio-economic status factors, respondents with lighter skin continue to have spouses with more education and higher occupational prestige.

Other mate selection studies have focused more broadly on the relationship between skin tone and perceptions of desireability and attractiveness. Experiments conducted by Porter (1991) not only support earlier findings that children develop skin tone preferences during identity formation, but also suggest that attitude development is associated with gender and age. When children ages 6-13 were presented with a vignette that asked what is the best skin-tone to have, 85% of all boys sampled felt that medium or lighter skin was most preferred, while 100% of girls in the sample said the same. Further, as age cohort increased, children developed more elaborate impressions of skin tone as a potential desirability resource or handicap. Porter explains, "reasons stated by children of 9-11 years were primarily clustered in the category of desire for sameness (e.g. "other children are that color and he feels left out"). Older children, those 12-13 years of age, gave reasons for their skin tone preferences that not only invoked issues of physical attraction (e.g. "probably thinks she is ugly with that color,") but also the possibility that people are discriminated against on the basis of skin tone ("could get more jobs and people would talk to her more.") (Porter, 1991, p. 153). A recent study by Bond and Cash (1992) sampled 66 African American undergraduate females attending a southeastern, urban university to further examine perceptions of skin tone as a desirability factor and influence on mate selection. They found that, regardless of their own skin tone, most of the female subjects believed African American men prefer women with lighter complexions. Also, through the use of an elaborate skin tone assessment procedure, these researchers observed that the lighter the skin tone subjects perceived men to prefer, the lighter these subjects viewed themselves relative to skin-tone appraisals from "judges" in the experiment.

Overall, these studies indicate that skin tone influences mate selection by helping to determine the characteristics and resources of one's spouse and shaping the traits deemed most desirable by members of the both genders. Age-related phenomena, such as the cohort to which an individual belongs and the period in which one makes selection decisions, may also be factors in the relationship. These studies, however, do not address how skin tone may influence mate selection in non-heterosexual relationships or marriages.

Resource Attainment

During the antebellum period, free Blacks were more likely to be light-skinned than dark and those lighter-skinned Blacks who were enslaved often received more social privileges and better working conditions relative to their darker peers (Reuter, 1918). E. Franklin Frazier (1957) has written that in 1860, the free mulatto class of Blacks in New Orleans, known affectionately as "gens of color," owned real estate and slaves valued between ten and fifteen million dollars. By virtue of their family ties to White fathers, many (though hardly all), lighter African Americans had an advantage over others in obtaining access to education, trade-skills, property, and social support. Frazier observed that as, "the majority of prominent Negroes, who were themselves mulattos, married mulattos," familial resources were transferred to successive generations of lighter African Americans (Frazier, 1957, pp. 32-33). More recent data suggest, however, that several variables, in addition to socio-economic background, significantly predict income, educational, and occupational status outcomes for Black women and men across skin complexion categories. Table 5 provides an overview of these data.

Based on a 1965 study of 312 Black male heads of households between ages 18 and 65 living in Los Angeles, Ransford (1970) found significant relationships between skin tone, education, occupational status, and employment. Even when educational attainment was considered, lighter respondents were more likely to be in white-collar positions and higher income categories than those of darker skin. Among high school graduates, skin tone was predictive of blue collar vs. white collar occupational status but was not significantly related to employment status. Dark high school graduates (33%), however, were nearly four times more likely to be underemployed (less than $5,000/year in 1964) than were their light counterparts (9%). Finally, dark respondents were almost three times more likely to be unemployed than light respondents when neither completed high school.

Other studies support Ransford's findings that dark-skinned African Americans are disadvantaged relative to lighter-complexioned people for resource attainment. Edwards' (1973) analysis, conducted with data from a 1968 racial attitude survey administered in 15 American cities, reportedly found dark respondents to be more likely to live in low income census tracts than lighter respondents. Conversely, lighter African Americans were more likely to have attended college and hold white-collar occupations than their darker counterparts. Differences among these results are not completely clear because of inadequate statistical analyses. Nonetheless, other studies report similar findings, including an unpublished study (Walker and Karas, 1994). In their analyses, Walker and Karas measured effects of skin tone (Dark vs. Not Dark) and age cohort (under 25 in 1965 vs. 25 or older in 1965) on income, occupational, and educational attainment. In the case of each "resource attainment" dependent variable, dark skin tone corresponded with relative disadvantages. For the elder age cohort, more than 90% of the zero-order correlation between skin tone and income was mediated through status attainment processes. In the younger cohort, approximately one-third of this correlation was mediated through the same processes. While "dark" respondents in the elder cohort had lower occupational prestige scores than those with lighter skin tones, the effects of skin tone on occupational attainment were not significant for the younger cohort. These findings are confounded further by the observation that skin color had no appreciable effect on educational attainment in the elder cohort, yet, among younger respondents, "dark" respondents completed significantly fewer years of schooling than did those with lighter skin. Clouding the picture, two subsequent studies of skin color and resource attainment used alternative analytical models in this same dataset and obtained contradictory results.

Hughes and Hertel (1990) used interviewer-reported skin tone in five categories ranging from "very dark" to "very light", unlike Walker and Karas (1994) who had dichotomized this measure. Similar to Walker and Karas (1994), Hughes and Hertel reported that light skin tone was significantly and positively correlated with education, occupational prestige, personal income, and family income. Furthermore, they corroborated the finding that these relationships were not diminished by the introduction of controls for gender, age in years, and parental socio-economic status. In opposition to earlier findings, however, Hughes and Hertel reported that for younger respondents the effect of skin tone on education was negligible, yet

Table 5
Resource Attainment

Study	Sample	Finding(s)
Keith & Herring (1991)	1979-80 National Survey of Black Americans (N=2107)	—Each increment of interviewer skin color rating corresponds to about1/2 an additional year of education. On average, Very Light respondents attain more than 2 additional years of education than Very Dark respondents. —Very Light respondents most likely to be employed as professionals and technical workers. Very Dark people most likely to be laborers. —Family incomes of Very Light respondents more than 50% greater than those of Very Dark respondents. —Personal incomes Very Light respondents almost 65% higher than those of Very Dark respondents.
Edwards (1973)	2809 Blacks in 15 American cities	—Greater proportions of interviewer-rated lighter Blacks attended college, in upper-income categories, white-collar occupations, and from families where parents are better-educated. —Dark respondents more likely to live in low-income tracts.
Ransford (1970)	312 Black male heads of household	—Controlling for education, interviewer-rated Light respondents have white-collar positions and higher income categories than those darker (particularly true for those with education less than college graduation.) —Dark respondents were almost 3 times more likely to be unemployed than Light respondents. —Dark high school graduates were almost 4 times more likely to be underemployed than Light counterparts.
Walker & Karas (1994)	1979-80 National Survey of Black Americans (N=812: All persons either working or laid off/complete data)	—Interviewer-rated Dark Blacks completed fewer years of schooling, worked in lower-prestige occupations, and earned less than lighter Blacks. —For elder cohort (25 or older in 1965), no relationship between skin color and educational attainments. For younger cohort (less than 25 in 1965), Dark Blacks completed significantly fewer years of schooling than those with lighter skin. —For elder cohort, Dark Blacks have lower occupational attainments than those with lighter skin tones. For the younger cohort, skin color did not have a significant effect on occupational attainments.
Hughes & Hertel (1990)	1979-80 National Survey of Black Americans (N=2107)	—Skin color has significant relationships with education, occupational prestige, personal income, and family income, even controlling for gender, age in years, and parents SES. Lighter-skinned individuals were higher for each indicator. —For young people, effect of skin color on education was negligible but increased with age, so that older people with lighter skin have more education. —For education and occupation, skin color differences, comparing dark to light, were nearly identical to race differences, comparing Black to White.

increased with age such that lighter skin, among older respondents, was associated with higher levels of educational attainment. Hertel and Hughes (1990) also made the striking observation that, in terms of educational and occupational attainment levels, skin tone group differences, comparing "dark" to "light," are nearly identical to racial group differences between Blacks and Whites in this country.

Using a similar five-level categorical skin tone variable and 1979-80 NSBA data, Keith and Herring (1991) obtain further evidence of light-skin privilege and dark-skin disadvantage with respect to Black women in particular. Their analyses indicate that very-light respondents attain, on average, more than two additional years of education than dark respondents; each unit of lighter skin tone corresponds to approximately one-half of an additional year of education. In terms of occupational attainment, Keith and Herring (1991) found very-light respondents more likely to be employed as professional and technical workers than people with darker complexions. The "very-dark" respondents were most likely of all complexion categories to be employed as laborers. Mean family income for very light respondents was more than fifty percent greater than that for the very dark group and personal income levels were nearly sixty-five percent higher for very-light respondents. Tests of statistical significance revealed, however, that skin tone is only a marginal predictor of personal income for women and men. More significantly, Keith and Herring report that only in the case of Black women was skin tone a statistically significant stratifying agent for education, occupation, and family income.

These studies of skin tone and resource attainment compose the core of empirical work on such questions to date. While the analytical models and results of successive studies reveal the promise and significance of this research endeavor, they also reveal a need for further model specification and perhaps new approaches that consider the relationship between skin tone and important socio-economic indicators. While it is clear that between 1950 and 1980 notable shifts in skin tone and resource attainment relationships occurred to the advantage of Black men, it is also true that Black women continue to bear the brunt of dark-skin stigmatization in both the social (i.e. attractiveness perceptions) and economic (i.e. family income) arenas.

Racial Identity

To this point, we have reviewed empirical studies involving the effects of skin tone on various aspects of African Americans' lives. In addition to research on preferences for specific skin tones, stereotyping, psychological and social functioning, mate selection, and resource attainment, empirical work also has been done concerning racial identity. Before discussing these studies, a brief explanation of our conceptualization of racial identity is necessary.

Racial identity has been defined in many ways by numerous authors depending upon which aspect of identity was pertinent for their investigation. For our review of the studies concerning the direct influence of skin tone on racial identity, we have chosen to employ the Multidimensional Model of Racial Identity, or MMRI (Sellers et al., 1996), as an organizational framework. The MMRI specifies four dimensions which shape how African Americans will express their identity: racial salience, racial centrality, regard, and ideology. Racial salience is the relevance of the identity to the individual. Salience is both subject to environmental influences capable of temporarily heightening or lowering relevance (situational) and more enduring individual differences (chronic). Racial centrality refers to the hierarchical ordering of the constellation of identities applicable to the individual. The regard dimension encompasses the views held about African Americans as a group. Regard consists of how the individual sees African Americans (private) and how other ethnic or racial groups are believed to view African Americans (public). The final dimension, ideology, refers to how individuals believe African Americans should act in various domains, particularly political/economic development, cultural/social activities, inter-group relations, and interaction with the dominant group (for more detailed explanation of each of the four dimensions and their domains, refer to Sellers et al., 1996).

Table 6 contains a summary of empirical studies that have been conducted explicitly to investigate the relationship between African Americans' skin tone and aspects of racial identity. Based on the MMRI, only the regard and ideology dimensions have been the focus of attention of the empirical studies; the salience and centrality dimensions have not been empirically researched.

Both aspects of regard, public and private, are related to an African American's skin tone. For public regard, dark-complexioned African Americans are likely to be more aware of racial discrimination from society in general (Edwards, 1973) and sense that White Americans are hostile toward Blacks (Edwards, 1973; Ransford, 1970; Freeman et al., 1966). These findings may be influenced by the individual's social class and amount of social contact with White Americans (Ransford, 1970).

The private domain of the regard dimension has a different relationship with African Americans' skin tone. Hughes & Hertel (1990) find a weak relationship between skin tone and an individual's self-rating of the closeness of his or her ideas and feelings to other Blacks. This relationship disappears when demographic factors such as age, gender, education, occupational prestige, and parents' socio-economic status are considered in addition to skin tone. These results are tempered, however, by a gender-skin tone interaction, which reveals that for women, but not for men, having a lighter skin tone is associated with lower closeness to other Blacks. A gender-age-skin tone interaction reveals that for young adult males, lighter skin tone is associated with greater closeness to other Blacks, but for older men, closeness scores are higher for those who are darker (Hughes & Hertel, 1990). On another measure of private regard, researchers found no relationship between skin tone and endorsement of stereotypical characteristics associated with Blacks as a group (Hughes & Hertel, 1990).

Finally, studies examining measures of the ideology dimension of the MMRI indicate that individuals rated as dark-complexioned show a greater willingness to shop in Black-owned shops, have children learn an African language, and participate in other separate institutions or practices than lighter African Americans (Edwards, 1973; Ransford, 1970), though these findings are influenced by social contact with Whites (Ransford, 1970). Another study combining elements from the political/ economic development, cultural/social activities, and interaction with dominant group domains of ideology into a separatism scale found a weak but significant relationship between endorsing separatist practices and skin tone that becomes non-significant when various demographic factors, like age, gender, and education, are also considered (Hughes & Hertel, 1990).

These findings provide a starting point for additional study. To date, empirical work involving more than two dimensions of racial identity has not been done. In particular, the salience and centrality dimensions have not been investigated. Also, the disparate samples employed in each study present a dilemma for specifying the link between African Americans' skin tone and racial identity. In only one of the reviewed studies (Hughes & Hertel, 1990) was a national representative sample of Blacks in the United States used. This introduces the possibility of bias due to regional and local differences and thus difficulty in generalizing to the African American population in this country.

Driven by concerns about the above limitations, we conducted a study using a national representative sample of African Americans (Jackson, Tucker & Gurin, 1987) to discern the relationship between skin tone and multiple measures of racial identity. We chose to examine each of the four theoretical dimensions specified by the MMRI and, when possible, the domains within each dimension. To this effect, we explored the relationships between skin tone and chronic salience, centrality, private and public regard, political/economic development ideology, cultural/ social interaction ideology, and ideology concerning interactions with the dominant group in society.

Findings on the Relationship between Skin Tone and Racial Identity

Data to explore the relationship between skin tone and theoretical components of the Multidimensional Model of Racial Identity came from the National Survey of Black Americans, NSBA, collected in 1979 and 1980. The NSBA is based upon a cross-section national probability sample of self-identified Black Americans over 18 years of age, who are United States citizens and living in non-institutionalized housing in the continental United States. Black interviewers conducted over two thousand interviews (N=2107) with an overall response rate of approximately 67%.

In the NSBA, we identified a set of variables which would serve to clarify the relationship between skin tone and racial identity when entered into the analyses. These control variables consisted of several demographic factors: the respondent's

Table 6
Racial Identity

Study	Sample	Finding(s)
Edwards (1973)	2809 Blacks in 15 American cities	—Interviewer-rated Dark Blacks showed a slightly greater consciousness of racial discrimination than those of lighter complexion. —Dark-complexion individuals sensed greater hostility on the part of Whites than those of lighter complexion. —Dark individuals demonstrated greater sense of Black pride or identification with Blackness.
Ransford (1970)	312 Black male heads of household	—Interviewer-rated Dark Blacks showed more hostility and endorsement of separatism than Light Blacks. Those relationships were weaker or non-existent for middle-class respondents.
Freeman, Ross, Armor & Pettigrew (1966)	250 wives of Black middle-class	—Skin color was associated with anti-White feelings. Dark-skinned Blacks were most likely to be anti-White.
Hughes & Hertel (1990)	1979-80 National Survey of Black Americans (N=2107)	—Weak but significant zero-order relationship between closeness to other Blacks and skin color rating. —Weak but significant zero-order relationship between separatism and skin color rating. —No relationship between skin color and racial self-esteem.

age in years, imputed family income for 1978, gender, and marital status, the number of years or grades of education completed by the respondent, and the region of the country in which the respondent was raised.

Near the end of the interview, interviewers assessed the shade of skin tone possessed by the respondent. Five possible categories could have been chosen to represent skin tone: Very Dark Brown, Dark Brown, Medium Brown, Light Brown (light-skinned), and Very Light Brown (very light-skinned).

In addition to skin tone, we chose nine measures to approximate the various domains contained within the four MMRI dimensions: Salience, Centrality, Regard — both Private and Public, and Ideology — Political/Economic development, Cultural/Social interaction, and Interaction with the dominant group. The exact wording of the questions for the four dimensions of racial identity are provided in

Table 7. Also contained in the chart are the range and response categories for each variable, as well as the coefficient Alpha in the case of the closeness (private regard) scale.

We used hierarchical analysis of covariance (ANCOVA) to test the relationship between skin tone and racial identity. For each dimension of racial identity, the demographic control variables were entered as covariates followed by skin tone. The results of these analyses are shown in Table 8.

Chronic Racial Salience

The results of the ANCOVA for our measure of the chronic racial salience dimension of the MMRI reveal that, controlling for education, age, family income, gender, region, and marital status, the five different skin tone groups do not differ significantly from one another in their likelihood to state that their chances in life depend more on Blacks as a group. Though there does seem to be pattern of lower likelihood to envision Black identity as being relevant for one's chances in life as skin tone goes from very dark to very light, we must conclude that this measure of chronic racial salience is not directly affected by one's skin tone.

Racial Centrality

When education, age, family income, gender, region, and marital status are entered as covariates, a marginally significant difference between the skin tone groups is observed for racial centrality. Though statistical tests to differentiate the groups from one another yielded no conclusive results, the group rated as Light Brown expresses the greatest likelihood of saying that being Black is most important to them. The groups rated as Very Dark, Dark, and Medium Brown are almost indistinguishable in their scores on this measure of centrality, while the Very Light Brown group is least likely to place being Black as higher in their hierarchy of identities.

Private Regard

The results of the analysis for the private domain of the regard dimension show that, even controlling for the demographic variables, a significant difference in the means of the skin tone groups can be observed. Individuals rated as possessing Dark Brown skin tones demonstrate the greatest closeness to the feelings and ideas of other Black people. It should be noted that though relative to other skin tone groups, the scores of Light and Very Light Brown individuals are the lowest, they still exhibit the overall tendency to rate one's self as being "very close" to the feelings and ideas of other Black people. Nevertheless, it is clear from the data that skin tone

Table 7
NSBA Questions Approximating MMRI Dimensions

MMRI Compent	NSBA Question	Response Range
Salience	Do your chances in life depend more on what happens to Black people as a group, or does it depend more on what you do yourself?	0=What R does 1=Black people as a group (or Both)
Centrality	Which would you say is more important to you — being Black or being American, or are both equally important to you?	0=Being American, Both, or Neither 1=Being Black
Private Regard	Now read this list of different kinds of Black people. For each one, indicate how close you feel to them in your ideas and feelings about things: Black people who are poor; religious church-going Black people; young Black people; middle-class Black people; working class Black people; older Black people; Black elected officials; and Black doctors, lawyers, and other Black professional people.	Cronbach's Alpha = .819 For each subgroup: 1=Not close at all 4=Very close To receive score for Closeness scale, respondent had to have answered 5 or more of the original items.
Public Regard	On the whole, do you think most White people want to see Blacks get a better break, or do they want to keep Blacks down or don't they care one way or the other?	0=Better break or Don't care 1=Keep Blacks down
Political Ideology	Blacks should always vote for Black candidates when they run.	1=Strongly disagree 4=Strongly agree
Economic Ideology	Black people should shop in Black-owned stores whenever possible.	1=Strongly disagree 4=Strongly agree
Cultural Ideology	Black children should study an African language.	1=Strongly disagree 4=Strongly agree
Ideology of Interaction with Dominant Group	Black women should not date White men. Black men should not date White women.	1=Strongly disagree 4=Strongly agree

influences our measure of private regard. This finding is both supported and contradicted by Hughes & Hertel's (1990) study in which they examined the relationship between skin tone and closeness. While the researchers found a significant negative zero-order relationship between skin tone and closeness, they also found that this relationship disappears when age, gender, education, occupational prestige, and parents' socio-economic status are entered as covariates. In our analyses, our covariates included age, gender, education, family income, marital status, and region. The difference in covariates employed in each study may account for the different analytical outcomes. The exact role that co-variates may play in influencing the tie between skin tone and closeness needs further investigation.

Public Regard

Different results are found for our measure of public regard. Here the analysis of variance indicates that when controlling for several demographic factors, there is no difference in the means of the skin tone groups. Though individuals in the Very Light Brown group show a much lower agreement with the view that Whites want to keep Blacks down, statistical tests failed to support that this group differed from the other four skin tone groups.

Political/Economic Development Ideology

Despite the numerous demographic variables entered as covariates before considering differences between the skin tone groups, a marginally significant relationship between skin tone and the political/economic development ideology variable is evident. An almost linear decline from the Very Dark to the Very Light Brown groups exists for agreement with the statement that Blacks should always vote for Black candidates who run for public office.

Cultural/Social Interaction Ideology

Significantly different mean scores for the skin tone groups are not present for the cultural ideology measure that we chose. A rating as Very Dark, Dark, Medium, Light, or Very Light Brown does not greatly influence an individual's support of Black children studying an African language.

Ideology of Interaction with the Dominant Group

Table 8 shows the ANCOVA results for the two questions concerning interaction with the dominant group. A marginally significant difference in the mean scores of the skin tone groups is present when respondents consider whether Black women should date White men. The greatest opposition to this type of interaction concerning Black women comes from those in the Very Dark and Dark Brown groups. The table also shows that when the focus shifts to the question of Black men dating White women, a slightly stronger difference in the means occurs, despite controlling for several demographic variables. Here, somewhat stronger opposition is expressed by those rated Very Dark and Dark Brown. Similar to their responses regarding Black women dating dominant group members, lighter skin tone groups show lower levels of opposition when considering Black men's dating White women. From these two analyses, it is plausible to conclude that one's skin tone has an influence over ideology concerning interaction with the dominant group in close personal relationships.

Table 8
ANCOVAs by Skin Tone Group for Racial Identity Dimensions

MMRI Dimension: NSBA Question	Interviewer Rating of Respondent Skin Tone					
	Very Dark (N)	Dark (N)	Medium (N)	Light (N)	Very Light (N)	F
Chronic Racial Salience: Chances in Life Depend on Blacks as a Group	52% (170)	55% (596)	49% (896)	46% (292)	45% (53)	1.49
Racial Centrality: Being Black Is Most Important	21% (171)	19% (593)	19% (886)	26% (287)	13% (53)	2.18+
Private Regard: Closeness in feelings and Ideas to Other Black People	3.37 (172)	3.42 (605)	3.35 (901)	3.27 (292)	3.28 (52)	2.54*
Public Regard: Whites Want to Keep Blacks Down	45% (163)	41% (571)	41% (840)	44% (275)	28% (47)	1.39
Political/Economic Development Ideology: Blacks Should Always Vote for Black Candidate	2.62 (164)	2.54 (582)	2.43 (869)	2.31 (286)	2.37 (51)	5.31**
Cultural/Social Interaction Ideology: Black Children Should Study an African Language	2.75 (160)	2.72 (548)	2.70 (811)	2.71 (278)	2.61 (49)	.17
Ideology of Interaction with Dominant Group: Black Women Should Not Date White Men	2.49 (154)	2.52 (514)	2.34 (765)	2.31 (257)	2.39 (41)	2.23+
Ideology of Interaction with Dominant Group: Black Men Should Not Date White Women	2.52 (154)	2.55 (521)	2.36 (773)	2.30 (260)	2.38 (42)	3.91**

+ $p<.10$ * $p<.05$ ** $p<.01$

NOTE: All group means and differences determined after entering demographic covariates (age, family, income, gender, marital status, education, and region)

Based on the hierarchical analysis of covariance to detect mean differences by skin tone group for various measures of racial identity, we found no significant differences for the measures of chronic racial salience, public regard, and cultural/social interaction ideology. For the measures of racial centrality and ideology concerning interaction with the dominant group for the dating behavior of Black women, marginally significant differences were present. Finally, significant mean differences by skin tone group were evident for private regard, political/economic development ideology, and interaction ideology for the dating behavior of Black men.

Conclusion

In this chapter we have attempted to provide a research framework for understanding the myriad ways in which skin tone may influence African Americans. Without a doubt, there are other areas which could be explored and included in our framework. From our review of the skin tone literature, a few areas in particular seem promising for extending the research framework: age- and gender-related effects and social psychological interpretations of skin tone as a status characteristic.

Many researchers contend that changes in the way in which skin tone operates among African Americans has occurred at various points in time. Particularly, during the mid-1960's and early 1970's, researchers fashioned hypotheses to ascertain the exact nature in which the dominant slogan of "Black is Beautiful" may have altered thinking and behaviors surrounding skin tone. Other researchers have claimed that while slight deviations from the historical trends favoring light-skinned people may have occurred, those differences have not been so great or enduring that the overall bias has changed. The results from the reviewed studies support both positions, depending upon which aspect of African Americans' lives is under investigation. More research disentangling the age-related effects of the period in which views are assessed, the unique experiences associated with the cohort to which an individual belongs, and the developmental impact of aging needs to be conducted before a clear answer to this issue will emerge.

A second theme in need of more investigation is gender. Many effects common to both men and women in the realm of skin tone consequences have been demonstrated. The stronger impact of skin tone for women compared to men, however, has been a dominant theme throughout our review. Whether the researcher has explicitly posited a differential relationship based on gender or happened to discover a glaring discrepancy in the course of their study, women have been shown to be detrimentally affected to a much greater extent than men. Some explanations for this highly influential gender difference have been put forth, but systematic investigation based upon these theories have been rare.

Finally, the majority of researchers have explicitly or implicitly conceived of skin tone strictly as a status characteristic initiated by Whites during slavery and continued by both the White and Black communities since emancipation to stratify individuals and regulate resources. Many findings, particularly in the resource attainment literature, support this notion. Also, historical accounts have repeatedly indicted both racial groups in perpetuating a hierarchy based on skin tone in this nation (Davis, 1994). This approach has provided firm theoretical support at the societal level for understanding the maintenance of skin tone bias. It does not, however, address the phenomenological experience of skin tone bias for the individual. The strict status approach to skin tone characterizes the individual as buffeted by structural influences beyond his or her control, without taking into account the diverse experiences and socialization which individuals may have encountered in regard to coping with skin tone bias from other Blacks, as well as dominant groups in this country. This approach presents a monolithic view of African Americans and does not address possible social and psychological mechanisms that may mediate society's biases. Taking into account how an individual may conceive of the societal messages and discrimination based on skin tone would provide critical information for understanding the role of skin tone in the identity development and other important social and psychological domains of life among African Americans.

References

Anderson, C., & Cromwell, R.L. (1977). "Black is beautiful" and the color preferences of Afro-American youth. *Journal of Negro Education, 46* (winter), 76-88.

Bond, S., & Cash, T.F. (1992). Black beauty: Skin color and body images among African-American college women. *Journal of Applied Social Psychology, 22(11)*, 874-888.

Boyd-Franklin, N. (1991). Recurrent themes in the treatment of African American women in group psychotherapy. *Women & Therapy, 11(2)*, 25-40.

Clark, K.B., & Clark, M.P. (1947). Racial identification and preference in Negro children. In T.M. Newcomb and E.L. Hartley, *Readings in Social Psychology* (pp. 169-178). New York: Holt.

Cross, W.E., Jr. (1991). *Shades of Black: Diversity in African American identity.* Philadelphia: Temple University Press.

Davis, F.J. (1993). *Who Is Black? One Nation's Definition.* University Park, PA: Penn State Press.

Drake, S., & Cayton, H. (1945). *Black Metropolis.* New York: Harcourt Brace.

Edwards, O.L. (1973). Skin color as a variable in racial attitudes of Black urbanites. *Journal of Black Studies, 3(4)*, 473-483.

Frazier, E.F. (1957). *The Black Bourgeoisie.* New York: Free Press.

Freeman, H.E., Ross, J.M., Armor, D., & Pettigrew, T.F. (1966). Color gradation and attitudes among middle-income Negroes. *American Sociological Review, 31*, 365-374.

Goering, J.M. (1971). Changing perceptions and evaluations of physical characteristics among Blacks. *Phylon, 33*, 231-241.

Hall, R.E. (1992). Bias among African Americans regarding skin color: Implications for social work practice. *Research on Social Work Practice, 2 (4)*, 479-486.

Hamm, N.H., Williams, D.O., & Dalhouse, A.D. (1973). Preferences for Black skin among Negro adults. *Psychological Reports, 3(2)*, 1171-1175.

Harvey, A.R. (1995). The issue of skin color in psychotherapy with African Americans. *Family in Society, 76(1)*, 3-10.

Holtzman, J. (1973). Color caste changes among Black college students. *Journal of Black Studies, 4(1)*, 92-101.

Hughes, M., & Hertel, B.R. (1990). The significance of color remains: a study of life chances, mate selection, and ethnic consciousness among Black Americans. *Social Forces, 68(4)*,1105-1120.

Jackson, J.S., Tucker, B., & Gurin, G. (1987). *National Survey of Black Americans*. Ann Arbor: Institute for Social Research.

Keith, V.M., & Herring, C. (1991). Skin tone and stratification in the Black community. *American Journal of Sociology, 97(3)*, 760-778.

Marks, E.S. (1943). Skin color judgments of Negro college students. *Journal of Abnormal and Social Psychology, 38*, 370-376.

Neal, A.M., & Wilson, M.L. (1989). The role of skin color and features in the Black community: Implications for Black women and therapy. *Clinical Psychology Review, 9*, 323-333.

Okazawa-Rey, M., Robinson, T., & Ward, J.V. (1987). Black women and the politics of skin color and hair. *Women & Therapy, 6(1-2)*, 89-102.

Porter, C.P. (1991). Social reasons for skin tone preferences of Black school-age children. *American Journal of Orthopsychiatry, 61(1)*, 149-154.

Ransford, H.E. (1970). Skin color, life chances, and anti-White attitudes. *Social Problems, 18*, 164-179.

Reuter, E. (1918). *The Mulatto in the United States*. New York: Negro Universities Press.

Robinson, T.L., & Ward, J.V. (1995). African American adolescents and skin color. *Journal of Black Psychology, 21(3)*, 256-274.

Russell, K., Wilson, M.L., & Hall, R.E. (1992). *The Color Complex: The Politics of Skin Color Among African Americans*. New York: Harcourt Brace Jovanovich.

Seeman, M. (1946). Skin color values in three all-Negro school classes. *American Sociological Review, 11*, 315-321.

Sellers, R.M., Shelton, J.N., Cooke, D.Y., Chavous, T.M., Johnson Rowley, S.A., & Smith, M.A. (1998). A multidimensional model of racial identity: Assumptions, findings, and future directions. In R.L. Jones (Ed.), *African American Identity Development*. Hampton, VA, Cobb & Henry.

Udry, J.R., Bauman, K.E., & Chase, C. (1969). Skin color, status, and mate selection. *American Journal of Sociology, 76*, 722-733.

Walker, H.A., & Karas, J.A. (1994). *The declining significance of color?: Race, color, and status attainment*. Unpublished manuscript.

Author

Kendrick T. Brown
Department of Psychology
Macalester College
1600 Grand Avenue
St. Paul, MN 55105-1899
Telephone: (612) 696-6000
E-mail: knbrwn@mich.edu

Cultural Identification and Cultural Mistrust: Some Findings and Implications

Francis Terrell and Sandra L. Terrell

Introduction

During the late 1960s and early 1970s, considerable emphasis was placed upon Blacks identifying members of their own culture and distrusting Whites. While this trend was in progress, insufficient attention was given to exactly what effect adopting a pro-Black attitude would have upon that Black individual's behavior. We have been especially interested in the outcome of these attitudes on the behavior of Black children and adolescents as it relates to their performance in academic and achievement settings. The present chapter summarizes some of our findings in these areas as well as findings which have been reported by others. In addition, we will suggest areas which require examination by other investigators.

Black Identification

It is generally agreed that professionals first became seriously interested in the Black self-concept and extent to which Blacks identify with their ethnic group as a result of the pioneering studies published by Kenneth B. Mamie Clark. In general, the Clarks found that Black children preferred to play with White, rather than Black dolls (Clark, 1943). The Clarks interpreted this finding to imply at least two things. First, Black children had a low self-concept. Second, since previous empirical findings had already indicated that children in general with a low self-concept performed poorly in academic situations and on standardized tests, then Black children would do poorly in these areas. As a consequence, it was argued that the Black self-concept should be enhanced. However, few actual studies were done to actually examine whether a strong relationship exists between one's Black self-concept and academic performance. Consider the following cases of two Black adolescents.

Case #1. Sheila is the oldest of eight children who was born and raised in Chicago. The father is a construction worker and is employed on seasonal basis. The mother is a housewife. Sheila's entire life was spent within a one hundred mile radius of where she lived. Sheila constantly heard her father say that it was both hopeless to try to improve their economic condition because they were Black and Blacks were not very smart. But even if they were smart, Whites would not permit them to own too much. In school, Sheila really didn't try to get good grades because she didn't think she could and because even if she did, she would probably still have considerable difficulty obtaining a high paying prestigious job. She completed school by getting marginal grades. After high school, Sheila got married. She has one child. Sheila, her husband, and the child live in a one bedroom apartment. The husband is employed as a movie projectionist at a local theatre. Sheila feels that she is successful.

Case #2. Maurice is the third oldest of five children. His father is a mechanic and runs his own repair shop in a small garage which he rents. The mother is employed as a teacher's aid at a local public elementary school. The mother encourages all of her children to take pride in themselves. Maurice begins to attend an African Arts Center. There he is exposed to other Blacks who have come to despise Whites. They also advocate rejection of all White literature and economic institutions. During school, Maurice continuously gets failing grades, sleeps during school and was held back twice. Maurice admits that he does not try hard in school and that if he did, he could probably get acceptable grades. However, Maurice is disinterested in school because he views it as a White institution where Black students are taught nothing but lies and half truths. Maurice quit school at 15 years of age. Since then, he has worked at odd jobs including a fast food restaurant, gas station attendant, and helper on a moving van.

The previous two cases represent a Black adolescent with a low Black self-concept and another with an extremely high level of ethnic identity. However, both were poorly motivated to achieve in academic settings and the outcome for both, as far as their economic future is concerned, does not appear promising. In the latter case, therefore, it seems important that a better understanding of the ways of both enhancing one's self-concept and motivating them to perform at their peak is of importance.

Cultural Identification and Mental Abilities

Although recent studies have indicated that differences are diminishing, a relatively consistent finding is that Black children receive lower scores on intelligence tests relative to White children (Loehin, Lindzey, & Spuhler, 1975). Several explanations have been postulated to account for the difference in performance between Black and White children on mental abilities tests. Deutsch (1965) and

Jensen (1969, 1974) have proposed that Black children are intellectually inferior. That is, the poorer performance of Black children on intelligence tests reflects a genetic deficiency. In contrast to this so-called deficiency model, other investigators have suggested that Black children obtain lower scores because items composing the test are culturally biased against Blacks (Williams, 1974). A third, less often considered explanation for the difference between the performance of Black and White children on intelligence tests may be that they are simply not motivated to perform at their peak during testing.

In a study by Terrell, Terrell & Taylor (1981a), it was reasoned that many Black adolescents obtain low scores on mental abilities tests because they are not motivated to perform at their potential. To explore this hypothesis, a group of Black children was given a standardized intelligence test and each time they got a question correct they were given what we referred to as culturally relevant reinforcement. This consisted of saying such things as "good job young blood" and "well done brother."

Findings of this study seem to suggest that some Blacks may not be performing at their potential because they view their performance on cognitive tests as irrelevant. However, when motivated to do so, they can score significantly higher. It is important that Blacks demonstrate their ability since major decisions are often made if they do not. In the area of intelligence testing, Blacks are often labeled as being mentally retarded when their performance is especially low. We wondered if at least some Black children, because they were unmotivated, had indeed been diagnosed as being retarded because of low performance on mental abilities tests. To explore this, Terrell, Terrell, & Taylor (1981b) replicated the study previously described using Black children who had been diagnosed as being borderline mentally retarded and placed in special education classes. In this study somewhat similar results were found. That is, Black children who had been diagnosed as being retarded scored significantly higher on a standardized intelligence test when given culturally relevant reinforcement than comparable children given traditional social reinforcement. Furthermore, the children given culturally relevant reinforcement scored significantly higher during this subsequent testing than they did on the earlier test used to diagnose them as being retarded during which traditional social reinforcement was used. The results of the two studies just described strongly suggest that many Black children are being mistreated because of a strong identity with the Black community. This creates additional problems later in life because these children are blocked at an early age from the opportunity for a quality education.

Ethnic Identity and Interpersonal Behavior

In addition to the implications of the impact of Black identity on intellectual and academic performance, it is also important to examine the impact of this attitude upon other behavior. One area which has been of special concern to us as well as to the Black community in general, is the extraordinarily high rate of Black on Black crime. Various investigators have attempted to account for this phenomena by maintaining that the high incidence of Black on Black crime, to a large extent, may be attributed to limited economic opportunities for Blacks. As a consequence, Blacks are often propelled into criminal activity in order to meet their day-to-day living needs. However, this argument does not account for the high frequency of senseless crimes many Blacks commit against each other (i.e., random fights, theft of useless items, and fighting without provocation). Others have maintained that Blacks commit these crimes due to frustration. A weakness in explanations of this type is that it fails to account for the reason Blacks specifically commit crimes against each other. If it were a need to ventilate pent-up emotions then one would conclude that the crime would be directed toward anyone who was available at the time of frustration. In many instances, the source of frustration is not Blacks. Rather, institutionalized and individual incidents of racism tend to be the primary contributors to frustration in the Black community. Still others have suggested that the rate of Black on Black crimes is simply artificially inflated because there is an increased likelihood that Blacks will be arrested and convicted due to flaws and biases in the legal system. While this may indeed be the case, such an explanation is in conflict with others who have proposed that Blacks are less likely to be arrested if they commit a crime against another Black and are less likely to be given stiff sentences when Blacks commit crimes against one another. Such an explanation also contradicts the commonly heard complaint that legal authorities are less inclined to act when crimes occur within the Black community. One argument for the high incidence of Black-on-Black crime which does seem to have some credence is that Blacks commit crimes against each other because they do not respect or identify with their culture. We examined the feasibility of this interpretation as a contributor to Black-on-Black crime. Terrell and Taylor (1980) selected a group of Black adolescents who had been convicted of committing property crimes against other Blacks and another group of adolescents who had been convicted of committing physical crimes against other Blacks. It was then hypothesized that Blacks who committed the more serious crime of physically injuring another Black would have a lower level of identification with the Black culture than those who engaged in crimes involving the property of other Blacks. It was found that Blacks convicted of committing property crimes did indeed have a better level of identification with the Black community than those who had physically injured another Black. Thus, these findings suggest that a lack of cultural identification is related to deviant behavior among Blacks.

One way in which Black parents have attempted to enhance the extent of cultural identification among their children has been assigning them Afrocentric names or names related to their culture. This became a very popular trend during the early 1960s and early 1970s. However, there is a paucity of studies examining what, if any impact this practice has had upon various behaviors of these Black children. One study by Terrell, Terrell, and Taylor (1988) compared the level of cultural identification of Black adolescents with and without African names. As suspected, adolescents with African names tended to have a higher level of cultural identification than those with traditional, European names.

Further Directions in Black Consciousness

Considerable progress has been made in our knowledge of the relationship between Black consciousness and various behaviors of Blacks. While this is indeed commendable, much more exploration is needed. Among some of the issues, from our perspective, requiring relatively immediate attention are continued studies within the area of academic performance and mental abilities testing. For example, several Black parents who gave their offspring either African or Muslim names have complained that their children are often treated unfairly by teachers. Research is needed to examine whether indeed this practice exists as well whether a relationship exists between children with African names and academic performance. Failure to do so could result in the ruination of promising Black children and adolescents as well as undermine efforts by Black parents to enhance the ethnic identity of their offspring.

Perhaps an area requiring most attention is a better clarification of Black consciousness and the impact different components of this personality construct has upon behavior in different areas. More specifically, many investigators in their research have examined correlates of Black consciousness as a single, unified construct. This is a relatively simplistic approach. Black consciousness is multifaceted and is composed of many dimensions. For example, an individual may have a high sense of ethnic awareness relative to the appreciation of Black art. However, that individual's identification politically and economically with his or her ethnic group might be underdeveloped.

Finally, an implicit assumption is that once an individual has established a heightened sense of awareness and appreciation of the Black community, this awareness continues and does not decline. This assumption may not be entirely warranted. We have observed many Blacks, whom we refer to as "Cultural Backsliders." These are individuals who were once committed to their ethnic group but for various reasons, rejected their cultural heritage. It seems important that we turn our attention to identifying those variables which produce, maintain, and take away from one's identity with his or her ethnic group.

Cultural Mistrust

As mentioned previously, concomitant with the trend toward identifying with the Black culture, Blacks also began to develop an increased suspicion of Whites. This was not a new idea. Grier and Cobbs (1968) have pointed out that many Blacks have long been wary of Whites. However, empirical studies examining whether Blacks are suspicious of Whites and the way in which Black wariness of Whites affects behavior, until recently, has been neglected. Therefore, a program of research was initiated designed to explore the extent to which Blacks mistrust Whites and the relationship of this construct with various behaviors.

In an early study, Terrell and Barrett (1979) selected Black males and females from upper and lower socioeconomic classes. These subjects were then given the Rotter Interpersonal Trust Inventory. Their scores on this test were then compared with those of a similar group of White males and females. It was found that in general Blacks were considerably less trusting than Whites and Black females tended to be less trusting of Whites than did Black males.

An important question is exactly how does this mistrust of Whites come about. Several causes for this tendency have been proposed. However, the most common explanation is that Blacks mistrust Whites as a result of being discriminated against. Although this had been proposed as an explanation, surprisingly, no research had been done to actually examine whether indeed racial discrimination was an important contributor to the onset of mistrust among Blacks. Therefore, a subsequent task which we decided to undertake was to examine whether indeed racism was a major contributor to mistrust of Whites by Blacks. To do this, Terrell and Miller (1979) first developed the Racial Discrimination Index (RDI). This is a 20 item inventory which consists of examples of situations in which Blacks are being discriminated against. Respondents are asked to fill out this inventory by indicating the number of times they have been discriminated against in a way similar to that depicted in each item on the RDI and to also rate the extent to which it is disturbing to them each time they have been confronted with a similar form of racism. Respondents' scores on the RDI were then correlated with their scores on the Cultural Mistrust Inventory (CMI). It was found that the more individuals had been discriminated against, the more mistrusting of Whites they were. Additionally, Blacks who reported that being discriminated against was highly disturbing to them tended to be more mistrustful of Whites than those who less disturbed when being discriminated against (Terrell & Terrell, 1981).

Cultural Mistrust and Mental Abilities

Given that mistrust does seem to be relatively common among Blacks and this mistrust seems to originate at least in part from racism, an important question is what impact does this trait have upon the intelligence test performance of Black children.

To examine this question, Terrell, Terrell, and Taylor (1981) selected a group of adolescents with high and low levels of mistrust of Whites. Half of the participants in these two groups were then administered an intelligence test by a Black examiner and the remaining sample was administered the test by a White examiner. It was found that students with a high level of mistrust who were tested by a White examiner had lower IQ scores than any other group. This study was replicated using elementary school children and similar results were found (Terrell & Terrell, 1983). Thus our findings indicate that being mistrustful of Whites can have an adverse effect upon intelligence test performance.

Cultural Mistrust and Interpersonal Behavior

The extent to which Blacks trust Whites also seems to be related to both whether, and the way they interact with Whites. One study indicates that Blacks who are mistrustful of Whites will avoid contact with them. For example, Terrell and Terrell (1984) found that Blacks who are highly mistrustful of Whites will refuse to seek counseling if the therapist they are assigned to is White. Similar results have been found in other studies (Watkins & Terrell, 1988; Watkins, Terrell, Miller, & Terrell, 1989). These studies indicate that Blacks who are experiencing emotional problems might prefer to retain their difficulties rather than attempt to resolve them if that requires interacting with Whites.

The single best indicator of intelligence is one's vocabulary. That is, the larger one's vocabulary, the more intelligent that individual is assumed to be. Studies have shown that relative to Whites, Blacks have a more restricted vocabulary. More precisely, Blacks tend to use fewer words than Whites (e.g., Deutsch, Katz, & Jensen, 1968). If the findings reported by these investigators consisted of language samples from Black children who were highly suspicious of Whites, then the low word production of these Black children may have been due to being mistrustful of Whites rather than a true reflection of their vocabulary.

Do our findings in the area of mental abilities testing and interpersonal behavior mean that being mistrustful of Whites is undesirable? There is some controversy among investigators as to whether or not cultural mistrust is pathological. On the one hand, Grier and Cobbs (1968) maintain that cultural mistrust is a healthy, adaptive attitude. Others, such as Kardiner and Ovesey (1951), have insisted that the lack of trust is indicative of an unhealthy, pathological personality. It is likely that in some instances, trust does have survival or facilitative value while in other instances, it can be counterproductive. However, being excessively trustful of Whites can be potentially harmful. It is our belief that being overly trusting of Whites can place a Black at risk and conversely, being too distrustful of Whites can also lead to disastrous consequences. Consider the following two cases.

Case #1. Roland is a 28-year-old inmate at a state correctional facility who is serving two life sentences for multiple armed robberies. Roland is a middle child born into a family a four children. The father has his own business as an auto mechanic and the mother works part time at a dry cleaning shop. During childhood and early adolescence Roland spent considerable time in the evenings and on weekends hanging around his father's garage. The garage was a favorite place for Black males in the community to gather to play checkers, cards, and talk. A frequent topic of conversation among these men were reasons why Whites could not be trusted. They would often be given examples of attempts by Whites to deceive them and how they avoided these attempts. In school, Roland's performance was not outstanding. He generally received grades which were barely passing. Roland felt that his grades would be much better if he were treated fairly by his teachers who were predominantly White. Roland complained that teachers often gave him lower grades on his paper than he should have received, that his report card contained grades which were lower than his test scores, and that teachers often asked him more difficult questions than White students. Roland also complained that his teachers often accused or punished him for things which were not his fault even when they knew he was not guilty. Because Roland felt he was treated unfairly in school he did not try very hard to get good grades and wanted to quit when he reached the tenth grade but at his parents' insistence, finally graduated from high school. Following graduation, Roland held three jobs. The duration of these jobs was from 4 months to 11 months. Roland quit his first job because he felt that he was being made to do more work than his White counterparts, he quit the second job because he felt that he was being required to perform more demeaning tasks than his fellow workers, and on the third job, he was fired because of poor evaluations from his White supervisor. In this instance, Roland claimed that the verbal reports he received from this employer were good and he could not understand why he was given bad written reports. Following his dismissal from the last position, Roland did not seek additional work because he was convinced that he would not be treated fairly by his White employers even if he did get a job. Roland then turned to stealing and robbery to get money. These later activities resulted in his current circumstances.

Case #2. Rhonda is the only child of an upper middle class family. The father is a physician and the mother is a nurse. The family has lived in a rather exclusive, but liberal, almost totally White community since Rhonda was four years of age. Rhonda has also attended an elementary and high school where the teachers and students were almost completely White. During her years in school, Rhonda's academic performance was outstanding. In fact, she was on the honor roll during the entire time she was in high school. During her senior year in high school, she was elected to the National Honor Society. After high school, Rhonda attended a small, predominantly White college and majored in business. Following college, Rhonda was offered a position as a junior executive in a large company. Rhonda accepted this job because she felt there was considerable room for advancement. Rhonda worked hard at her career. Her supervisor promised her that she would be promoted. However, after working for the company for two years, a White male and female who joined the company at the same time Rhonda did, were promoted while Rhonda was not. Rhonda became upset about this matter and asked her supervisor why she was not promoted. He informed her that she was doing excellent work but needed additional experience and probably would be promoted the following year. After staying with the company another year, a White individual who joined the company after Rhonda was hired, received a promotion. Rhonda again asked why she had been passed over for advancement. This time, the supervisor informed her that he had another more important new position in mind for her and that he was presently developing it. He assured Rhonda that she most likely would be recommended for this position. Rhonda has been with this same company for almost ten years and still has not been promoted. Three years ago, Rhonda discovered that many ideas she thought of had been implemented and her supervisor had been given credit for these accomplishments. Coupled with that, she discovered that other employees who had been with the company less than five years earn considerably more money than she does. Approximately two years ago, Rhonda began drinking heavily to the point that she has several Blackout spells. Her drinking had become so excessive that her employer has threatened to terminate her. Rhonda is currently undergoing psychological treatment for alcoholism and depression.

Both cases just described are actual individuals. Although specific background components may vary, we have encountered many Blacks with similar ideological characteristics of one of the two individuals described above. For the first individual, Roland demonstrated an excessive amount of mistrust to the extent that it not only interfered with his capacity to function effectively, but ultimately contributed to a deviant lifestyle. In the case of Rhonda, her willingness to trust Whites played a major role in ruining what appeared to be a very promising career. As with ethnic identification then, it seems advisable that an excessive amount of this trait or the lack of it can have debilitating or indeed disastrous consequences. If it is agreed that mistrust of Whites, to some extent is not only desirable but necessary for the survival and growth of Blacks, an important question is what would be an ample amount of mistrust of Whites? Research in this area would be useful. Some suggested research projects designed to examine the extent to which mistrust may be adaptive will be proposed next.

Further Directions in Cultural Mistrust

Systematic exploration into the area of cultural mistrust must be considered as being in its infancy stage and extensive research is needed in this area. Some areas requiring relatively immediate attention are research designed to explore whether mistrust of Whites is pathological or a healthy survival tool. One way in which this question may be addressed is by examining the extent to which successful and unsuccessful Blacks mistrust Whites. We suspect that Black individuals with extraordinary high levels of mistrust will be less than optimally successful while Blacks with a moderate level of mistrust are functioning more effectively. It is also anticipated that findings will indicate that those Blacks who are highly trustful of Whites will report being less successful.

Finally, it has long been recognized within the Black community that not only are there Blacks who do not trust Whites, but many Blacks are also wary of other Blacks. If the Black community is to become unified and prosper, research examining the extent to which Black mistrust of Blacks exists and correlates of this tendency must be examined. This should then be followed up by studies exploring ways of ameliorating this tendency.

Summary and Conclusion

Over the years we have engaged in a program of research designed to examine the effects of the Black Consciousness, a trend which began in the 1960's and continued into the 1970's. During this era, many suggestions were made by Black leaders which they thought would enhance the pride, autonomy, and abilities of Blacks. However, little empirical research followed which examined what, if any, effect, adhering to these guidelines had upon those who adopted them. Our own research in the area of mental abilities seems to indicate that individuals with either high levels of Black Consciousness or Cultural Mistrust tend to perform better when in the presence of other Blacks. However, their performance deteriorates when tested in the presence of Whites. Studies examining other behaviors as a function of level of Black Consciousness and trust level has been too limited for any firm conclusions to be drawn. But our preliminary findings suggest that either an excessive or insufficient amount of these variables are related to poorer levels of functioning.

In conclusion, although many Blacks adopted a heightened sense of awareness, the effects of this trait may not have had the expected effects. Our research has suggested that Black researchers must study the effects differing levels of ethnic identity has upon a variety of behaviors.

References

Atkinson, D. R., & Thompson, C. E., (1992). Racial, ethnic, and cultural variables in counseling. In S.D. Brown, & R.W. Lent, (Eds.), *Handbook of Counseling Psychology,* (2nd ed., pp. 349-382). John Wiley & Sons, Inc.

Clark, K. B., & Clark, M. P. (1947). Racial identification and preference in Negro children. In T. M. Newcomb, & E. L. Hartley, (Eds.), *Readings in Social Psychology.* New York: Holt.

Cross, W. E. (1980). Models of psychological nigrescence: A literature review. In R. L. Jones (Ed.), *Black Psychology* (2nd ed.). New York: Harper and Row.

Deutsch M. (1965). The role of social class in language development and cognition, *American Journal of Orthopsychiatry, 25,* 78-88.

Deutsch, M., Katz, I., & Jensen, A. R. (1968). (Eds.). *Social class, race, and psychological development.* New York: Holt, Rinehart, and Winston.

Grier, W. W., & Cobbs, P. M. (1968). Black Rage. New York: Bantam Books.

Jensen, A.R., (1969). How much can we boost IQ and scholastic achievement? *Harvard Educational Review, 39,* 1-23.

Jensen, A.R. (1974). The strange case of Dr. Jensen and Mr. Hyde. *American Psychologist. 29,* 467-468.

Kardiner, A., & Ovesey, L. (1951). *The mark of oppression.* New York: Norton.

Loehin, J.C., Lindzey, G., & Spuhler, J.N. (1975). *Race Differences in Intelligence.* San Francisco: Freeman.

Terrell, F., & Barrett, R.K. (1979). Interpersonal trust among college students as a function of race, sex, and socioeconomic class. *Perceptual and Motor Skills, 48,* 1194.

Terrell, F., & Taylor, J. (1980). Self Concept of juveniles who commit Black on Black crimes, *Corrective and Social Psychiatry, 26,* 107-109.

Terrell, F., & Terrell, S.L. (1981). An inventory to measure cultural mistrust among Blacks, *Western Journal of Black Studies, 5,* 180-185.

Terrell, F., Terrell, S.L., & Taylor, J. (1981a). Effects of race of examiner and cultural mistrust on the WAIS performance of Black students. *Journal of Consulting and Clinical Psychology, 49,* 750-751.

Terrell, F., Terrell, S.L., & Taylor, J. (1981b). Effects of type of reinforcement on the intelligence test performance of retarded Black children. *Psychology in the Schools, 18,* 225-227.

Terrell, F., & Terrell, S.L. (1983). The relationship between race of examiner, cultural mistrust and intelligence test performance of Black children. *Psychology in the Schools, 20,* 267-269.

Terrell, F., & Terrell, S.L. (1984). Race of counselor, counselor sex, cultural mistrust level, and premature termination of counseling among Black clients. *Journal of Counseling Psychology, 31,* 371-375.

Terrell, F., Terrell, S. L., & Taylor, J. (1988). The self-concept level of Black adolescents with and without African names. *Psychology in the Schools, 25,* 65-70.

Terrell, S. L., & Terrell, F. (1993). African-American cultures. (1993). In Battles, D.E. (Ed.), *Communication Disorders in Multicultural Populations,* (pp. 3-37). Boston: Andover Medical Publishers.

Watkins, C. E., & Terrell, F. (1988). Mistrust level and its effects on counseling expectations in Black client-White counselor relationships. *Journal of Counseling Psychology, 35,* 194-197.

Watkins, C.E., Terrell, F., Miller, F.S., & Terrell, S.L. (1989). Cultural mistrust and its effects on expectational variables in Black client-White counselor relationships. *Journal of Counseling Psychology. 36,* 447-450.

Watkins, C.E., Terrell, F., & Miller, F.S. (1990). *The relationship between level of cultural mistrust and academic achievement.* Presented at the Annual meeting of the American Psychological Society. Dallas Texas

Williams, R.L. (1974). Scientific racism and I.Q. : Silent mugging of the Black community. *Psychology Today, 7,* 32-41.

Author

Francis Terrell, Ph.D
Psychology Department
University of North Texas
Denton, Texas
Telephone: (817) 565-2678
Fax: (817) 565-4682

Part 4

Health Psychology

Chronic Pain and Health Psychology: Implications for African Americans

Louis P. Anderson and Gary T. Miles

Case 1. C.J. is a 37 year old construction worker who began complaining of pain in his back, hip and legs after falling seven feet from a ladder that gave way while he was working on a house that was being built. After his accident he was taken to a local emergency room where he was x-rayed, given pain medication, and told to stay in bed for a few days. One week later he began noticing that his physical condition had worsened. He now experienced pain while sitting, standing, walking, and coughing. He then went to an orthopedic hospital where he was given a complete neurological examination, a myelogram, and an electromyogram. His examination was unremarkable and he was prescribed pain medication. A brace and bed rest were also recommended. Two weeks passed and C.J.'s employer began to question his willingness to work. This came as a shock to C.J. because in his 18 years on the job he had missed very few days at work. Even though he still experienced severe pain in the lumbar region, C.J. decided to return to work. He worked his shift and when he returned home went immediately to bed. He began to drink alcohol in order to control his pain. In the beginning, C.J.'s wife was very sympathetic. However, she began to become increasingly irritated at her husband's behavior and perceived him as being unwilling to help out with the children and the household chores. Her favorite comment was "I have to work just like you." Within the two months that followed, C.J. made repeated visits to the hospital and saw no less than eight physicians. C.J. did not understand much about his condition and was unsure of what types of questions to ask his physicians. Surgery was suggested and after some deliberation and under extreme pressures to return to work decided on surgery. He had a spinal fusion of the lumbar region and then was again placed in a brace. After surgery and rehabilitation, C.J. still continued to experience pain. A second surgery was performed, but the pain continued. Since the pain had not remitted his physician began to feel that the pain was psychosomatic and suggested that C.J. should see a psychiatrist. C.J. decided to file for disability compensation.

    Case 2. H.R. is a 60 year old widow living in a home for the elderly. She suffers from arthritis. Her family became increasingly unable to care for her and decided that her medical and psychological condition (e.g., she is depressed) dictated that she be placed in a nursing home. She noticed that her condition worsened when her husband of 38 years suddenly died.

231

Case 3. B.J. is a 33 year old African American woman with a five year history of severe bilateral headaches. She described her headaches as a throbbing sensation and notes that her neck and shoulder are often sensitive to touch. Within the past two years she has been treated with valium, barbiturates and fiorinal. She has been married for seven years and has two children ages 6 and 5. Except for her headaches her health is unremarkable. She has refused psychological help.

Case 4. A.M. is a 25 year old single, upwardly mobile professional African American woman. She is described by all who know her as an assertive, independent and highly successful woman. Recently, however, she has been experiencing low back pain, weight loss, numbness and tingling in the extremities and anxiety. She briefly mentioned these symptoms to her private physician during her recent annual checkup but all that was recommended a reduced workload and a vacation. She took a week off from work but continued to experience joint pains, anxiety and other symptoms of autonomic hyperactivity. When A.M. began to experience some problems in falling asleep she reluctantly began to talk to friends about her symptoms. Apparently everyone knew her as a strong, healthy woman with little in the way of weaknesses so they could not conceive of anything being wrong with her. A.M. began to experience interpersonal conflicts at work and in her intimate relationships which further increased her tension level. She became more and more distressed over her condition. Thereafter she called a local mental health center and saw a therapist for several sessions . When she did not show improvement after two months her therapist referred her to an internist for an evaluation. She was diagnosed as having systemic lupus erythematosus.

Case 5. J.J., age 8, came to the emergency room with his mother complaining of severe arm and leg pain. This was an all too frequent scene for J.J. who, at the age of 2, was diagnosed as having sickle cell anemia. J.J's parents were unaware that they had sickle cell trait and when they learned of J.J.'s condition felt shocked and guilty. During the 8 years since J.J.'s birth, he has had no less than 30 hospitalizations and/or emergency room visits. J.J. was his parents' first child and they were not prepared for the changes that he brought to their relationship. Although there is no known cure for sickle cell anemia, J.J.'s parents continued to hold hope that something could be found to relieve his suffering. The medical bills forced J.J.'s father to take on a part-time job. The illness caused J.J. to tire easily, this along with his being smaller than other children his age led to some limitations placed on his physical activities. Although he seemed to have a good self-concept, he often discussed the anxiety he experienced as a result of his condition and his fears of having to go to the hospital.

As social scientists interested in research on African Americans our focus primarily has been on their mental health. It is widely held, however, that African Americans suffer from a very high incidence of acute and chronic medical illnesses such as hypertension, diabetes, cancer and chronic pain (USNCH, 1982). Nonetheless, current texts (Smith, Burlew, Mosley, & Whitney, 1978; Williams, 1981; Jones &

Korchin, 1982; Jenkins, 1981; Powell, 1983; and White, 1984; Jones, 1991, 1998) in the social sciences which focus on ethnic minority issues have paid limited attention to the application of behavioral and social science principles to the understanding, prevention, and treatment of physical disorders. For the most part our graduate training traditions have dictated our research and applied interests. Thus there has been little interest in health care issues African Americans experience. Although physical illnesses primarily require treatment and monitoring by physicians, there is increasing evidence that significant improvement in one's physical health can result from incorporating medical procedures with scientific knowledge derived from the behavioral and social sciences (Million, Green & Meagher, 1982). Moreover, the success of medical interventions is highly dependent on the age of onset of an illness.

It is currently believed that the severity of medical conditions is exacerbated by such factors as age, lifestyle, response to stress and the type of interpersonal relationship in which an individual is involved (Stone, Cohen & Alder, 1979). Psychosocial and contextual factors can also influence the treatment effectiveness of most medical conditions (Gentry, 1984). During the past decade applied and basic research have demonstrated that the debilitating effects of medical conditions for both the young and elderly can be significantly reduced by integrating behavioral and biomedical scientific knowledge and techniques (Schwartz & Weiss, 1978). It is important to note that we are not implying that energies have been wasted or misdirected by primarily studying the mental health of African Americans but instead that the same research, clinical and theoretical skills can also be applied to health care issues as well.

The five cases presented above are typical examples of the pain and health care issues facing African Americans. It is unfortunate, however, that we know very little about health care reactions of the African American. The area of health care is too large and amorphous to be adequately addressed here. We will, therefore, use pain as an exemplar in order to discuss the unique contributions that psychologists can make to the health care issues of African Americans.

The purpose of this review is threefold. Our goal primarily is to review the literature and provide a concise description of pain, while illustrating how painful states change into chronic conditions. Second, we will attempt to provide a theoretical account of the psychological reactions to pain. In order to advise and treat African American individuals with chronic pain we must gain insight into the origin of both the physical and psychological aspects of the disorder and how it affects the life of the patient and the lives of persons intimately involved with the patient. Consequently, the third purpose of this review is to examine treatment strategies used by health psychologists. Again, the intent here is to use a model of chronic pain to discuss the unique clinical and research contributions social and behavioral scientists can make to the health care of the African American patient.

The Cost of Pain to the Individual and to Society

"Why focus on pain?" you may ask. Simply, pain is the emotional state that leads to an individual's decision to seek medical care. Moreover, the health care system is based on reducing physical pain. Pain is perhaps the most potent motivator of behavior known to human beings. Each day approximately 90 million people in the United States suffer from a variety of painful conditions that require medical attention (Rosse & Lawson, 1970). It is estimated that Americans spend over 90 million dollars each year on non-prescription pharmaceutical agents such as aspirin, analgesics, ointments, and heating pads (Koenig, 1973; Turk, Meichenbaum & Genst, 1983). With increasing age, there is a tendency to use more pharmaceutical agents. Exact figures are not known but it is estimated that approximately 14% of the 42 million sufferers of headaches are black Americans (Adams, Feuerstein & Fowler, 1980). Systemic lupus, a variant of arthritis, affects African American women four times as often as Whites (Arthritis Foundation). Sickle cell anemia, a genetically transmitted painful disease, affects 1 in 600 African Americans (McElroy, 1980). Moreover, because of their occupations, African Americans are at risk to suffer from the debilitating effects of arthritis and back injury. The elderly are most vulnerable to arthritis and lower back pain. It has been estimated that the costs to society for treating a single chronic pain patient with regard to hospitalization, insurance benefits and unemployment can go as high as $100,000 (Bonica & Albe-Fessard, 1976).

Although concern with pain is as old as the field of medicine, only recently has attention focused on nonmedical approaches to chronic painful disorders. As a result, clinics and medical centers have emerged which focus exclusively on the treatment of one or more of the varieties of chronic pain conditions. The American Pain Society (Turk et al., 1983) found that within the past five years 800 new pain clinics have been developed.

Defining Pain

A number of terms have been used and will be used in the following sections to point out the extent of the problem with which we are faced. It is important, however, to clarify some of the terms that are being used to define pain. As Figure I illustrates, pain can result from a multitude of factors.

When we say that we are in pain, we are conveying a state of unpleasantness, suffering and distress. Consequently, it is important to note that pain is an emotional state. To communicate to someone that we are in pain we are, by and large, communicating a negative emotional condition, albeit a state of suffering. Pain is an elusive concept and most definitions contains many contradictions. Sternbach's (1968) definition of pain, although incomplete, probably comes closest to providing a broad-based model for understanding pain. According to Sternbach: "Pain is an

Figure 1
Four Levels of Pain

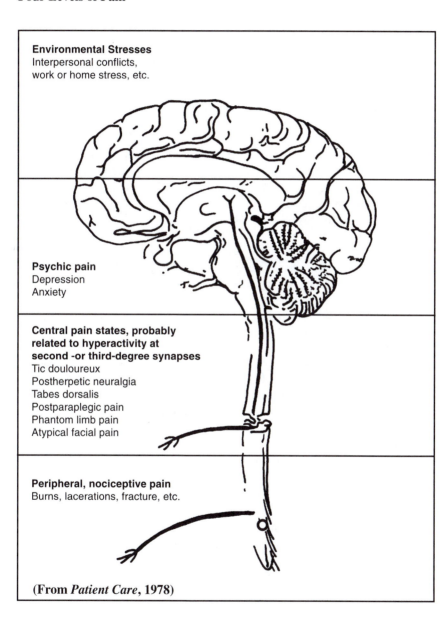

Environmental Stresses
Interpersonal conflicts,
work or home stress, etc.

Psychic pain
Depression
Anxiety

**Central pain states, probably
related to hyperactivity at
second -or third-degree synapses**
Tic douloureux
Postherpetic neuralgia
Tabes dorsalis
Postparaplegic pain
Phantom limb pain
Atypical facial pain

Peripheral, nociceptive pain
Burns, lacerations, fracture, etc.

(From *Patient Care*, 1978)

abstract concept which refers to 1) a personal sensation of hurt; 2) a harmful stimulus which signals current or impending tissue damage; or 3) a pattern of responses which operate to protect the organism from harm" (p. 12).

Of importance, according to Sternbach's definition, is that pain is a private subjective experience. In addition, there is both functional and adaptive value to pain. The experience of pain appears to alert the organism to the possibility of tissue damage (Melzack, 1973). This would allow the individual to then engage in the behaviors necessary to prevent and/or reduce his/her suffering. Therefore, pain not only serves as an internal cuing mechanism that warns the individual that something is wrong, but it also triggers interpersonal behaviors as well. Illness related behavior such as grimacing, moaning, crying, posturing are but a few symptoms of pain used to elicit helping behaviors from others (Fordyce, 1976). Implicit in any model of pain is the view that pain is mediated by higher cortical functions. As revealed in Figures 1 and 2, although the determinants of pain are diverse, all painful impulses are regulated by the brain. In broad terms, the experience of pain begins when a stimulus (see Figure 2) excites sensory receptors located on the base of the skin which in turn send sensory information to the thalamus via the spinothalamic tract (Melzack, 1973). The process just described is referred to as nociception. A nociceptive stimuli refers specifically to the external agent that causes the trauma. Accordingly, nociception is the process whereby nerve fibers send to the central nervous system information that tissue damage has occurred or is imminent. Pain, therefore, is immutably linked to nervous system reactivity and is considered a learned response to trauma.

As the definition implies, nociception represents a conscious perceptual process. This is an important point because nociception can exist in the absence of pain (Melzack, 1973). For example, the nerve fibers of a paraplegic will continue to respond to nociceptive input and fire nerve impulses toward the brain but the paraplegic since his/her pathway is severed will not experience pain. Conversely, (see Figure 1) pain can also occur in situations where there is no sensory input from the periphery (e.g., chronic pain, phantom limb pain).

Up to this point, we have focused primarily on the easiest type of pain to detect, nociceptive pain. It is not useful, however, to view pain primarily as a physical disturbance. For example, in all 5 cases presented at the beginning of this chapter, pain affected the sufferer's personality and interpersonal relationships. It is most useful to view pain as a result of physiological and psychological determinants or both (Melzack & Torgerson, 1971). Although emotional reactions to pain may be a motivating factor in an individual seeking medical treatment, it does not necessarily follow that psychological factors in of themselves solely cause pain. When pain results primarily from psychological factors (see Figure 2) such as depression and muscle tension due to worry and anxiety we refer to this particular type of pain as psychogenic. Psychogenic pain is also a label used by health care professions to

Figure 2
Illustration of the Three Major Structures Involved in the Pain Experience

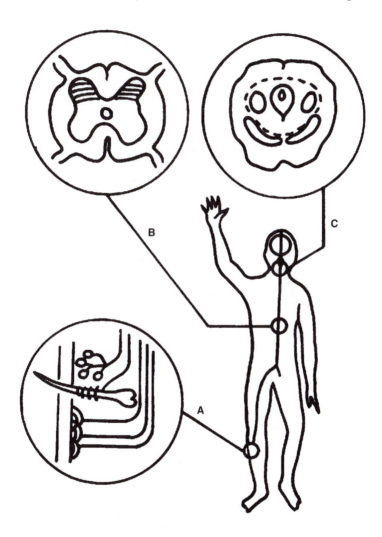

A represents the free nerve-endings, B is the cross section of the spinal chord and C represents the brainstem (taken from Melzack, 1973.

refer to a discrepancy between a patient's complaints of pain and physiological evidence derived from medical procedures (Fordyce, 1976). In this chapter we will not focus on psychogenic pain. Most contemporary theorists have not found this label to be very useful. In the sections to follow, we will clarify these points. We will begin by discussing issues relating to physical illness and pain through the life span.

Pain: A Life Span Perspective

It can be argued that a major variable which differentiates an individual's response to pain is his/her age group. In other words, the perceptions, behavior, and needs of the middle aged and elderly may differ from that of the young adult. Since African Americans are living longer, it is important that some consideration be given to a life span perspective.

The case of H.R. described previously is a good example. In addition to the pain that she experienced, H. R. had to contend with the death of her husband of thirty-eight years and her increased dependency on her grown children.

Erickson (1950) was one of the few psychologists to articulate the normal developmental tasks faced by people during their life span. Erickson's stages are based on major challenges or life crises. Our success in resolving these major encounters contributes to our well-being, sense of self and future development. Thus, Erickson's perspective has relevance for the experience of physical illness and pain because his theory would predict that the impact of chronic pain will have different meanings and will provide different challenges depending on the individual's developmental stage. For example, the elderly because of the natural aging process would be more prone to experience pain associated with chronic illnesses such as arthritis and angina.

Briefly, Erickson outlines eight stages of development. These stages extend from infancy to later adulthood. During early development, our task is to develop trust and autonomy . The young child is highly dependent on his/her parent. As such, children lack the capacity to understand why the environment is not responsive to their needs. The child is self-centered. Consequently, if the child's pain and suffering are not tended to, then feelings of helplessness and fear may develop and extend into adulthood. In addition, since social interactions are important at this stage, a parent who is physically incapacitated, grimacing, anxious or complains about pain would not be able to readily attend to the child's need and may unwittingly model maladaptive pain behaviors.

According to Erickson, the task of adolescence, is to learn appropriate social roles. The adolescent's self concept could easily be lowered if severe pain is experienced. During adulthood, the achievement of a committed relationship is the major task, while in mid-life, the challenge is to guide, encourage and support the development of the younger generation. At this stage, chronic pain and/or physical disability would limit the individual's capacity to meet normal developmental challenges. As illustrated in the case of C.J., with severe injury, the individual may experience a loss or reduction in his/her capacity to pursue vocational interests. If this occurs, goals would have to be redirected because career options would no longer be feasible. For men like C.J., a reduction in self-concept occurs particularly if the male's economic role in the family is surrendered. Role reversal occurs when the adult switches from the role of a provider-nurturer, to one of the nurtured. Physical illness and pain may even alter sexual functioning, adding to marital difficulties.

Physical illness and pain are common among the elderly. As such, vocational issues, sexual functioning and childrearing are not major factors. At this stage, depression and suicide are concerns. In fact, the suicide rate is two to six times as high among the elderly when compared to other age groups (Kanin, 1978). Chronic illness, a loss of a significant other, and forced retirement are the strongest predictors of suicide.

The effects of chronic pain across the life span is an area that deserves more attention. Chronic pain can strike at any point in the life span, but it's effect on the sufferer, and his/her family unit is variable. Research is needed to specify those developmental factors which place the individual at risk for developing chronic maladaptive behavioral patterns. Toward this end, health and medical psychologists have been interested in the characteristics of acute and chronic pain sufferers. In addition, they are interested in how acute pain is transformed into a chronic maladaptive pain syndrome. Thus far, in this section, we have focused on conceptualizing pain within a life span framework. Now, the focus will turn to specific factors which influence our experience of pain.

Acute Versus Chronic Pain: Psychological Contributions to the Understanding of Pain

Three major areas exist in which acute and chronic pain can be distinguished: functional, behavioral and psychophysiological. Acute pain typically warns the organism that something is wrong (Casey, 1977). For example, after a motor vehicle accident a severe back pain may indicate a herniated disc. Acute pain is readily identified because it is often the result of identifiable tissue damage (Melzack, 1973). Chronic pain, on the other hand, usually has no associated tissue damage and no apparent functional value once the initial pain has served the function of alerting the organism of some injury (Gorsky, 1980).

As discussed in the previous section, pain is the result of nociception and functions as a warning mechanism. Most medical theories of pain are based on nociception and thus are hard pressed to explain chronic pain, since neither tissue damage nor nociceptive stimuli are present in chronic pain conditions. The assumption is that when acute pain changes into a chronic state, psychological factors contribute significantly to an individual's adjustment. The treatment of chronic pain therefore has been greatly influenced by psychological theories.

Typically, researchers not only distinguish between acute and chronic pain but also view pain along a continuum of which acute and chronic pain are two broad categories. The major work in understanding pain as it relates to the behaviors these patients manifest has been done by behavioral psychologists, e.g., Sternbach (1974), Fordyce (1976) and Keefe (1982).

Bonica and Albe-Fessard (1976) pointed out that in acute pain, the subjective response on the part of the individual is adaptive. Anxiety is the chief subjective response. The individual views his/her pain as some sort of warning that something physical is wrong. Cogswell and Weir (1964) suggest that in an acute condition the physician does something to the client who is a passive recipient. The individual by and large expects that with proper medical care and/or home remedies the pain will be relieved within a short period of time. The acute pain usually causes only a temporary disruption in the individual's activities (Keefe & Brown, 1980).

Physicians often immobilize the acute pain patient in order to utilize the therapeutic benefits of rest (Hilton, 1950). With regard to behaviors, the individual with acute pain usually: (a) avoids physical activities; (b) reduces his/her activity level; and (c) rests (Fordyce, 1976). Pain medication is often given to the patient with acute pain, but prescription of the analgesic is time-limited.

Psychophysiological changes also occur. As pain becomes severe, physiological mechanisms increase in the form of increased blood pressure, heart rate and respiration (Hassett, 1978). Laboratory and clinical reports support this point. Beecher (1966) and Lutterbeck and Triay (1972) found that reducing anxiety, as indicated by autonomical arousal, decreased a subject's reaction to pain. In addition, Sternbach (1968) discovered that high trait anxious patients overreact to painful stimulation.

Keefe and Brown (1981) have posed the view that a pivotal point exists in the pain experience. They hypothesized that as the patterns of pain behavior become entrenched as part of the individual's lifestyle (i.e. continuing use of pain medication, bed rest, reduction in activities) the individual enters a pivotal point (from 3 to 6 months after onset of pain) which determines whether she/he becomes a chronic pain patient. Little has been written about the pre-chronic pain stage in the pain literature, nor does any research directly verify its existence. However, variables such as race, sex, age, modeling of pain behavior and personality have been suggested as determinants of whether individuals in the pre-chronic pain stage become chronic pain patients (Weisenberg, 1977; Anderson & Rehm, 1984). Mersky (1965) found that patients who report pain for at least a 3 month duration tend to fall in the 45 and above age group. Similarly, Sternbach (1974) has observed that the mean age of the chronic pain patient in most of the studies he reviewed was about 42 years. Middle aged individuals may be prone to chronic pain because they are most vulnerable to disruptions in social roles, occupation and failure to meet challenges of their own developmental stage. Mersky (1965) has shown that greater chronic pain behaviors occur in (a) lower-class individuals, (b) women with a prior history of negative physical findings, (c) depressed individuals, and (d) individuals with a family history of chronic illness. Moreover, chronic pain patients who receive preferential treatment from their family because of their illness display more frequent chronic pain behaviors (Block et al., 1980).

Craig and Weiss (1972) found that the pain behaviors of subjects are greatly influenced by modeling. Mothers who showed extreme anxiety during tooth extraction had children who exhibited similar behaviors (Johnson & Baldwin, 1968; Weisenberg, 1978). Buss and Portney (1967) found that the stronger the identification the person has with his/her group, the more willing he/she is to tolerate pain. Given the limited amount of research in this area, the precise degree to which modeling influences chronic pain behaviors remains unknown. However, young children may be influenced by how mothers model pain behavior.

Most experts have described the chronic pain stage as occurring approximately 6 to 12 months after the initial onset of acute pain. Individuals who accept the limitations that their pain places upon them realize that there is no medical cure, adjust to the pain. This may be easier for the elderly and middle aged than for young adults. Those who do not adapt will more than likely become chronic pain patients. In part, some of the problems of chronic pain conditions occur because the chronic pain patient is encouraged to be responsible for a considerable portion of his/her care. Quite possibly, those individuals regardless of age, who are not sufficiently independent or responsible to perform such a function will have problems (Croog, Shapiro, & Levine, 1971). For example, Anderson and Rehm (1984) found that those African American chronic pain sufferers who were more independent manifested less helplessness, dependency and clinging behaviors. Moreover, those individuals who were more independent experience less pain.

In comparison to the acute and pre-chronic stages where anxiety reduction leads to less pain perception, anxiety for the chronic pain patient persists and may eventually evolve into feelings of helplessness. Vegetative symptoms of depression are prevalent in this population, as is suicidal ideation. Behaviorally these individuals are inactive and tend to stay in bed for the major portion of normal waking hours (Fordyce, 1976). As a result of the reduction in anxiety, the chronic pain patient shows a deteriorating physical condition. In reflecting on C.J. in our first case study, you begin to see how from his initial acute organic condition, emotional states of anxiety and depression increased to the point where his impairment worsened.

In summary, it appears as though there are several stages in the pain experience which can be distinguished. Pain patients are highly variable in the extent to which their ailments become translated into a chronic syndrome. Although research has identified several contributing factors, the degree to which these factors influence chronicity is still not clearly understood. Still a major question to be answered concerns the African American pain patient.

African American Patient's Response to Pain

As we have illustrated in previous sections, pain is a very complex phenomenon. Individual variation in both the expression and perception of pain goes far beyond etiology and involves a number of psychosocial and cultural factors (Melzack, 1973). In order to communicate one's experience of pain to a health professional, the individual must exhibit certain behaviors known as pain behaviors. Pain behaviors such as grimaces and medication use are certainly not entirely mechanical and, in part, are due to learned ways of responding (Fordyce & Steger, 1976). By and large, these patterns of responding are shaped by our family, culture, and environment. In other words, it appears as though it is nearly impossible to obtain a pure pain reaction to a nociceptive stimuli uncontaminated by psychosocial factors (Weisenberg, Kreindler, Schachet, & Werboff, 1975).

As in the case with most issues we have touched on in this chapter, very little is specifically written about ethnic pain response patterns. One of the first, if not the first, study in this area was done by Chapman and Jones (1944). These researchers, using a laboratory device known as the Hardy-Wolff-Goodell heat apparatus, found pain tolerance of "Negro" students to be significantly below that of Whites. Similarly, Woodrow, Friedman, Siegelaub and Collen (1972) found a trend for Whites to tolerate more pain than African American subjects. In order to determine pain tolerance these investigators applied pressure to the achilles tendon . Mersky and Speer (1964) using yet another mechanical device reported no difference between African American and White male subjects to pressure applied to the forehead.

Tolerance, or the highest intensity of a stimulus that the subject can withstand, is viewed to be the closest to clinical pain. The external validity of analogue pain studies is very questionable and may add very little to our understanding of pain (Weisenberg, 1977). Moreover, it has been found that physiological arousal of African American subjects is higher when the experimenter is White (Sattler, 1970).

In contrast to laboratory pain, Winsberg and Greenlick (1967) report no differences in the pain ratings of African American and White obstetrical patients. Moreover, medical staff evaluated each group's behavioral response as being similar. The authors concluded that similar factors determine each ethnic group's pain reactions. Flannery, Sosand McGovern (1981) using behavioral observation, self-report and attitudinal scales to determine tolerance to episiotomy pain did not find differences among African American, Italian, Jewish, Irish and Anglo-Saxon obstetrical patients. African American spinal cord patients were also found not to differ from other ethnic groups in their self-reports and response to ischemic pain (Lawlis, Achterberg, Kenner & Kopetz, 1984). Moreover in this study, the author was found that African American women rated their pain higher than males. The higher pain ratings of women, in part, may explain the reason why women receive more and higher doses of pain medication than men (Pillowsky & Bond, 1969).

African American dental patients when faced with dental procedures appear to be concerned about threats to their self-esteem. Weisenberg et al. (1975) argue that African American patients may be threatened by a White dentist and therefore, health care professionals in order to reduce the anxiety associated with the situation should be sensitive and express a very respectful attitude toward the African American client. We know from testing (Sattler, 1970) and therapy situations (Banks, 1980) that African American consumers often manifest increased anxiety and lower functioning when interacting with White professionals.

Taken together, these studies seem to imply that there are some differences in the tolerance of laboratory pain between ethnic groups. On the other hand, few ethnic differences in response to clinical pain have been demonstrated. The response patterns of African Americans may depend on situational factors. Anxiety derived from the social encounter and the perceived threat when interacting with a White health provider may contribute more to African American patient's pain behavior than the pain itself. Research in this area is sorely needed.

Correlates of Pain

Several specific factors have been implicated in determining how individuals react to pain. These variables apparently interact in a continuing and complex manner. In this section the variables are divided into four major areas: (1) mood; (2) physiological state (e.g., anxiety and attention); (3) cognitive coping strategies; and (4) illness behavior and social support.

Much of the research reported in this section focuses on non-Black populations. Nonetheless, the variables that will be presented here have a bearing on the understanding of the African American pain patient and more broadly on increasing our knowledge of the applied and research strategies available to social and behavioral scientists interested in the general area of health psychology.

Factors Influencing Pain: Mood

Unquestionably, depressive syndromes are common in patients with chronic pain (see cases 1 and 2). However, clear separation of the affective response to the pain itself from the response to other associated factors such as the patient's reaction to an illness (e.g., cancer, sickle cell anemia) is difficult. Nonetheless, depression does apparently relate in some way to the duration as well as to the severity of pain. When pain is relatively constant, habituation of the autonomic responses leading to vegetative symptoms of depression usually occurs (Sternbach & Timmermans, 1975).

Virtually no empirical research has been reported on the relationship between chronic pain and depression. Research has shown that even in " acute" pain states, depression is present (Timmermans & Sternbach, 1976). Moreover, a reduction in pain is usually associated with the alleviation of depression (Sternbach & Timmermans, 1975). In addition, treating depression with tricyclic antidepressants in some cases reduces the pain (Bradley, 1963). Some researchers (i.e., Sternbach, 1978) have suggested that a common mechanism may underlie the two phenomena. This belief is based on the evidence which points to the part that biochemical factors play in both the experience of pain and depression. It has been hypothesized that a decrease in amines such as dopamine and serotonin is associated both with the onset of pain and pain tolerance (Welch, Hashi & Meyer, 1973; Welch, Spira, Knowles & Lance, 1974) . Moreover, tricyclic antidepressants are known to increase the amount of amines in the brain. Together, these separate findings form the basis for the speculation that a common mechanism accounts for depression and pain.

In a related line of investigation, Nadel & Portadin's (1977) retrospective study of 22 African American patients with sickle cell disease showed that in 50 percent of the patients, the onset of painful crises was preceded by severe depression and response to different types of loss. This retrospective study indicates that, at least in the case of sickle cell disease, biochemical changes associated with depression may provide an environment for the onset of painful crises. A premorbid history of depression and a family history of depression (Mohamed, Weisz, & Waring, 1978) appear to play a strong role in pain tolerance, pain expression, and complaints of pain. These authors found that individuals with depression and persistent pain had significantly more evidence of depression in their families and in the families of their spouses than a matched control group. Schaffer, Donlon, & Brittle (1980) found that a significant proportion of pain patients without contributing medical pathology experienced clinical depression and had a positive family history of depression.

Although little research has focused on the relationship of depression to chronic pain, behavioral psychologists, particularly Fordyce and his colleagues (Fordyce et al., 1968, 1973), have offered one possible connection. These theorists suggest that a key element in the chronic pain syndrome is the absence of effective positive reinforcement. They claim that the sudden shift in the lifestyle of the person with chronic pain typically results in a reduction in those daily activities which were sustained by reinforcers (Fordyce et al., 1973).

Interestingly enough, studies have shown that tranquilizers such as diazepam or chlordiazepoxide increase depression (Fauman, 1980; Adler, 1978). Apparently, initial improvement occurs because the medications relax tight muscles and reduce some of the causes of discomforts. The basic pain problem, however, often persists. In explaining the poor outcome due to the medication, physiological explanations not withstanding, behaviorists may speculate that the medication adversely blunted the patients' general responsiveness to their surroundings so that they are less able to function in their routines. It is speculated that the more the pain condition interferes with the premorbid behavioral repertoire of the individual, the greater the deprivation of reinforcement and the greater the amount of depression (Sternbach, 1974; Fordyce, 1976). Empirical data have shown that increasing the activity level of chronic pain patients reduces both pain and depression (Fordyce et al., 1978).

Physiological State

Most individuals who experience pain will readily acknowledge that their pain is much worse when they are anxious. Results in the area of experimental pain have consistently shown that whatever reduces anxiety in subjects also reduces the intensity of pain they experience and the magnitude of pain responses, whether the anxiety is reduced by hypnosis, self-control, or cognitive strategies (Sternbach, 1968). Anxiety as a response has been particularly associated with acute pain. During the acute stage, anxiety appears to take a cyclical course and decrease in relationship to pain sensation. In chronic pain, however, anxiety persists and may coexist with depression (Fordyce et al., 1978).

In clinical populations, reports of pain appear to be lower when individuals are anxious than when they are in a relaxed state (Beecher, 1966). Individuals who are sensitized to surgical procedures by being exposed to specific information regarding the pain and discomfort of the surgical procedure showed better adjustment to surgery than did those groups of patients who received no information (Langer, Janis, & Wolfer, 1975). The amounts of analgesic medication used for the control of pain was substantially reduced when relaxation procedures and patterned breathing were implemented (Egbert, Battit, Welch, & Bartlett, 1964).

The literature on the role attention plays in pain perception is incomplete. A direct relationship should exist between pain intensity and an individual's awareness of pain. Attention provides a basis for increased clarity of perception. Thus, increased focusing on an irrelevant stimulus reduces awareness of the sensation of pain (Hilgard, 1969). When an individual's concentration is affected, then she/he may be able to tolerate pain at higher levels. This is the principle behind many techniques such as hypnosis that are now in use in pain management clinics. Berlyne (1951), among others, found that an individual's pain tolerance can be increased if his or her attention is distracted away from the painful stimulus. Similarly, Kanfer and Goldfoot (1966) found that subjects who were distracted by viewing slides during the experiment showed the most pain tolerance. Horan and Dilinger (1974) effectively used emotive imagery to increase pain tolerance. Cognitive strategies when compared with psychotherapy appear to be a superior technique (Chaves & Barber, 1974).In a related line of research, MMPI results have consistently revealed that individuals in the most pain have the higher elevations on scales which indicate obsessional and ruminative traits (Sternbach, 1974).

Cognitive Coping Strategies

The body of research on human pain responses permits the generalization that the effects of cognitive variables may influence the perception and sensation of pain. Rosenbaum (1980), in two experiments found that subjects who scored high on self- control (i.e., individuals who are able to regulate personal action so as to cope effectively with a given situation) endured experimentally induced pain longer than low self-controllers. Anxiety appears to be important in pain perception, in part because it affects a person's feeling of control. Along this line, Staub, Tursky, and Schwartz (1971) in a laboratory experiment found that uncertainty increased anxiety and reduced pain tolerance. Therefore, when subjects were given control over the intensity of pain, their anxiety decreased and their pain tolerance increased. Sternbach (1978) argued that lack of control increases anxiety which decreases pain tolerance.

The aforementioned studies have implications for African American individuals who at times are found to be anxious when being treated by non-African American health care professionals (Weisenberg et al., 1975). Since anxiety is often associated with lack of control, it is important therefore for the African American patient to learn strategies to control his/her anxiety (these strategies will be discussed in the treatment section). Along this same line, health care professionals should strive to provide a relaxing environment for consumers of health services.

Control over pain can also be understood in terms of general attributions of the person. Nisbett and Shacter (1966) studied the attributions which subjects made to body arousal in relation to the level of tolerance. They found that subjects who tolerated the most shock attributed their body arousal more to the effects of a drug than did subjects who attributed their arousal to the electric shock. Davison & Valins (1969) found that subjects who made self-attributions in pain control had a high tolerance for pain. Averil (1973) reported that individuals with an internal locus of control orientation recover from dental surgery quicker than externals. Apparently, control over pain does not necessarily have to be exercised by the individual but can be increased if the person facing the stress is able to trust the controller of the stress, or is prepared with information concerning the stress (Leventhal, Singer & Jones, 1965).

The importance of cognitive factors in the experience of pain has been examined in an interesting study by Rybstein (1979). Experimental conditions were manipulated to examine the influence of the following types of cognitive strategies: (a) reinterpreting the pain stimuli; (b) diverting attention from the pain; and (c) concentrating on the sensation itself. Results of the study demonstrated a significant reduction in pain in the group that used reinterpretive cognitive instructions. However, when the effectiveness of a self-management treatment program was compared with a program of coping self-statements, the self- management program produced the greatest reduction in pain even after the treatment was ended (Turk et al., 1983).

Efforts to determine successful coping characteristics of pain sufferers have led researchers to two major concepts: coping and avoiding (Petrie, 1967; Goldstein, 1973). These two variables reportedly refer to individual differences in ways of responding to pain. Apparently, avoiders use denial, rationalizations and avoidance behaviors, while copers use predominantly approaching mechanisms such as intellectualization and obsessive-compulsive behaviors. Although research in this area is far from conclusive, avoiders tend to have a higher pain tolerance (Davidson & Babey, 1970), and require more medication following surgery (Andrews, 1970). Moreover, individuals who use avoidance and denial as coping strategies show good post-surgical adjustment to pain only when they are not exposed to information regarding the surgery (De Long, 1970). Copers, on the other hand, adjust well for surgery only if they are given specific information concerning the surgery. Those who were given general information exhibited poor postsurgical adjustment (De Long, 1970; Cohen & Lazarus, 1973).

Pain, Illness Behavior and Social Support

Mechanic (1976) like Parsons (1958) before him, differentiates between the characteristics of disease and illness. Disease, according to Mechanic (1974) implies an underlying biological condition, whereas illness involves a subjective decision, based on the kinds of behavior being emitted, that an individual is not healthy. Although there is a direct relationship between disease and illness, the reverse cannot be stated because illness involves a subjective inference based on behavior that can be due to functional causes or structural alterations. The health care system is oriented toward treating the underlying disease or organic pathology and pays little attention to the social context and illness behavior. Illness related behavior and social context are areas of increasing importance to social scientists.

In a seminal paper, Moos and Tsu (1977) outlined seven strategies individuals use to adapt to illness. The strategies are as follows:

Illness related:

1. Dealing with pain and incapacitation
2. Dealing with the hospital environment and special procedures
3. Developing adequate relationship with the professional staff
4. Preserving a reasonable emotional balance
5. Preserving a satisfactory self-image
6. Preserving relationship with family and friends
7. Preparing for an uncertain future

The strategies outlined by Moos and Tsu (1977) point out the multiple and interacting factors which contribute to effectively coping with an illness. While the precise role of each of these strategies is unknown, it is safe to say that effective copers are those who have appropriate inter- and intrapersonal skills and competencies necessary to meet the demands of the illness. Although Moos and Tsu (1977) focus on the individual and how illness affects behavior, their model is invaluable for pointing out the fact that pain and illness occur within social contexts and are embedded in social relationships.

Families, in general, and the African American family in particular, determine many health related beliefs and behaviors (Allen & Stukes, 1982). The extended African American family has been noted for its strong kinship bonds, role flexibility, high network and insularity (Hill, 1971; Nobles, 1974). We know very little about the African American's health belief practices. Since they value the development of a strong extended family network and the maintenance of their cultural heritage, it should follow that the health practices and beliefs of African Americans should be highly consistent within families. Likewise it would also seem there would be a rapid and easy flow of health related information and practices between family members.

Interestingly enough, Janzen (1978) found that a continuing African tradition is for the clan or family group and not the individual to decide the health care activity of the sick person. Nobles (1974) has long contended that African Americans have held on to their African traditions. As with mental health concerns, African American family members may depend on older members of the family to help them with decisions regarding advice and referrals. African American families typically have specialists who provide informational and emotional support (Baer, 1981).

The type of support available to the individual appears to influence health related behaviors. Lafarge (1981) found that African American women are more likely to seek medical treatment if a friend accompanies them. Although the family and friends seem to influence health seeking behaviors, African American patients when given a choice to comply with recommendations from experts or their peer group choose experts (Ross, 1973).

One would think that the family along with the network of friends and acquaintances provide an individual with the emotional material and informational support needed to adjust to pain and illness. Although as logical as this may seem, we know very little about the relationship between social support, adjustment to illness and the influence of culture. Broadly speaking, we do not know how social support systems work, how people perceive supportive acts or precisely what type of support is most effective with whom and in what situations. For example, among the plethora of studies in the area there is some evidence to suggest that a spouse's post-surgical care and support predicted adjustment following onset of angina (Medalie & Gouldbort, 1976). In addition, lack of support is associated with complications in pregnancy (Nuckolls, Cassell, & Kaplan, 1972). On the other hand, Anderson and Rehm (1984) found that higher degrees of support adversely affect certain chronic pain groups. Likewise Reif (1976) found disability among men suffering from myocardial infarction to be related to high degrees of emotional support. Although contradictory findings exist within the literature, for the most part, social support is viewed as being beneficial to the sick person. Since adjustment to pain and illness is related, in some way, to psychosocial factors, more attention should be placed on research in this area. This has relevance for African Americans since the African American family system is the central source of support for an African American individual.

In summary, personality, mood, physiological states, cognitive coping strategies and social support appear to influence the degree to which a person responds to pain. One could ask, to what extent these variables differ with regard to racial and ethnic group status. Comparisons could be made of individuals from different groups. However, in making such comparisons it is our feeling that there will always be substantial individual variation within groups. Although we suspect that personality, patterns of mood, physiological states, and cognitive strategies vary as a function of ethnicity, it is our feeling that these aforementioned variables contribute significantly to an individual's (regardless of race) reaction to pain. Research directed at clarifying the interaction of these correlates of pain with coping and adaptation should lead to a better understanding of chronic painful states. In addition, we encourage more efforts aimed at assessing individual variation among African American clients and not those strategies aimed at comparing African American and White pain sufferers. We will now turn our attention to treatment issues.

Review of Treatment Strategies

Methodological Issues

A critical issue encountered in evaluating the effectiveness of any treatment program for chronic pain concerns an adequate selection of outcome criteria. Individuals coming in for treatment are quite heterogeneous on most measures. In addition, as pointed out in previous sections, pain patients differ on a number of dimensions. As such, these differences make them differentially receptive to different forms of treatment strategies. In carrying out research in this area, some have argued (Weisenberg, 1977) that it is desirable to clearly delineate the criteria of pain being assessed.

In review, the experience of pain can be broadly divided into cognitive, subjective-emotional and behavioral dimensions. By and large, increases in activity levels, primarily measured as up-time are the criteria used in most studies (Keefe, 1982). Clinical changes are typically operationalized around specific behaviors (e.g. walking, sitting, and grimacing). The emotional- affective dimension of pain is generally believed to be unreliable, primarily because it involves subjective evaluation. Thus, the best designed research studies tend to make the assumption that pain behaviors are direct reflections of underlying pathophysiology which is elicited by the sensation of pain.

A second major task in research on chronic pain treatment programs involves the selection of patient samples. Often researchers indiscriminately include in their sample, subjects with a mixture of painful conditions. There are some drawbacks to this kind of selection procedure. Since we know that treatment effectiveness is dependent on the type of pain syndrome (Keefe, 1982), it is feasible to assume that any treatment effects present in studies using subjects with a mixture of painful conditions may be masked due to the differential response patterns of these subjects. It is therefore extremely important for researchers to select a homogeneous sample of pain patients for their studies. This strategy would allow meaningful comparisons to be made across studies. Also, results from studies are easier to interpret and generalize thus leading to studies which would clearly delineate patterns of successful treatment for each pain syndrome.

For the most part, the chronic pain treatment literature is replete with case studies. Major problems exist in that no control or placebo-control groups were used. Furthermore, some researchers combine a variety of treatment strategies, thus not allowing for a determination of the ingredients which contribute to the treatment effects. The best studies in this area are those which use various kinds of control groups such as untreated controls, waiting-list controls, placebo controls and crossover controls. In addition, the choice when researching small samples is clearly single case methodologies. Multiple and extended baseline should be implemented in order to reasonably assess treatment effects (Kazdin, 1980).

With the aforementioned in mind, we will now discuss what we think are some of the best studies of treatment strategies.

Cognitive Therapy

Cognitive behavioral techniques have been used for pain, e.g., migraine and tension headaches, low-back pain, and myofascial pain dysfunction syndrome. Cognitive behavioral strategies are designed to help patients prevent or short circuit noxious sensations before they crystallize into severe pain. Treatment focus is on factors that contribute to pain and on those factors that contribute to dysfunctional physiological processes, e.g. excessive muscle contraction (Turk et al., 1983; Turner, 1982). Cognitive behavioral techniques tend to incorporate distraction, suggestion, anxiety reduction, and an increased sense of self-control. Each program emphasizes and depends on the active participation of the patient(Turk et al., 1983). A principle underlying all behavioral medicine/health psychology programs is that the individual is responsible for his/her health and not the health care professional.

In one of the best studies in this area, chronic low back pain outpatients were randomly assigned to cognitive behavioral group therapy. Patients showed significant improvement on self- report measures of pain, depression, disability, and on a significant other rating of physical and psychosocial dysfunction. These patients continued to demonstrate further improvement on several measures of pain, depression, and disability at 12 and 18 month follow-ups. In addition, there was a marked reduction in health care use and an increase in time spent working (Turner, 1982).

Headache patients have been treated successfully with cognitive coping strategies. Treatment rationales presented to patients by Holyrod et al. (1977) and Bakal et al. (1980) explained how disturbing moods and behaviors result from certain thought processes or cognitions. By utilizing cognitive coping skills training, patients were induced to attribute their headaches to specific maladaptive thought patterns.

Results indicated that cognitive coping skills training proved effective with significant improvement in headache (Bakal et al., 1980) with a concomitant reduction in medication usage (Holyrod et al., 1977). Taken together, their data suggest that cognitive coping skills training may be useful in the management of severe chronic problems by producing a significant symptomatic reduction in chronic pain.

Thompson (1981) reported that cognitive strategies have been shown to increase one's tolerance to pain, but not the self-reported measure of pain. Cognitive control appears to have uniformly positive effects on the experience of an aversive event. Such strategies appear to lessen anticipatory anxiety, and reduce the impact of the stimulus. In a study which employed a two group crossover design, Hartmann and Ainsworth (1980) compared stress inoculation with alpha biofeedback. Results revealed that the group receiving biofeedback first experienced the greatest reductions in their self-report of pain.

In summary, the evidence does suggest that cognitive strategies can be effective in the treatment of some types of pain syndromes. Headache sufferers seem to respond well to this approach. One must warn the reader, however, that in some of the studies reviewed, cognitive approaches were not the sole strategy used.

Biofeedback and Relaxation Procedures

In a literature review on the applicability of biofeedback techniques, Yates (1980) noted that the promotional literature invariably refers to the usefulness of biofeedback in treating chronic pain. However, Yates noted, the empirical literature on biofeedback contains few studies relating to the efficacy in treating chronic pain. This fact is interesting in that prior to Yates' review, biofeedback techniques had been investigated in the treatment of Raynaud's disease, tension headache, vascular headache, and chronic back pain (Haynes et al., 1975; Cox et al., 1975; Martin & Matthews, 1978; Blanchard e tal., 1978a 1978a; Birk, 1973a, 1973b).

Andrasik & Holyrod (1980) treated tension headache sufferers with electromyographic (EMG) biofeedback. And found that these procedures directed at reducing frontal muscle tension levels produced similar effects on headache at both post-treatment and 6-week follow-up assessments. Their results suggested that the learned reduction of frontal EMG activity may play only a minor role in the biofeedback treatment of tension headache.

Ford (1982) compared biofeedback training alone versus biofeedback and psychotherapy versus biofeedback and relaxation techniques. He found that biofeedback combined with psychotherapy resulted in higher success rates than either biofeedback alone, or relaxation techniques combined with biofeedback. Other studies have found biofeedback training to be equivalent to other forms of relaxation procedures for the treatment of tension headache, vascular headache, and primary Raynaud's disease (Haynes et al., 1975; Cox et al., 1975; Martin & Matthews, 1978; Blanchard et al., 1978; Silver et al., 1979; Jacobsen et al., 1979; Reinking & Hutchings, 1981). Fior et al. (1983) studied patients suffering from chronic rheumatic back pain being treated with EMG biofeedback, pseudotherapy, or conventional medical treatment during a four week inpatient stay at a Rheumatology Clinic. At the end of the treatment phase, the biofeedback group showed significant improvements in the duration, intensity, and quality of their back pain, as well as their EMG levels, negative self-statements, and utilization of the health care system. These improvements were maintained at a four month follow up assessment. The pseudotherapy group showed minimal, nonsignificant improvements and the medically treated group remained unchanged. This study illustrates that EMG biofeedback can be a useful and effective method to treat chronic back pain.

Cram & Freeman (1984) presented evidence contradicting the use of EMG biofeedback in the treatment of chronic back pain. They assessed the effects of three types of EMG biofeedback training on patterns of change in neuromusculature activity in chronic pain patients. They concluded that EMG biofeedback treatment procedures for chronic back pain need to be seriously reconsidered. The EMG assisted relaxation training approaches created more than an decade ago for headache patients may not be the best approach for chronic back pain patients. Cram and Freeman (1984) argue, based on the results of their study that EMG assisted relaxation training protocols conducted in static posture are only marginally effective for chronic pain patients due to poor generalization, and that more dynamic postural approaches may be more effective.

The use of relaxation is rapidly expanding in treatment areas ranging from dentistry to the control of chronic pain. Practicing relaxation before childbirth resulted in significant pain reduction during childbirth among women who elected such preparation (Cogan & Kluthe, 1981).

In a study cited earlier in this chapter, Turner (1982) treated chronic low back pain outpatients with group progressive relaxation training, cognitive behavioral group therapy, or a waiting list condition. Only the relaxation training and cognitive behavioral therapy patients showed significant improvement at post-treatment and at both 18 and 24 month follow-up.

In summary, research has shown that chronic pain sufferers can experience relief from pain with the use of biofeedback or relaxation procedures. Headache sufferers, in particular, can benefit from these approaches. Although research has shown that relaxation procedures can reduce the experience of pain, it still is unclear if these differences can lead to significant changes in pain and related behaviors.

Transcutaneous Electrical Nerve Stimulation

Electrical stimulation has been utilized as a method of pain control since late in the nineteenth century. As of late, this method has been gaining in popularity as a viable treatment alternative. Transcutaneous electrical nerve stimulation has been used effectively to treat both acute and chronic pain sufferers, but it is most effective with acute pain (Breckner & Breckner, 1978; Coffey & Mahon, 1982).

Transcutaneous electrical nerve stimulation (TENS) transmits electrical stimulation cutaneously to the appropriate underlying nerves to prevent the message of pain from reaching the brain. It is believed that TENS selectively stimulates and overloads the large sensory fibers, thus relieving pain as postulated by the central inhibitory and/or gate control theories. Usage is contraindicated in patients with psychogenic and/or psychiatric disturbances, pregnancy, and pacemakers. Positive treatment outcomes are indicated for those patients with chronic pain not amenable to conservative therapies and/or poor surgical risks. This has later been expanded to include patients with acute pain (Coffey & Mahon, 1982).

Sternbach (1978) utilized a transcutaneous neurostimulator as an alternative for many patients on analgesics. The transcutaneous neurostimulator (TNS) is a possible electrical stimulator which seems to provide relief from pain by direct action on peripheral nerves, blocking transmission in pain fibers and by stimulating central descending inhibitory processes. Patients wear the stimulator inconspicuously throughout the day. Electrodes are taped into place and batteries can be recharged during the night. Sternbach found that the TNS aided in minimizing the development of dependence and tolerance to analgesic medication.

Behavioral Programs

About 65% of chronic pain patients who receive contingency management show significant improvement. Many, if not most, are able to return to normal social and recreational functioning. If carried through to successful conclusion, treatment typically results in a reduction in physical pain and an improved physical function ing. There also tends to be an increase in psychological well-being, self-esteem and personal happiness (Unikel, 1978). Thus, behavioral approaches influence the response to pain in a number of areas.

Operant techniques require that goals desired by patients are contingent on activities that will lead to improved health and adjustment. Undesirable behaviors are eliminated, while drug abuse and excessive verbalization of pain are not rewarded (Fordyce, 1976). Treatment goals typically include: the reduction of pain behaviors, increased levels of physical activity, reduction of pain related health care utilization behaviors, and the promotion and maintenance of effective well behavior (Fordyce, 1976). The major focus of an operant behavioral program is on encouraging the chronic pain patient to get out of bed and lead as active a life as possible.

Contingency-management programs are unique in that the chronic pain patient is required to maintain daily diaries. Information is requested on the specific time patterns in which pain occurs. Whether the pain is better or worse in the morning or evening and when, what, and how much medication is taken to control pain. "Uptime" or the amount of time during the day that is spent sitting, standing, or walking, and reclining is also recorded. Weekly total average uptime is 112 hours. Weekly totals less than 80 hours indicates significant impairment (Fordyce, 1976). In order to increase uptime, patients are given specific daily assignments to perform, i .e ., exercise, walking, sports, or household chores . Patients are given tasks within the limits of their capabilities, with preference going to activities one enjoys or would like to do. It is understood that the activities must be carried out for a prescribed period of time before they are given medical treatment for pain relief. As treatment continues, the patient is required to become progressively more active until suitable activity levels have been reached (Unikel, 1978).

Fordyce (1976) indicated that patient selection for a contingency management treatment program must consider: (A) Which pain behaviors or functional impairments are to be decreased, and which activities are to be increased by the patient, spouse or others? (B) What reinforcers hold promise of effectiveness in treatment, particularly in the early phases? (C) Which post-treatment activity is reasonably to be expected from patient and spouse? Are those behaviors in their repertoires? Are they accessible? (D) Are spouse and family ready, willing, and able to participate in treatment and support change?

Psychological Treatment of the African American Pain Patient

Not much has been written specifically about the treatment of the African American chronic pain patient. We do know that the health care professional should be careful in his assessment of the African American patient. As stated previously, the anxiety that the African American patient experiences may be due to the situation and not the pain itself. In addition, since African American clients tend to have high MMPI scale elevations, the health professional may have to rely more on self-report and behavioral monitoring approaches. Along this same line, the Back Pain Classification Scale (BPCS) developed by Leavitt and Garron (1979), should be favored over other pain instruments since it reportedly is not affected by age, education, race, sex or religion.

Family is very important to African Americans. Therefore, the entire family should be involved in the treatment of African American patients. The involvement of the family in the treatment of the chronic pain patient is the most effective treatment strategy known (Fordyce, 1976). Consequently, the strengths of the African American family in providing emotional and tangible support should be an advantage for the African American chronic pain sufferer. Most standard pain treatment programs involve behavioral contingency strategies. A typical behavioral contingency management program would allow limited use of medication for pain and make the medication contingent upon desirable activities such as walking and light exercise. By and large, within such a program, the patient and his spouse usually are asked to monitor all activities in order to determine the patient's optimal level of functioning. Once this is determined, then a contingency schedule is worked out which would allow the patient to gradually increase his well behaviors while decreasing his sick role or illness behaviors. It is our assumption that such a program would provide little difficulty for the African American patient.

Conclusion

Pain is probably the most potent motivator of behavior known to man. The once widely accepted belief that the experience of pain is purely a sensory experience is no longer acceptable. The understanding of how an individual perceives, experiences and reacts to pain and physical illness are important areas of study . Pain and illness related behaviors are determined in part, by psychosocial and cultural factors. Health care professionals are trained to focus on and specifically alleviate the underlying cause of pain. For the most part, cultural, contextual and psychosocial factors are ignored by health care professionals. As suggested by this review, successful treatment of a patient in pain often requires some appreciation of how the individual patient perceives and copes with his/her condition . Thus, since the patient's perception and coping strategies are influenced by psychosocial, contextual and cultural factors, social scientists can make unique contributions to the health care field and in particular to the control of pain.

Social scientists interested in ethnic minority issues however, have not paid much attention to the area of pain in particular, and in health care issues in general. In this chapter, we have attempted to use pain as an exemplar in order to examine psychosocial concomitants to physical illness and to demonstrate how integrating behavioral and biomedical knowledge and techniques can be beneficial to African Americans. The review of the clinical and research literature on pain provide the health care professional with a holistic framework to assess and treat chronic painful conditions. In addition, acute and chronic pain are differentiated within a transitional framework. Such a framework should provide a heuristic model for the understanding of how certain acute stages change into chronic conditions. Although our review is incomplete in many ways, just the same, we hope that it can stimulate future ethnic minority research efforts in the area of health care and health psychology.

References

Adams, H. E., Fuerstein, M., & Fowler, J. L. (1980). Migraine headache: Review of parameters, etiology and interventions. *Psychological Bulletin, 87*, 217-237.

Adler, R. N. (1978). Psychotropic agents in the management of chronic pain. *Journal of Human Stress, 4(2)*, 13-17.

Agnew, D. C., & Merskey, N. (1976). Words of chronic pain. *Pain, 2(11)*, 73-81.

Allen, W. R., & Stukes, S. (1982). Black family lifestyles and the mental health of Black Americans.In F. U. Munoz & R. Endo (Eds.), *Perspectives in minority group mental health*. Washington, D.C.: University Press of America.

Anderson, L. P., & Rehm, L. P. (1984). The relationship between strategies of coping and perception of pain in three chronic pain groups. *Journal of Clinical Psychology, 40(3)*, 1170-1177.

Andrasik, F., & Holyrod, K. A. (1980). A test of specific and nonspecific effects in the biofeedback treatment of tension headache. *Journal of Consulting and Clinical Psychology, 48(5)*, 575-586.

Andrews, J. M. (1970). Recovery from surgery, with and without preparation. Instructions for three coping styles. *Journal of Personality and Social Psychology, 15*, 223-226.

Armentrout, D. P. (1979). The impact of chronic pain on the self-concept. *Journal of Clinical Psychology, 35(3)*, 517-521.

Arthritis Foundation (1973). *Primer on the rheumatic diseases.* Washington,D.C.: Author.

Averil, J. R. (1973). Personal control over aversive stimuli and its relationship to stress. *Psychological Bulletin, 80*, 286-303.

Baer, H. A. (1981). Prophets and advisors in Black spiritual churches: Therapy palliative or opiate? *Culture, Medicine and Psychiatry, 5(2)*, 145-170.

Bakal, D. A., Demjen, S., & Kaganov, J. A. (1982). *Cognitive behavioral treatment of headache.* Unpublished manuscript, University of Calgary. In R. Roy

& E. Turks (Eds.), *Chronic pain: Psychosocial factors in rehabilitation*. Baltimore: Williams and Wilkins.

Banks, W. M. (1980). The social context and empirical foundations of research on Black clients. In R. L. Jones (Ed.), *Black Psychology*. New York: Harper and Row.

Bartol, C.R., & Costello, N. (1976). Extraversion as a function of temporal duration of electrical shock: An exploratory study. *Perceptual and Motor Skills, 42(3)*, 1174.

Beecher, H. K. (1966). Pain: One mystery solved. *Science, 151*, 840-841.

Berlyne, D. E. (1951). Attention, perception, and behavior therapy. *Psychological Review, 58*, 137.

Birk, L. (1973a). Tension headache. In L. Birk (Ed.), *Biofeedback and behavioral medicine*. New York: Grune and Stratton.

Birk, L. (1973b). Migraine Headache. In L. Birk (Ed.), *Biofeedback and behavioral medicine*. New York: Grune and Stratton.

Blanchard, E. B., Theobal, D. E., Williamson, D. A., Silver, B. V. & Brown, D. A. (1978). Temperature biofeedback in the treatment of migraine headache. *Archives of General Psychiatry, 35*, 581-588.

Block, A. R., Kramer, E. R., & Gaylor, M. (1980). Behavioral treatment of chronic pain: The spouse as a discriminate cue for pain behavior. *Pain, 9*, 243-252.

Bonica, J. J., & Albe-Fessard, D. (1976). *Advances in pain research and therapy, Vol. 1*. New York: Raven Press.

Bradley, J. J. (1963). Severe localized pain associated with the depression syndrome. *British Journal of Psychiatry, 109*, 741-745.

Breckner, V. L., & Ferrer-Breckner, T. (1978). Three alternatives to surgery and drugs in pain control. In S. F. Brena (Ed.), *Chronic pain: American's hidden epidemic*. New York: Antheneum.

Buss, A. H., & Portnoy, N. W. (1967). Pain tolerance and group identification. *Journal of Personality and Social Psychology, 6*, 106-108.

Butcher (Ed.), *MMPI: Research developments and clinical applications*. New York: McGraw-Hill.

Carson, R. C. (1969). Interpretive manual to the MMPI. In J. N. Butcher (Ed.), *MMPI: Research developments and clinical applications*. New York: McGraw-Hill.

Casey, K. L. (1971). Somatosensory responses of bulboreticular units in awake cats: Relationship to escape-producing stimuli. *Science, 173*, 77.

Chaves, J. F., & Barber, T. X. (1974). Cognitive strategies, experimenter modeling and expectation in the attenuation of pain. *Journal of Abnormal Psychology, 83*, 356-363.

Cinciripini, P. M ., & Floreen, A. (1981) . An evaluation of a behavioral program for chronic pain. *Journal of Behavioral Medicine, 5(3)*, 375-389.

Coffey, G. H., & Mahon, M. V. (1982). Pain: Theories and a new approach to treatment. *Journal of the National Medical Association, 74(2),* 147-153.

Cogan, R., & Kluthe, K.B.(1981).The role of learning in pain reduction associated with relaxation and patterned breathing. *Psychosomatic Research, 25(6),* 535-539.

Cogswell, B. E., & Weir, D. D. (1964). A role in process: The development of medical professionals in long-term care of chronically diseased patients. *Journal of Health and Social Behavior, 12,* 66-72.

Cohen, F., & Lazarus, R. S. (1973). Active coping processes, coping dispositions, and recovery from surgery. *Psychosomatic Medicine, 35,* 375-389.

Cox, D. J., Freundlich A., & Meyer, R. G. (1975). Differential affectiveness of electromyographic feedback, verbal relaxation instructions, and medication placebo with tension headaches. *Journal of Consulting and Clinical Psychology, 43,* 892-898.

Craig, K. D., & Weiss, S. M. (1972). Verbal reports of pain without noxious stimulation. *Perceptual and Motor Skills, 34,* 943-948.

Cram, J. R., & Steger, J. C. (1983). EMG scanning in the diagnosis of chronic pain. *Biofeedback and Self-Regulation, 8(2),* 229-241.

Cram, J. R., & Freeman, C. W. (1984). *Specificity in EMG biofeedback treatment of chronic pain patients.* Unpublished manuscript. Seattle, WA: Swedish Hospital Pain Center.

Croog, S . H ., Shapiro, D. S ., & Levine, S . (1971) . Denial among male heart patients. *Psychosomatic Medicine,* 385-397.

Davison, G. C., & Valins, S. (1969). Maintenance of self-attributed behavior change. *Journal of Personality and Social Psychology, 11,* 25-33.

Davidson, P. O., & Bobey, M. J. (1970). Repression-sensitizer differences on repeated exposures to pain. *Perceptual and Motor Skills, 31,* 711-714.

DeLong, R. D. (1970). *Individual differences in patterns of anxiety arousal, stress relevant information and recovery from surgery.* Unpublished doctoral dissertation, University of California, Los Angeles.

Demjen, S., & Bakal, D. A. (1979). A cognitive-behavioral treatment program for chronic pain. *Headache, 19,* 249.

Engel, G. (1959). Psychogenic pain and the pain-prone patient. *American Journal of Medicine, 26,* 899.

Evaskus, D. S ., & Laskin, D. M. (1972). A biochemical measure of stress in patients with myofascial dysfunction syndrome. *Journal of Dental Research, 51,* 1464-1466.

Flannery, R. B., Sos, J., & McGovern, P. (1981). Ethnicity as a factor in the expression of pain. *Psychosomatics, 22(11),* 39-50.

Flor, H., Haag, G., Turk, D. C., & Koehler, H. (1983). Efficacy of EMG biofeedback, pseudotherapy, and conventional medical treatment for chronic rheumatic back pain. *Pain, 17,* 21-31.

Ford, M. R. (1982). Biofeedback treatment for headaches, Raynaud's disease, essential hypertension, and irritable bowel syndrome: A review of long-term follow-up literature. *Biofeedback and Self-Regulation, 7(4)*, 521-536.

Fordyce, W. (1976). *Behavioral methods for chronic pain and illness.* St. Louis: C.V. Mosby.

Fordyce, W. E., & Steger, J. C. (1979). Chronic pain. In O. F. Pomalreou & J. P. Brady. *Behavioral medicine theory and practice.* Baltimore: Williams and Wilkins.

Gentry, W. D. (1984). *Handbook of behavioral medicine.* New York: The Guilford Press.

Gentry, W. D., & Thomas, M. (1974). Chronic low back pain: A psychological profile. *Psychosomatics, 15*, 174-177.

Gessel, A. H., & Alderman, M. M. (1971). Management of myofascial pain dysfunction syndrome of the temporomandibular joint by tension control training. *Psychosomatics, 12*, 302-309.

Goldstein, M. J. (1973). Individual differences in response to stress. *American Journal of Community Psychology, 1*, 113-137.

Gorsky, B. H. (1981). *Pain: Origin and treatment.* New York: Medical Examination Publishing Co., Inc.

Gorsky, B . H. (Oct.1979). Chronic pain: A management plan based on experiences in a pain clinic. *Postgraduate Medicine, 66(4)*, 147-154.

Greene, C. S., Lerman, M. D., & Sutcher, H. D. (1969). The TMJ pain dysfunction syndrome: Heterogeneity of the patient population. *Journal of the American Dental Association, 79*, 1168-1172.

Greenhoot, J. H., & Sternbach, R. A. (1974). Conjoint treatment of pain. *Advances in Neurology, 4*, 595-603.

Harding, H. C. (1967). Hypnosis in the treatment of migraine. In J. Lassner (Ed.), *Hypnosis and psychosomatic medicine.* New York: Springer-Verlag.

Hartman, L. M., & Ainsworth, K. D. (1980). Self-regulation of chronic pain. *Canadian Journal of Psychiatry, 25*, 38-43.

Haynes, S. N., Griffin, P., Mooney, D., & Parise, M. (1975). Electromyographic biofeedback and relaxation instructions in the treatment of muscle contraction headaches. *Behavior Therapy, 6*, 672-678.

Hilgard, E. R. (1969). Pain as a puzzle for psychology and physiology. *American Psychologist, 24*, 103-113.

Hill, R. (1971). The strength of the Black family. New York: Cognitive control of tension headache. *Cognitive Therapy Research, 1*, 121-133.

Horan, J. J., & Dellinger, J. K. (1974). "In vivo" emotive imagery: A preliminary test. *Perceptual and Motor Skills, 39*, 359-362.

Hudgens, A. J. (1977). The social worker's role in a behavioral management approach to chronic pain. *Social Work in Health Care, 3(2)*, 149-157.

Jacobsen, A. M., Manschrenck, T. C., & Silverberg, E.(1979). Behavioral treatment for Raynaud's disease: A comparative study with long-term follow-up. *American Journal of Psychiatry, 136*, 844-846.

Jacox, A. (1980). The assessment of pain. In W. L. Smith, H. Merskey, & S . C. Gross (Eds.), *Pain: Meaning and management*. New York: SP Medical and Scientific Books.

Janzen, J. (1978). *The quest for therapy in lower Zaire*. Berkeley, CA: University of California Press.

Jenkins, A. H. (1981). *The psychology of the Afro-American: A humanistic approach*. New York: Pergamon Press.

Johnson, R., & Baldwin, D. C., Jr. (1968). Relationship of maternal anxiety to the behavior of young children undergoing dental extraction. *Journal of Dental Research, 47*, 801-805.

Jones, E. E., & Korchin, S. J. (Eds.)(1981). *Minority mental health*. New York: Praeger.

Jones, R. L. (Eds.) (1991). *Black psychology*. Hampton, VA: Cobbs & Henry Publishers.

Jones, R. L. (Eds.) (1998). *African American Mental Health*. Hampton, VA: Cobbs & Henry Publishers.

Kalla, J. M. (1978). The effects of premorbid adjustment upon treatment outcome of chronic pain patients. *Dissertation Abstracts International, 10(10-B)*, 5025-5026.

Kanfer, F. H., & Goldfoot, D. A. (1966). Self-control and tolerance of noxious stimulations. *Psychological Reports, 18*, 79-85.

Kanin, G. (1978). *It takes a long time to become young*. New York: Doubleday.

Kazdin, A. E. (1980). *Research design in clinical psychology*. New York: Harper & Rowe.

Keefe, F. J. (1982). Behavioral assessment and treatment of chronic pain: Current status and future directions. *Journal of Consulting and Clinical Psychology, 50(6)*, 896-911.

Keefe, F. J., & Brown, C. (1981). Behavioral treatment of chronic pain. In P. Boudewyns & F. Keefe (Eds.), *Behavioral medicine in general medical practice*. Menlo Park, CA: Addison-Wesley.

Knapp. P. H. (1981). Core processes in the organization of emotions. *Journal of American Academy of Psychologists, 9*, 415-434.

Koenig, P. (April, 1973). The placebo effect of patient medicine. *Psychology Today, 7*, 60.

Lafargue, J. (1981). *Those you can count on: A social network study of family organization in an urban population*. Ph. D. dissertation, University of Washington.

Lawlis, F. G., Achterberg, J., Kenner, J., & Kopetz, K. (1984). Ethnic and sex differences in response to clinical and induced pain in chronic spinal pain patients. *Spine, 9*, 751- 754.

Leaventhal, H., Singer, R. E., & Jones, S. (1965). Effects of fear and specificity of recommendations. *Journal of Personality and Social Psychology, 2*, 20-29.

Levine, F. M., Tursky, B ., & Nichols, D. C. (1966). Tolerance for pain, extraversion and neuroticism: Failure to replicate results. *Perceptual and Motor Skills, 23(3)*, 847-850.

Linton, S. J., & Gotestam, K. G. (1983). A clinical comparison of two pain scales: Correlation, remembering chronic pain and a measure of compliance. *Pain, 17*, 57-65.

Ljunggren, A. E. (1983). Descriptions of pain and other sensory modalities in patients with lumbago-sciatica and herniated intervertebral discs. Interview administration of an adapted McGill Pain Questionnaire. *Pain, 16*, 265-276.

Martin, P. R., & Mathews, A. M. (1978). Tension headaches: Psychophysiological investigation and treatment. *Journal of Psychosomatic Research, 22*, 389-399.

Maruta, T., Swanson, D. W., & Swenson, W. M. (1979). Chronic pain: Which patients may a pain management program help? *Pain, 7*, 321-329.

McElroy, S R. (1980). *The handbook of the psychology of hemoglobin: A perspicacuous view of sickle cell disease.* Lanham, MD: University Press of America.

Mechanic, D. (1976). Stress, illness and illness behavior. *Journal of Human Stress, 2*, 2-6.

Medalie, J. H., & Goldbourt, U. (1976). Angina pectoris among 10,000 men: II. Psychosocial and other risk factors as evidenced by a multivariate analysis of a five year incidence study. *American Journal of Medicine, 60*, 910-921.

Melzack, R. (1973). *The puzzle of pain.* New York: Basic Books.

Melzack. R., & Torgerson, W.S. (1971). On the language of pain. *Anesthesiology, 24*, 50-59.

Melzack, R., & Wall, P. D. (1982). *The challenge of pain.* New York: Basic Books.

Mersky, H. (1978). Diagnosis of the patient with chronic pain. *Journal of Human Stress, 4(2)*, 3-7.

Merskey, H. (1978). IASP subcommittee on taxonomy. Pain terms: A list with definitions and notes on usage. *Pain, 6*, 249-252.

Merskey, H. (1973). The perception and measurement of pain. *Journal of Psychosomatic Research, 17*, 251 -256.

Merskey, H. (1968). Psychological aspects of pain. *Postgraduate Medicine, 44*, 297-306.

Millon, T., Green, C., & Meager, R. (1982). *Handbook of clinical health psychology.* New York: Plenum Press.

Mitchell, K. R., & White, R. G. (1977). Behavioral self-management: An application to the problem of migraine headaches. *Behavior Therapy, 8*, 213-222.

Mohamed, S . N., Weisz, G. W., & Waring, E. M . (1978). The relationship of chronic pain to depression, marital adjustment, and family dynamics. *Pain, 5(3)*, 285-292.

Moos, R. H., & Tsu, V. D. (1977). The crises of physical illness: An overview. In R. H. Moos (Ed.), *Coping with physical illness*. New York: Plenum Press.

Nadel, C., & Portadia, C. (1977). Sickle cell crisis: Psychological factors associated with onset. *New York State Journal of Medicine, 57*, 114-118.

Nisbett, R. E., & Schacter, S. (1966). Cognitive manipulation of pain. *Journal of Experimental Social Psychology, 2*, 227-236.

Nobles, W. W. (1974). Africanity: It's role in Black families. *Black Scholar, 5*, 18-25.

Nuckolls, C. G., Gassel, J. B., & Kaplan, B. H. (1972). Psychosocial assets, life crises, and the prognosis of pregnancy. *American Journal of Epidemiology, 95*, 431-441.

Parsons, T. (1958). Definitions of health and illness in light of American values and social structure. In E. G. Jaco (Ed.), *Patients, physicians and illness*. Glencoe, IL: The Free Press.

Petrie, A. (1967). *Individuality in pain and suffering*. Chicago, IL: University of Chicago Press.

Pillowsky, I., & Bond, M. R. (1969). Pain and it's management in malignant disease: Elucidation of staff-patient transactions. *Psychosomatic Medicine, 31*, 400-404.

Pinsky, J. J. (1978). Chronic intractable benign pain: A syndrome and it's treatment with intensive short-term group psychotherapy. *Journal of Human Stress, 4(3)*, 17-21.

Powell, G. J. (1983). *The psychosocial development of minority group children*. New York: Bruner & Mazel.

Reading, A. E., & Martin, R. (1976). The treatment of mandibular dysfunction pain . *British Dental Journal, 140*, 201-205.

Reif, L. J. (1975). *Cardiacs and normals: the social construction of a disability*. Doctoral dissertation, University of California, San Francisco.

Reinking, R. H., & Hitchings, D. (1981). Follow up to "Tension headaches: What form of therapy is most effective?" *Biofeedback and Self-Regulation, 6*, 57-62.

Robins, A. H. (1973). Functional abdominal pain. *South African Medical Journal, 47*, 832-834.

Rosenbaum, M. (1980). A schedule for assessing self-control behaviors: Preliminary findings. *Behavior Therapy, 11*, 109-121.

Rosenthal, R. (1966). *Experimenter effects in behavioral research*. New York: Appleton-Century Crofts.

Ross, J. (1973). Influence of experts and peers upon Negro Mothers of low socioeconomic status. *Journal of Social Psychology, 89*, 79-84.

Rosse, C., & Lawson, D. K. (1970). *Introduction to the musculoskeletal system*. New York: Harper & Rowe.

Rybstein-Blinchik, E. (1979). Effects of different cognitive strategies on the chronic pain experience. *Journal of Behavioral Medicine, 2*, 93-102.

Sattler, J. (1970). Racial experimenter effects in experimentation, testing, interviewing, and psychotherapy. *Psychological Bulletin, 73*, 137-160.

Schafter, C. B., Donlon, P. T., & Bittle, P. M. (1980). Chronic pain and depression: A clinical and family history survey. *American Journal of Psychiatry, 137*, 118-120.

Schwartz, G. E., & Weiss, S. M. (1978). Behavioral medicine revisited: An amended definition. *Journal of Behavioral Medicine, 1*, 249-251.

Schwartz, G. E., & Weiss, S. M. (1977). What is behavioral medicine? *Psychosomatic Medicine, 34*, 377-381.

Shealy, C., & Maurer, D. (1974). Transcutaneous nerve stimulation for control of pain. *Surgical Neurosurgery, 2*, 45-47.

Silver, B. V., Blanchard, E. B., Williamson, D. A., Theobold, D. E., & Brown, D. A. (1979). Temperature biofeedback and relaxation training in the treatment of migraine headaches. *Biofeedback and Self-Regulation, 4*, 359-366.

Smith, W. D., Burlew, A. K., Mosley, M. H., & Whitney, W. M. (1978). *Minority issues in mental health*. Reading, MA: Addison-Wesley.

Speigel, D., & Albert, L. H. (1983). Naloxone fails to reverse hypnotic alleviation of chronic pain. *Psychopharmacology, 81*, 140-143.

Srenn, P. G., Mothersill, K. H., & Brooke, R. I. (1979). Biofeedback and a cognitive behavioral approach to treatment of myofascial pain dysfunction syndrome. *Behavior Therapy, 10*, 29-36.

Staube, E., Tursky, B., & Schwartz, G. E. (1971). Self-control and predictability: Their effects on reactions to aversive stimulation. *Journal of Personality and Social Psychology, 18*, 157- 162.

Sternbach, R. A. (1968). *Pain: A psychophysiological analysis*. New York: Academic Press.

Sternbach, R. A. (1974). *Pain patients: Traits and treatment*. New York: Academic Press.

Sternbach, R. A. (1978). Treatment of the chronic pain patient. *Journal of Human Stress, 4(3)*, 11-15.

Sternbach, R. A., & Timmermans, G. (1975). Personality changes associated with reduction of pain. *Pain, 1*, 177-181.

Thompson, S. C. (1981). Will it hurt less if I can control it? A complex answer to a simple question? *Psychological Bulletin, 90(1)*, 89-101.

Timmermans, G., & Sternbach, R. A. (1976). Human chronic pain and personality: A canonical correlation analysis. In J. J. Bonica & D. G. Albe-Fessard (Eds.), *Advances in Pain Research (Vol . 1)*. New York: Raven Press.

Turk,D.C.,Michenbaum,D.,& Genest, M.(1983). *Pain and behavioral medicine: A cognitive behavioral perspective.* New York: The Guilford Press.

Turner, J. A. (1982). Comparison of group progressive-relaxation training and cognitive-behavioral group therapy for chronic low back pain. *Journal of Consulting and Clinical Psychology, 50(5),* 757-765.

Turner, J. A. (1979). Evaluation of two behavioral interventions for chronic low back pain. In D. Turk, D. Michenbaum, & M. Genest (Eds.), *Pain and behavioral medicine: A cognitive behavioral perspective.* New York: Guilford Press.

Unikel, I. P. (1978). *Behavior modification to control pain.* In S. F. Brena (Ed.), *Chronic pain.* New York: Antheneum

Weinsberg, B., & Greenlick, M. (1967). Pain response in Negro and White obstetrical patients. *Journal of Health and Social Behavior, 8,* 222-228.

Weisenberg, M.(1975). *Pain:Clinical and experimental perspectives.* St.Louis:C.V. Mosby.

Weisenberg, M.(1977). Pain and pain control. *Psychological Bulletin, 84,* 1008-1044.

Weisenberg, M., Kreindler, M. L., Schachat, R., & Werboff, J. (1975). Pain: Anxiety and attitudes in Black, White, and Puerto Rican patients. *Psychosomatic Medicine, 37(2),* 123- 135.

Welch, K. M. A., Spira, P. J., Knowles, L., & Lance, J. W. (1974). Simultaneous measurement of internal and external carotid blood flow in the monkey. *Neurology, 24,* 750-757.

Welch, K. M. A., Hashi, K., & Meyer, J. S. (1973). Cerebrovascular response to intracarotid injection of serotonin before and after middle cerebral artery occlusion. *Journal of Neurology, Neurosurgery and Psychiatry, 36,*724-735.

Williams,L.(1981). *Black psychology: Compelling issues and views.* Washington, DC: University Press of America.

White, J. L. (1984). *The psychology of Blacks: An Afro-American perspective.* Englewood Cliffs, NJ: Prentice Hall, Inc.

Woodrow, K. M., Freidman, G. D., Siegelaub, A. B., & Collen, M. F. (1972). Pain tolerance: Differences according to age, sex and race. *Psychosomatic Medicine, 34(6),* 548-556.

Yates, A. J. (1980). *Biofeedback and the modification of behavior.* New York: Plenum

Author

Louis P. Anderson, Ph.D
Department of Psychology
Georgia State University
University Plaza
Atlanta, GA 30301
Telephone: (404) 651-1615
Fax: (404) 651-1391
E-mail: Psylpa@panther.gsu.edu

Improving the Health of African Americans: Research, Perspectives and Policy

William Martin

The purpose of this chapter is to provide a conceptual overview of issues related to the physical and mental health of African Americans, with particular attention given to specific recommendations that respond to the wide array of health challenges African Americans face. These recommendations will be framed from a perspective that honors and embraces an African worldview (Nobles, 1991). The chapter is organized into six major sections: Expanding the Definition of Health, a Brief History of African American Health, Race Differentials in Mortality and Morbidity, Mental Health Practitioners' Role in African American Health, Approaches to Improving African American Health, African American Health Care Delivery System, and Conclusion. Although the chapter is sequentially organized, the concepts form a web of ideas, challenges, and, hopefully, well grounded solutions and intervention strategies.

Expanding the Definition of Health

The definition of health has mirrored the trends of diseases over the centuries. The word health can be traced back to Old High German and has the same origin as the words whole. The ancient Chinese conceived of health as balance with nature (Stone, 1979) while the Greek conception of health was similar to that of ancient Africans which embraces the concept of wholeness—as opposed to the European definiton of health which espouses wholeness but practices fragmentation. A central tenent of the present chapter is that African Americans should begin with a definition of health that embraces the African worldview as described by Nobles (1991). As I will explicate in the present chapter, the African conceptualization of health has become more and more an integral part of the mainstream health care delivery system.

Shifting epidemiological patterns have resulted in the redefinition of health. In the early 1900s, most persons died from infectious diseases; thus, the germ theory of disease took center stage. Today, most individuals die from chronic, lifestyle related diseases; thus, the biopsychosocial theory of disease has taken center stage. Baker (1994) argues that Engel's model of biopsychosocial health has immediate relevance for the psychiatric assessment and treatment of older African Americans, but unfortunately, this more inclusive definiton of health has gradually become tainted with a "blaming the victim" tone that summarily ignores or minimally emphasizes the relevance and importance of social, economic, and political forces as the etiological roots of disease. The World Health Organization's definition captures these non-medical aspects of health. The World Health Organization's definition of health acknowledges that health is a resource that enables individuals and groups to meet their needs and achieve their aspirations (1991). This broadened definition has led to the inclusion of psychiatric disorders, emotional problems, alcoholism, violence, and toxic dumping as health problems to be prevented, managed, treated, cured, and healed.

In an attempt to recapture the balance and wholeness of health care, Knowles (1977) advocated less reliance on medical services and more reliance on individual and social responsibility. Mental health research acknowledges that a public health approach to preventing and treating mental illness is a complementary strategy to providing direct patient care (Snowden, 1982; Hilliard, 1981) and, furthermore, that "African Americans have to become more responsible for their health, not only at the individual level but also at the other interfacing levels involving organizations and the environment" (Livingston & Carter, 1992, p. 413).

A Brief History of African American Health

Ten to twelve million Africans physically, psychologically, and spiritually survived the middle passage (Palmer, 1992) and millions of descendants of the middle passage survived the atrocities of slavery, Jim Crow, and the more subtle forms of contemporary racism and discrimination. While immigration to the U.S. by ethnic groups has generally been to escape political or religious oppression, poverty, or to improve the quality of life (Myers, 1991), those of African ancestry immigrated by force (Palmer, 1992).

Attempts at the destruction of African people were systematically begun from the day they were captured and enslaved, packed into shipping vessels, sold on auction blocks, and forced to labor in a strange land. They were in fact treated as animals, not humans. The slave traders and owners tried to justify the inhuman conditions slaves experienced with respect to safety, comfort, and health by reaching the theological conclusion that descendants of Ham were destined to suffer (Frazier, 1966). Moreover, the slave owners labeled adaptive behaviors demonstrated by slaves as pathological. Specifically, Cartwright (1851) described in the medical literature a psychiatric diagnosis called draptomania which means runaway slave. It is evident that draptomania was a form of medical enslavement because this diagnosis "pathologized" an adaptive response, that is, to escape inhuman conditions.

The social, economic, educational, and legal barriers to full participation in the society of the United States of America have resulted in psychophysiological processes that ultimately lead to disease. Sherman (1994) posits that John Henryism plays a role in the disparities between African Americans and Whites with respect to health status. John Henryism:

> . . . assumes that lower SES individuals in general, and African Americans in particular, are routinely exposed to psychosocial stress (e.g., chronic financial strain, job insecurity, and subtle or perhaps not so subtle social insults linked to race and social class) that require them to use considerable energy each day to manage the problems generated by these conditions. (p. 167)

Furthermore, Sherman suggests that John Henryism was a cultural adaptation strategy which can be traced back to Reconstruction.

Most would agree that slavery, reconstruction and Jim Crow characterize situations that shaped the social environment in which African Americans have lived, worked and played since the Middle Passage. These events profoundly impacted the health status of African Americans. Sherman (1994) described the psychophysiological linkage between biosocial events and mental illness. This linkage recognizes that the quality of one's personal environment represents a risk factor for mental illness. Over time, biosocial events have resulted in disparities in health status between African Americans and other populations of the United States.

Race Differentials in Mortality and Morbidity

Dating back to the 1800s, when health records were first collected, substantial racial differences were observed between the health status of African Americans and Whites. More specifically, over the past one hundred years, African Americans have been labeled as suffering from more psychopathology than Whites (Pasamanick, 1963). Differential mortality and morbidity rates in the U.S. are assumed to be closely connected to race as well as to ethnicity (Plepys & Klein, 1995). According to Bragg (1982), African Americans continue to receive more diagnoses of schizophrenia than do Whites. Reducing these and other health disparities among Americans has again become a national goal as exemplified in Healthy People 2000 (McGinnis & Foege, 1993).

The source of race differentials in mortality, morbidity, and quality of life is primarily rooted in the sociocultural structure of U.S. society. The social fabric of the U.S. was and continues to be a tapestry of prejudice and discrimination. Blustein (1994) established an interactive effect between racial differences and social system exploitation.

Historical as well as contemporary forces have affected the health status of African Americans. Some would argue, however, that history has not made a significant difference due to the unchanging character of the sociocultural fabric of the United States. Pouissant (1990), who comprehensively surveyed mental health related variables since 1969 concluded that over the next few years the mental health status of African Americans is forecasted to be poor.

Poussaint's reflection on the 1969 Joint Commission of Mental Health of Children's statement is as real today as it was in 1969. The original statement reads: "The racist attitudes of Americans which causes and perpetuates tension is patently a most compelling health hazard. Its destructive effects cripple the growth and development of millions of our citizens, young and old alike. Yearly, it directly and indirectly causes more fatalities, disabilities, and economic loss than any other factor" (Subcommittee to the President's Committee on Mental Health, 1978, p. 822).

The impact of race must not be ignored in "reinventing" the health care delivery system if the health status of African Americans is to improve. Race, however, is not the only critical variable in the development and perpetuation of excess illness and death experienced by African Americans. For example, Pouissant (1990) argues that, " . . . while poverty does not necessarily result in poor mental health, it is a significant contributing factor" (p. 18). Green (1994) establishes that the racial differences in the leading economic indicators describe disparities in health status. According to the National Center For Health Statistics (1990), the poverty rate of African Americans and Whites was 32% and 10% respectively. The median income of African Americans was $16,400 compared to $28,000 for Whites in 1990 (Bureau of Census, 1990). In spite of certain gains, the African American unemployment rate beginning in the mid 1950s has remained double that of White as well as the infant death rate (Jacob, 1986). Manton, Patrick, and Johnson (1987) argue that racial discrimination is simply a natural characteristic of capitalism which affects health. W.E.B DuBois sums up the relationship between economics and disparities in health status when he observed that, "To be a poor man is hard, but to be a poor race in a land of dollars is the very bottom of hardships" (1903/1961, p. 20).

Disparities in health status are as distinct as differentials in access to appropriate health care services. Russell and Jewell (1992) highlighted the following barriers to health care services for African Americans: financial, transportation, child care, poor understanding of treatment plans, inability to adhere to treatment plans, and African American cultural habits as well as health practices. Willie, Reiker, Kramer, and Brown (1995) present a host of data highlighting the well-documented finding that African Americans are "underrepresented among those receiving psychotherapy" (p.12).

Mental Health Practitioners' Roles in African American Health

Mental health practitioners who develop interventions for members of the African American community must not only avoid falling into the trap of "blaming the victim" but must also focus on the broader context in which African Americans live, work, do not work, and play. As such, Joceyln Landrum-Brown (1995) argues that mental health professionals should focus on liberation from internalized oppression, self-transformation, and resource development at the individual, social, family, and organizational level.

Landrum-Brown (1995) clearly calls for mental health practitioners to add to their arsenal in the war against declining health status in an environment of escalating racial and class polarization. This call is not limited to African American mental health practitioners for two reasons. First, racism is the sole burden of those who are oppressed but also the burden of those who oppress and/or receive privilege from the perpetuation of racial oppression. Second, there is a shortage of African American mental health professionals (Willie et al., 1995). It must be emphasized that all mental health practitioners will need to "value diversity and multiculturalism" (Turner & Kramer, 1995, p. 19). Thus an ecological perspective should be emphasized that embraces the Afrocentric worldview (Akbar, 1976; Nobles, 1974). Those who adopt this perspective must recognize that understanding individuals in sociocultural context is directly related to the design of successful intervention programs and that such high impact systems as school and health care delivery systems need to consider how their norms and service orientation mesh with their views of their consumer (Kelly, 1966).

Not only must mental health practitioners avoid "blaming the victim" because of the danger of developing inappropriate interventions, but within the African American community, "blaming the victim" takes on a special meaning. Specifically, "blaming the victim" is perceived as a dysfunctional and maladaptive coping mechanism (Ramseur, 1991).

Approaches To Improving African American Health

There are numerous approaches to improving the health of African Americans as individuals, families, communities, and as a people. Mental health practitioners are equipped with an assessment and therapeutic arsenal to improve the health of African Americans. This arsenal reflects the way health care is being delivered today which is a combination of individual effort, organizational effort, and community effort (Johnson, 1992). For purposes of conceptual and organizational clarity, I have organized the approaches under four categories: health policy, community development, service delivery, and self-care.

Health Policy

In spite of the glowing appraisals of managed competition, recent national surveys indicate that both the quantity and quality of medical care varies among racial and ethnic groups. Blendon, Aiken, Freeman, & Corey (1989) found that African Americans are almost twice as likely as Whites to receive medical care in hospital clinics, emergency rooms, and academic medical centers. Care delivered in these settings is fragmented due to scheduling and a higher percentage of health care providers who are in training, thereby minimizing the health enhancing effects of continuity of care.

Care is not only delivered differentially across racial and gender lines but also across diagnostic groups. Glass (1995) posits that the cause of discrimination towards the mentally ill is based upon not only attitudes but also upon discriminatory policies regarding the treatment of mental disorders that are based on persistent stigmas about psychiatric disorders and outdated myths about efficacy of treatment.

Social Darwinism applied to health policy not only compromises the health of African Americans, but of all Americans categorized as poor. Unlike the United Kingdom, the United States is reluctant to incorporate social class as a determinant of health status because this would clash with the commonly held fantasy of "the land of opportunity." As such, health scholars and practitioners involved in the intramural and extramural grant funding systems of government, corporate, and private corporations must advocate for the inclusion of social class as both an independent and dependent variable in the study of health care. Scholars and practitioners who sit on peer review panels of refereed journals must also communicate to those submitting manuscripts that they explore the impact of social class as well as the influence of race, gender, and ethnicity on health care delivery. The lack of the systematic inclusion of social class in the national health data bases has resulted in a lack of understanding of the social determinants of disease and is a potential barrier to developing a more informed health policy (Krieger & Fee, 1994).

Scholars and practitioners seeking to improve the health of African Americans should find ways to achieve the Seven Point Plan described by the President of the National Medical Association (Walton, 1994). This would require that mental health practitioners collaborate with other health care professionals in a way that focuses on a web of knowledge, experience, resources, and support. The Seven Point Plan suggests that health care providers: require cultural representation among providers and consumers, protect against discrimination in health care reform, lobby for federal direction to oversee states, advocate for health care as a right, establish privileges for "essential" community providers, expand health care human resources, and design African American networks.

Community Development

There is a key link between health policy and community development. Semmes (1996) described this relationship as follows: "Public policy should enhance the capabilities of communities to develop and maintain viable health-giving infrastructures. A community based health program ethic is critical but cannot replace necessary structural changes that need to be made in institutional, communal, and societal life" (p. 153). Community approaches to improving the health status of African Americans rest on the foundation that health status is socially constructed. Cassel (1976) argues that groups undergoing rapid social change become increasingly vulnerable to disease because of the inherent stress of the change itself. Moreover, he suggests that it takes generations for some populations to adapt to the new circumstances and thereby improve their health prospects. The community development perspective argued for in this chapter is very similar to the African proverb, "It takes a whole village to raise a child." This phrase and underlying philosophy was addressed as part of the Democratic platform in the 1996 Presidential Elections.

The challenge is that many African American communities have lost the capacity, infrastructure, and resources to develop a sense of community. It is necessary therefore that mental health providers trained in the social and behavioral sciences apply their theoretical and technical arsenal to develop Community Involvement in Health (CIH) programs in facilitating the improvement of health outcomes in the African American community. CIH is a participatory approach to health care that recognizes the recipient rather than the provider as central to the process. As health care professionals involve the communities and individuals in their health and health care, they need to adapt approaches that emphasize the roles of negotiation, compromise, advocacy, teaching, and self-care (Hildebrandt, 1994).

This approach to improving the health status of African Americans recognizes that governmental resources and powers are finite, that government programs are often socially inappropriate, and that doing something for people is a less effective strategy than enabling people to do more for themselves (WHO, 1991). The approach also recognizes that the health care delivery system has to become less hospital-centered and more community-centered (Righetti, 1994).

Implementation of Community Involvement in Health programs requires that health care professionals build on the strengths of existing programs, provide monetary support, link the knowledge of community health workers with mainstream health providers, document the role of community health workers, educate community health workers, and develop career plans for community health workers (p. 53). Minkhoff (1994) challenges community mental health professionals to become community organizers and activists in order to have an impact on what is fundamentally a political process. This calling should not be restricted to community mental health professionals but should be extended to include all mental health practitioners. Sherer (1994) highlights the focus of the community organization and activism as emerging from the same mission, that is to connect potential health care consumers with providers, and promote resource allocation among groups that have traditionally lacked access to adequate care.

Mental Health Service Delivery

Access is one of the foremost challenges in the mental health care delivery system. It must be recognized that even if access did not represent a formidable challenge in the delivery of behavioral health care services, that excess morbidity and mortality would continue to exist. Why? There is more to excess morbidity and mortality than the delivery of services. National Center for Health Statistics (1993) indicated that health status is impacted by both medical and non-medical factors. However, it must be acknowledged that the payoff for the African American community will be higher than average if access is significantly improved (Johnson, Anderson, Bastida, Kramer, Williams, & Wong, 1995).

It is not likely, in the near future, that access will significantly improve for the African American population in light of the current demand for services and the advent of managed behavioral health care. Sharfstein, Stoline, & Koran (1995) have noted that of the approximately 35.1 million Americans with a mental disorder, and the 15 million with a substance use disorder, only 9.4 million Americans receive services in the specialty mental health sector and 20% of those afflicted receive no services (p. 246). It is evident that the vast majority of Americans with mental and substance use disorders are assessed and treated outside the mental health delivery system. However, Minkhoff (1994) has forecasted that managed care will gradually bring more and more African Americans into the mainstream health care delivery system as the boundaries between public and private sector disappear. An illustrative example is Medicaid managed care. Minkhoff characterizes the new mental health system as private sector firms competing to become public providers and community mental health centers actively competing for HMO contracts in the private sector. It is imperative that psychologists and other mental health service providers become not only managed care tolerant but also managed care enthusiasts. In fact, Lathrop (1996) predicts that one of the emerging competitive strategies in the managed care industry is market segmentation, in which market data on consumer behavior is used to develop products tailored to particular needs, e.g., designing new products and testing their marketability with groups of targeted consumers.

African Americans present a unique challenge to service providers. This unique challenge is the accurate diagnosis and treatment of African Americans and other culturally different populations (Comas-Diaz & Griffith, 1988). Giordano (1994) suggests "ethnically sensitive" mental health services can be delivered by validating and strengthening ethnic identity; being aware and making use of patient's support system; playing the role of cultural broker; being sensitive to "cultural camouflage;" understanding the pros and cons of therapist/patient ethnic match; and respecting and working within the limits of your knowledge of other ethnic groups.

Self-care

Self-care represents a psychological approach to improving the health of African Americans as individuals, families, communities, and as a people. African Americans are not strangers to the concept of self-care. African American Christians are familiar with the saying-God helps those who help themselves. African Americans who are Muslim have heard Malcolm X, the Honorable Elijah Mohammed, and the Honorable Louis Farakhan ask the question: What have you done for yourself?

Self-care is critical for several reasons. First, the technologies of the health care delivery system do not adequately address the health challenges faced by African Americans. Otten, Teutsch, Williamson, & Marks (1990) found among African American adults between the ages of 35 to 54 that 31% of the excess mortality was due to commonly known risk factors, 38% due to family income factors, and the remaining 31% was not accounted for but hypothesized to be due to difference in health care access and other unknown factors.

The second factor highlighting the importance of self-care in the promotion of African American health is the finding that 75% of community dwelling adults reported having at least one symptom in the last month, yet only 25% sought health care, and only 1% were admitted to a community hospital or referred to another physician (White, Williams, & Greenberg, 1961). It appears, therefore, that the vast majority of Americans who experience symptoms rely on self-care as the first line of defense. Thus, African Americans, like other Americans, seek health care services in the formal health care delivery system almost as a last resort, thereby suggesting that most of the diagnostic and treatment interventions occur outside the purview of the formal health care community. In addition, many African Americans continue to practice traditional African religious and folk medicine practices. This practice dates back to slavery times when slaves relied upon herbal remedies (Stewart, 1971).

Many African American health care professionals are concerned about the use of self-care approaches in the prevention and treatment of diseases, among them the President of The National Medical Association who proclaims:

As great as this event (Million Man March) was, however, as a health care provider, I had a concern. If we were in fact, willing to take on the responsibility of improving the social ills, why are we, as African Americans, so unwilling to assume responsibility for our own health and well-being? Mind you, this neglect of one's physical self is not exclusive to the African American individual or community. However, historically this is the population that physicians of the NMA have served. I cannot count the many times that I have spoken with colleagues who offered example after example of patients who could have avoided life-threatening or debilitating diseases if only they had come in for yearly check ups. If only they had taken their prescribed medicine, or had followed the proper diet, or had some form of regular exercise, many of the diseases they contracted could have been avoided. The use of stress relief tools and techniques, followed by good advice about preventive health care such as no smoking and moderate consumption of alcohol would have served as a safety net to illness and disease. (Veal, 1996, p. 13)

African American Health Care Delivery System

The creation of an African American health care delivery system is essential if the health status of African Americans is to improve significantly before the beginning of the 21st Century. Landrum-Brown (1990) argues that any mental health delivery system must reflect the model of mental health functioning of the population it serves. Moreover, African American mental health theorists, researchers, and practitioners are called to develop innovative ways to promote the total well-being of African Americans. Existing models of mental health prevention and treatment are limited in their applicability to African American populations. Landrum-Brown (1990) reminds us that the present mental health delivery system has failed to fully understand mental health from an Afrocentric perspective that offers constructive coping strategies for adapting to acute and chronic racial stressors.

With an increased understanding of the psychodynamics of African Americans, a rare opportunity to develop new products and services that are tailored to the needs of African Americans exists. Not only is this a rare opportunity but an emerging competitive strategy in the managed care industry with respect to market segmentation and new product development (Lathrop, 1996). Thus, an African American health care delivery system would embrace the more holistic definition of health which includes physical and mental health as one and not as separate entities as described by those who subscribe to the doctrines of Cartesian philosophers. It is incumbent upon African Americans who have the theoretical knowledge and practical technology to apply the principle of self-determination of Nguzo Saba (Karenga, 1971) to design an egalitarian health care delivery system (Green, 1994) for African Americans that attempts to undo the negative effects of brainwashing in White supremacy. This represents a daunting and formidable task. However, prior to the 1960s, African Americans had an African American health care delivery system that provided a continuum of services. In fact, at the beginning of the century there were well over 200 African American hospitals (Hopkins, 1994). As of 1998, there exist only three remaining African American hospitals. The design of African

American networks as promulgated by The President of The National Medical Association as part of their Seven Point Plan for Health Care Reform (Walton, 1994) only reinforces the commitment of many African Americans to make this happen. The development and continued application of NTU psychotherapy (Phillips, 1990) represents a real world example of an African-centered therapeutic technology applied to individuals, families, communities, and organizations.

The vision of an African American health care delivery system must emerge from the knowledge that our ancestors were pioneers in medicine, medical education, and health care delivery. This knowledge should transform our individual and collective despair and restlessness into power. African American health professionals are obligated to redefine empowerment so that health administrators, health educators, medical suppliers, insurance brokers, and health educators will not simply wait for power to be given to them but recognize that power is to be taken individually and collectively to set and achieve your own agenda.

African American health professionals have an important role to play in building the foundation of an African American health care delivery system by "...assisting individuals and communities in articulating both their health problems and the solutions to address those problems by providing access to information, supporting indigenous community leadership, and assisting the community in overcoming bureaucratic obstacles to action," (Robertson & Minkler, 1994, p. 301); the design of an African American health care delivery system must address the pluralistic needs of African Americans as providers and consumers.

Role of Mental Health Professionals in the Design of An African American Health Care Delivery System

There are at least three strategic roles for mental health providers in the establishment of an egalitarian African American health care delivery system: entrepreneur, organizer and consultant. Semmes (1996) emphasizes the importance of health activism among African American health care professionals. More specifically, Semmes describes the role of African American health care activists as requiring the organization and support of African American health professionals and educators who should lend their support to enhancing the health awareness, knowledge, and self-help capabilities of African American communities through lectures, demonstrations, voluntary activism, and personal transformation and who are active in reforming their own professions and making them more responsive to the health needs of African American communities.

Many existing health structures for African Americans are experienced as racist and as such, alternative structures have to be designed and constructed. The operating vision of such a health care delivery system is based on the assumption that health care is a right not a privilege and that health care is more than simply a commodity to be bought and sold in the marketplace. Green (1994) outlines the architecture of an operating vision which should serve as an organizational template in the design of an African American health care delivery system organized to improve outcomes of care, quality, satisfaction, morbidity, mortality, accessibility, appropriateness, and affordability. The essential components of an Egalitarian Model of Health Care include: (1) equal access to health care, (2) full employment, (3) comprehensive, integrated occupational and safety programs, (4) preventive services, (5) health promotion, (6) scientifically based health education and prevention programming for children, (7) comprehensive care for all regardless of ability to pay, (8) easy access to the full continuum of health care services, and (9) easy access to culturally appropriate health care information (Green, 1994).

Entrepreneur role. George Fraser (1994) declared that entrepreneurship represents the next wave of the Civil Rights Movement. More specifically, he cited the enormous growth in the number of African American owned businesses and has noted that African American entrepreneurs are no longer limited to a few niche markets. Entrepreneurship holds promise for the health status of the African American community. The creation and management of Afrocentric health care delivery systems can facilitate an optimal match between the needs of those seeking services and those providing services. There are a host of barriers to entrepreneurship for African Americans ranging from access to capital to a "can-do" attitude.

African American mental health providers are best equipped among African American professionals to develop the entrepreneurial attitude needed for success. Below are three tactics to be employed by African American mental health professionals to promote entrepreneurship: (1) as a scholar, conduct applied research on entrepreneurship as an attitude and behavior; (2) as a health care provider, create alliances and build a managed behavioral health care practice through the application of Umoja [Unity] (Karenga, 1971); (3) as a community builder, challenge other African American professionals to apply the principle of Ujamaa [Cooperative Economics] (Karenga, 1971).

Organizer role. Afrian people have built great civilizations from Timbuktu to Egypt. The development of an African American health care delivery system is no different. Critics would argue that African Americans lack economic resources. According to Akbar (1994), "African Americans have the eighth or ninth wealthiest economy in the world, so our struggle is not an economic struggle but a psychological struggle." It is for this reason that the foundation of an African American health care delivery system does not include economics alone; leveraged financial capital is also necessary.

After African Americans have individually and collectively embraced the vision of entrepreneurship and the transformation of that vision into an operating vision, then all of the tactics used to realize that vision will have to be set into motion. Karenga (1971) stresses the importance of Ujima (Collective Work and Responsibility) which has been defined as the building of community which can also be translated into the building of organizations. Schein (1970) reminds us that:

The effective utilization of people in organized human effort has always been a pressing problem. The pharaoh building a pyramid face problems fundamentally similar to those faced by the corporation executives or university presidents of today. Each must figure out (1) how to organize work and allocate it to workers; (2) how to recruit, train, and effectively manage the people available to do the work; (3) how to create work conditions and reward and punishment systems which will enable workers to maintain high effectiveness and sufficient morale to remain effective over long periods of time; (4) how to adjust that organization to changing environmental conditions and technological innovations; and (5) how to cope with competition or harassment from other organizations or groups within their own organizations. (pp. 1-2)

African American mental health practitioners and scholars can ensure the organizational development of an African American health care delivery system by (1) conducting applied research on the efficiency and effectiveness of African American organizations; (2) seeking assistance from the Minority Business Development Association of the U.S. Department of Commerce; and (3) building bridges between professional and convene summits and work groups.

Consultant role. African American mental health practitioners should explore developing consulting firms dedicated to establishing health care delivery networks, building alliances, conducting health care market research, negotiating international health care relationships with our brothers and sisters in Africa, and Latin America. Markarian (1994) suggests forming strategic alliances with other consulting firms to improve business and to diversify the client mix. The essence of the consulting role that African American mental health practitioners have to play is eloquently described by Robertson and Minkler (1994) who state that the emerging role for health care professionals consists of " ...assisting individuals and communities in articulating both their health problems and the solutions to address those problems by providing access to information, supporting indigenous community leadership, and assisting the community in overcoming bureaucratic obstacles to action" (p. 301).

Conclusion

The design, delivery, and maintenance of an African American health care delivery system represents an opportunity to push the educational, economic, sociocultural, political, and other agendas forward in the pursuit of improved morbidity and mortality rates among African Americans. The design of such a system should not be viewed as purely reactionary. Drucker (1994) proposed that a new sector, called the social sector, is emerging to meet the needs of human beings. In this sector:

"What matters is not the legal basis but that the social-sector institutions have a particular kind of purpose. Government demands compliance; it makes rules and enforces them. Business expects to be paid; it supplies. Social sector institutions aim at changing the human being. The "product" of a school is the student who has learned something. The "product" of a hospital is a cured patient. The product of a church is a churchgoer whose life is being changed. The task of social sector organizations is to create human health and well-being" (p. 76).

The ecological perspective and the African-centered perspective of an egalitarian African American health care delivery system offers one of the emerging types of social sector organizations. Certainly, the final outcome of such a health care delivery system is a healthy and well individual, family, group, community, and people.

The challenges of designing a health care delivery system are daunting but the risk of apathy is even more frightening. It has been suggested that by the year 2000 almost all Americans will be enrolled in some form of managed health care and that African American hospitals will be excluded from these networks (Hopkins, 1994). To the extent that African Americans are excluded in this era of national conservatism and uproar regarding government funded "entitlement" programs, then the very health and well being of the African American community is at serious risk. Not all African American health care professional are skeptical of the possibilities of designing an African American health care delivery system. For instance, among them Dr. Jocelyn Elders, former Surgeon General of the United States of America. Elders states:

"I think that African American hospitals and African American physicians are groups who want to get together and form a group, an alliance. They need to begin to look at that and form groups now. If not, they'll end up having to join other groups. And if they choose not to do that, well then they may be left outside of the loop. And I don't think they can afford to be left outside of the loop, so I think it's very important that they begin to come together and talk and unite. That's what other groups are doing. And so they're going to do the same thing" (Robinson, 1994, p. 24).

A challenge to American mental health professionals has been presented. Will we respond or continue to be victims? It is imperative that an African American health care delivery system that provides a continuum of services is designed. The elements of such a system and a call for action have been presented in the present chapter.

References

Akbar, N. (1976). *Natural psychology and human transformation.* Chicago, IL: World Community of Islam in the West.

Akbar, N. (1994). *Personal communication.*

Ashanti, F. K. (1993). *The psychotechnology of brainwashing: Africentric passage.* Durham, NC: Tone Books.

Baker, F. M. (1994). Psychiatric treatment of older African Americans. *Hospital and Community Psychiatry, 45(1),* 32-37.

Blustein, B. E. (1994). Interdisciplinary approaches to biological concepts of race. *Working Paper 93-4.* Collaborative Core Unit in Labor, Race, and Political Economy. Washington, DC, Graduate School of Arts & Sciences, Howard University.

Bureau of Census (1992, May). Health insurance coverage: 1987 to 1990. Selected data from the survey of income and program participants. *Current Population Reports.* Series P-70, No. 29, Washington, DC.

Bureau of Census (1990). Trends in income by selected characteristics: 1947 to 1988. In *Information Plus,* Edited by C. D. Foster, A. Landes, S. M. Binford. Wylie, TX.

Cartwright, S. A. (1851). Report on the diseases and physical peculiarities of the Negro race. *New Orleans Medical and Surgical Journal, 7,* 691.

Cassel, J. (1976). The contribution of the social environment to host resistance. The Fourth Wade Hampton Frost Lecture. *American Journal of Epidemiology, 104,* 107-123.

Comas-Diaz, L., & Griffith, E. E. H. (1988). *Clinical guidelines in cross-cultural mental health.* New York: Wiley.

Drucker, P. (1994). The age of social transformation. *The Atlantic Monthly, 274(5),* 53-94.

Dubois, W. E. B. (1961[1903]). *The souls of Black folks.* Greenwich, CT: Fawcett.

Fraser, G. (1994). *Success runs in our race.* New York: Morrow.

Frazier, E. F. (1966). *The Negro family in the United States.* Chicago, IL: University of Chicago Press.

Giordano, J. (1994). Mental health and the melting pot: An introduction. *American Journal of Orthopsychiatry, 64(3),* 342-345.

Glass, R. M. (1995). Mental disorders: Quality of life and inequality of coverage. *Journal of the American Medical Association, 274(19),* 1557.

Green, L. D. (1994). Health care reform or revolution. *Working Paper 93-2.* Collaborative Core Unit in Labor, Race, and Political Economy. Washington, DC: Graduate School of Art & Sciences, Howard University.

Hildebrandt, E. (1994). A model for Community Involvement in Health (CIH) program development. *Social Science in Medicine, 39(2),* 247-254.

Hilliard, T. (1981). Political and social action in the prevention of psychopathology of Blacks: A mental health strategy for oppressed people. In J. Joffee & G.

Albee (Eds.), *Primary prevention of psychopathology: Prevention through political action and social change*. Hanover, NH: University Press of New England.

Hopkins, T. (1994). Life or death for Black hospitals? *Black Professional, 5(2)*, 30-34.

Jacob, J. E. (1986). Overview of Black America in 1985. In J. B. Williams (Ed.), *The state of Black America: 1986*. Washington, DC: Urban League.

Johnson, J. (1992). State health reform: Five trends that will transform hospitals. *Hospitals*, 2638.

Johnson, K. W., Anderson, N. B., Bastida, E., Kramer, J., Williams, D., & Wong, M (1995). Panel II: Macrosocial and environmental influences on minority health. *Health Psychology, 14(7)*, 601-612.

Karenga, M. (1971). *Kwanzaa: Origin, concepts, practices*. Los Angeles, CA: Kawaida Publications.

Kelly, J. G. (1966). Ecological constraints on mental health services. *American Psychologist, 21*, 535-539.

Knowles, J. H. (1977). The responsibility of the individual. In J. H. Knowles (Ed.), *Doing better and feeling worse: Health in the United States*. New York: Norton.

Krieger, N., & Fee, E. (1994). Social class: The missing link in U.S. health data. *International Journal of Health Services, 24(1)*, 25-44.

Landrum-Brown, J. (1995). Black mental health and racial oppression. In C. V. Willie, P. P. Rieker, B. M. Kramer, & B. S. Brown (Eds.), *Mental health, racism and sexism*. Pittsburgh: University of Pittsburgh Press.

Lathrop, J. P. (1996). Competitive strategies for the next generation of managed care. *Healthcare Forum Journal, 39(2)*, 36-39.

Livingston, I. L., & Carter, J. J. (1992). Improving the health of the Black community: Outlook for the future. In I. L. Livingston (Ed.), *Handbook of Black American health*. London: Greenwood Press.

Manton, K., Patrick, C., & Johnson, K. (1987). Health differentials between Blacks and Whites: Recent trends in mortality and morbidity. *The Milbank Quarterly, 65*, 129-199.

Markarian, N. (1994). Growing your consulting business. *Black Enterprise, 25(4)*, 108-116.

McGinnis, J. M., & Foege, W. H. (1993). Actual causes of death in the United States. *Journal of the American Medical Association, 270*, 2207-2212.

Minkhoff, K. (1994). Community mental health in the nineties: public sector managed care. *International Journal of Mental Health, 23(1)*, 39-59.

Myers, W. D. (1991). *Now is your time: The African American struggle for freedom*. New York: Harpertrophy.

National Center for Health Statistics. (1990). *Health, United States*. Hyattsville, MD: National Center for Health Statistics.

Nobles, W. (1974). Africanity: Its' role in Black families. *The Black Scholar, 5(9)*, 10-17.

Nobles, W. (1991). Extended self: Rethinking the so-called Negro self-concept. In R. L. Jones (Ed.), *Black psychology*. Hampton, VA: Cobb & Henry.

Otten, M. W., Teutsch, S. M., Williamson, D. F., & Marks, J. S. (1990). The effect of known risk factors on the excess mortality of Black adults in the United States. *Journal of the American Medical Association*, 845-850.

Palmer, C. (1992). African slave trade: The cruelest commerce. *National Geographic*, 64-91.

Pasamanick, B. (1963). Misconceptions concerning differences in the racial prevalence of mental diseases. *American Journal of Orthopsychiatry, 33*, 72-86.

Phillips, F. (1990). NTU psychotherapy: An Afrocentric approach. *The Journal of Black Psychology, 17(1)*, 55-74.

Pouissant, A. F. (1990). The mental health status of Black Americans, 1983. In D. S. Ruiz (Ed.), *Handbook of mental health and mental disorder among Black Americans*. Greenwood Press: New York.

Ramseur, H. P. (1991). Psychologically healthy Black adults. In R. L. Jones (Ed.), *Black psychology*, Hampton, VA: Cobb & Henry.

Righetti, A. (1994). The psychiatric service as entrepreneur/social enterprise. *International Journal of Mental Health, 23(1)*, 39-59.

Robertson, A., & Minkler, M. (1994). New health promotion movement: A critical examination. *Health Education Quarterly, 231(3)*, 295-312.

Robinson, L. S. (1994). Dialogue with Dr. M. Joycelyn Elders. *Emerge, 5(10)*, 20-28.

Russell, K., & Jewell, N. (1992). Cultural impact of health care access: Challenges for improving the health of African Americans. *Journal of Community Health Nursing, 9(3)*, 161-169.

Semmes, C. E. (1996). *Racism, health, and post industrialism: A theory of African American health*. Westport, CT: Praeger.

Sharfstein, S. S., Stoline, A. M., & Koran, L. (1995). Mental health. In A. R. Kovner (Ed.), *Health care delivery in the United States*. New York: Springer Publishing Company.

Sherer, J. L. (1994). Neighbor to neighbor. *Hospital & Health Networks*, 52-56.

Sherman, J. (1994). John Henryism and the health of African Americans. *Culture, Medicine, & Psychiatry, 18*, 163-182.

Snowden, L. (1982). *Reaching the underserved*. Beverly Hills, CA: Sage.

Stone, G. C. (1979). Health and the health system: A historical overview and conceptual framework. In G. C. Stone, F. Cohen, & N. E. Adler (Eds.), *Health psychology: A handbook*. San Francisco: Jossey-Bass

Subcommittee to the President's Committee on Mental Health (1978). *Task Panel Reports* (Vol. 3). Washington, DC: U.S. Government Printing Office.

Veal, Y. S. (1996). A million voices for health care: Strengthening the health values and behaviors of African Americans. *Journal of the National Medical Association, 88(1)*, 13-14.

Walton, T. M. (1994). Health care reform: The NMA's Number 1 Priority. *Journal of the National Medical Association, 86(10)*, 735-736.

White, K., Williams, T., & Greenberg, B. (1961). The ecology of medial care. *New England Journal of Medicine, 265*, 885-892.

Willie, C. V., Reiker, P. P., Kramer, B. M., & Brown, B. S. (1995). *Mental health, racism, and sexism*. Pittsburgh: University of Pittsburgh Press.

World Health Organization Technical Report Series. No. 807 (1991). *Environmental health in urban development*. Report of a WHO Expert Committee. WHO, Geneva.

Author
William "Marty" Martin, Psy.D., M.P.H.
Department of Health Systems Management
Tulane University School of Public Health
1430 Tulane Ave., SL-29
New Orleans, LA 70112
Telephone: (504) 588-5428
Fax: (504) 584-3783
E-mail: wmartin@aol.com.

Part 5

Mental Health

African American Definitions of Self and Psychological Health

Karen L. Edwards

Introduction

There have been numerous orientations designed to conceptualize psychological health, such as humanistic formulations which stress creativity, love and self understanding (Fromm, 1965; Maslow, 1962); behavioral approaches which consider competence (White, 1960); adaptation to one's environment (Ullman and Krasner, 1969); social modeling (Bandura, 1969); the absence of mental illness (Ausubel, 1961; Kubie, 1975); and socio-cultural approaches which examine the social context (Offer & Sabshin, 1974). These traditional conceptions have generally failed to consider the influence of race and racism (Pettigrew, 1973) and the distinct cultural heritage of African Americans (Jones, 1972; Ramseur, 1991, 1998; Wilcox, 1973). There is a continuing need for definitions or orientations toward understanding and conceptualizing Black/African American psychological health (Akbar, 1979; Gary, 1978; Jones, 1980; Ramseur, 1991, 1996; Thomas and Comer, 1973; White, 1970; Wilcox, 1973), and to avoid the conceptualizations which view Black/African American mental health from supposed universal European assumptions (Wilson, 1980). The present chapter describes an exploratory qualititve study on African Americans at several developmental levels addressing the question of how African Americans, as an oppressed group, self-define psychological health.

Although there does not seem to be agreement regarding the best theoretical formulation of mental health, there does seem to be agreement regarding some of it's global aspects. In reviewing the literature, several variables were consistently noted irrespective of orientation. Most definitions made mention of the necessity of having: 1) a realistic orientation toward the social and physical environment; 2) social skills in interpersonal relations; 3) an emotionally satisfying personal life; 4) internal control; 5) responsibility; 6) an integrated self-image; and 7) a vitality toward life. Each orientation, within its own framework made some reference to: 1) the individual's ability to adequately cope with both the internal and external environments; 2) the influence of environment and one's accurate assessment of it; and 3) the maintenance of balance (i.e., health) between the two. However, while recognizing these influences, the predominate theories of psychological health have failed to consider the influence of an oppressive environment which exists for African Americans and others who are visibly different from the dominant culture, via racism.

African American psychologists have recognized this void and have begun addressing the need for models of psychological health based on African American realities (Gary, 1978; Jones, 1972, 1980; Ramseur, 1991, 1996; Wilcox, 1973; Wilson, 1980). For example, Wilcox proposed ten components of psychological health for Black Americans which stand in contradiction to traditional approaches. The components are: 1) conscious awareness of a hostile society; 2) the need for a constant state of dynamic tension; 3) the ability to deal with subordinates; 4) the lack of desire to oppress or be oppressed; 5) involvement in shaping Black destiny; 6) self-confrontation; 7) identity of own culture, e.g., its history and values; 8) knowledge of destructive societal "isms;" 9) the ability to see the humanity of oppressed people; and 10) non-fragmentation of self into emotion, intellect and action. While these characteristics address more accurately the skills and awarenesses needed to function effectively as an African American, they nevertheless are the author's interpretation of what is required or necessary for Black/African American mental health. Thomas and Comer (1973) also offered a definition of Black American psychological health in which Blacks were considered in relationship to their total cultural/societal system e.g., the political, economic and social. Gary and Jones (1978) proposed that for Blacks to be mentally healthy, they need to: 1) experience efficacy in modifying the environment to accomplish such tasks as promoting one's growth; 2) have an integrated self-image; 3) exercise sound and realistic judgment; and 4) satisfy basic needs. Ramseur (1991, 1998) provides an extensive review of theory and research on psychological health among African Americans, including universal models of psychological health, theories of Black personality and identity with psychological health implications, empirical research on self-conception, the competent personality, and Black coping resources and styles. He determined that there are six (6) issues central to the development of a model of Black adult psychological health: 1) a positive self concept; 2) positive group (Black) identity and community connection; 3) accurate perception of the social environment; 4) effective adaptation to the social environment (e.g., need to be bi-cultural); 5) development and maintenance of emotional intimacy with others; and 6) maintenance of a sense of competence and ability to work productively.

The present study took a phenomenological, introspective (Jenkins, 1991) and symbolic interactionist view of psychological health. It thus proposed a process whereby African Americans would self-define psychological health from within groups of other African Americans. The goal was to provide a forum where they could come together in an interactive (i.e., shaping) mode to define mental health from a Black/African American cultural approach (Jackson, 1976; Nobles, 1973; White, 1972). Gary (1978) stated that "the mental health of Blacks must be viewed within the context of the total cultural and societal systems as well as within the perspective of the Black group" (p. 14). A total of 117 subjects participated in the study (male and female college students, adults, and elderly). From a guided fantasy procedure (See Appendix A: Methodology), participants arrived at the highest ranked characteristics of psychological health. Results were content analyzed. Because there was such a volume of data, only the most consistent trends will be reported.

Self Conceptions

Two indices of self concept were obtained from the "Who Am I" (Kuhn & McPartland, 1954), which provided a general definition of self conception, and a measure of self-esteem from the "actual-ideal" discrepancy method (Rogers & Dymond, 1954). Data from these indices were analyzed in the following manner: college students as a group; college students by gender; all adults; adults based on gender; the elderly as a total group; and the elderly based on gender; all females; and all males.

In response to the "Who am I" question, college students used primarily sex and then race descriptors, such as "I am a man or woman," first, then, "I am Black or African American." Other descriptor categories were: competence, such as "talented, successful, intelligent," and self-determination, e.g., "strong-willed, striving, hard worker or struggling to get ahead;" and interpersonal style, e.g., "shy, outspoken, opinionated or kind/softhearted." Gender differences for college students reflected that women students made significantly more interpersonal style references such as outspoken and soft-hearted, than did men; and women students showed a sense of interpersonal balance in that they could be both "outspoken and opinionated as well as caring and soft-hearted." College men made more age references, e.g., "young" or specific age references, than did women. Mixed gender student groups mentioned their student status and interpersonal style descriptors.

The actual-ideal self discrepancy indicator of self-esteem for the college student groups showed competency themes increasing from actual to ideal, whereas interpersonal, psychic style and determination themes decreased; ideal competency themes reflected increased knowledge, being wiser and self sufficient; and ideal interpersonal themes reflected dynamic and powerful styles; ideal determination themes reflected greater ambition, more persistence and being driven. Gender differences for self-esteem showed women students with more references to psychic style descriptors such as "emotional, insecure, and lonely for actual self, and optimistic, confident, and very happy" for the ideal-self, than did men (e.g., actual selves as "tranquil, and good natured, and flexible and happy" for male ideal). Men made more references to competence themes such as "observant" for actual, and "increased knowledge of life" for the ideal, than did women (e.g., "naive, strong" for actual, and "greater consciousness, professional" for ideal selves). Mixed gender groups were consistent with total college sample.

The adult group responded to the "Who am I" question like the student group, with sex and race descriptors. Other adult responses were kinship, e.g., "mother, father, husband, wife," and ideological, e.g., "concerned about society's imbalance and injustice." The only gender difference noted for the adults was that men frequently mentioned their occupations, whereas women did not. There was almost no discrepancy between the actual and ideal self descriptors; the adult men and women saw themselves as being strong, prosperous, secure within, dynamic, loving and "having it together."

The elderly group gave sex descriptors most frequently to the "Who am I" question. Additionally, they gave their names. Gender differences reflected women giving ideological descriptors, e.g., "concerned about racism," more than men. Actual and ideal descriptors for both men and women showed interpersonal style decreasing from actual to ideal, and moral worth increasing in frequency. Qualitatively, however, the ideas expressed were about the same.

Fantasies

Rather than imposing a coding scheme on the guided fantasy material, emergent theme analyses were made. It is interesting that intimate relationship themes became more salient across the age groups, such as the college students talked about their dating behaviors, or the lack of them; the adults referred to their desires to have mates; and the elderly reminisced about their marriages and departed spouses. There was little mention in the fantasy material of relationships with other Blacks outside of the family or friendships; nor issues regarding political or social awarenesses such as racism or sexism. Religious themes were only mentioned by the elderly group. Primary emergent themes for the groups were: college students/self-orientation themes, e.g., what they intended to do with their lives, and health and physical themes, e.g., physical appearance; adults: mentioned intimate relationships, and living atmosphere themes, e.g., homes they would like to own; and the elderly: their intimate relationships, e.g., departed spouses, family, and children.

The fantasies coded by gender showed that women tended to see their lives revolving around their families, physical appearance, combined health\physical, and their homes, or living atmosphere; whereas men's fantasies reflected their intimate relationships, personal orientation-self themes, e.g., themselves and their personal goals, and their material possessions, e.g., cars. Women mentioned family relationships, whereas men seldom did; women mentioned work relationships, e.g., co-workers being pleasant, whereas men rarely did. However, men mentioned spirituality themes, e.g., being one with the Creator, with greater frequency than did women.

Characteristics of Psychological Health

The data are from the final study procedure in which every member in each group rank ordered and weighted the top five characteristics from a list of characteristics developed by the group. These data were then coded for each group. Group data were compiled on the age and gender variables. The age variable data are presented first; meaningful groupings of themes coded by the Gordon (1968) (see Appedix A: Data Analysis) scheme are presented.

Themes characterized as moral worth and ideological and belief references showed increased importance across all three age groups, with the adults ranking morality somewhat higher than the other two groups. For the college student groups, the coding category moral worth, referred to specific aspects of morality, e.g., "self-respect, self-love and truth;" whereas the ideological/belief category referred to the theories and philosophy or worldviews, providing the framework for morality, e.g. "spiritual guidance, needing a belief in God, and strong cultural identity." The adult group thought of morality in terms of "self-love, self-worth and satisfaction with God-created self;" and the elderly spoke of "love, being honest, and being born of the spirit." Ideological themes for the adults referred to "treating one's fellow men correctly, being in touch with Supreme Being, and having a pragmatic approach to life;" while the elderly spoke of "being Black and proud, realizing that not all days will be happy, being what you are, and blessings will come from God."

A second meaningful theme grouping was the competence-determination category. Competence was particularly important for the college student groups and adults, whereas determination was more salient for the college students than the adults, and not mentioned by the elderly. Competence themes for the college students focused on "intelligence, knowing limitations, and mental strength;" for the adults, competence referred to "survival skills, adaptability, resilience, and intelligence;" and for the elderly, it related to "being educated and reading a lot." Determination themes for the students focused on "will-power, control over one's life, and being goal-oriented and determined;" and for the adults, it referred to "being goal-oriented, having and being true to objectives;" there were no determination themes for the elderly.

A third theme of some importance across groups was the interpersonal (style) category. It was most salient for the adult group who listed items like "communication: being able to express yourself, communicating true feelings, talking to get across a message and feelings, and having secure relationships; assertiveness, and needing to be with someone or being married." Interpersonal themes for the elderly focused on "going it alone, letting others alone and not arguing and fighting, being easy to get along with, showing love and having a wife, a relationship, or being married." College student interpersonal themes referred to "interpersonal communication to strengthen relationships, assertiveness, caring and loving, ability to deal with other races/sexes, and being surrounded in love with someone else."

Other themes relating to psychological health were physical, unity and kinship. Similarity of content was noted for the physical category such that college students mentioned "beauty of self, especially with darker skinned women, physical beauty and good health;" adults mentioned "appearance, health and diet;" and the elderly referred to "cleanliness and personal hygiene." Unity, which would encompass themes relating to internal harmony, were mentioned primarily by the college student groups, e.g., "inner peace, inner beauty, self-knowledge and control, and striving to fullest potential." The adults also mentioned "understanding self;" the elderly had no themes so coded. Kinship themes were mentioned by the elderly in terms of the "importance of family and being married and having a wife or relationship;" by the college students as "being family oriented, and having family values such as being married and staying together;" and the adults mentioned kinship themes the least, but did refer to being married.

Gender differences on the characteristics of psychological health showed most clearly in the areas of moral worth, interpersonal style, and unity. Moral themes were significantly more frequent for all women in the study, e.g., "self-worth, self-respect, self-love;" than for all men in the study, e.g., "responsibility, self-worth, and truth;" as were interpersonal themes more frequently mentioned by women, e.g., "caring, loving, communication;" than men, e.g., "understanding significant others, assertiveness." The men however, mentioned unity themes significantly more, e.g., "understanding self, inner peace, know yourself, sense of who one is;" than did women, e.g., "inner beauty." Ideological belief references shared the same frequency for both women and men as did competence themes. Determination themes were quite close in frequency. Less salient themes sharing the same frequencies were physical, psychic style, describing the predominant way of thinking or personality, and kinship themes.

Compiling frequencies, as an indicator of salience, for all groups across age and gender, the following order of characteristics of psychological health were found for this sample: 1) Ideological/Belief references: "spiritual guidance, needing a belief in God, treating fellow man correctly, being in touch with Supreme Being, being what and who you are and getting blessings from God, putting Christ Jesus at the head of house, strong cultural identity, being Black and proud, being pragmatic, common sense to life, and realizing that not all days will be happy;" 2) Moral Worth: "self-respect, self-love, good esteem, strong self-worth, satisfied with God-created self, truth, honesty, responsible, to love, being happy with what you do, being true to self and others, respect for others, compassion, empathy, understanding, caring, God, Godliness;" 3) Interpersonal Style: "Communication to strengthen relationships, to express yourself and your true feelings and a message, assertive, respect for others, caring, loving, secure relationships, understanding significant others, having compassion, being friendly;" 4) Competence: "intelligent, able, mentally strong, adaptable, resilient, survival skills, educated, reading a lot, know limits;" 5) Determination: "determined, will-power, control over one's life, goal-oriented, working toward objectives and being true to objectives;" 6) Unity: "inner peace and beauty, know yourself, understand yourself, strive for fullest potential;" and 7) Health/Physical: "good health, health and diet, appearance, beauty of self (especially with darker skinned women), cleanliness, and personal hygiene."

Discussion

The objective of this qualitative study was to allow African American women and men of different age groups to define psychological health from their unique perspectives and globally for all African Americans. The design was proposed as facilitating this process by having African Americans define the concept in groups with other African Americans, as it in fact occurs in reality through the sharing of symbols of reality. The design also allowed for the many strands and themes of thinking to emerge and to be put into a meaningful whole. The specific procedure called for participants to propose five key characteristics (components) of African American psychological health as they evolved from their own personal experience (fantasy) as their most psychologically healthy selves. The richness of the data obtained lies behind the coding scheme, to the specific examples given as aspects of this concept. For the sake of economy the discussion will focus on the key characteristics of African American psychological health, with age and gender dimensions discussed with respect to each characteristic and the general definition. Fantasy materials will only be discussed if they stand in contradiction to or highlight any of the other findings.

The highest ranked characteristic of psychological health for this study was Ideological and Belief Reference. Within this category as the primary characteristic of African psychological health, the participants shared their worldviews and philosophies regarding spirituality/religion, culture, and personal orientations for daily existence as healthy African Americans. They stated that to be psychologically healthy one had to have a spiritual awareness; an awareness of who one is as an African American and in relation to others, and strategies for daily existence. While the ideological belief reference category was important as a characteristic of African American psychological health across age and gender, it should be noted that it gained in salience across age, with the elderly group stressing this aspect a bit more than the students and adults. This suggests that one's philosophy of life, as a guiding force, gains in prominence with the maturity to assess its value. It is also common to become more globally philosophical about life as one matures and seeks to place a myriad of experiences into a meaningful whole or framework.

The spiritual aspect of the study's ideological and belief reference component finding while developmentally rational, may be contaminated by the fact that the elderly sample was obtained from a church-run nursing home. However, that the college students and adults also frequently mentioned religious philosophies tends to ameliorate that fact. It could also be suggested that there is a relationship between political inactivity (recall the feelings about society scales in which the study sample showed non-political activity towards eliminating racism and sexism) and religiosity. Numerous studies have suggested that there is an inverse relationship between political activity and religiosity (Hilliard, 1972; Howard, 1970; Marx, 1967); and others have addressed the negative effects of religion on psychological health in general (Anderson, 1971; Frazier, 1964; Grier and Cobbs, 1971). Hilliard found that activists (as opposed to non-activists) were more independent and needed less external reinforcement. While there were frequent responses relating to having a strong cultural identity and pride in being Black as philosophical orientations, the action or behavioral components suggesting political activity, as defined by this study were muted.

Locus of control theorists (e.g. Rotter, 1966) would perhaps suggest greater externality than internality for this sample in the sense that they look to an omnipotent, omniscient God-figure, rather than developing internally motivated self-strategies for coping (Gore and Rotter, 1963; Strickland, 1965). Along this locus of control dimension, de Charms (1968) stated that "origins" (internal LOC) exert more personal control over their environments than "pawns" (externals). It was additionally noted that lower class Blacks tend to be more external (Rotter, 1966). This is supported by an "access to societal spoils" notion which states that those with limited access to those spoils tend to be more external. Thus the study sample may reflect some hesitancy and doubt regarding actual goal attainment consistent with their social status, but certainly their awareness of the importance of self-determination (as action component) was clear (i.e., it was one of the highest ranked characteristics of psychological health). The locus of control hypothesis with reference to this study would be negated based on where God was located for them, i.e., internally (within) or externally (outside of self). However, the study did not address this issue.

Many have examined the positive mental health benefit of a religion for Blacks/African Americans (Akbar, 1979; Edwards, 1987; Gary, 1987; Griffith, English & Mayfield, 1980; Smith, 1981). Thus, it is not surprising that one of the primary (first ranked characteristics) components of African American psychological health would be a spiritual/religious ideology. The centrality of spirituality for all participants further supports the proposition and reality that Africans and African Americans are a spiritual people (Gyekye, 1996; Mbiti, 1970; Paris, 1995). Paris defines spirituality as the

> "animating and integrative power that constitutes the principle frame of meaning for individual and collective experiences . . . the integrating center of their power and meaning. The distinguishing feature of African spirituality, as opposed to other groups, is that it is always integrally connected with the

dynamic movement of life....in the struggle for survival . . . [as well as] the union of those forces of life that have the power within to threaten and destroy life . . . or to preserve and enhance it" (p. 22).

One should recall that within the category of ideological and belief reference component, participants combined the desire for spiritual guidance with having a strong cultural identity as well as having a pragmatic approach to life. Thus they were aware of the necessity for the union of spirit with the struggles of their people.

As a note, it can be said from the responses that the elderly group could be characterized as "religious," whereas the college students and adults tended to be more "spiritual," with a focus on the global teachings of religion without as frequent reference to denominational creeds and regular church attendance. As you may recall, there were no gender differences for the ideological/belief component in general. However, the issue of gender and religiosity/spiritually will be discussed further, below.

The second highest ranked characteristic of African American psychological health was moral worth. The moral worth dimension used generalized cultural symbols as universalistic value standards to evaluate the actions of self and others in social interaction. For this study the moral worth component was closely related to the ideological and belief component, in that moral worth provided the specific aspects of participants' broader philosophy of psychological health, e.g., respect for self and others, satisfaction with God-created self, Godliness and compassion (moral worth); and provided aspects of a general philosophical orientation which called for needing a belief in God, seeking spiritual guidance, and a need for treating one's fellow man correctly (ideological/belief). Thus in seeking spiritual guidance and treating others correctly (ideological) one would need to value truth, be honest and to love self and others (moral) much like the concept of Maatian ethics (Karenga, 1990). It should be noted that not only did the study participants stress moral principles for themselves, but for others as well. There is some indication that to be psychologically healthy one must respect, love, have esteem for, be satisfied with, and show compassion and empathy for one's self first, which would then enable one to be equally moral to others. Spirituality as linked to morality (i.e., judgments and valuations of right and wrong), and ethics (i.e., the standards of right and wrong) are significant to any definition of psychological health, particularly African/African American psychological health. Yet, it is sorely absent in traditional definitions (e.g., Ausubel, 1961; Fromm, 1965; Jahoda, 1958; Thomas and Comer, 1973; Wilcox, 1973; Wilson, 1980), in Black cultural definitions (e.g., Gary, 1978) and even in models currently proposed for Black/African American psychological health (Ramseur, 1991, 1998). Too often in modern conceptualizations, as opposed to ancient African ones, psychological health as well as spirituality as foundational to psychological health, is devoid of a moral and ethical base (within a social, moral, ethical and practical context), which these study participants found necessary to include. It has become fashionable to speak of being "spiritual," yet the concept has been conveniently divorced from its ethical and moral moorings, such that one can be spiritual and engage in covetous, avaricious, hateful, vengeful and illicit behaviors in practice, with ostensibly no diminution to the quality of one's presumed spirituality.

Gyekye (1996) in addressing Akan moral values, proposes that they are the social rules and norms employed by persons to guide conduct within a society. Morality, from an Akan perspective then, is viewed as a "social phenomenon," in which there is concern for harmonious and cooperative living, consideration for others' interests, social responsibility, good character, and a sense of duty to others. Thus morality, according to Gyekye, derives as a natural vs. a revealed religion from a people's experience and view of the world. This view of morality is consistent with Maatian ethics (Karenga, 1984; 1990). Maat, which stands for divine order in a cosmic, natural and social sense, also refers to balance, truth, virtue and righteousness. In essence, the concept of Maat was the moral and spiritual impetus of ancient Egyptian (Kemetic) sacred literature (Karenga, 1984). Further, African morality as a necessity, requires proof in practice (Karenga, 1990). Thus, one was taught "to think [M]aat, speak [M]aat and do [M]aat in secular and sacred situations" . . . to accomplish both "a mutually beneficial community" as well as "everlasting life" (Karenga, 1984, p. 40). While current notions of psychological health and spirituality have become bastardized versions of the ways of the ancients, these African American study participants, unwittingly and subconsciously have called forth a re-connection of spirit to ethics and morality, in a more balanced and comprehensive view of psychological health.

While moral worth was an important component of psychological health across age groups, there was a tendency noted for the college students and adults to mention more "self-principles" for morality such as self-love, self-respect; than the elderly group who defined moral worth more globally as, "to love and be loved and being honest." This finding would be consistent with developmental theory which describes the elderly as being more concerned with global evaluations of their lives, which they sense are near completion; as opposed to the college students who are just beginning to define their philosophies of life, and the adults who are actively practicing those philosophies in the interpersonal and work environments. It should also be noted that women significantly more than men, contributed moral worth themes to the conception of psychological health. If moral worth represents a major aspect of spirituality, then women, as "bearers of the culture," would provide and be concerned with the specific mechanisms (moral issues) by which the people are spiritual or express a spiritual ideology. The hieroglyphic symbol for the Kemetic goddess Isis, stands for "seat or throne" (Budge, 1969, 1988; Walker, 1983), and the symbol has been further related to the Maatian motherhood principle of right, justice and truth. It could be said that these African American women study participants are providing the lap or foundation, on which "spirituality" and the concept of morality is made manifest. The morality expressed and provided by the study women is as it states in Psalms 89:14 and Psalms 97:2 that "Righteousness and justice are the foundation of Thy throne" (New American Standard Bible, 1990).

An additional finding complicates the above explanation: men mentioned more spiritual themes than did women in defining psychological health. Recall however, the finding that men ranked ideological and belief references as their highest component of psychological health, whereas women ranked moral worth as their highest component; and the previous discussion regarding the ideological component as providing the overall philosophy of spirituality, whereas moral worth served to provide the specific prescriptions to actualize the ideology. This additional finding could then serve to further support and explicate the results, rather than refute or complicate them. The rationale for the above may be that as African American men and women share the basic ideology of life (spirituality), it is the added responsibility of women in their child bearing and perhaps more often child-rearing capacities, to provide the details and specific moral aspects (the seat, lap or foundation) actualizing the philosophy. It should also be noted that in general, women made more references to "religious" themes of psychological health, such as, the importance of religion, a belief in God (denomination not important), being in touch with the Supreme Being, and "one can't do anything without the Lord" and prayer/Godliness; whereas men more often spoke of "spiritual" themes, such as having spiritual knowledge, spirituality in general and the need to have a spiritual foundation. It is possible to think of spirituality as the fruit of religion (Edwards, 1987); thus it could be conceived that the women study participants speak to the root or trunk of the moral aspects of religion, whereas the men speak to the fruit of religion, or the spirit (Edwards, 1987).

The above gender-related finding may also be explained by the fact that women attend and play a more significant supporting role in organized religious activities, than do men in general (Cleage, 1972; Grant, 1993), except for the predominance of the male religious leadership (i.e. pastors, deacons, trustees) in the Baptist church (study sample was primarily of Baptist faith). As Grant states: "women are not full members [of the church] because they are not given opportunities for full participation at all levels of the church, particularly at the decision-making levels...they are only permitted to become servants" (p. 214). For many men in fact, it is considered less than manly to attend organized religious services as merely a lay attendee (61% of the adult males and 43% of the college student men had minimal or no church attendance). Thus, it is significant that this study shows that non-religious attendance in no way lessens or minimizes the importance of the "fruit" of religious worship, which is spirituality (Edwards, 1987). Further, it has been noted that there is a difference between African and African American spirituality. The foundations of African spirituality have been delineated by beliefs in: 1) an active presence of the Creator God in the world; 2) a unified sense of reality encompassing both divinity and humanity; 3) life as the ultimate gift; 4) importance of kinship and community; 5) the active role of ancestors; 6) an oral tradition in reverence to the spoken word, good speech, the power of heka and divine speech; and 7) beliefs in the sacredness of nature and the environment in recognition of the divine in all creation (Downey, 1993; Mbiti, 1988); whereas African American spirituality, a term more recently used than that of religion, is said to be more scripturally based, concerned with the prayer and God-conscious experiences of Black people in the United States, and focused on social concerns, social justice, practical charity and political involvement (Downey, 1993) necessitated by an African American cultural history of oppression. Thus, if one views African American spirituality as being more scripturally based and indeed "religious," then African American women in this study would reflect that orientation more than the men in the study.

The interpersonal style component of psychological health was ranked third by the study sample. This component is related to the previous two components in that it further defines the specific interpersonal dictates required of the more global ideological/philosophical orientation and more specific moral stance toward psychological health. It should be noted that several of the responses were coded in more than one of the above three component categories; such as "respect for others" was coded under both interpersonal style and moral worth; and was also closely related to "treating one's fellow man correctly," which was coded as an ideological and belief reference. This multiplicity of coding enmeshes the three components further. However, the interpersonal style component did provide distinctive themes with reference to communication and relationships, such as understanding significant others, expressing one's self, having secure relationships and communicating to strengthen relationships. Interpersonal style themes relating to communication and relationships were most frequently provided by the adult participants in general and the adult women in particular. This finding can be explained by the fact that the adult women were mostly divorced, widowed or separated, and thus had the experience, good or bad, of having a mate (whereas the women college students were never married), and were still at an age where the possibility of finding a mate was still salient (as opposed to the elderly women). An interesting finding related to relationships was found within the women college students, who expressed more hopelessness and irrelevancy with regard to relationships. Rather than relationships, college women tended to focus more on professional and career aspirations. Interestingly enough, college women in mixed groups with males, tended to express the above more so than college women in all female groups. Perhaps this attests to the difference between holding abstract ideas about relationships, without the male presence (i.e., in all female college student groups), than with males present (i.e., in mixed gender groups of college students). Fleming (1983) in a study of Black women on both Black and White campuses, found that Black women on White campuses expressed more hopelessness regarding marriage than Black women on Black campuses, which is supported by this study.

Competence was the fourth component of psychological health and self-determination was the fifth. While important across all age groupings, the competence component of African American psychological health showed increased salience for the college student and adult participants. Qualitatively there were some differences in the definitions of competence. For example, both the college students and the elderly made references to academic themes, such as formal education, knowledge of heritage (college students) and needing an education and reading a lot (elderly); whereas the adults spoke of survival skills, adaptability and resilience. Clearly the adults defined competence in more practical and applied ways than the students. However, both the college students and the adults made frequent references to intelligence, being able, and mentally strong. It is interesting that the most frequent competence reference was intelligence. It is very understandable that the college students, within an academic environment where their basic intellectual capacities are challenged daily, would define competence in intellectual ability terms. What this study shows is that perhaps even beyond the academic environment, adult Blacks interacting in the work environment are also challenged. Of course the literature is voluminous regarding the existence or non-existence of the basic intellectual capacities of Blacks (e.g., Jensen, 1969; Shuey, 1958).

The fifth characteristic of African American psychological health, self-determination, showed a precipitous decline across age groups, with the elderly making no references to this theme. Thus, it can be said that the motivation and sustaining energy (self-determination) required to promote and maintain competence declined with age. This was also evident in the self-determination themes, in which college students spoke of will-power, determined, control over one's life (suggesting concerted effort); whereas the adults made references to being goal oriented, working toward and being true to objectives. There were no gender differences with regard to either competence or self-determination components of psychological health. Both men and women tended to rank competence higher than self-determination.

There were other components of psychological health which did not make the top five rankings but are of value to mention. The sixth and seventh ranked components were unity, such as the need for inner peace and beauty, self-knowledge, and striving to fullest potential; and physical, such as good health, diet, beauty of self, and cleanliness and personal hygiene. Only the college students gave prominence to the unity concept; the adults made one reference to it, and the elderly made no references. Interestingly, college men made significantly more unity references than did college women; internal harmony and cohesion may then be viewed as an aspect and benefit of spirituality, which was also more salient for males in general, than females. The seventh ranked physical references made by the study sample may be an expression of a more holistic view to psychological health which recognizes the mind-body-spirit interconnection.

The eighth component of psychological health for this study was psychic style which refers to one's personality, or how one typically thinks and feels. It was defined as having a positive attitude, being happy, open-minded and non-judgmental. The ninth component, kinship, was surprisingly not ranked higher given the African cultural tradition of being family/tribe oriented (e.g., Mbiti, 1970; Nobles, 1980). However, the single status of the sample must be considered (the majority of the sample was not currently married); thus the sample expressed kinship at a non-legal-intimate level or through the interpersonal component practiced in the context of the community.

In addition to the study goal of defining African American psychological health, the study also attempted to describe the persons (study sample) offering the definition. Who we are, and how we perceive ourselves, determines how we view "external" reality (e.g., definition of psychological health). Thus there was an attempt to describe the self-conceptions and esteem of the participants. There are many references in the literature regarding the negative self-concepts of Blacks (e.g., Baldwin, Brown & Hopkins, 1991; Clark & Clark, 1947; Grier & Cobbs, 1968; Kardiner & Ovesey, 1951; Poussaint & Atkinson, 1970; Rainwater, 1967; Vontress, 1971) and Black women specifically (Collins, 1990; Green, 1994, Grier & Cobbs, 1968; Kardiner & Ovesey, 1951; Pettigrew, 1964; Ruffin, 1989). Other researchers such as McCarthy and Yancy (1971) and Nobles (1980) have re-evaluated both the theory (faulty assumptions of) and research (methodological problems) which fail to consider the ethos and unity (African centered) of African Americans. The African American women and men in this study appear to have healthy self-concepts. Two indices of self-concept were employed, a third, indirectly through the fantasy material. Both the African American women and men responded to the "Who Am I" indicator of self-concept in terms of gender and race. However, their statements reflect a deeper meaning associated with these factors, such as: "I am a proud Black woman;" or "Black woman with goals;" "African male;" "a Black man in the U.S. who has a chance" (these statements also allowed for multiple coding). How the women and men defined themselves was very similar.

The components of competence, determination, interpersonal, moral and kinship were salient across gender. However, gender differences could best be observed when comparing the component of competence. Competence was of greater salience to the self-conception of African American men, while psychic style or personality factors were salient for women. This distinction may address the normative socialization differences for men and women. The components of self-concept for the African American women in this sample reflected an attempt at integrating the traditional and non-traditional norms for women such that the traditional feminine expectations (interpersonal, personality, morality) were ranked higher than the non-traditional (competence, self-determination), although they both were highly ranked. Both the African American men and women were ranked highly (the highest) on interpersonal components of self. The morality component of self for African American women was consistently significant (for self-concept and psychological health). This may be indicative of an overall cultural norm for women to be "good" and "respectable;" however, it gains in meaning when the subcultural reality of the stereotypes regarding African American women and morality are considered, and the African heritage linkage of spirituality and morality.

The self-esteem, as measured by consistency between actual/real and ideal selves, of the sample was not low or negative as some literature suggests. Reviewing the components for both sexes, they saw themselves as competent and determined, linked to intimates and family in positive (morality) terms. The fantasies corroborated this perhaps more for the women than men. From a symbolic interactionist perspective (incorporating the views of the "other") the assessments from the fantasies showed African American women expending quite a bit of their energies on work relationships. Many of the fantasies at first glance seemed rather unrealistic, reflecting more pure fantasy/ideal wish material (daughter of the richest man in the world or having a limousine take them to work). More importantly, the fantasies suggested that the reference group was not just the middle or upper class, but the "power elite" (the super rich). The literature suggests that the potential for lower self-image is greater when Blacks use European American standards/values as a reference (Kardiner & Ovesey, 1971; McCarthy & Yancy, 1971; Proshansky & Newton, 1968). This notion could be further supported by fantasy material in which the following type of statements were made: "As high as I was in the fantasy, I felt that low in reality;" "when the fantasy ended, I was a poor struggling working woman on I-75 [an interstate highway] going to work." However, on the more positive side, others made comments such as: "I need to try harder to make my fantasy come true" (saw fantasy as being possible). The self-concept and fantasy material in relationship to the definition of psychological health, suggests that this sample is "striving." While their self conceptions in general were good, there existed the element of "from whence they were/are striving." Stated differently, they are aware of the obstacles (racism, sexism) but are choosing to overcome them.

Thus, in particular reference to the fantasies of the women study participants, three interpretations might be offered: 1) that they had the White power elite as a reference group with the problems and difficulties associated with that circumstance; or 2) that the fantasies reflected attempts to overcome the depressive conditions and realities of being Black, female, marginally above the poverty level, oppressed and alone; and or 3) as Linda Leonard (1990), a Jungian analyst might suggest, especially for the woman who saw her father as the richest man in the world, that an attempt was made to redeem the personal and cultural father from their perceived inabilities and inadequacies magnified by racism, to thus rescue her feminine self from the depths of despair. This redemption would entail re-fathering, as in the case cited, by obtaining a powerful father or masculine principle both external (through the father) and internal (through the masculine principle within the self) which theoretically would lead to a healthier balance with the feminine self.

The purpose of the study was to define Black/African American psychological health from an African American perspective. The definition primarily expressed the need to have some philosophical orientation toward one's Creator and one's self and others in relationship to this Creator; having a code of moral standards for self and others; specific codes for interacting and communicating with others, especially intimates; adequate strategies for coping and adaptation such as common sense and intelligence; and some orientation regarding goal attainment. The study sample showed that African American men and women do in fact share a spiritual ideology which is manifested in different ways based on gender. Further, it was found that non-religious attendance does not lessen or minimize spirituality. The study definition differs from many of the other definitions of psychological health in that it shows a definite awareness of African American reality (e.g., racism, relationships) however, the focus is less on racism and "others", than it is on self, and self-knowledge and respect as the foundation for understanding and interacting with others. It provides an overall framework for "living in the world" or worldview which recognizes the interconnectedness of self and others. A significant distinction of the study definition is that it links spirituality, morality and ethics to the concept of psychological health, which traditional European American and Black American conceptions lack.

The definition of psychological health proposed by this study reflects what West (1977) would consider as an "African American philosophy." West defined the concept as: "the interpretation of African American history, highlighting the cultural heritage and political struggles, which provides desirable norms that should regulate responses to particular challenges presently confronting African Americans" (pp. 122-123). West further proposed that there are two basic challenges confronting African Americans: self-image, which considers the "perennial human attempt to define who and what one is;" and self-determination, which addresses the "political struggle to gain significant control over the major institutions that regulate people's lives" (pp. 123). For West, the challenges can be distinguished, but they are inseparable. Thus inherent in the study definition of psychological health is in fact, an explanation of who, as Black African Americans, the participants are; the struggles against racist and sexist oppression they face; and their best solution for how the challenges must be faced both personally and for the African American community. The balance presented by them (including both positive and negative aspects of self) demonstrated a belief that an African American self-image begins with critical introspection and self-examination, or self knowledge. The participants are in the process of "becoming" who and what they ultimately want to be through a process of self-definition (the process or "path" being more highly valued and vital than the result), embodied within an African American philosophy, which recognizes spirituality, as distinct from religiosity, as a way to meet the challenges above.

The study participants would also be classified as humanists (West, 1977; Jenkins, 1991). West stated that: "The humanistic self-image of African Americans is one neither of heroic super humans untouched by the experience of oppression nor of pathetic subhumans devoid of a supportive culture....This tradition...accepts this culture for what it is, the expression of an oppressed human community imposing its distinctive form of order on an existential chaos, explaining its political predicament, preserving its self-respect and projecting its own special hopes for the future" (p. 139). Jenkins' (1991) "telic-humanistic" psychological perspective might view the striving, efficacy and competence motivational themes found in the study as reflecting participants' powerful motivating intentions to become more competent in their physical world transactions.

Additional support for the above notions yet with a caveat of caution regarding strivings for materialistic competence was also expressed by an adult male participant who was an artist by occupation (obtained from a tape of the session): "At some other time we had the picture of the church, with the preacher and the good sisters. The brothers weren't as religious, but were getting their strength internally. Spirituality may be the solution to the problem. Spirituality (meaning life itself) not religion. You can't get that much from organized religion because of the hypocrisy. We as Blacks are creating our own environment that's helping to destroy our collective base, through our attitudes regarding striving [materialism], which has cost us. We're paying a heavy price for it. Now in the 70's and 80's [90's] we're beginning to say that this costs too much; we each need to rethink our direction as a person [s]."

The study components of psychological health were found in general to be similar to those of Jahoda (1958) and other theorists, such as having awareness of self, unified outlook on life, autonomy, clear reality perception, and mastering of environmental challenges. What is suggested here is that the components (characteristics) of psychological health may be the same across race, however, the specific interpretations and manifestations of them may differ. Stated differently, being Black or White may not change the basic components of health, only the processes employed to go about this understanding. In this latter sense, the proposed study definition of psychological health is Black/African American.

The study definition also expressed distinctive relevance to African Americans. The spiritual component of psychological health is a distinguishing feature from European American definitions. Self-knowledge and other references to self (respect, acceptance, etc.) were seen by the participants as aspects of that spiritual orientation (rather than as separate). Self, in relationship to, and embedded within spirituality as an overriding framework, would potentially negate "self-centered" and "narcissistic" strivings and interpretations of psychological health. The proposed definition is also distinctive from other European American and Black culturalist definitions in that it links psychological health with spirituality, ethics and morality. Thus, the definition may be considered as a re-awakening of ancient African values, not merely African American ones; a truer picture perhaps, of an African cultural heritage defined conception of psychological health. This is evident when comparing the Ramseur (1991, 1998) model consisting of issues/components of psychological health, with the components/characteristics from this study. While addressing virtually the same issues, the definition herein proposed offers a Maatian-like link of psychological health to moral and ethical as well as spiritual issues, with a further added dimension of the need for self-knowledge and inner harmony (as defined within the category of unity). Perhaps the study participants were anticipating the evolution of Black consciousness to a more balanced and healthy consciousness of being both African and American.

African American psychological health herein defined, also points to the suggestion made by several theorists (e.g., Akbar, 1979; Gary, 1978; Smith, 1981) that mental health professionals need a clear understanding of the role which spirituality plays (and in some cases religion), in African American life. It is further proposed that there exist greater potential benefits for mental health professionals in understanding spirituality and spiritual principles, than perhaps in religiosity/ religion, thus allowing for broader therapeutic applicability with clients of all faiths. Spiritual principles transcend individual denominational beliefs (which can serve a divisive function vs. a cohesive one). In fact, it has been proposed that intrinsically (at the core), all religions espouse the same basic ideology, but as variations on a theme (al-'Ashmawi, 1986). While the majority of African Americans are of the Baptist faith (as was this sample), there are also Blacks within Catholic, Islamic, Judaic, Buddhist and other denominations/faiths. Thus a knowledge of spiritual principles which transcend the specifics, would be critical.

Future studies may want to consider a quantitative examination of the components (characteristics) of African American psychological health espoused here, to validate their broader relevance to the African American community. Other themes suggested for further study are: Black men and spirituality; indicators of spirituality; fantasies of Black men and women vis-à-vis the African American community; social awareness and spirituality among Black men and women; and developmental issues associated with the conceptions of African American psychological health.

Appendix A

Methodology

An exploratory study was conducted (Edwards, 1987) to determine self-defined components of psychological health for African Americans. The sample consisted of only 25 persons in three groups representing students (2 groups) and adults (1 group). The methodology was the same as that used currently. Several interesting themes emerged and varied according to level of maturation and gender, and were thought to be important factors influencing African American psychological health. However, with the small size it was impossible to know if these themes were merely unique to this sample. Thus gender and age became a major focus of the second study (independent variables), and the sample size was increased.

Subjects

A total of 117 subjects participated in the present study. Three age (developmental) levels were represented: young adult (College student), 17-24 years; mid-adult (Adult), 40-59 years; and older adult (Elderly), 65-94 years.

The ages of the sample clustered around 20-24 years for the college students (51%); 40-49 years for adults (45%); and 70-79 years for the elderly (43%). Each age group was considered on a gender variable of women, men and mixed gender for the students and adults. A mixed gender group for the elderly was not obtained. A total of 26 groups were conducted; 14 student groups; 7 adult groups and 5 elderly groups. A network method was employed (Goetz & LeCompt, 1984) to obtain subjects. This strategy called for each successive participant(s) to have been named by a preceding participant(s). Student subjects were obtained at a large midwestern (predominately White) university; the adults from the community, and the elderly from a nursing home. All were in a mid-sized, urban midwestern city.

Measures

Subjects completed a questionnaire which contained the following:

1) Cultural Attitude Survey, which was based on Cross' (1972) model of Stages of Black Identity. Because items were found ambiguous to many subjects, data from this survey were not used. 2) Feelings About Society: Race; and Feelings About Society: Sex. There were four items for each topic, e.g., "I have never been discriminated against because of my race" to "I am actively involved in political activities to eliminate racism." There were similar questions regarding feminist\womanist activities. Strength of attitude (political involvement) was indicated by these items. 3) Who Am I Method - Self Concept (Kuhn & McPartland, 1954). A modified version of the Who Am I/Twenty Statements test was employed as a projective-like assessment of self-concept. Rather that twenty statements however, subjects were allotted three spaces on which to respond. A value of this test is that it allows for free subject response with minimal experimenter influence as well as allowing subjects to determine the salience of characteristics defining the self-image (order-position dimension). 4) Self-esteem was indicated by requesting that subjects use six adjectives (three each) to describe their "Actual" and "Ideal"

(self-ideal discrepancy) selves (Rogers and Dymond, 1954). Theoretically, it is proposed that the degree of correspondence between the two, indicates self-esteem. 5) Demographic items regarding: age, education, parental education, occupation and income, marital status, children, and religious preference and attendance.

Procedure

1) Guided Fantasy (Singer, 1974; Morgan & Skovholt, 1976): Subjects were asked to imagine themselves going through a typical day as their ideal of a psychologically healthy African American\Black person. Each participant then described his/her fantasy to the group, while the facilitator wrote each description on newsprint. The group then brain stormed as many additional characteristics as possible. In a nominal group process, each member then contributed to the list, the one essential characteristic. Each participant then selected from the list, the five (rank ordering) essential characteristics of a psychologically healthy African American\Black person. All rankings were weighted and summed to produce a final group list of the five most valued characteristics. The entire group process, which varied in length from 2 to 3 hours, was taped recorded.

Data Analysis

Content analyses were used to analyze the data from the 1) self concept indices; 2) fantasies; and 3) highest ranked characteristics of psychological health. The self-concept and psychological health characteristics were coded on a schema developed by Gordon (1968) to analyze free response self-representations. There were eight primary categories with specific sub-categories:

1) Ascribed Characteristics - social identity designations, conferred at birth, which remain throughout life. These characteristics serve to locate individuals in terms of society: i.e., Sex, Age, Race, Name, Religion.

2) Roles and Memberships - social identity under individual control: i.e., Kinship, Occupational, and Student roles; Political Affiliations; Social Status, Citizenship and Membership in an Actual interacting group.

3) Abstract Identifications - abstract and private identities which defy global (social) identification, or place an individual in a universal, very large abstract category, or associates the individual to some comprehensive idea system (e.g. political, ideological, philosophical). Existential Individuating (e.g., me, an individual, undefinable, unique); Membership in an Abstract category (e.g., a person, human being); and Ideological Belief References (a Christian, liberal).

4) Interests and Activities - includes judgments of quality, meaning and substance, such as Judgments and Tastes, Intellectual Concerns, Artistic Activities and Other Activities.

5) Material References - such as Possessions and Resources (owner of a building) and Physical Self or body image.

6) Four Systemic Senses of Self - suggesting that every human system or person must solve the problems of adaptation, goal attainment, integration and pattern maintenance (Parsons, 1961). Each corresponds to a sense of self, i.e., a) Moral Worth: indicating pattern maintenance in which the self is seen as good, bad, honest, etc.; b) Self-Determination: indicating goal attainment and striving to get ahead; c) Sense of Unity: reflecting integration at the person level (e.g., harmony, cohesion and continuity of self); and d) Sense of Competence: indicating adaption (e.g., coping resources and capacities).

7) Personal Characteristics - Interpersonal Style, describing one's typical manner of acting and interacting, and Psychic Style, or personality.

8) External Meanings - represented one's assessment of the attitudes others hold toward self and references to the testing situation itself, i.e., Judgments Imputed to Others, Situational references (i.e., testing situation), and Uncodable responses.

The fantasy coding schema emerged from the content or themes of the fantasies. Major categories with subcategories were: 1) Work, Career and Education, i.e., Status Symbols (perks of work\school\career), Type (specific career, and/or major), Commitment to work\career (e.g., working long hours and energy expended), and Environment or nature of work\school; 2) Relationships which were Intimate, Friendships, Work related, with Family, with Others in general, with Other Blacks, and Uncommitted or Alone; 3) Personal Orientation including Self references, and references to Others; 4) Health (e.g., physical and mental status) and Physical self (e.g., physical beauty); 5) Leisure Activities or recreational pursuits; 6) Political and Social Awareness (references to any of the "isms") with specific categories for Racism, Sexism and Other awarenesses; 7) Spirituality (i.e., global concept) and Religion (i.e., specific activities surrounding organized religious beliefs and practices); 8) Living Atmosphere or references to one's living environment; and 9) Material Values and Possessions.

In both coding schemes, statements could be coded as belonging to more than one category (frequencies do not equal number of subjects). Inter-coder reliabilities were: .95 (self-concept); .89 (fantasy); .93 (characteristics of psychological health).

References

Akbar, N. (1979). Awareness: The key to Black mental health. In W. D. Smith, K.H. Burlew, M.H. Mosley & W.M. Whitney (Eds.), *Reflections on Black psychology* (pp. 13-21). Washington, DC: University Press of America.

al-'Ashmawi, S. (1986). Three cultures: Judaism, Christianity and Islam. *The Jerusalem Quarterly, 38*, 138-144.

Anderson, G. (1971). Maturing religion. *Pastoral Psychology, 22*, 17-20.

Ausubel, D.P. (1961). Personality disorder is disease. *American Psychologist, 61*, 69-74.

Baldwin, J.A., Brown, R., & Hopkins, R. (1991). The Black self-hatred paradigm revisited: An Africentric analysis. In R. Jones (Ed.), *Black psychology* (3rd ed., pp. 141-165). Hampton, VA: Cobb & Henry.

Bandura, A. (1969). *Principles of behavior modification*. New York: Holt, Rinehart and Winston.

Budge, E.A.W. (1969). *The gods of the Egyptians: Studies in Egyptian mythology* (Vol. 2). New York: Dover Publications.

Budge, E.A.W. (1988). *From fetish to God in ancient Egypt*. New York: Dover Publications.

Clark, K.B., & Clark, M.P. (1947). Racial identification and preference in Negro children. In E. Maccoby, T. M . Newcomb, & E. L. Hartley (Eds.), *Readings in social psychology* (pp. 602-611). New York: Holt, Rinehart and Winston.

Cleage, A., Jr. (1972). *Black Christian nationalism*. New York: Morrow & Co.

Collins, P. H. (1990). *Black feminist thought: Knowledge, consciousness, and the politics if empowerment*. New York: Routledge.

Cross, W.E., Jr. (1971). The Negro-to-Black conversion experience. *Black World, 20(9)*, 13-27.

Davis, J., & Weaver, J. (1982). Dimensions of spirituality. In C. Spretnak (Ed.), *The politics of women's spirituality: Essays on the rise of spiritual power within the feminist movement* (pp. 368-370). New York: Anchor Press/Doubleday.

de Charms, R. (1968). *Personal causation*. New York: Academic Press.

Downey, M. (Ed.). (1993). The *new dictionary of Catholic spirituality*. Collegeville, MN: The Liturgical Press.

Edwards, K.L. (1987). Exploratory study of Black psychological health. *Journal of Religion and Health, 26(1)*, 73-80.

Edwards, K.L. (1994). The kindred fields of Black liberation theology and liberation psychology: A critical essay on their conceptual base and destiny: A response . *Journal of Black Psychology. 20(3)*, 360-363.

Edwards, K.L. (1998). A cognospiritual model of psychotherapy. In R. Jones (Ed.), *African American Mental Health*. Hampton, VA: Cobb & Henry.

Fleming, J. (1983). Black women in Black and White college environments: The making of a matriarch. *Journal of Social Issues, 39(3)*, 41-54.

Frazier, E.F. (1964). *The Negro church in America*.. Chicago, IL: University of Chicago Press.

Fromm, E. (1965). *The sane society*. New York: Holt, Rinehart and Winston.

Gary, L. (Ed.). (1978). *Mental health: A challenge to the Black community*. Philadelphia, PA: Dorrance and Company.

Gary, L. (1987). Religion and mental health in an urban Black community. *Urban Research Review, 11(2)*, 5-7, 14.

Gary, L.E., & Jones, D.J. (1978). Mental health: A conceptual overview. In L. E. Gary (Ed.), *Mental health: A challenge to the Black community* (pp. 1-25). Philadelphia, PA: Dorrance and Company.

Goetz, J.P., & LeCompte, M.D. (1984). *Ethography and qualitative design in educational research.* New York: Academic Press.

Gordon, C. (1968). Self-conceptions: Configuration of content. In C. Gordon and K. L. Gergen (Eds.), *The self in social interaction* (pp. 115-136). New York: John Wiley and Sons, Inc.

Gore, P., & Rotter, J. (1963). A personality correlate of social action. *Journal of Personality, 31*, 58-64.

Grant, S. (1993). The sin of servanthood: And the deliverers of discipleship. In E. M. Townes (Ed.), *A troubling in my soul: Womanist perspectives on evil and suffering* (pp. 199-218). New York: Orbis Books.

Greene, B. (1994). African American women. In L. Comas-Diaz and B. Greene (Eds.), *Women of color: Integrating ethnic and gender identities in psychotherapy* (pp. 10-29). New York: Guilford Press.

Grier, W.H., & Cobbs, P. M. (1968). *Black rage.* New York: Basic Books.

Grier, W. H., & Cobbs, P. M. (1971). *The Jesus bag.* New York: McGraw-Hill.

Griffith, E.H., English, T., & Mayfield, V. (1980). Possession, prayer and testimony: Therapeutic aspects of the Wednesday night meeting in a Black church, *Psychiatry, 43,* 120-128.

Gyekye, K. (1996). *African cultural values: An introduction.* Philadelphia, PA: Sankofa Publishing.

Hilliard, T.O. (1972). Personality characteristics of Black student activists and non-activists. In R. Jones (Ed.), *Black psychology* (pp. 136-144). New York: Harper & Row.

Howard, J. (1970). How to end colonial domination of Black America: A challenge to Black psychologists. *Negro Digest, 19*, 4-10.

Jackson, M.R. (1984). *Self-esteem and meaning: A life historical investigation.* Albany: State University of New York Press.

Jahoda, M. (1958). *Current concepts of positive mental health.* New York: Basic Books.

Jenkins, A.H. (1991). A humanistic approach to Black psychology. In R. Jones (Ed.), *Black psychology* (3rd ed., pp. 79-98). Hampton, VA: Cobb and Henry.

Jensen, A.R. (1969). How much can we boost IQ & scholastic achievement? *Harvard Educational Review, 39*, 1-123.

Jones, F. (1972). The Black psychologist as consultant and therapist. In R. Jones (Ed.), *Black psychology* (pp. 363-374). New York: Harper & Row.

Jones, R.L. (Ed.). (1980). *Black psychology* (2nd ed.). New York: Harper & Row.

Kardiner, A., & Ovesey, L. (1951). *The mark of oppression.* Cleveland, OH: World.

Karenga, M. (1982). *Introduction to Black studies*. Inglewood, CA: Kawaida Publications.

Karenga, M. (1984). The book of Khun-Anup. In M. Karenga, *Selections from the husia: Sacred wisdom of ancient Egypt*. Los Angeles, CA: Kawaida Publications.

Karenga, M. (1990). Towards a sociology of Maatian ethics: Literature and context. In M. Karenga (Ed.), *Reconstructing Kemetic culture: Papers, perspectives, projects* (pp. 66-96). Los Angeles, CA: University of Sankore Press.

Kubie, L.A. (1975). The language tools of psychoanalysis: A search for better tools drawn from better models. *The International Review of Psychoanalysis, 2*, 11-24.

Kuhn, M.H. (1960). Self-attitudes by age, sex and professional training. *The Sociological Quarterly, 1*, 39-55.

Kuhn, M.H. & McPartland, T. S. (1954). An empirical investigation of self-attitudes. *American Sociological Review, 19*, 68-76.

Leggon, C.B. (1980). Black female professionals: Dilemmas and contradictions of status. In L. F. Rodgers-Rose (Ed.), *The Black woman* (pp. 189-202). Beverly Hills, CA: Sage Publications.

Leonard, L.S. (1990). Redeeming the father and finding the feminine spirit. In C. Zweig (Ed.), *To be a woman: The birth of the conscious feminine* (pp. 125-136). Los Angeles, CA: Tarcher Press.

Lichtheim, M. (1976). The instruction of Amenemope. In M. Lichtheim, *Ancient Egyptian literature: The new kingdom* (Vol. 2, pp. 146-163). Berkeley: University of California Press.

Marx, G T. (1967). Religion: Opiate or inspiration of civil rights militancy among Negroes. *American Sociological Review, 32*, 64-72.

Maslow, A. (1962). *Toward a psychology of being*. Princeton, NJ: Van Nostrand.

Mbiti, J.S. (1970). *African religions and philosophy*. New York: Anchor Books.

Mbiti, J.S. (1988). *African religions and philosophy*. London: Heinemann.

McCarthy, J.D., & Yancy, W.L. (1971). Uncle Tom and Mr. Charlie: Metaphysical pathos in the study of racism and personal disorganization. *American Journal of Sociology, 76*, 648-672.

Morgan, J.I., & Skovholt, T.M. (1976). Using inner experience: Fantasy and daydreams in career counseling. *Journal of Counseling Psychology, 24(5)*, 391-397.

New American Standard Bible. (1990). *The new open Bible: Study edition*. Nashville, TN: Thomas Welson.

Nobles, W.W. (1980). African philosophy: Foundations for Black psychology. In R. Jones (Ed.), *Black psychology* (2nd ed., pp. 23-36). New York: Harper & Row.

Nobles, W.W. (1973). Psychological research and the Black self-concept: A critical review. *The Journal of Social Issues, 29 (1)*, 11-31.

Offer, D., & Sabshin, M. (1974). *Normality* (Rev. ed.). New York: Basic Books.

Parsons, T. (1961). Outline of the social system. In T. Parsons, W. Shils, K. D. Waegele, & J.R. Pitts (Eds.), *Theories of society* (Vol.1). Glencoe, IL: Free Press.

Pettigrew, T.F. (1964). *A profile of the Negro American.* New York: Van Nostrand Reinhold.

Poussaint, A., & Atkinson, C. (1970). Black youth and motivation. *Black Scholar, 1*, 43-51.

Proshanky, H., & Newton, P. (1968). The nature and meaning of Negro self-identity. In M. Deutsch, I. Katz, & A. Jensen (Eds.), *Social class, race and psychological development.* New York: Holt, Rinehart and Winston.

Rainwater, L. (1967). Crucible of identity. In T. Parsons, & K. B. Clark (Eds.), *The Negro American* (pp. 160-204). Boston, MA: Beacon.

Ramseur, H.P. (1991). Psychologically healthy Black adults. In R.L. Jones (Ed.), *Black psychology* (3rd ed., pp. 353-378). Hampton, VA: Cobb & Henry.

Ramseur, H.P. (1998). Psychologically healthy African American adults. In R.L. Jones (Ed.), *African American mental health* (pp. 3-32). Hampton, VA: Cobb & Henry.

Rogers, C., & Dymond, R. (Eds). (1954). *Psychotherapy and personality change.* Chicago: University of Chicago Press.

Rotter, J. (1966). Generalized expectancies for internal versus external control of reinforcement. *Psychological Monographs, 80*, 609.

Ruffin, J. E. (1989). Stages of adult development in Black professional women. In R. Jones (Ed.). *Black adult development and aging* (pp. 31-61). Berkeley, CA: Cobb & Henry.

Shuey, A.M. (1958). *The testing of Negro intelligence.* Lynchburg,Va: J.B. Bell.

Singer, J.L. (1974*). Imagery and daydream methods in psychotherapy and behavior modification.* New York: Academic Press.

Smith, A., Jr. (1981). Religion and mental health among Blacks. *Journal of Religion and Health, 20*, 264-287.

Strickland, B. (1965). The prediction of social action from a dimension of internal-external control. *Journal of Social Psychology, 66*, 353-358.

Thomas, C.S., & Comer, J.P. (1973). Racism and mental health services. In C. Willie, B. Kramer, & B. Brown (Eds.), *Racism and mental health* (pp. 165-181). Pittsburgh, PA: University of Pittsburgh Press.

Ullman, L.P.,& Krasner, L. (Eds.). (1969). *A psychological approach to abnormal behavior.* NJ: Prentice-Hall.

Vontress, C.E. (1971, June). The Black male personality. *Black Scholar, 2*, 10-16.

Walker, B. (1983). *The women's encyclopedia of myths and secrets.* San Francisco, CA: Harper & Row.

Walsh, R.N., & Vaughan, F. (Eds.). (1980). *Beyond ego:Transpersonal dimensions in psychology.* Los Angeles, CA: J. P. Tarcher, Inc.

West, C. (1977). Philosophy and the Afro-American experience. *Philosophical Forum,* Spring, 117-148.

White, J. (1972). Toward a Black psychology. In R. Jones (Ed.), *Black psychology* (pp. 43-50). New York: Harper & Row.

Wilcox, P. (1973). Positive mental health in the Black community: The Black liberation movement. In C. Willie, B. Kramer, & B. Brown (Eds.), *Racism and mental health* (pp. 463-524). Pittsburgh, PA: University of Pittsburgh Press.

Wilson, G.L. (1980). The self/group actualization of Black women. In L.F. Rodgers-Rose (Ed.), *The Black woman* (pp. 301-314). Beverly Hills, CA: Sage Publications.

Author

Karen Lenore Edwards
Department of Psychology
M. L. #376
University of Cincinnati
Cincinnati, OH 45221-0376
Telephone: (513) 556-0648
Fax: (513) 556-1904
E-mail: karen.edwards@u.c.edu.

Therapeutic Processes for Health and Wholeness in the 21st Century: Belief Systems Analysis and the Paradigm Shift

Linda James Myers
The Ohio State University

with case presentations by
Flavia Eldemire
University of Massachusetts, Amherst

As our understanding of the world and human behavior increases, we are seeing a paradigm shift occurring in the discipline of psychology (Manicas & Secord, 1983). Over the past twenty-five years the shift has meant movement toward a more holistic and integrative understanding that place consciousness and relationships at the center of well-being and a healthful humanity (Myers, 1988; Myers & Diener, 1995; Uchino, Cacioppo, & Kiecolt-Glaser; Weil, 1997). In part the shift has been fostered in the West by recognition that most modern crises are man-made (Mesarovic, Mihajlo, and Psetel, 1974) and that there is a mismatch between the demands of the planetary culture and our capacity to respond (Kegan, 1994). Suggestions that our reactions to the modern world are often inappropriate because of the nature of our minds and the training we give them (Ornstein & Ehrlich (1989), foster the need for alternatives for our learning challenged culture (Elias, 1997) and are the spawning ground for movement beyond the limitations of the currently dominant worldview. African-American psychologists have played significant roles in this shift, ranging from critique and refutation to innovative reconstructions and conceptualizations (Akbar, 1976, 1981; Azibo, 1992; Bynum, 1994; Karenga, 1982; Myers, 1980; Myers, 1988; Nobles, 1970, 1980; Wilson, 1978, 1981).

As the status of conventional models came under severe criticism, the foundation of Black psychology and the methodological perspectives that guide its research and therapeutic practices were formed (Banks, 1982). Today, alternative models from outside and within the "mainstream" are beginning to converge. These perspectives acknowledge that both individuals and societies are unprepared to meet the challenges posed by global issues because learning processes are lagging

313

appallingly behind new demands (Botkin, Elmandjra, & Malitza, 1979). Emerging to address these needs and as a part of the paradigm shift was a "oneness" model of psychological functioning (Myers, 1980). This model of psychological functioning is based on a theory of optimal consciousness (Myers, 1988). The model has a corollary psychotherapeutic/psychoeducational approach called Belief Systems Analysis (Myers, 1981). Each was propelled by the need to develop a more comprehensive and unified understanding of human experience that could promote increased individual and collective health and well-being.

This paper will present a brief overview of Optimal Theory (Optimal Theory) and its corollary therapeutic approach, Belief Systems Analysis (BSA), a method with a process for the expansion of consciousness towards healing in any human system through transforming basic worldview and specific capacities of the self. Focusing on the habits of mind that produce the limiting norms, practices, policies, and objectives of human experience, BSA opens inquiries into the underlying whys' of human functioning and encourages transformative learning akin, to that described by Bateson (1979) as level three and as triple-loop learning by Argyris and Schon (1978). The assumptions, tenets, methods and processes of Optimal Theory and BSA will be illustrated.

Historical Sequence and the Context of Self Knowledge

As a woman of both African American and Native American descent, I grew up in the sixties in a very nurturing, supportive, functional familial environment. However, I was acutely aware that something about the larger society was very much out of order. When it came to people of my ancestral heritages, this country demonstrated little or no understanding. Nor was there evidence of justice and harmony as foundational beliefs in mainstream American culture. Yet America claimed to be a land of freedom and justice for all. My dismay at these contradictions led to my interest in understanding the dominant societal worldview, its blatant contradictions and their ramifications. Often a disorienting dilemma in a person's life prompts engagement in the kind of critique of the contemporary social world that lays the ground for transformative learning (Elias, 1997), such was the case in my experience.

A few characteristics of the dominant worldview became readily apparent upon critical reflection, among them was its fragmented, externally-oriented, superficial nature. This dominant worldview has fostered an incapacity or unwillingness to acknowledge and resolve destructive inconsistencies in our social, political, educational and helping systems. For example, pre-Emancipation America enslaved Africans who tried to escape their enslavement were diagnosed as mentally ill. The escapees were given the diagnosis of *draptemania*. In short, the American mental health system defined the self-actualizing behavior of enslaved

Africans as pathological deviance. By implication this has meant that enslaved Africans who assimilated/internalized their subordinated status, engaged in accommodating behaviors, or identified with their aggressors, were deemed normal, if not healthy.

Are contemporary circumstances much improved? For African American's psychological health continues to be defined by individuals who have assimilated/ internalized the mainstream mindset. For example, the educational system is dominated by a monocultural worldview instilling assumptions, beliefs and values promoting White privilege and Black disenfranchisement Americans of African descent (and others) are more likely to be tapped for positions of leadership by the white power structure, if their views are in concert with the ones fostered by the structure. To the extent one of the views being fostered by the mindset is that African Americans are inferior and that European Americans and their culture is superior, the African American will inherently be at risk to the conscious and unconscious influences of the White supremist view. It's internalization will be reflected in devaluing perceptions of other African Americans, the distancing of oneself from other African Americans, making choices and decisions that would negatively effect African Americans as a group, and other destructive actions (e.g., anti-Black sentiments and policies often come from other Blacks). However, these perceptions, choices and actions will be seen by the benefactors of the White power structure as normal, healthy, reasonable, congruent and reinforcing of the ones they inhere. By identifying the deep structure or the assumptions in the conceptual system fostering the mental state and underpinning the worldview, it became clear that those assumptions yielded the same outcomes irrespective of who held them. I came to describe the set of assumptions and principles comprising the conceptual system of the aforementioned mindset as suboptimal because although they play integral roles in the functioning of the human psyche, they yield consequences reflective of fragmentation, disharmony, alienation, greed, imbalance, and a lack of reciprocity, lack of compassion, and lack of self-awareness.

Within contemporary psychology we are led to believe that this suboptimal mindset is simply a consequence of human nature. Optimal Theory concedes that individuals in all cultures have the *capacity* to inhere a suboptimal mindset and in this relative sense it is universal. However, suboptimal functioning is not an inevitable or necessary outcome. I was personally aware of another way of being in the world which emphasized the holistic interrelatedness and interdependence of all things; the oneness or the unity of all things with the good (Myers, 1980). This alternative mindset made the dominant institutional structures seem horribly irrational, if not unethical or insane. Given my cultural reality and experiential knowledge base, my efforts to understand human behavior in this social context have proceeded as those of a stranger in a strange land. Seeing the world differently, I was able to identify the philosophical assumptions and principles or conceptual system characterizing my own mindset or mental state and that perpetuated by the dominant culture. The assumptions of each mindset seemed to lead to different outcomes, (e.g., hegemonic privilege versus reciprocity, disharmony versus harmony, imbalance versus balance, violence versus peace, compassion exhaustion versus compassion expansion).

Through a set of interrelated constructs, definitions and propositions, Optimal Theory (Myers, 1988) was designed to explain the structural underpinnings of human consciousness and its functioning at both higher and lower levels. The goal of Optimal Theory is to enhance pure knowledge of how to increase postive human relational capacities. Optimal Theory presumes potential for both suboptimal and optimal consciousness exists within each individual. Social learning is seen to shape the nature and extent to which either orientation is fostered (along with the predisposition's to either mindset inherited from the past). By specifying relationships among various philosophical assumptions, values, beliefs about self and the world, and so on, a systemic view of human experience is presented for the purpose of clarifying and predicting intrapersonal, interpersonal and sociocultural phenomena, which is one of the objectives of Optimal Theory. Self-knowledge and explorations of the interrelationships between and interdependence of forces of consciousness reflected in all phases of life provide the epistemological and methodological frameworks of Optimal Theory. The purpose of Belief Systems Analysis (BSA), as a therapeutic strategy, is the amelioration of relational incapacities on intra- and inter-personal levels. Sperry (1983) notes that the prime hope of tomorrow's world lie s not in outer space or improved technology, but rather in a change in the kinds of value-belief systems we live and govern by.

Need for Holistic View of Mental Health

Utilizing Optimal Theory, our approach to solving problems and mental health will of necessity be holistic because to engage a discourse without a holistic perspective is to risk a symptom-focused analysis of behavior and exposure to influences outside of ones conscious awareness. By framing the examination broadly enough to question previously held assumptions, both implicit and explicit, the space is created for assessing a wider range of data to be incorporated in our analysis. The mental health of African Americans (this heterogeneous population will be treated as a group) will be used in example. We will address the following questions: What is mental health? According to what criteria does one assess the status of mental functioning? How does one achieve mental health in a pathogen ridden, toxic environment? What, if any, is the relationship between conceptions of health and standard of ethics? Addressing these questions from the perspective of Optimal Theory will expose us to a type of thinking that will enable us to make more successful responses to the complex difficulties facing us as a humanity. In addition, it will speak to the urgency of connecting the positive institution of the unconscious and the wisdom of the conscious, provide an opportunity to explore development of the wisdom of human systems at individual as well as collective levels, and offer a framework of values that can provide direction and boundaries for future development of mental health and well being.

According to Elias, (1997) one cause of the troubles afflicting the contemporary world is the quality of mind that we have perfected in European American cultures. He states, European Americans have perfected mental capacities that produce technological wonders accompanied by runaway ecological and social crises. If a problem cannot be solved with the type of thinking that created it, the most fruitful way to resolve these dilemmas simply may be to change the way we think. For the most part mainstream Western psychology (that academic discipline whose objective is the understanding of human behavior) has been functioning with restrictions on the mechanisms for such analyses. The fragmented nature of the prevailing quality of mind in the European American cultural and academic worldview (primarily suboptimal) is evident in the nature of its disciplinary foci. Even within the discipline of psychology itself, the artificial but virtually complete division of the social, individual, clinical, health, and organizational aspects of human functioning are pervasive.

This same socio-cultural characteristic of fragmentation can also be seen on the individual level in a resistance to the kind of awareness that would acknowledge the role of self in constructions of reality, or put one in touch with a sense of respect, if not reverence, for those aspects of life that are shared by all human beings. All too often in such a cultural system, assumptions, beliefs, attitudes and aspects of lived experience are denied and left unexplored or uninterrogated, especially if they are inconsistent with the dominant worldview. The means for holism and reintegration comes with the capacity for diunital logic. Diunital logic refers to a system of reasoning that allows one to see the dualities in all things, process the polarities as mutually creative resources rather than exclusive or competitive options, and to unify them through knowledge and understanding of their interrelatedness and interdependence. Through this process we achieve the ability to contain dualities and go beyond an oppositional framework. Only recently in social psychological literature have some of the characteristics of the ability to evaluate beyond bipolar conceptualizations and the evaluative errors that are inherent in the inability been studied in detail (Cacioppo, Gardner & Bernston, 1997).

Diagnosis and assessment of psychological disorder in this society have consistently been restricted to the level of the individual. In addition, notions of pathology and health have been defined from the experiential realities and perspectives of the dominant group, primarily European Americans, A broader, fuller, multi-level analysis of mental health is needed. Optimal Theory (Optimal Theory) can be used to meet this need, because it allows for the adaption of a transcultural perspective rooted in the worldview of our collective African ancestors, which is universal.

Roots of Theoretical Orientation

As I began to explore the cultural roots of the worldview I came to describe as optimal, I first looked to my own ancestral heritage as an African American.[1] I began with that aspect of my identity because it was the one made most salient to me by virtue of the ethnic orientation characterizing familial socialization, the pervasive and oppressive nature of White supremacy in the larger society, and the prevailing community focus and zeitgeist. Like many scholars, I saw the necessity of going back to at least pre-colonial Africa to discover an "authentic" African heritage. My own holistic perspective supported going back to the earliest historical records, as Africa was said to be the home of all human culture and civilization (Bynum, in press; Diop, 1974). Some with a more segmented worldview may not see the relevance of ancient history (or mythology) to the contemporary study of the mind. However, given the role of consciousness in a holistic, integrative worldview (more about that later), and the timeless dimension of the unconscious (Taub-Bynum, 1984), awareness of the beginning is invaluable.

Evidence of the beginning of a wisdom tradition is found in the Pyramid Text of ancient Africans, dating back to 2052 B.C. (Obenga, 1991). In this text a definition of the wise provides the cultural historical foundation for a universal orientation and understanding that appears holonomic and that supports the thrust of Optimal Theory. The idea that all is contained and reflected in each aspect of everything else (Mackenzie, 1991), is found in Obenga's discussion of the use of the term "he," which was commonly understood in the worldview of the ancients to be inclusive of the female, depicting an integrative mindset in which there could be no conception of male without female (Obenga, 1991).

> [S]he is the one who has the heart informed about those things that we otherwise do not know. [S]he who has lucidity when [s]he deals with an idea or problem, who is enlightened, moderate in action and familiar with old writings. [S]he is well informed enough to solve problems, instructed, educated, his mind has been educated. [The wise] stays awake at night seeking the correct ways which surpass what [s]he did the day before, seeks always to improve, wiser than the wise person having elevated themselves to wisdom; seeks advice and sees to it that people go to them for advice, as they are informed about any and everything. The wise know tradition by studying our ancestors ancient texts. They have experience in human matters and can solve problems. Day and night they have had to meditate in order to find out the correct ways. They are always eager to go for the best (Obenga, 1991).[1]

According to Cacioppo, Gardner and Bernston (1997) among the tasks confronting social scientists are sorting through axioms, developing theories that specify the conditions under which each holds, and devising measures that illuminate the psychological operations underlying the obvious. The Seven Hermetic Principles (Bynum, in press; Frye, 1987), or the laws of life as taught by Tehuti, also known as Thoth and as Hermes by the Greeks (Schwaller de Lubicz, 1982), provide anxioms that span across time and that are theorized to be universal (Bynum, in press; Myers, 1988). Optimal Theory has been developed and can be used to specify the conditions under which the Principles of Djehuti and other maxims hold in contemporary times in their relationship to healthy human functioning and an improved ordering of the universe.

The first of the Seven Hermetic Principles holds that all is mind. This principle places consciousness at the center of the largest macro-system on the human plane of existence. Optimal Theory, grounded in this premise, posits the spiritual/material unity of the cosmos, an idea which is also supported by similar assumptions in quantum physics, cognitive neuroscience and many Eastern philosophies (Bynum, in press; Capra, 1975; Chopra, 1995). This convergence is important because Optimal Theory would predict that the heights of knowledge across the broadest range of fields of study and cultures would yield the same conclusions or, equally appropriately, point in the same direction.

Allowing that all is mind or consciousness, Optimal Theory emphasizes the power of attention, thoughts and feelings. Your experience is created by virtue of that to which you attend. That to which one does not attend will have less bearing on experience (except when inattention is forced, as in repression). Consciousness in this instance is meant to be inclusive of the conscious, the subconscious, and the unconscious, as well as the holonomic flow between these levels of consciousness (flow of worlds within worlds). The unconscious aspect is important because of the commonly held awareness that greater is that which is unknown (as aspect of the unconscious), than that which is known (an aspect of the conscious). Consciousness (not just human consciousness, although that is our point of emphasis at this time) is assumed to be infinite, and can be said to diminish or expand into infinity. At any given time all thoughts and feelings exist in consciousness.

Optimal Theory acknowledges the various domains of consciousness, and the nature and characteriistics of each. This cohesive approach allows more ready access to those aspects of human functioning identified with different frequencies of electromagnetic waves produced by the brain, and, so-called extra-sensory or psychic experiences, such as anomalous cognition or psychic reading, remote viewing and spiritual healing.

We note that in the language of Optimal Theory, reality is conceived as a spiritual/material unity. From this vantage point, the material aspect can be seen as symbolic of or as a representation of the spiritual. This language also brings to the fore the spiritual, implicate, inner, unseen order of thoughts, feelings, intuition, and revelations, reinforcing their connection to the explicate (outer, visible) order of the five senses. With such a shift in perspective, that which appears holds deeper meaning than the surface appearance might inform, and unifies external perception with inner awareness. Historically, such unity has been characteristic of many traditions of knowledge and wisdom. Optimal Theory supports the development of the various manifestations of these traditions as they emerge within each cultural group and heritage. As each (individually and collectively) brings the height of their knowledge to the collective, the opportunity for the greatest good for all humanity is expanded. In order to accomplish this task, identifying and studying the characteristic attributes that have persisted over time toward optimal outcome, noting the conditions under which they resurge to point us toward the future, and illuminating the psychological operations underlying the attributes, can be helpful (Cacioppo et al., 1997).

The second principle of which Djehuti speaks is the principle of correspondence. This principle states that as above, so below. This principle describes the nature of the relationships among configurations of energy, suggesting that particular similarities, patterns or truths found on one plane or level of existence will have their corollaries on the other. So for example, if it can be observed in nature in general that life passes through seasons or cycles, the same would be expected to be true for individual and collective human development. This principle fosters the use of analogies, metaphors, and symbols to provide deeper insight into essential relationships among configurations and the value of knowing how one's assumptions are shaping one's perspective on reality. This principle can be the basis of prediction. For example, if on the physical plane of existence in outer space we find that black holes are the source of stellar life systems, we would expect to find a similar pattern working in a similar way on the spiritual plane of existence in inner space (e.g., black holes would be the source of life in inner subatomic space). Physicists who present an aspect of this premise conjecture on entangled particles, which accounts for communication between particle of the same origin across time and space (Giueffre, 1998). This finding would predict similar capacities for information transfer on the human plane.

The third principle, the principle of vibration, states that nothing rests. This principle is consistent with the process orientation of Optimal Theory which acknowledges the dynamic nature of being and explores the appearance of the static. The idea that everything moves is consistent with current scientific understandings of the subatomic activity of matter. In terms of human functioning, we would see that change and growth are constant and dynamic.

The fourth principle is the principle of polarity or duality, which speaks to the realization that everything can be seen as dual. Optimal Theory is guided by the awareness that opposites identical in nature but different in degree or vice versa, are the basis from which life is generated. We can see this principle at work from the electrical and magnetic fields where impulses to movement are governed by interactions of opposites. We would want to reason about said dualties with a unity that contains and transcends oppositions in order to avoid the traps of dualism and dichotomous logic. In other words, moving beyond bipolar conceptualizations in evaluative processes toward a bivariate evaluative space model would be consistent with Optimal Theory.

The fourth Hermetic Principle, that of duality, affords us the power of choice within any given context to either focus on the positive or the negative. The common sense would inform the value of seeing the good. However, common sense becomes uncommon in a suboptimal environment of socialization. More often an emphasis is placed on the lower rather than the higher functioning of consciousness, the more coarse versus refined, the more superficial versus substantial, the more expedient versus moral or correct, the more obvious versus subtle. The therapeutic modality called Belief System Analysis derived from Optimal Theory, emphasizes and draws upon the concept of polarity in the process of unifying, containing and transcending the primary oppositions of good and not good in human experience. Belief System Analysis achieves this end through a strategy called the optimization process. Diunital logic is essential to this capacity.

The fifth principle that everything has gender is an extension or elaboration on the dual nature of things. Masculine (e.g., hard, aggressive, external, territories, unemotional) and feminine (e.g., soft, gentle, receptive, internal, emotional) attributes can be identified in all aspects of life. Men and women have both masculine and feminine attributes. These attributes are complementary, and are needed for the greater good of the whole and for regeneration.

Rhythm is the sixth principle. This principle suggests that in the flow of life forces there will be recurrent patterns of alternating elements. Optimal Theory acknowledges that rhythm permeates being. Further, Optimal Theory acknowledges that when identified, accommodated or synchronized, rhythm can be used to regulate, balance and restore order. Concepts such as synchrony, synergy, and being in the flow emerge from this principle. Optimal Theory incorporates awareness of natural phenomena such as rhythm, which can contribute to an understanding of patterns within a system.

Principle number seven is that of cause and effect. Everything happens according to law and it has been said that chance is the name for a law unrecognized. Optimal Theory places high value on reason (not to be understood as exclusive of intuition, or seen solely in the mode of logical positivism), and supports the idea that for every effect there is a cause, and for every cause there is an effect. Akin to this principle are those of reaping what you sow; what goes around, comes around; and for every action there is a reaction. The exploration of optimal functioning may mean pursuit of that which some may consider unknowable. Optimal Theory assumes knowledge is infinite, but the interrogation of any and all ideas and phenomena is valid. Wisdom is defined as reason illuminated by science. Optimal Theory is rooted the wisdom tradition of African deep thought.

Bynum (in press) in his study of the African unconscious notes:

Both contemporary quantum mechanics and ancient meditational discipline overtly accept the quantum interconnectedness of all things in the universe. The physicists speak of non-locality and experimentally point to Bell's Theorem as "proof." The Mahayana Buddhist refer to the doctrine of dependent origination. The root idea here is the hidden resonance of all things.

The convergence of modern scientific data coming from many independent sources indicates and urgent need for a drastic revision of our fundamental concepts about human nature and the nature of reality (Grof, 1979). Optimal Theory supplies such a revision. Optimal Theory provides an alternative method for understanding and exploring the structure of consciousness. BSA challenges the assumptions which comprise one's conceptual system and creates one's worldview. In so doing BSA opens one up to new awarenesses. Theorizing that one's reality and experience are contingent on the nature of one's conceptual system, Optimal Theory provides a framework for selecting among the multitude of stimuli to which one attends. Optimal Theory also provides a framework for understanding how energies will configure, their rhythm, flow, and qualities, as well as the cumulative state of being and covariant attributes, affinities and conduits in one's experience. Within Optimal Theory two conceptual systems, the suboptimal and optimal, have been identified. Each of these systems has consequences or outcomes which have implications for the creation and transformation of life. The optimal worldview is holistic, integrative and transformative, it is as ancient as it is new, as non-local as it is local; it seeks to incorporate the implicate order into conscious experience to the extent possible; and acknowledges the hidden resonance of things.

The Evolution of Theory

Optimal Theory evolved in the vein of the wisdom tradition to seek to predict how human consciousness can be structured with observation and reason to be in union with the divine or supremely good. The records left by our ancient ancestors (the African mothers and fathers of all human culture and civilization) reinforce a conception of the timelessness of the universe and a holistic perspective which recognizes the interrelatedness and interdependence of all things. This orientation is paradigmatically distinct from Western psychology. Emphasizing a perspective that holistic and integrative rather than fragmented and disintegrative. Optimal Theory conceives of a dynamic, spiraling, evolutionary cycle of consciousness for which the double helix of DNA or, on the individual level from the wisdom tradition of the ancient Egyptians, the Kundalini rising, might be reasonable visual images.

When I first began to discuss Optimal Theory, one of the questions that I was asked is, "who thinks this way?" At the time I was only able to point out that we see remnants everywhere throughout the world in the teachings of virtually every cultural group. Further, among African Americans, this pattern of thinking has been central to survival of enslavement and oppression. Optimal Theory assumes the evolutionary nature of consciousness across generations. One proposition in Optimal Theory is that the optimal mindset that was known to our ancestors in the beginning, should be in existence now, and can be traced among those of African descent in America as well as among others. These propositions have been supported by research into the wisdom tradition of African deep thought (Carruthers, 1995). Teachings that exemplify the optimal mindset in contemporary African American culture can be found in this social context from organized religion as would be expected when a fragmented worldview is dominant. One unique example has been identified in the teachings of Prophet G.W. Hurley, as he is known by his followers, whose doctrine centered on realizing the God within. Although the leader had desired to start a school of psychology, in the early twenties in Alabama, he found it more practical to spread his work through the development of the Universal Hagar Spiritual Church. This group's philosophy and teachings mirror those of ancient Africans in ways that can be readily identified and are in complete concert with those of the teachings of Jesus the Christ or Buddha and Mohammed, when interpreted from a holistic and integretative worldview.

As human consciousness evolves and our awareness and understanding of the nature of the interrelatedness and interdependence of all things increases, we will find that our worldview will reflect fewer contradictions, less fragmentation and discontinuity, it will become more cohesive. The worldview dominant in Western culture seldom acknowledges the holonomic (all in is everything) aspect, even in the context of psychology. Due to the ontological separation of the spiritual and the material, the traditional Western paradigm of the nature of the universe has been incomplete, segmented and reductionistic in its approach to mind, life and spirit. In the Western tradition a form of reason devoid of intuition, revelation and spirit has become synonymous with order and science (Schwaller de Lubicz, 1982). In the African tradition spirituality and science have been compatiable (Finch, 1998), not mutually exclusive. Western science is now revealing a holistic and interconnected picture of the universe. That is, science is beginning to reveal an indivisible reality that closely resembles the ancient descriptions characteristic of the East (Capra, 1975; d'Espagnat, 1976; d'Espagnat, 1979), African included (Finch, 1998). However, psychology's failure to articulate a holistic model of behavior has proved problematic. Optimal Theory recognizes that each culture, and each individual, is unique, having its special contribution to make to the greater good of the whole (Myers, 1985). Everybody does not need to do the same thing in the same way, nor can they. According to an Ashanti proverb, no man's path crosses another, everyone has a direct path to the Supreme Being. However, when the prevailing mindset is exclusionary, preventing exposure to and understanding of the unique contributions and value of others, potential for the greater good is lost. Limitations become manifest to the extent that the value of diversity and pluralism is not seen.

To the extent that the cultural limitations of traditional Western paradigms are acknowledged, the way is opened for an expanded view of psychological theory (Walsh & Vaughn, 1980). Concern that the three major models of Western psychology — psychoanalysis, behaviorism, and humanistic psychology — were limited in their recognition of the upper reaches of psychological development (Walsh & Vaughn, 1980) led to the emergence of transpersonal psychology. Not yet fully accepted by the mainstream, the transpersonal school has struggled to develop its legitimacy. One source of difficulty has been the concern expressed by May and others that focus on the upper reaches of development might prompt us to ignore or deny the pathological or negative aspects of psychological functioning (May, 1989). Optimal Theory solves that dilemma by recognizing the necessary role of the "negative" in realization of the positive and for the purpose of growth, thereby affirming the dual nature of experience. Optimal Theory fits within the transpersonal school in that it allows for: 1) going beyond the limits of individual ego and identity, (this particularly is relevant in the context of the holonomic construct of a multi-dimensional or extended self that is inclusive of one's ancestors, community, future generations, and nature); 2) emphasis on maximal states of psychological well-being (again in effort to be consistent with a wisdom tradition whose earliest educational systems taught the achievement of everlasting peace and happiness); and, 3) the development and support of a more balanced, holistic, integrated and cohesive state of consciousness which is an alternative to the norm in this culture.

A natural outcome of a wisdom tradition which concentrates on and is always eager for the development of the "best," is the search for a conscious union with the divine or supremely good. The role of the Optimal Theory as a theory of divine consciousness, has been to explore and explicate a perspective that assumes that peace and happiness known now can be carried into eternity; and, that increased understanding of the omnipresent intelligence, which has unlimited power to govern experience, can be achieved. Learning to think, harmonize, and flow with nature through this life force of intelligent energy is not only possible, but mandatory, if health and balance are to be restored individually and collectively. Health and balance are restored when the higher, more optimal consciousness within the individual or collective unifies, contains and moves beyond the lower, more suboptimal. The corollary epistemological position of Optimal Theory's spiritual/material ontology is that through knowledge of this force, which is in self (in a multi-dimensional sense), all knowledge can be realized. Practitioners of the optimal mindset who are coming into greater self knowledge, recognize that the pattern of transformation is part of a necessary natural order.

Optimal Theory posits that a suboptimal conceptual system creates a way and view of being in the world that is oppressive and the cause of pathology, be it mental or physical in nature. This suboptimal system, through its externalized focus on ego, personality and outward appearances, alienates one from his/her inner being and the implicate order from which the connecting life force emerges. To the extent that this view is dominant in a society or culture, because of its inherent fragmentation and alienation of self from the finer forces (peace, harmony, balance, compassion, etc.), racism, sexism, classism, elitism, regionalism, imperialism, materialism, tribalism, heightism, weightism, violence, depression, chemical dependency and other addictions, and so on are the result (Myers, 1988). Just as a steady diet of empty calories driven by focus on false sense of temporary pleasure leads to obesity and other physical health problems in the physical realm, so does a psychological diet that is spiritually depleted lead to the degeneracy, dysfunction and moral bankruptcy we see in the spiritual realm of individual, familial and social life.

In essence, this vibratory universe of trans-temporal and trans-spatial relations is literally alive on every level and capable, at least on some subtle level, of interaction with human consciousness. This was the insight of the ancient seers on the banks of the Nile and Indus River Valley over five millenia ago. Their intuition was that matter was actually repressed or entombed spirit and that spirit was a profoundly personal process. ...Implicit in Hermetic Philosophy and science was the notion that each area of the body, each area of life enfolding, each other area of life and that all was animated by consciousness, vibration, and force... "balance" was needed not only physically but in a moral sense. Imbalance in one's ecology, not only local but more vast and solar, that is to say the ecology of one's community and one's relationship to the gods and pharaoh, was absolutely necessary or else symptomatology would arise (Bynum, in press).

Movement away from a suboptimal worldview to a more optimal one, or from lower consciousness to higher, is the objective of BSA, the therapeutic modality derived from Optimal Theory. In this context, power becomes the ability to define reality, to control one's thoughts and actions. As no one can make any one of us think or feel anything we do not choose to, each of us has the same amount of power; what differentiates us is the fact that some of us more readily give up our power to someone else. Equally important, there is a tendency for social and institutional structures to support a definition counter to one's own. This latter tendency need not be prohibitive, as we shall discuss later. However, empowered by the adoption of an optimal conceptual system designed to maximize the potential for positive experience, movement toward liberation and higher consciousness is facilitated.

The Optimally Functioning Human Being

What would be the characteristics of an optimally functioning individual? First it warrants reiteration that becoming optimal is a process that is dynamic and transformative, rather a state that is achieved and remains static. However, in process, the optimal functioning individual is more concerned about substance than form. A worldview giving primacy to the implicate order of values for peace, harmony, balance, compassion, truth, justice and reciprocity reduces the degree of external, superficial focus significantly. More attention is placed on increased knowledge, wisdom and understanding of self and others. Reasoning with the unity that contains and transcends all oppositions, this individual can see both sides of a situation. The individual appreciates that something could be both true and not true at the same time due to shifts in perspective, (*anyo kweli enyo*), two relative truths, yet one absolute at the same time.

Essential to optimal development is disidentification from a sense of ego and personality, which would see itself as separate from the universal, infinite source of all good. A false sense of self is forsaken in order to facilitate identification with higher consciousness. This leads to a unity with the universal good of which the individual is a unique expression. One recognizes one's self as a vessel for the supremely good and this recognition prevents one from getting caught up in issues of false pride and power. When the revelation of oneness or unity consciousness is experienced, it is often as the result of a sincere desire to know and seek truth. Through critical self-examination and introspective self-analysis of the impact of his/her belief system, thoughts/feelings and intra-personal communication or self-talk, the optimally functioning individual uses these mechanisms to help stay on the path and insure that self-knowledge is enhanced.

This awareness is not without purpose. Self knowledge moves in a consistent, spiraling pattern from the most inward to the most outward. As self-love, the basis of all love, is increased, the outcome will be increased love for others. The same is true for self-respect. That is, good begins within and evolves to encompass the farther, more external, distal formulations of being, (e.g., from intra-psychic to interpersonal, from cellular to tissue/organ/system/body, from individual to familial/cultural/global), only to reencounter itself once again. Acknowledging the multi-dimensional nature of our being, and accepting out connection to the infinite through our ancestors, our children, nature and our communities, reverence for each dimension is fostered.

Recognizing that each person is unique and special and should be acknowledged for their contributions to the greater good, the optimal functioning individual (OFI) embraces the higher consciousness of truth, justice, harmony, balance, order, compassion, reciprocity and propriety. Taking a stand for those principles in a suboptimal environment may mean that, for a time, the OFI is seen as a trouble maker or as one who refuses to "play the game." For those who observe and interpret the world from a suboptimal framework, the behavior of the OFI will likely be totally misinterpreted or misunderstood without the opportunity for effective communication. The OFI is likely to champion the cause of the most vulnerable or so-called "under-dogs." Standing up for what is just and right may "rock the boat," although the OFI seeks justice and righteousness with love, peace, and harmony in mind.

According to folklore, the pathway to higher consciousness is through the heart. Ancient Kemites (Egyptians) are said to have depicted this truth symbolically through pyramid architecture. Optimal Theory supports this axiom and, as such, the OFI pursues a clean, pure heart—a heart filled with love and free from wrong doing. The OFI works to overcome his/her lower nature, rebuking jealousy, envy, greed, and wanton self-interest. He/she knows that without self-mastery, self-destruction is inevitable. The awareness that the source of all satisfaction is within, brings a homeostasis of being, which is internal and spiritual in origin, accessed through thought/feeling of a deep nature. As knowledge, wisdom, and understanding are shared, the sharer experiences an increase in the same, as do others.

The OFI is careful to insure that his/her good is not defined primarily by his/her senses (i.e., appearance, feeling, tastes, smells, sounds, and looks) and that his/her behavior is not geared toward pursuit of the external and superficial. Without the anchoring of a conscious desire for deeper knowledge, wisdom and understanding, insatiable appetites for more and/or greater sensation, drives behavior to addictions. As the OFI gains experiential knowledge, consciously and deliberately seeking and practicing wisdom, s/he eventually learns to discern the energies coming into his/her vibration with increasing clarity. At this point correct insights, intuitions, and other anomalous cognitions become more prevalent.

The OFI is free thinking and avoids getting caught up in the illusions of others. S/he processes the negative behaviors of others as expressions of their inner selves and does not give them the power to disturb or disrupt. Negativity is used as an opportunity to grow. The OFI searches his/her heart for what is right and what is wrong. Answers to ethical questions are first addressed through examination of his/her motivations and intentions, to insure they are in line with the greater good for all.

In previous works (Myers, Speight, Highlen, Cox, Reynolds, Adams & Hanley, 1991; Myers; 1988), I discussed the application of Optimal Theory to identity development (Optimal TheoryAID); its relationship to moral development, as proposed by Kohlberg (1981); faith development as proposed by Fowler (1976); and intellectual and ethical development as put forth by Perry (1970). Suffice it to say here that as one becomes an OFI, the transformation of consciousness that takes place readily supports positive development in each of these areas of life.

Implementing Optimal Theory through BSA

A Dynamic BSA Model

It is from the heritage of African-American psychology that the psychotherapeutic approach called Belief System Analysis (BSA) first evolved over nineteen years ago (Myers, 1980). With the development of the oneness model, BSA was created as a broad-based therapeutic strategy for restoring health and balance to people whose mental health had been impaired by the psychological oppression of a worldview that is antithetical to that holistic understanding which can be traced back to the wisdom tradition in the beginning of human culture and civilization. BSA was designed to address the difficulties that emerge as people desirous of justice, balance and order seek mental health in a society where injustice, imbalance and chaos thrive. BSA provides a therapeutic framework for maximizing positive experience and empowerment.

It was clear that BSA could not be restricted to individual and group psychotherapeutic modalities. The model of humanity embedded within Optimal Theory's orientation has determined which human capacities would be studied and cultivated, and which would be ignored and go undeveloped (Norcross, 1985). "Treatment" interventions must, by definition, flow from the underlying conceptions of pathology, health, reality, and the therapeutic process (Kazdin, 1980). Optimal Theory requires a holistic, integrative, multi-level therapeutic approach consistent with the resurgence of the paradigm shift previously described.

Belief Systems Analysis is designed to be comprehensive in orientation, and dynamic in methodology. It has been developed as a psycho-educational process to be used individually or with groups in a wide variety of forums. Success with this modality had been realized with various populations from groups of men incarcerated for acts of violence and for substance abuse issues (Myers et al., 1991), to women's support groups and teen pregnancy prevention programs. In addition, its use in the development of an Africentric school and use in a corporate setting in leadership, ethics training and team building will be explored later in this chapter. Aimed at those in pursuit of developing higher consciousness, BSA utilizes self-exploration and self-knowledge as the foci to begin to change our world.

BSA in concerned with the transformation of consciousness. It is a therapeutic tool for life enhancement in the general human movement toward higher consciousness and divinity and increased emotional intelligence (Goleman, 1995). The Ten Cardinal Principles, which reflected the steps that an initiate must take to achieve self-mastery and higher consciousness (James, 1954), provide the guidelines to the processes of BSA. Other ancient texts, such as the Teachings of Ptah Hotep provide direction for positive interpersonal relationships, building good character, and other positive manifestations of the consciousness doctrine (Hilliard, 1997). These ancient documents have relevance today in terms of developing psychological practice based on the wisdom tradition of restoring health and wholeness.

BSA builds upon the wisdom tradition of learning self-mastery in the process of moving from lower (fragmented, disintegrative or suboptimal) consciousness to higher (holistic, integrative or optimal) consciousness. In the initial stages of the therapeutic process after a commitment to growth is made, the Ten Cardinal Principles represent the primary areas in which self-mastery must be demonstrated. Given that the nature and role of consciousness in human experience is primary, mastery of these principles insure increased mindfulness (Langer, 1989), emotional intelligence (Goleman, 1995), and resilience. The principles will be discussed later.

Realizing Healing and Divine Order in a Suboptimal Context

Strupp and Binder (1984) acknowledge that a basic ingredient of psychotherapy is the healing quality of good human relationship. This healing quality can not be replaced or compensated for by cleverness, astuteness, or technical expertise. Belief System Analysis acknowledges that this is a truth based on our self-knowledge epistemology. While BSA emphasizes the healing aspect of good human relationship, BSA sees good relationship as a goal as well as the process of healing. According to Optimal Theory, pathology reflects a disjuncture in human relationship, intra-individually, inter-individually, or both. In contrast, mutual respect, trust, loving acceptance, honest caring feedback, guidance and support form the foundation for healthful, healing relationships within and between individuals.

In an optimal environment, all relationships would be healthy and healing (i.e., therapeutic). The ability to foster these kinds of relationships depend on the degree of self-knowledge and mastery possessed by the individuals involved. Given this potential for healing, the success of the therapeutic process is contingent upon the readiness and willingness of the participants to work on themselves and their relationships.

Utilizing BSA, the first phase of the therapeutic relationship is geared toward helping the participants to see the relationship between their current belief systems and their experiences. The suboptimal/optimal continuum is used to help the participants to see how their conceptual systems dictate the nature and quality of their experiences. On-going assessments are made of the degree of change, if any, the participants desire to make in their conceptions and their experiences.

Participants constantly reflect their underlying assumptions or conceptual frameworks in their functioning. BSA highlights this point by comparing and contrasting the consequences of differing belief systems and assumptions. In this way, participants are in a better position to consciously choose their preference, and maintain responsibility for their choices. Those participants who effectively utilize BSA will gradually begin to identify alternatives that are more conducive to healthful growth. Self-knowledge must be sought. The desire to seek comes from within the participants. Once initiated, the process is heuristic, and becomes self-perpetuating and self-correcting. As participants come to know more about their true identities, having had the revelation and/or experienced the intuition of its correctness, they will come to rely on that inner knowledge more fully. At this point the principle goal of the therapeutic relationship will be to provide supportive reinforcement and clarification.

As the pathway to higher consciousness is through the heart, successful participants in BSA will generally feel more secure, relaxed, enthusiastic, loving, confident, honest, and just. Change will be manifested in three areas of life. First, the participant will cease to base his/her worth on external criteria. Self worth will become intrinsic. Second, participants will cease letting appearances, circumstances, and conditions determine the nature of their thoughts/feelings. Individuals will be empowered to define reality healthfully and resourcefully for themselves. Third, participants will learn to rely on positive beliefs and in unity with infinite spirit as the source of all. They will also learn to rely on patience to insure positive outcomes. Engagement in therapeutic relationships will build a strong sense of community.

You will note that we have carefully avoided the use of both the term "client" and "therapist," and have opted to continually speak of "participants." This break with mainstream labels is necessary for three reasons. First, it reflects our acknowledgment of a more holistic, integrative awareness. That is, the term "participants" acknowledges that what is at issue is much more complex and multi-layered than the patient-therapist dichotomy accommodates. It acknowledges that the paid relationship is, on some level, the outcome of a dysfunctional and failed social system of organization, in that if relationships were healthier, professional service may not be needed. Second, the rejection of mainstream labels acknowledges that the scope of the causes of pathology and relational dysfunction are far too perpervasive to confine to the narrow contexts defined by professional standards of practice. The causes of pathology are also too complex to be effectively understood by a fragmented disintegrative worldview. Third, the construct of participants is broad, stable, and fluid enough to accomplish our aim of identifying those engaged in a therapeutic, healing relationship. BSA, a developmental, psychoeducational process, accepts and acknowledges that participants cannot move beyond the order of their own creation until they are ready. However, when consciously defined and mutually agreed upon, that relationship will move any professional to a higher standard of practice and ethics than normally defined. Whole context may require response to conventional diagnoses and professional practices, participants engage in such with awareness of the bigger picture.

A key technique of BSA is the optimization process. This process is designed to help participants to transition from a suboptimal to optimal consciousness. Optimal Theory posits that the role of negativity in human experience is to provide the opportunity to grow into greater self-knowledge. This realization allows for the ability to unify, contain, and transcend all oppositions. The optimization process works such that once I choose to define reality based on an optimal conceptual system, I will likely bring into my experience something to cause me to feel separate from my unity consciousness. I will know that I have been separated when I become conscious of my "negative" feelings (e.g., anxious, fearful, guilt, angry, jealous, etc.). The challenge of the optimization process is to examine my assumptions, self-talk, feelings, and circumstances to master the lesson for which the "negative" experience was created. Once the lesson has been mastered, the experience will not need to be recreated. Over time as lessons are mastered, less "negativity" is brought into our experience, because it is no longer needed. We will also learn to stop defining difficult and/or painful experiences as negative; experiences will be described as "challenges" or as opportunities. These challenges will ultimately be seen as blessings. While most of us may not achieve that level of transformation in this life time because the process of perfecting oneself is a long and arduous one, Optimal Theory posits that knowing what is possible increases the probability of, and potential for, achievement. Thus a cyclic, self-perpetuating, self-correcting process has been set into play which, in time, insures success.

This lofty vision for humankind acknowledges both the continuous nature of the process of growth, and the fact that few may fully achieve the envisioned state. By the same token, according to Optimal Theory, as a result of our interconnectedness or oneness, when one of us achieves this level of knowledge or being, we all do benefit. When optimally functioning people are in leadership, a shift of the entire culture and society is possible.

Getting Outside the Box of Intellectual Imperialism and Conceptual Incarceration

Belief System Analysis is a tool that can be used to develop our capacities for self-healing and sustained development throughout life. Individuals who choose to use BSA, necessarily subscribe to a view of the world which is compatible with this vision. Such individuals must overcome the intellectual imperialism and conceptual incarceration that comes with living in a suboptimal environment.

Activities and techniques that may be applied in the therapeutic process include hypnosis, dream analysis, relaxation exercises and biofeedback training, astrology, and other strategies useful in increasing self-knowledge. Infusing consciousness with reading in the areas of ancient history and philosophy, religion, metaphysics, the human potential movement, and other areas of literature emphasizing healthful growth can prove helpful. Observation and analysis of popular culture can also be a useful method for increased self-awareness and human understanding.

In this context of becoming an OFI the images that one perceives becomes symbolic of spirit (energy as information, consciousness, God/dess), and the rhythm or vibration of spirit is recognized and acknowledged. That is, any image perceived by the OFI is interpreted as divine consciousness seeking to reveal itself. Even if it appears as not good, a challenge or trouble, the OFI has a steadfast commitment to the truth that s/he knows will bring that which appears into line with the positive vibration s/he is sending. The concept of rhythm connects the relationship between what is (the truth one knows) and what is becoming (the way things fit together to form the world representative of divine spirit). The inseparable interplay between cognition and emotion, thought and feeling, good and not good, respond to the experience of the optimal unity consciousness. Learning how to perceive and interpret this interplay is the aim of the therapeutic process.

The goal of BSA is to improve the quality of life of each participant (as well as the quality of life of those around him/her) by raising his/her level of consciousness toward the optimal. This goal is far-reaching, yet consistent with wisdom tradition. Life is revered and conceived as inseparable from cohesiveunity consciousness. Harmony among all life forces is valued. From this perspective, we begin with self-love and work outward. When people really feel good about themselves, they will begin to feel better about others; so, in terms of goal achievement and evaluation, how one feels about oneself and others becomes the criterion for health and well-being. The value of a transcendent belief systems has been noted (Fine, Schwebel & Myers, 1985; Propst, 1982). BSA has been found to be particularly effective with those experiencing depression, posttraumatic stress, chemical dependency, violence and conflict, or desiring self-esteem building, improving quality of relationships and stress reduction (Myers et al., 1991). If one is too highly fragmented and disintegrative (suboptimal) in worldview, and/or if one does not wish to grow, optimal consciousness may temporarily be unachievable. Such a person would not be a good candidate for participation in BSA at his/her current level of functioning.

Belief System Analysis should support and enhance experiences with other consciousness disciplines. The teachings of Jesus Christ, Buddha, Mohammed, and other sages and prophets, converge with the spiritual principles of an optimal conceptual system. The Bible, Koran, and other ancient books of wisdom, including Eastern philosophies, can be useful tools in the therapeutic process, depending upon the prior beliefs the participants bring. The nature of supreme reality, as the source of all things good, is supported by all ancient sages and prophets (Graves, 1975). BSA does not seek to interfere with the individual's religious beliefs. Rather, it seeks to enhance functional understanding of that omniscient, omnipotent, omnipresent creative force which is sometimes called energy, consciousness, God, Amen, Ra, Allah, Oludamare, Buddha, Aset, Krishni, Tao, Jahwey, Hurley, or Jesus. We will know that we are on the path (i.e., that our worldview is consistent with wisdom tradition) as long as peace, love, harmony and balance guide our hearts.

Belief System Analysis teaches the value and mechanism for building community by opening lines of honest, forthright communication and constructive criticism. It does so through steadfast adherence to principles of good. The height of human experience is to be of service to others. In the light of the reciprocal relationship between self and other, and the law of reciprocity known in African American folk culture as, "what goes around, comes around," as just universe is realized. As one learns more about and embraces the whole of one's being, (including of one's perceived shortcomings), one comes to understand that no man or woman has all advantages. Each, in his/her own way, is unique, special and needed for the greater good of the whole. One has no difficulty in acknowledging the strengths, and giving proper respect to the brilliance of others.

Participation in BSA is transformative. The role of revelations and conversion experiences are valued. BSA is not authoritarian. Although preferable directions may be indicated based upon predictable consequences, participants make all choices (in this system there is no error, only potentials for growth). Belief System Analysis is informative and has much in common with many conventional psychotherapies, as discussed in previous works (Myers, 1988).

Optimal Theory — and, by extension, BSA — does not artifically separate the cognitive from the affective, nor does it ignore the unconscious. The multi-sensory level of functioning allowed by an optimal conceptual system accommodates divination (in this instance defined as communication with higher powers for the purpose of fostering greater good), spiritual healing and other forms of communication with forces normally inaccessible to a fragmented, non-cohesive consciousness. With long-term participation in BSA, these skills will evolve as self-knowledge increases to more advanced levels. As mentioned previously, the Ten Cardinal Principles are used as guidelines in BSA to ensure proper alignment with the forces of the implicate order. The utilization of the more advanced processes such as divination requires demonstrated mastery of these principles to support balance and harmony in working with others. One must demonstrate that one can control one's thoughts and actions, one must have devotion of purpose, faith in oneself to assimilate and will the truth. One must be free from resentment under persecution and the experience of wrong, and must be able to distinguish between right and wrong, and, between the real and unreal.

Training in BSA involves long-term participation in therapeutic relationships and in the process of optimization. The purpose of this process is to facilitate becoming one who consciously and deliberately is seeking to elevate oneself as a healer. One must have a commitment to pursuing optimal, cohesive consciousness (Myers, 1981, 1988). One must demonstrate in one's own life that which one is seeking to assist others in achieving. The aim of BSA — to teach a way of being in the world whereby one can achieve maximally positive experience through unity consciousness —must be modeled with the full realization that we are all in process.

Resurging in contemporary times through the experiential knowledge and cultural reality of a woman of African and native American descent, Optimal Theory and its therapeutic method BSA, fully incorporate the knowledge, wisdom, and understanding gained by our ancestors who underwent the Middle Passage and some 400 years of enslavement. These ancestors survived without the benefit of maintaining the surface structure manifestations of their indigenous culture, but were intensely connected with the deep structure manifestations. Optimal Theory posits that the deep structures of culture sustained them. Incorporating the law of opposites and other principles of the Hermetic tradition, BSA fosters the learning and practice of healing methods revealed directly by our revered ancestors and by knowledge and understanding of the implicate order.

African Americans: A Case Study of Nature Versus Nurture

In scholarship about what is typically thought of as the East, and the West, we find that Africa is frequently excluded. However, if one properly orients oneself toward humankind's point of origin, it is from African civilization that other cultures and civilizations evolved. Africa cannot be overlooked if we want a complete understanding of humanity. For a truly holistic view we must go back to the genesis, which can prvide us the basis for a transcultural perspective. In so doing, we will find that therein are many of the answers to questions facing us at the dawn of the 21st century. Questions such as, how can we restore order in the midst of chaos? In this section of the paper, Optimal Theory will be used to expose patterns brought now to conscious awareness, as well as a new depth of understanding illustrated through the trials and triumphs of African Americans, as humanity evolved. Once unconscious and not fully developed at the dawn of civilization, our knowledge of ourselves, and of the world, is coming full circle.

To better understand mental health, the African American case can be used in example. Knowledge of the history of African people in America and the enslavement process through which they were taken is important. Woodson (1933) noted our miseducation and the negative consequences of adopting the mindset of the group dominant in the United States. Cautioning that whoever controls the way a people think, controls the people, Woodson (1933) admonished African Americans to be mindful of psychological oppression. Referred to by Myers (1993) as the psychology of oppression, the process was initiated with terrorism, forging the belief that the physical survival and well-being of the enslaved African was in the hands of the slave captor. Next the denial of access to and negation of African history and culture, as well as the elevation of the history and culture of the slave captor, left the enslaved African cut off from normal opportunities for cultural carry-over. Never before in the history of humankind had people been denied for such an extended period of time access to basic human rights to the extent of having no control over what happened to their bodies, or with whom they were to have sexual intercourse, or which language they spoke. Africans were treated as chattel.

Should it be the case that such a people survive physically, what might one expect to be the initial psychological impact and/or the impact over several generations? What of the physical and mental status of the dehumanizers and their progeny? If one as a member of the group whose disenfranchisement was once so formalized, that one's dehumanization was legally institutionalized, what is the credibility of the legal and social institutions for such individuals? What can be said of the ethics and mental health of the law makers and those operating the social institutions? Moreover, what happens when the mindset which was at the core of the pathology which fostered your enslavement, is now predominate, and the one into which you continue to be socialized? Most would agree that answers to these questions could provide insight into the dynamic complexities of the psychological experiences and mental health of all Americans (Grier and Cobbs, 1968: Kramer, Rosen & Willis, 1973). Indeed, answers to these questions may well have implications for humanity as a whole (Myers, 1988). However, such questions are seldom raised in mainstream psychology in this country. Awareness of these socio-historical realities is seldom factored into the analysis of health issues for African Americans or people of other cultures.

Seeing Self Through the Eyes of Others

In 1857, the United States Supreme Court stated in its opinion in the case of Dred Scott versus John Sanford, that African Americans were "so far inferior that they had no rights which a White man was bound to respect." While the Fourteenth Amendment calling for "equal protection" under the law was passed in 1868 by the first Reconstruction Congress, and its ratification was made a condition of reinstatement into the Union, written and unwritten "Black Codes" aimed at restricting the rights of African American citizenship abounded for almost another hundred years.

Optimal Theory holds that African Americans existing under such oppressive conditions for extended periods of time survived by virtue of the depth and breadth of their worldview, which afforded them to live above brutal conditions. As early as 1890's, W.E.B. DuBois articulated the reality of seeing self through the eyes of other, when the other does not see clearly. His identification of the nature of a potential double consciousness in our psyches reflects but one of the possible psychological consequences of being African in America. Seeing self through the eyes of the other differs experientially from being aware of how others might see oneself given their limited worldview. While assimilation into the worldview of the dominant culture did not happen over night, it did bring with it alienating self perceptions. The gradual erosion of the cultural deep structure of the dislocated African, becomes even more apparent in American culture with the advent of school desegregation and television. As a consequence, an increase in self destructive behavior could be predicted.

While we must acknowledge that there is as much diversity within groups as between groups, the point remains that, en masse, African Americans have had (and many would argue still have) a shared experience of oppression. The long-term consequence of the oppression process is mentacide (Wright, 1979), the systematic destruction of a people's mind and culture. Mentacidal people are self-destructive; they suffer from the various categories of mental disorder described by Akbar

(1984). Examples of mentacide among the African American population are many, cutting across lines of socio-economic standing, color, and education. At the lowest socio-economic levels mentacide may play out as hopelessness and helplessness in the revolving door of incarceration, youth killing one another for material goods, gang acceptance, young mothers selling their bodies and children for drugs, and men killing each other over any provocation which connotes disrespect.

Among the more economically advantaged and educated classes, we see other manifestations of internalized oppression of mentacide. The "overseer syndrome" is acted out time and time again, as the White power structure identifies and materially rewards African Americans, who have adopted a suboptimal conceptual system will do their bidding. Such collaborators serve to oppress other African Americans, holding back African Americans' progress toward equality and self-determination, and ensuring the perpetuation of the status quo. Clarence Thomas would be a prime example of an African American who was so identified for leadership, and who by virtue of internalized inferiority, identification with the aggressor, and mentacidal condition of oppression, engages in behaviors characteristic of one with an anti-self disorder. However, these circumstances can also be seen as a prime opportunity for transformation for Justice Thomas. Historically, the overseer was often the "mulatto" off-spring of the slave captor and enslaved African woman. "Mulattos" emerged as a class of lighter complexioned African Americans to whom some privilege was extended. Internalized oppression is further reflected in our belief that whiteness signifies superiority while blackness signifies inferiority in all of its subtle forms and fashions; in color consciousness and in our reluctance to support one another professionally and as community. However, not all African Americans are mentacidal. Many avoid succumbing to the oppressive worldview. Several factors seem to contribute to the strength and resilience of these African Americans. A clear understanding of the nature of the oppressor and the process of oppression helps inoculate such people by invalidating the assumptions of white supremacy and fostering internal reserve.

In addition, it is important to note the relationship between oppression and depression in their social context. Among psychologists depression is known as "the common cold of mental health" (Kleinman, 1986). Optimal Theory posits that it is the faulty, suboptimal conceptual system and worldview that make both depression and oppression so common-place in this culture (Myers, 1988). The disenfranchisement, suppression, and repression which results from oppression leads to depression. However, depression is commonly undiagnosed and underdiagnosed among African Americans, because we have yet to fully determine the appropriate diagnostic criteria for depression among non-dominant and oppressed groups. Optimal Theory would suggest that such behaviors as violence (manifestations of extreme irritability, if not rage), substance abuse (self-medication), and anti-social/anti-self actions (hopelessness, internalized oppression, etc.), should be explored as manifestations of depression.

While some acknowledge the special difficulties of being healthy in a "sick" society in general (Fill, 1974; Ryan, 1971), the most disenfranchised and oppressed people need more and better clinical care, yet they often receive culturally irrelevant, inferior service (Hollinghead & Redlich, 1958; Ruiz, 1992). Inadequate service is very much related to the recurring themes of African American inferiority, such as lower intelligence and violent or criminal predisposition. The insidious suboptimal assumptions that frame the service delivery, research and conclusions of Western models of psychology regarding African Americans and their mental health leave little room for accurate perception. The failure in the field of psychology, with respect to meeting the needs of African American populations is predictable, seldom acknowledged, and has received very minimal attention in terms of structuring training programs, social policy or mental health delivery systems. Improvement in these areas will require openness to cultural pluralism versus cultural imperalism.

Optimal Theory and BSA are effective tools for exploring the nature human resiliency in the face of experiencing some 400 years under a system of socially mandated and legislated dehumanization. Belief System Analysis and Optimal Theory conclude that restoring health and balance means eradicating the fragmented, suboptimal worldview, and restoring an optimal conceptual system consistent with the teachings of the wisdom tradition of those who have gone before us. While the situation may appear hopeless to some, there is a Yoruba proverb which says that "God does not allow flies to bite a tailless cow." In other words, a divine order would have it that in each set of circumstances we will find we have what we need.

Overcoming the Mental and Spiritual Bondage of Oppression

Optimal Theory (Optimal Theory) posits that our ancient ancestors were correct in their proposition that our purpose in being (with each incarnation) is to come to know more and more fully who we are as manifestations of an infinite, omnipresent, creative energy whose every aspect has intelligence—omniscience, and omnipotence. Given that the historic cultural tradition of African people has emphasized both transcendent and immanent aspects of God, the imperative for acknowledgment of this perspective in psychological study, if we are to allow for pluralism, is crucial. People acknowledging African descent (all people are of African descent from the most holistic perspective, not all acknowledge that ancestry) have not only embraced the implicate order in traditional culture, but, according to Optimal Theory, have drawn upon the realization of that order in the effort to survive enslavement and brutal, dehumanizing oppression. Lawrence Levine (1977) noted evidence of that tradition in his commentary on Black culture and Black consciousness.

But de good Lawd gibs us eyes t'see t'ings dey doan see, an' he comes t' me, a poor brack slave woman, an' tells me be patient, 'cause dar's no wite nor brack in hebbin. An' de time's comin' when he'll make his brack chillums free in dis yere worl', an gib' em larnin', an' good homes, an' good times. Ah! honey, I knows, I knows! "Aunt Aggy"—an enslaved African woman in Virginia in 1840's (Levine, 1977).

At the point where one begins defining one's reality based on an optimal conceptual system, mental bondage, which Hilliard (1970) describes as invisible violence, is reduced. BSA, when participated in, continues to enhance experience and the transformation that takes place is consistent with that the wisdom tradition has spoken about over the millenia. Indeed, the practice of a theory of optimalization has been our salvation as African people in America. Developed more consciously, deliberately and precisely through BSA, an optimal worldview when put into practice, assures our survival of the chaos created by the suboptimal orientation in the past, present and future. The suboptimal view serves the purpose of providing the mechanism for growth in self-knowledge, greater wisdom and understanding. In short, the suboptimal worldview/experience is a phase in the process of optimization that helps us to see that all is good.

Conclusion

Most theories of personality posit a single fundamental human need that is causal in shaping human behavior. From a psychoanalytic perspective the need is to maximize pleasure and minimize pain; for phenomenologists the need is to maintain a relatively stable, coherent conceptual system; for object-relations theorists the need is for relatedness; others suggest the need to overcome feelings of inferiority and enhance self-esteem (Epstein, 1994). Optimal Theory recognizes that each of these needs can be met with the realization of conscious union with one's supremely good, infinite, spiritual essence. Through the insights of Optimal Theory, and the practice the therapeutic process of Belief Systems Analysis, progress toward the fulfillment of primary needs can be made.

According to Myers (1998), experiential knowledge of one's connection to the divine comes by revelation. This spiritual awareness, combined with the will to align oneself with forces of good, becomes the basis for a deep, eternal inner strength. BSA emphasizes teaching participants to bring their assumptions to conscious awareness and juxtapose them against those assuming divine order. At the point of becoming aware of one's powers to choose one's assumptions, learning to reason out of one's higher consciousness or that creating the greatest good, becomes a developmental process.

Socio-psychological pursuit of a fuller understanding of the implicate order and of spiritual development, allows for the examination and application of principles and values without regard to specific religious doctrine or dogma. While Optimal Theory and BSA were developed based upon careful study, observation and examination of the experiences of African Americans in the United States, they are applicable to oppressed people wherever they might be. The vast majority of cultures throughout the world at this point in our human evolutionary cycle suffer from maladies which derive from suboptimal conceptual systems. Optimal Theory and BSA can be used to restore order in the midst of personal as well as collective chaos and destruction.

On the Horizon

While we have written about a theory and therapeutic practice based on the awareness of a paradigm shift, there are those for whom no shift has taken place. Our target audience is those people for whom the limitations of the old paradigm of materialism, fragmentation, and alienation have become unbearable, and for whom there is an awareness that there must be a better way of living. Those possessing knowledge of another way of being in the world must stand up for that which is true, just, loving, peaceful, harmonious, and balanced, so that they stay connected to the source of all good. Optimal Theory and BSA provide understandings to be explored as we pursue wellness and seek to restore harmony, balance, and order to ourselves and the universe.

The theme of Optimal Theory has been that each, in his/her own way, must bring his/her gifts (e.g., knowledge, wisdom and understanding) to the celebration of our humanity. Optimal Theory argues for a new sense of cultural identity based on the deep structures of a cultural heritage rooted in oneness with peace, harmony, balance, order, reciprocity, compassion, justice and truth, a potential transcultural identity. At that point our culture, our way of life, will be identified with our character and by our actions, rather than by the more common surface structure aspects that now dominate our thinking. Optimal Theory is a special call which cuts across ordinary human diversity markers to identify those sharing the desire (motivation) and will (intentions) to pursue the greater good for all humankind. This process will require honest acknowledgment of our past shortcomings. Understanding that there is already an order to the universe, we are seeking to create harmony while remaining aware of the fact any "negative," if used for its purpose, will result in an upliftment bringing us closer.

There is an old proverb which says that if you don't know where you are going, any road will take you there. Belief System Analysis, based on Optimal Theory as a theory of health, well-being, and supremely good cohesive consciousness, is specific with regard to where it is going, and equally specific in terms of the markers for the correct path. For some, Optimal Theory will present a radical departure from mainstream Western psychological approaches to human development. However, given our current state of crisis, a radical departure may be exactly what is needed.

We shall see those who are of like mind coming together to pool their knowledge, answer questions and solve problems. Will psychology as a discipline develop to the point of being open to, and inclusive of, an alternate frame of reference based on the wisdom tradition? Will some areas of African and African American Studies be similar? Only time will reveal the answers to these questions. However, the evolution of Optimal Theory and BSA allows that we no longer have to wait, and so far the reception from the people we are trying to reach has been most favorable. The choice is yours, right here, right now. I have the honor to be your most humble servant. Peace and blessings.

Case Studies in Belief Systems Analysis

This section of the paper will present a brief discussion of six case studies using Belief System Analysis as a psychotherapeutic/psychoeducational modality in the traditional sense and in terms of restoring healthy functioning in a broader social context. The first two cases were longer term individual psychotherapy cases seen by Dr. Myers, the therapist developing the therapeutic model. The third is a summary of the application of BSA in a public educational setting. The last three cases will be those engaged by a practitioner in training, utilizing BSA as the psychotherapeutic modality for the first time. These cases will be presented by Flavia Eldemire, a graduate student in counseling psychology from the University of Massachusetts-Amherst, who worked with Prof. Myers for two years in order to learn more about optimal psychology and be trained with supervision in BSA. She will present three shorter term cases she engaged during the first year of training.

Several things are noteworthy as we begin to explore the application of the BSA model and processes. First, the current prevailing professional guidelines from training to professional licensure and third party paying systems, still respond to traditional models of individual, family or group therapy. We will therefore accommodate that reality by providing a few examples of the BSA model. However, the new paradigm requires the addition of a new mode of therapeutics and the development of new systems of practice, exchange and accountability. The new paradigm which Optimal Theory supports also emphasizes process versus outcome, indeed at some level the process is the outcome from an optimal vantage point. Consequently, from the outset it must be noted that besides the encouragement to turn within, most critical differences between BSA and other therapeutic approaches occur at the level of worldview or one's conceptual system and experiential knowledge, the perception and meaning of experiences and actions (rather than the snapshot in time of the experiences and actions themselves) are the points of focus and praxis. The development of healthier individuals in a larger social context can be achieved through the utilization of the therapeutic modality in group settings, with programs, or in institutional structures (Myers, 1989). BSA, as a therapeutic strategy, has proven quite effective in enhancing the daily lives of individuals and the functioning of groups, and has been used in a wide range of programs throughout the country.

Before turning to the case studies, it is important to add something about the practitioner and practitioner-in-training relationship. Nothing honors a teacher more greatly than a worthy student. Prof. Myers has been fortunate to have a great number of wonderful students. However, when a graduate student steps out on faith and travels to another institution to study without financial support with a faculty member because she admires her work, one senses the making of an unusual opportunity. Consistent with a self-knowledge epistemology, both the practitioner and practitioner-in-training must be engaged in the therapeutic process of BSA. Ms. Eldemire was able to demonstrate remarkable growth in the first year of training. In her second year she was able to translate that growth into practice in a corporate setting in the banking industry. She is now using her skills as an educational consultant in a large public school system. Without a doubt she has proven a credit to the model throughout her demonstrations of excellence.

Case 1

Helen P. was a middle-aged African American female, who decided to pursue individual psychotherapy after hearing the therapist speak at a women's conference. Returning to her hometown in the Midwest after having lived in the West Indies for several years, the twice divorced mother of three daughters and one adopted son, was suffering from severe depression, exacerbated in part by the empty nest syndrome, unresolved family of origin issues, and adjusting to a non-tropical climate.

Helen entered therapy as an eager learner, having already spent a considerable amount of time introspecting, reading and pursuing spiritual knowledge. At our initial session a heartfelt revelation, providing insight and deeper understanding of the concept of one love, unfolded. Helen's highly emotional and passionate nature is supported by the placement of cosmic energies at the time of Helen's birth. Learning to understand and control watery emotional energies was a key element in Helen's treatment. Given the long term of the treatment, I will discuss here only one aspect of the treatment focus: Helen's intimate relationships.

Helen was an attractive and out-going woman, whose second husband was a European American theology professor. Helen's husband had custody of their children until they reached their teenage years. One of the key issues in Helen's therapy was her relationships, particularly with men. Starting with her primary relationship with a man, her father, Helen experienced insecurity and the subtleties of manipulation in her intimate relationships. Always trying to gain approval, Helen tried to be the perfect daughter. She was exposed to a wide array of suboptimal socialization practices, from color to class and gender inferiority. She went to college, graduated with a degree in art and married a young, African American doctor right after graduation. Within two years she had a "nervous breakdown" and was divorced.

She had married based on the reality defined by others. Her husband was quite a "good catch" in the material sense, but, he was also caught up in the power/impotence drama of an externalized sense of self and reality. He took his self-alienation, the abuse of rigorous internship, and his rage out on Helen, abusing her physically and mentally. She was divorced within a year, disillusioned and numb, only to remarry, this time to a white theologian. Helen recounted, in retrospect, that her first husband wanted to be white. He took his inability to achieve this goal out on her. Rather than risk that same scenario with another African American man, she thought she would just take the original rather than the copy. Maybe he would be more whole. She quickly learned he could not be the complete package she was looking for. However, materially speaking she was living a "good life," playing the role of the professor's wife, mother and social activist comfortably in Canada. However, four children (three by birth, one adopted) later, she decided she could no longer tolerate the pretense of a relationship that she had long since outgrown. Leaving her husband and her children, Helen migrated to the West Indies, where she felt that she began to heal from the caustic consequences of living in an environment in which she was part of a non-dominant minority group.

Upon returning to the U.S., that initial healing made it possible for Helen to do some introspective work. She was able to examine her past relationships with men, explore the dynamics of attraction and reaction, and seek to prepare herself to be a better female role model for her children. More importantly, she became strong enough to look at herself honestly and openly confront (with the support of her therapist) the "demons in her closet," her suboptimal side. Helen was able to use these "negatives" for the purpose of creation, growth and self-mastery. In other words, she learned to engage in the optimization process and utilize it as a life-long learning and self-improvement process. Tarot cards, astrology, and other forms of divination were quite helpful as Helen continued on the path of self-development, mastering the process of optimization. Realizing that she is not all that she wants to be, but continuing to do the best she can, given where she is in her developmental process, Helen uses her "negative" experiences as stepping stones to higher consciousness. Practicing forgiveness (of self first), and increasing self-knowledge, harmony and balance may not always dominate Helen's experience, but they will become more dominant as she continues to work through her "lessons."

Case 2

Jesse R. was a 45 year old African American male, who was married and the father of three. Jesse R. was a police officer, whose major issues had to do with coping with oppression, harassment and discrimination on the job. He as diagnosed with depression and post-traumatic stress disorder. When participants seeking help utilize third-party paying systems, DSM IV diagnostic criteria can be used in response to the requirements of those systems.

Jesse was a very strong, committed, African American man, who was stylish and athletic in appearance. He was a family man and a member of the board of trustees in his church. His strong religious beliefs supported his commitment to honesty and justice. He often incurred the wrath of the power structure for being outspoken and for championing the underdog. Due to Jesse's role in an organization of Black police officers in a legal suit, he had been the target of retaliation. The focus of therapy was to strengthen Jesse's coping skills, and to help his work through issues that emerged with his family as a result of the undue pressure under which he was placed. As the lone voice for truth and justice in the face of a system against which most were too fearful to stand, Jesse needed deeper insight in order to create the internal fortitude he needed to sustain himself. In this process, a number of other issues emerged, primarily having to do with living above immediate circumstances or conditions, combating fear, and overcoming helplessness and hopelessness.

After several months of weekly therapy sessions designed to help Jesse to restructure his thinking about the oppression by deepening his understanding of the power he had and how best to wield it, on-going support was provided on an as needed basis. By identifying and reinforcing beliefs already existent in his Christian faith, awareness of what needed to be done was immediate and his faith sustained him to the limits of his understanding. The familiarity of a system that made existence tolerable may have also, at times, served to make the acquiring of greater satisfaction less accessible, to the extent that motivation to search deeper may have been circumvented. As Jesse's treatment progressed, his wife was included in several sessions. Jesse's coping skills improved as his understanding of the spiritual/material reality was deepened and expanded. He became much more relaxed and able to deal with hostile environment, placing the meaning and value of the situation in its proper context. Over time he was able to develop and implement a strategy to remove himself from the environment and continue his stand for justice with reduced stress and increased peace of mind. Jesse experienced knowledge of how to live above conditions and a new conviction to avoid giving power to external forces which did not serve his best interest. Likewise, he was able to learn to work productively in an oppressive, toxic environment.

Case 3

It is important to present at least one non-traditional application of Optimal Theory and BSA in order to provide a fuller picture of its salience for the healing of the African American community and society-at-large. A brief description of how it is being used to develop and Africentric school in a large metropolitan school district in the conservative Midwest allows insight into its breadth and depth as a strategy for collectively restoring health and balance. While we are looking at a long and slow developmental process to effect the desired changes, a brief introduction to the project can be of value.

One institution (outside of the family and church) whose responsibility is to socialize members into the worldview dominant in the society, is the formal educational system. Without intervention in the education of our young people, the suboptimal mindset will be assimilated, and hope for the restoration of health, balance and harmony in our communities will be lost. Efforts to develop and Africentric school whose mission it would be to educate our children based on our cultural realities and strengths, were very much enhanced by the adoption of Optimal Theory as the philosophical framework for educational program development. Fears and resistance to Africentric programming in the public school system were widespread, not only among Whites who saw the school as a move toward segregation, but among many Blacks as well. Many of the African American detractors had internalized the concept of black inferiority and did not want to support self-determination, but rather preferred the dictates of the white power structure, or feared such efforts could not be successful. The effort to provide African American children with a quality education in the face of a system that is not working, was made possible by the capacity of Optimal Theory to impart a fuller understanding of the wisdom tradition. As the imperative for culturally authentic programming to be shaped from the deep structure of African culture became apparent, BSA emerged as a necessary bridge to the implementation of programming and training of staff.

Utilized as a psychoeducational process for exploring differences in worldview and exposing the staff to concepts of miseducation and oppression, BSA provided a workable strategy for engaging in and sustaining the long-term developmental process of seeing and experiencing the world differently. Helping unseasoned staff to make the shift in perspective needed to develop and use African-centered pedagogy, was a major challenge. The optimization process was used as the formula for insuring ongoing improvement and processing. All along the way, issues of self-knowledge, relationship, values, character and trust had to be examined and worked through.

The school was opened successfully, and is in its second year of operation. Ongoing support and follow-up is being provided. Starting with how the staff, students, parents and the community saw themselves and each other, new ways of perceiving, thinking, feeling and behaving had to be introduced for the educational project to be successful. Belief System Analysis is requisite for each of these constituencies, and each person will need to undergo their developmental process individually and collectively. In this way we tried to create and educational environment and process in which truth, justice, and propriety could be administered with compassion and reciprocity, yielding harmony, balance and order. For, as long and difficult as the process was, BSA allowed for a method of guiding and monitoring growth irrespective of the phase in the developmental process. As predicted, relationships emerged as key to the success of implementing the education vision, and the primary force to emerge with the potential to destroy the vision, was ourselves. However, the forces for progress prevailed, and we made it through our first year of challenges with success. We can see clearly that we are getting better with each year by staying true to our course.

The next three cases will summarize the experiences of Flavia Eldemire, a doctoral student who worked with Prof. Myers for two years. Ms. Eldemire participated in her own therapeutic relationship and received supervision in individual psychotherapy and consulting: As a graduate student in training, my cultural reality and experiences were completely absent from discussions of psychological theory and treatment, until I was introduced to optimal psychology in a graduate seminar on the foundations and history of psychology. I wanted to learn more, so I took the opportunity to leave Amherst, Massachusetts with my two children and move to Columbus, Ohio to study with Dr. Myers (which became two). Having explored Optimal Theory and engaged in the optimization process of self-development, these two years have transformed every aspect of my life. Although one might expect in going through training and supervision to become a better psychologist/therapist, I did not expect that this training experience would make me a better person, mother, professional consultant, and student. Over the nine month period of working with the clients to be discussed, each client also evidenced tremendous growth in terms of their ability to explore, and to make meaning of their life experiences. As a result, each of them began to create new definitions and models for their future growth. Having learned so much the first year about how assumption, values, and decisions are made and constructed, I decided to stay another year to gain additional supervision in the application of Optimal Theory and BSA in my life as well as in corporate settings, examining corporate culture.

Case 4

Connie D. was a 40 year old, African American, and a first time college student. This vibrant, youthful, attractive mother of five children, had two small children in the home, the other three children were either in college or living on their own. When we first began therapy, Connie was working at three part-time jobs and managing her duties as student and parent. Her immediate issues centered on managing school work while managing a family. She lacked study skills, knowledge of the requirements to become a successful student, and self-confidence. Her motivation to succeed was extremely high, and she had extensive life skills and enormous potential for growth. Working with her was quite enjoyable. Connie was willing to work on multiple issues simultaneously, which served her well in her transition from home to work to school.

Growth for her came quite quickly; she attended all of our scheduled sessions ready to fully engage in the therapeutic process. What I was able to provide her was the space, the security and platform that allowed her to voice her concerns and criticisms of managing her multiple roles. Because she felt comfortable, she was able to communicate her needs in a clear and concise manner. Connie learned to easily determine where, when and what kind of help she needed, and, she practiced expressing those needs to me. As a team we were able to find the gaps in her education and her academic readiness. We were able to examine and create a more manageable work schedule to fit her academic hours. Her new schedule included time for her study, attend her classes and accommodate her children's school schedule. The flexibility allowed Connie to feel comfortable in both her roles as a student and parent. The new schedule also opened the door for us to address a variety of personal issues that were impetus for her lack of confidence and self-esteem.

As we explored and examined her history, it was evident that the fragmentation in her life was now being repaired and a new direction was at hand. Her ability to let go of past behaviors in relationships and in her actions and reactions to everyday situations, were strongly influenced by her inner strength and her spiritual awareness. In Connie's situation the challenge was to recenter her focus on what she really wanted for herself, to the point of realizing that the love she was seeking in multiple relationships was within herself and that she must start there and move outward. As Optimal Theory predicts, as one comes into greater knowledge of self, one's sense of alienation from the divine decreases, and self-acceptance increases. In time, Connie was able to try more things and learn to accomplish for herself what she had relied on the men in her relationships to accomplish for her. Connie's desire to understand herself more fully as a whole person was vital to her success. Her primary (and interrelated) goals were self-acceptance, seeing herself as capable of managing multiple roles, and learning new ways of being with a spiritual/material mindset. One of the pivotal points in our process was our sharing of ways to study, something many people take for granted. The freedom Connie experienced by opening up to share that she did not know, her ability to take the time to find out how and her willingness to put these things in practice, opened up a new world for her. Connie will no longer accept no for an answer to things that are important to her. She is committed to digging deep within for critique and inquiry. Finally, she will now assist her family in a more effective and healthy manner.

Case 5

Siswe T. was a thirty year old, Black, male doctoral student in the school of engineering. He was in his final year of his program. Siswe was from a very wealthy southern African family with very formal traditions, roles, customs and expectations. His presenting issues at our initial session were his inability to complete eight incompletes that he had received in his courses, his difficulties, anxieties about his wedding plans and future bride, and his family relationships back home in Africa. Siswe was bright and articulate, polished, and emotionally intense. He took his relationship to all things very seriously, and left little room for error and/or growth. Methodical and very critical of himself when he did not meet personal expectations, he felt under a lot of pressure from his family to return to Africa. He also experienced stress about finishing school, and about his future bride who was African-American and not from his ethnic group of origin. He also had to face his depression and its impact on his ability to complete his course work.

Prior to our initial session Siswe met with Dr. Myers to work on getting the time cleared to work on his mental health. After our initial session we began sorting out what issues were top priority. The first task was to reduce Siswe's anxiety so that he would not be overwhelmed by the multitude of issues he had to face. Because his doctoral education was his first priority, we began to focus upon what was needed to complete his work. He needed to face each of his professors, many of whom were questioning his ability because of his failure to complete his work in a timely manner. He had up to this point earned a 4.0 average.

Siswe was under severe stress, some of which was self-induced, while some of it was simply from the daily pressures of life in the Western world. Depression and anxiety had begun to affect his academic performance. Siswe carried his work in folders on a daily basis, in not so fruitful attempt to ease his anxiety. We developed strategies to break his projects into smaller, more manageable segments. We developed a plan to help him create a budget for his wedding to alleviate some of the financial pressures. With support to complete his work, Siswe was able to improve his performance at work and in school.

With clarity regarding how to complete his work and having his wedding plans in order and peace in his professional work arena, Siswe finally became less anxious. As therapy progressed, a smile began to appear upon his face. He became more confident and more at peace with himself. He began to worry less about his family and other issues over which he had limited or no control. Siswe was able to complete his incomplete grades, which helped to improve his self-esteem and his professional relationships within his department. At Siswe's place in the developmental process, little progress was made toward looking more deeply at causal issues, values and beliefs. He had not yet begun to see beyond the trappings of the American form of materialism in a way deep enough to see his own intrinsic worth. However, the principles and processes he learned in the therapeutic relationship will no doubt serve to support him with future challenges. Had I continued to work with him given more time, he would have been helped to see more clearly that with or without the degree he is a worthy human being destined for excellence.

Case 6

Kelly E. was an African American woman in her early thirties. She was referred for therapy by a friend of her mother. This attractive, youthful mother of three children, lived with the father of one of her children, and though the relationship was unsatisfactory to her, she stayed with him for material support. She had limited resources, limited educational experience and lacked self-confidence and life skills. Her coping skills were also limited. Kelly had a tendency to be nonverbal and aggressive. Reluctant to take responsibility for herself, Kelly longed for others to be responsible for her needs and desires. She had a negative view of herself and was often manipulative in her behavior to acquire the things she felt she needed.

As we began her therapeutic process, we examined several critical issues which were hindering her from maintaining a more balanced life, a life she so desperately wanted and needed to have. One of the first issues for us to work on as a team was the securing of reliable transportation that would allow for her to manage her life in a more orderly way without being totally dependent on others. Because of her limited resources she had the tendency to depend upon others to assist her in a variety of ways, (e.g., getting her to and from the grocery store, to the doctors and, to fulfill errands). At times she would appear very sweet and loving to those aiding her, yet there were times when she also appeared lazy and unmotivated or extremely angry.

After transportation was secured we then began to explore more effectively and deeply her relationships with the men in her life. She was separated from her husband, and was living with a man who was the father of her youngest child. It was concluded that it was best that she break her ties with both her youngest child's father and the man with whom she lived, and focus on herself, as it was clear she no longer desired the intimate relationship with him that he wanted with her. It was his ability to assist her materially that had initially attracted her to him in the first place. Kelly wrestled with the possibilities of reuniting with her husband whom she still cared for. However, it was his inability to support her financially that led her to leave her husband. Kelly had a variety of issues to face which played out in her relationships, staring with the poor relationship Kelly had with herself.

Despite Kelly having intellectual awareness of her worth and divinity due to her religious upbringing, she lacked an internalized, experiential knowledge of these truths. Through the therapeutic relationship, Kelly was able to confront the contradictions between her reputed beliefs and her actual practices. She learned that her capacity to love others, particularly her children, was very much tied to her capacity to love and accept herself. By the time of terminating therapy, Kelly had not only a clearer idea of how far she had to go to get where she desired to be, but also what she must do to get there. Having been able to help her assess where she was on the developmental path, Kelly was also made aware of the optimization process and she had committed to engage in it. She was grateful for the honest feedback and support. She committed to support her journey toward self-reflective behavior by reading a variety of texts and by attending local church services that would serve to reinforce her work.

Note

1. While I have Native American ancestry in both my paternal and maternal blood lines, like so may African Americans living west of the Mississippi, I do not have the privilege of direct experiential access to that part of my heritage. To a large measure the sociocultural circumstances of enslavement, genocide, and human bondage disrupted those line of transmission of culture, as well. Often family histories were not discussed and passed on, cultural ties were interrupted and transformed. Several years ago I had the opportunity to attend a healing ceremony and naming ritual with members of the Iroquois nation in Toronto, Canada. I was blessed to have the "grandfathers" give me my name and purpose, which immediately resonated with what my experiences had revealed previously. They informed from their cultural vantage point that my purpose was to help people understand God and bring healing.

References

Adler, A. (1927). *The practice and theory of individual psychology.* New York: Harcourt, Brace & World.

Akbar, N. (1976). *Natural psychology and human transformantion.* Chicago: World Community of Islan in the West.

Akbar, N. (1981). Mental disorder among African-Americans. *Black Books Bulletin, 1(2).*

Alexander, T. (1963). *Fundamentals of Psychoanalysis.* New York: Norton.

Asante, M.K. (1984). The African American Made Transcendence. *The Journal of Transpersonal Psychology, 16(2),* 167-177.

Asante, M.K. (1980). *Afrocentricity: The theory of social change.* Buffalo, New York: Amulefi Publishing Co.

Atkinson, D.R., Morten, G., & Sue, D.W. (1983). *Counseling American Minorities: A cross-cultural perspective.* (3rd ed.). Dubuque, IA: William C. Brown.

Baldwin, J. (1980). The psychology of oppression. In Asante, M. & Vandui, R. (Eds.), *Contemporary Black Thought*. Beverly Hills: Sage.

Banks, J.A. (1984). *Teaching Strategies for Ethnic Studies* (3rd ed.). Boston: Allyn & Bacon.

Banks, W.C. (1976). White preference in Blacks: A paradigm in search of a phenomenon. *Psychological Bulletin, 83*, 179-186.

Banks, W.C., McQuater, G.V., & Hubbard, J.L. (1978). Toward a reconceptualization of the social-cognitive bases of achievement orientations in Blacks. *Review of Educational Research, 48*, 381-397.

Banks, W.C., McQuater, G.V., & Ross, J.A. (1979). On the importance of white preference and the comparative difference of Blacks and others: Reply to Williams and Norland. *Psychological Bulletin, 86*, 33-36.

Barr, F.E. (1983). Melanin: The organizing molecule. *Medical Hypothesis, II*, 1-40.

Berry, J.W. (1980). Acculturation as varieties of adaptation. In A.M. Padilla (Ed.), *Acculturation theory, models, and some new findings*. Boulder, Colorado: Westview Press, Inc.

Bohm, D. (1986). A new theory of the relationship of mind and matter. *Journal of the American Society for Psychical Research, 80*, 113-135.

Bynum, E.B. (1994). *Transcending psychoneurotic disturbances: New approaches to psychospirituality and personality development*. Ithaca, New York: Haworth Press.

Bynum, E.B. (In press). *Oldawan: The African unconscious*. New York: Columbia University Teachers College Press.

Cacioppo, J., Gardner, W., & Bernston, G. (1997). Beyond bipolar conceptualizations and measures: The case of attitudes and evaluative space, *Personality and Social Psychology Review, 1(1)*, 3-25.

Capra, F. (1975). *The Tao of physics*. Berkeley: Shabala.

Carney, C. G., & Kahn, K.B. (1984). Building competencies for effective cross-cultural counseling: A development view. *The Counseling Psychologist, 12*, 111-119.

Carruthers, J. (1995). *Mdw Ntr: Divine speech*. London: Karnak House.

Cass, V.C. (1979). Homosexual identity formation: A theoretical model. *Journal of Homosexuality, 4*, 219-235.

Coleman, D. (1980). Perspectives on psychology, reality, and the study of consciousness. In R. N. Walsh & F. Vaughn (Eds.), *Beyond ego: Transpersonal dimension in psychology*. Los Angeles: J.P. Tarchar.

Cross Jr., W.E. (1991). *Shades of Black: Diversity in African-American Identity*. Philadelphia: Temple University Press.

Dohrenwend, B.P., & Dohrenwend, B.S. (1969). *Social status and psychological disorder*. New York: John Wiley & Sons.

Dohrenwend, B.P., & Dohrenwend, B.S. (1974). Social and cultural influences on psychopathology. *Annual Review of Psychology, 25*, 47-52.

Downing, N.E., & Roush, K.L. (1985). From passive acceptance to active commitment: A model of feminist identity development of women. *The Counseling Psychologist, 13*, 59-72.

Ellis, A. (1973a). *Humanities psychotherapy: The rational-emotive approach.* New York: Julian Press.

Ellis, A. (1973b). *Rational-emotive therapy.* In R. Corsini (Ed.), *Current Psychotherapies.* Itasca, Ill.: F.E. Peacock.

Fill, J.H. (1974). *The mental breakdown of a nation.* New York: New Viewpoints.

Finch, C. (1998). *The star of deep beginner: The genesis of African science and technology.* Decatur: Khenti, Inc.

Fine, M.A., Schewebel, A.I., & Myers, L.J. (1985). The effects of worldview on adaptation to single parenthood among middle-class adult women, *Journal of Family Issues, 6(1)*, 107-127.

Frankl, V.E. (1962). *Black self-determination.* Westport, Connecticut: Lawrence Hill and Co.

Frye, C., Harper, C., Myers, L.J., & Traylor, E. (1987). How to think Black: A symposium on Toni Cade Bambari's. *The Salteaters....Contributions in Black Studies, 6.*

Giorgio, A. (1987). The crisis of Humanistic Psychology, *The Humanistic Psychologist, 15(1)*, 15-20.

Giueffre, K. (1998). *Supraspatial reality with entangled particles: Quantum evidence for the possibility of extracerebral information transmission.* Towards a Science of Consciousness Conference, Tuscon, Arizona.

Goleman, D. (1995). *Emotional Intelligence.* New York: Bontain.

Gossm, W.E. (1978). Models of psychological nigrescence: A literature review. *Journal of Black Psychology, 5*, 13-31.

Graves, K. (1975). *The world's sixteen crucified saviors: Christianity before Christ.* New York: Free Thought Books.

Grier, W. & Cobbs, P. (1968). *Black Rage.* New York: Basic Books.

Grof, S. (1979). Modern consciousness research and the quest for the new paradigm, *Revision, 2*, 41-52.

Gwaltney, J.I. (1982). *Drylongso: A portrait of Black America.* New York: Random House.

Haggins, K. L. (1994). *An Investigation of Optimal Theory applied to identity development.* Unpublished doctoral dissertation, The Ohio State University.

Helms, J.E. (1984). Explanation of the effects of a model for race on counseling: A Black and White model. *The Counseling Psychologist, 2*, 153-165.

Helms, J.E., & Carter, R.T. (1990). Development of the White Racial Identity Attitude Scale. In J.E. Helms, (Ed.), *Black and White Racial identity attitudes: Theory, research, and practice* (pp. 67-80). Westport, CT: Greenwood Press, Inc.

Helms, J.E. (1989). Considering some methodological issues in racial identity counseling research. *The Counseling Psychologist, 17(2)*, 227-252.

Helms, J.E. (Ed.). (1990). *Black and White racial identity attitudes: Theory, research, and practice.* Westport, CT: Greenwood Press, Inc.

Highlen, P.S., Jecmen, D.J. & Speight, S.L. (1991). [Data from Female Identity Development study]. Unpublished raw data.

Hilliard, A. (1997). *The reawakening of the African mind.* Gainesville: Makers Press.

Hilliard III, A. (1992). IQ and the Courts Larry P. Wilson Riles and PASE v. Hannon, In H.P. McAdoo & D. Azibo et. al., (Eds.). *African-American psychology: Theory, Research and Practice.* Newbury Park: Sage Publications Inc.

Hollinghead, A., & Redlech, F. (1958). *Social class and mental illness.* New York: John Wiley & Sons.

Horney, K. (1950). *Neurosis and human growth.* New York: Norton.

Jecmen, D.J. (1989). *The development of an instrument to measure identity development in females: The femal identity development scale.* Unpublished master's thesis, The Ohio State University.

Jones, E., & Korchin, S. (1982). *Minority mental health.* New York: Praeger.

Jung, C.G. (1954). *Collected Works, Vol. 16. The Practice of psychotherapy.* New York: Pantheon.

Jung, C.G. (1973). *Letters* (G. Adler, Ed.). NJ Princeton University Press.

Karenga, M. (1982). *Introduction to Black Studies.* Los Angeles: Kawaida Publications.

Karenga, M. (1984). *The Husia: Sacred wisdom of ancient Egypt.* Los Angeles: Kawaida Publications.

Kazdin, A.E. (1980). *Behavior modification in applied setting* (revised edition). Homewood, Illinois: Dorsey Press.

Kohlberg, L. (1981). *The philosophy of moral development.* San Francisco: Harper & Row.

Kramer, M., Rosen, B.M., & Willis, E.M. (1973). Definitions and distributions of mental disorders in a racist society. In C.V. Willie, B.M. Kramer, & B.S. Brown (Eds.), *Racism and mental health,* Pittsburgh University of Pittsburgh Press.

Kuhn, S. (1970). *Structure of scientific revolutions.* 2nd ed. Chicago: University of Chicago Press.

Lakatos, T. (1970). Falsification and the methodology of scientific research programs. In Lakotos & A. Musgrave (Eds.), *Criticisms and the growth of knowledge.* London: Cambridge University Press.

Langer, E.F. (1989). *Mindfulness.* Reading, Mass.: Addison-Wesley.

Levine, L.W. (1977). *Black culture and black consciousness.* New York: Oxford University Press.

Maslow, A.H. (1960). *Toward a psychology of being* (2nd ed.). New York: Van Nostrand Reinhold.

Maslow, A.H. (1971). *The farther reaches of human nature.* New York: Viking.

Masterman, M. (1970). The nature of a paradigm. In T. Lakatos & A. Musgrave (Eds.) *Criticism and the Growth of Knowledge.* London: Cambridge University Press.

May, R. (1989). Transpersonal or transcendental? *The Humanistic Psychologist, 14(2),* 87-90.

Messer, A.B., & Winokur, M. (1980). Some limits to the integration of psychoanalytic and behavior therapy. *American Psychologist, 35,* 818-827.

Myers, L.J. (1981). *Oneness: A Black model of psychological functioning.* Southern Regional Education Board Black Psychology Task Force, Atlanta Georgia, December, 1981.

Myers, L.J. (1983). Transpersonal psychology: The role of the Afrocentric paradigm. *Journal of Black Psychology, 12 (1),* 31-42 and In A.K. Burlew, W.C. Banks, H.P. McAdoo, & D.A. Azibo (Eds.). (1992). *African-American psychology: Theory research and practice.* Newbury Park, Ca.: Sage.

Myers, L.J. (1984). The psychology of knowledge: The importance of worldview. *New England Journal of Black Studies, 4,* 1-12.

Myers, L.J. (1987). The deep structure of culture: Relevance of traditional African culture in contemporary life. *Journal of Black Studies, 18(1),* 72-85.

Myers, L.J. (1988). *Understanding an Afrocentric Worldview: Introduction to an optimal psychology.* Dubuque, IA: Kendall/Hunt.

Myers, L.J., Speight, S.L., Highlen, P.S., Cox, C.I., Reynolds, A.L., Adams, E.M., & Hanley, C.P. (1991). Identity development and worldview: Toward an optimal conceptualization. *Journal of Counseling and Development, 70,* 54-63.

Nichols, E.J. (1976). The philosophical aspects of cultural difference. World Psychiatric Association, Ibadan, Nigeria.

Nobles, W. (1980). Extended self: rethinking the so-called Negro self concept. In R. Jones (ed.) *Black Psychology* (2nd ed.). New York: Harper and Row.

Norcross, J.C. (1985). In defense of theoretical orientation for clinicians. *The Clinical Psychologist, 38(1),* 13-17.

Osipow, S.H., & Walsh, W.B. (1970). *Strategies in counseling for behavior change.* Englewood Cliffs, NJ: Prentice Hall.

Parham, T.A. (1989). Cycles of psychological nigrescence. *The Counseling Psychologist, 17(2),* 187-226.

Parham, T.A., & Helms, J.E. (1981). The influence of Black students' racial identity attitudes on preferences for counselor's race. *Journal of Counseling Psychology, 28(3),* 250-257.

Paterson, C.H. (1973). *Theories of counseling and psychotherapy.* (2nd ed.). New York: Harper & Row.

Pepinsky, H.B., & Pepinsky, P. (1954). *Counseling: Theory and practice.* New York: Roland Press.

Perry, W. (1970). *Forms of intellectual and ethical development in the college years.* New York: Harper & Row.

Pribram, K.H. (1991). *Brain and perception: Holonomy and structure in figural processing.* Hillside, New Jersey: Lawrence Erlbaum Associates.

Propst, L.R. (1982). *Cognitive therapy via personal belief structures. The newer therapies: A sourcebook.* New York: Van Norstrand Reinhold.

Reynolds, A.L., & Pope, R.L. (1991). The complexities of diversity: Exploring multiple oppressions. *Journal of Counseling and Development, 70,* 174-180.

Rogers, C.R. (1961). *On becoming a person.* Boston: Houghton Mifflin.

Rogers, C.R. (1951). *Centered therapy.* Boston: Houghton Mifflin.

Ryan, W. (1971). *Blaming the victim.* New York: Pantheon Books.

Sawchenko, P.E., & Swanson, L.W. (1981). Central noradrenergic pathways for the integration of hypothalamic neuroendocrine and autonomic responses. *Science, 214,* 685-687.

Schafranske, E.P., & Gorsuch, R.L. (1984). Factors associated with the perception of spirituality in psychotherapy. *Journal of Transpersonal Psychology, 16,* 231-241.

Schwaller deLubicz, R.A. (1982). *Sacred science: The king in pharaonic theocracy.* Rochester: Inner Traditions.

Sevig, T. (1993). The development and validation of the Self Identity Instrument. Unpublished doctoral dissertation, The Ohio State University.

Speilberger, C.D. (1983). *Manual for the state/trait anxiety inventory.* Palo Alto, California: Consulting Psychologists Press, Inc.

Strong, S.R. (1979). Social psychological approach to psychotherapy research. In A.E. Bergin & S.L. Garfield (Eds.), *Handbook of psychotherapy and behavior change* (2nd ed.). New York: Wiley.

Sullivan, H.S. (1953). *The interpersonal theory of psychiatry.* New York: W.W. Norton.

Sue, D.W. (1981). *Counseling the Culturally Different: Theory and practice.* New York: Wiley.

Sue, D.W., & Sue, D. (1990). *Counseling the culturally different: Theory and practice* (2nd ed.). New York: Wiley.

Sue, S., & Zane, N. (1987). The role of culture and cultural techniques in psychotherapy: A critique and reformulation. *American Psychologist, 42,* 37-45.

Terrell, F., & Terrell, S. (1984). Race of counselor, client sex, cultural mistrust level, and premature termination from counseling among Black clients. *Journal of Counseling Psychology, 31(31),* 371-381.

Tokar, D.M., & Swanson, J.L. (1991). An investigation of the validity of Helms's (1984) model of White racial identity development. *Journal of Counseling Psychology, 38(3)*, 296-301.

Vontress, C.E. (1971). Racial differences: Impediments to rapport. *Journal of Counseling Psychology, 18(1)*, 7-13.

Walsh, R.N., & Vaughn, F. (1980). A comparison of psychotherapies. In Walsh & F. Vaughn (Eds.), *Beyond ego: Transpersonal dimensions of psychology*. Los Angeles: J.P. Tarchers, Inc.

Wei Wu Wei (1970). *All else is bondage*. Hong Kong: Hong Kong University Press.

Wilson, A. (1978). *The developmental psychology of the Black child*. New York: Africana Research Publications.

Woodson, C. (1933). *The mis-education of the Negro*. Washington, DC: The Associated Publishers, Inc.

Author

Linda James Myers, Ph.D
Department of Black Studies
386 University Hall
The Ohio State University
Columbus, OH 43210
Telephone: (614) 292-3447
Fax: (614)292-2293
Email:

Name Index

Name Index

Subject Index

Subject Index